INTERCULTURAL PUBLIC RELATIONS

Intercultural Public Relations: Theories for Managing Relationships and Conflicts with Strategic Publics develops a coherent framework to unify the theories of public relations and intercultural communication, and, within the framework, examines empirical studies of intercultural interactions.

This book follows an intercultural approach, which considers how individuals and entities with dissimilar cultural identities interact and negotiate to solve problems and reach mutually satisfying outcomes. This work provides a theory-driven, empirically supported framework that will inform and guide the research and practices of intercultural public relations. Furthermore, it provides numerous levels of analysis and incorporates the use and challenges of social media.

The book examines theories and issues in three integrated processes:

- Identification of publics
- Relationship management
- Conflict resolution

These areas represent the most critical functions that public relations contributes to organizational effectiveness: scanning the environment, identifying strategic publics, and building long-term, quality relationships with these publics to reduce costs, gain support, and empower the publics themselves. In doing so, the book adopts simultaneously public-centered and organization-centered perspectives. This unique work will serve as an essential reference for students, practitioners, and scholars in today's global public relations environment.

Lan Ni, Ph.D., is Associate Professor at the University of Houston. Focusing on identification of publics, relationship management, and conflict management, she examines how public relations in intercultural settings can both benefit organizations and empower publics, especially immigrants and minority groups. Supported by multiple funding agencies, her research has been published in major journals and consistently shapes her teaching.

Qi Wang, Ph.D., is Associate Professor at Villanova University. She is interested in theorizing and observing interpersonal and intercultural communication in various contexts, with the goal of promoting individual, relational, and organizational wellbeing. Her research has won multiple awards and has appeared in top tier journals in the communication field.

Bey-Ling Sha, Ph.D., APR, is Professor at San Diego State University. She has been thinking about cultural identity since kindergarten and theorizing about intercultural public relations since her M.A. thesis at the University of Maryland. She is an award-winning public relations scholar, teacher and practitioner.

INTERCULTURAL PUBLIC RELATIONS

Theories for Managing
Relationships and Conflicts
with Strategic Publics

Lan Ni, Qi Wang, and Bey-Ling Sha

Routledge
Taylor & Francis Group

NEW YORK AND LONDON

First published 2018
by Routledge
711 Third Avenue, New York, NY 10017

and by Routledge
2 Park Square, Milton Park, Abingdon, Oxon OX14 4RN

Routledge is an imprint of the Taylor & Francis Group, an informa business

Library of Congress Cataloging in Publication Data
A catalog record for this book has been requested

ISBN: 978-1-138-18921-8 (hbk)
ISBN: 978-1-138-18922-5 (pbk)
ISBN: 978-1-315-64173-7 (ebk)

Typeset in Bembo
by Swales & Willis Ltd, Exeter, Devon, UK

Lan Ni

To my parents, for teaching me all the important components of intercultural communication competence.

To my husband, who has been with me every step of the way on the journey of intercultural adaptation and has always supported me emotionally and intellectually.

To my children, for giving me the precious opportunity to grow as a parent and to integrate my professional and personal goals in understanding intercultural identity issues.

Qi Wang

For Frankie, Aiden, and Avery.

Bey-Ling Sha

To my mother, who instilled in me at an early age the importance of identity and made me learn to communicate interculturally.

CONTENTS

Acknowledgments   *ix*

1 Introduction   1

PART I
Theoretical Foundations   **15**

2 Foundational Theories in Public Relations Management   17

3 History and Foundational Theories of Intercultural
   Communication   60

4 Conflict Management and Negotiation   116

PART II
Intercultural Public Relations at Various Levels   **149**

5 Interpersonal Level: Competencies and Practices   151

6 Intra-Organizational Level: Identifying and
   Communicating with Publics   184

7 Intra-Organizational Level: Relationship Management   209

8 Intra–Organizational Level: Conflict Management
   and Negotiation   232

9 Organizational Level: Organizational Identity and
   Identification   260

10 Social Media   279

11 Conclusions   302

Index   *311*

ACKNOWLEDGMENTS

The authors would like to acknowledge the support of each other in this journey of exploring intercultural public relations.

Lan Ni: I would like to acknowledge the life-changing influence from my mentors, Drs. James Grunig and Larissa Grunig, whose genuine, two-way symmetrical communication approach has shaped my research, teaching, and even parenting style. I would also like to acknowledge the generous support that I received from the following funding agencies: the Arthur W. Page Center for Integrity in Public Communication, Urban Communication Foundation, Public Relations Society of America Research Foundation, as well as the Asian American Studies Center, Center for Mexican American Studies, College of Liberal Arts and Social Sciences, and Division of Research at the University of Houston. Their support has greatly advanced my research projects on intercultural public relations, most of which have appeared in this book.

Qi Wang: Praise and thanks to God, for this life and being with me every step of the way. Thanks to Villanova University for granting me the sabbatical to work on the project and the support of my colleagues in the Department of Communication. Thanks to Lan Ni and Bey-Ling Sha for the mutual support and an unforgettable journey. Special thanks to the soul of the project, Lan, for her incredible leadership and perseverance.

Bey-Ling Sha: Thank you to my earliest scholarly mentors for starting me on this journey: Dick Crable, K. Sriramesh, Jim Grunig, and Lauri Grunig. And thank you to Lan Ni and Qi Wang for bringing me along on this ride.

1

INTRODUCTION

Background and Context of the Book

The journey of writing a book on intercultural public relations began back in 2001, when the first author of this book had just started her graduate program in public relations at the University of Maryland. Coming as an international student, she had great interest in and passion for public relations in intercultural settings. To get a general sense of public relations practices among organizations and publics across different cultural backgrounds, she searched for resources on this topic, starting with the library database. Although many articles and readings existed, the only books she could find at the time were the following two: *International Public Relations: A Comparative Analysis* (Culbertson & Chen, 1996) and *Multicultural Public Relations: A Social-Interpretive Approach* (2nd ed., Banks, 2000). While she was excited to find these two, she was also surprised that there were not more systematic explorations on this important topic.

Things changed tremendously over the past decades. As the trend in globalization continues, organizations face the challenge of how to identify, interact with, and manage relationships with publics from diverse cultural backgrounds. Such challenges exist both within a country and across borders. In response to these challenges, many more books on public relations across national boundaries have been published since then, including influential books by Sriramesh and colleagues (e.g., Sriramesh & Vercic, 2009).

In the following years, both in graduate school and beyond, the first author has been fortunate enough to have met and worked extensively with the second and third authors on this topic of common interest. The second author has in-depth knowledge and background in intercultural communication, which has been instrumental in their collaborative work on intercultural public relations.

The third author first proposed the concept of *intercultural public relations* (Sha, 1995, 2006) with a series of studies in the areas of cultural identity of both publics and organizations, consistently inspiring and contributing to this area of research.

Together, the three authors believe that systematic theorizing is still lacking with regard to the specific aspect of intercultural public relations practices, which is defined as "a special case of public relations in which the salient cultural identity avowed by the organization differs from the salient cultural identity avowed by the public" (Sha, 2006, p. 54).

The next section provides a brief review of the current books on researching public relations through the lens of culture, comparing and contrasting different approaches to culture in the context of public relations (i.e., cross-cultural, multicultural, and intercultural approaches), highlighting the lack of an existing theoretical framework for systematic examinations of *intercultural* interactions among publics and organizations, thereby introducing the need for the current book.

Current Status and Need for a New Book

Globalization

Much research in public relations has been inspired by the trend of *globalization*, which involves the increasing global interconnectedness that results from constant interchange of important factors across national borders such as economy, culture, technology, finance, and people. Globalization has immense and widespread consequences because any issue or activity in one part of the world could potentially influence that of another part, either instantly or eventually (Ni, 2013). It is noted that even though the term *globalization* was not widely recognized until it was coined by Theodore Levitt in 1983, globalization itself is not a new phenomenon, nor is it precisely defined by Western countries, according to Krishnamurthy Sriramesh and Dejan Vercic (2009). For more discussion on the connection between globalization and *global village*, see Chapter 3 of the current book.

Vercic, Zerfass, and Wiesenberg (2015) reviewed studies on public relations in the global environment and argued that both systematic empirical research and theory specific to public relations in global organizations are still lacking. In particular, they identified a major problem, where many studies done in countries other than the United States are placed under the "international public relations" umbrella even though those studies examined purely domestic public relations practices in a particular country. Very few studies were actually concerned with cross-cultural analyses, intercultural communication and relationships, or global issues or organizations (Jain, De Moya, & Molleda, 2014). This problem points to a fundamental need to understand and distinguish the different approaches to culture in the research of public relations, which is discussed below.

Distinction Among Terms

Many related but different terms are typically used to describe phenomena related to globalization. Examples include international, multinational, global, cross-cultural, multicultural, and intercultural. They are sometimes used interchangeably, which can lead to confusion. In this section, we define and differentiate several key terms commonly used from two broad categories. The first category refers to different countries or nation states, and the terminology used includes *international, multinational,* and *global* public relations, whereas the second category refers to different cultures that are more pertaining to group-oriented, social-interactive behavior. The latter terminology includes *cross-cultural, multicultural,* and *intercultural* public relations.

Although country or nation state undoubtedly constitutes an important aspect of cultural differences, the concept of culture entails much more than national boundaries alone. *Culture* is defined as "the collective of programming of the mind that distinguishes the members of one group or category of people from others" (Hofstede & Hofstede, 2005, p. 4). The mental programming consists of "attitudes, values, belief systems, disbelief systems, and behaviors" (Singer, 1998, p. 6). Any group that shares similar perceptions could be considered a culture, such as gender, sexual orientation, religion, and social economic status. Please refer to Chapter 3 for a more thorough discussion on the definitions and scope of culture.

Among the three terms in the first category (international, multinational, and global) that involves more than one country or nation, *multinational* is typically reserved to refer to a business or corporate setting. In the context of public relations literature, a distinction has been made between international and global. In examining different public relations practices and how such practices are or will be influenced by different factors, two main schools of thoughts emerged: international public relations and global public relations, also called and roughly equated with polycentric and ethnocentric, emic and etic, and culture-specific and culture-free approaches, respectively. The *international* approach to public relations emphasizes differences in practices in different parts of the world due to different cultural influences. The key assumption is that no universal rules or principles, mostly developed in the Western countries and thus likely to be ethnocentric, apply or should apply to such different practices. The *global* approach to public relations, however, suggests that universal principles of best public relations practices do exist and should be applied in different parts of the world, but with modifications based on and careful considerations of the local culture (Sriramesh & Vercic, 2009).

However, in the context of public relations, many issues that are of interest to diverse groups of people can either go beyond national borders or remain in the same country. Culture in its most comprehensive form consists of various levels, and country or nation is only one of the many levels. Therefore, it is important to consider the second set of terms on culture.

Following and adapting the distinction among terms in intercultural communication (see more in Chapter 3), we argue that the following three main approaches to public relations in the global environment are needed. Briefly, the *cross-cultural* approach focuses on cross-cultural or cross-national comparisons following established criteria and examines how different environmental factors influence public relations practices in different parts of the world. The *multicultural* approach focuses on the co-existence and representation of diverse cultures in the society, highlighting the importance of diversity in publics. Finally, the *intercultural* approach focuses on the actual process of interaction and communication among people from different cultural backgrounds both within a country and across borders. Again these three approaches in this second category are used to classify the approaches to the study of public relations in the global environment. Some variations among these approaches exist (see Chapter 3 for more discussion).

In general however, most of the existing theory books in this area take one of the following approaches: (a) a cross-cultural or cross-national approach with limited discussion on actual interaction processes, (b) a critical approach with a focus on power, and/or (c) a multicultural approach. Below is a more detailed review of the different books with the need for this current book proposed at the end.

Review of Current Books

First of all, both of the early pioneering books in this area mentioned in the beginning of this chapter provide tremendous help for students, scholars, and practitioners alike who want to learn and apply theories and practices of public relations on a global scale. They helped explore the landscape of intercultural public relations. Culbertson and Chen's (1996) is the first book that has provided not only theoretical foundation, but also cross-national or cross-cultural comparisons of public relations practices in different parts of the world. Banks' (2000) book also addresses using theories to communicate with diverse publics. However, it only contains one chapter on substantial theorizing, which focuses on diversity issues. The other chapters are focused primarily on different practices and contexts. Both books were published more than a decade ago and have not been updated since. Other research and books are reviewed below according to the different approaches taken.

Cross-Cultural Comparisons

In existing public relations research, cross-cultural comparisons share many commonalities with the international and global approaches discussed earlier. Most studies in this category examine the similarities and differences of public relations practices in different countries. In fact, Curtin and Gaither (2007) identified four main categories of such studies in *international* public relations:

1. Analyses of how national cultures influence public relations practice.
2. Analyses of the relevance of U.S.-centric public relations models in other countries.
3. Comparisons of public relations practices across regions or countries through case studies.
4. Studies of international public relations practiced by governments.

In terms of the *global* approach, James Grunig and his colleagues developed a global public relations theory of generic principles derived from the *Excellence theory* (e.g., L. Grunig, J. Grunig, & Dozier, 2002) and specific applications of these principles. Reflecting the idea of globalization, this global theory has been expanded and refined through studies in different parts of the world and has been heavily reflected in Sriramesh and Vercic (2009).

Principles of excellence feature five themes: management processes, two-way symmetrical processes, diversity, ethics, and social responsibility. Six specific variables that can influence public relations practices include *infrastructure*, which contains political system, level of economic development, level of activism, and legal system; *culture*, which includes both societal and corporate cultures; and *media environment*, which includes media control, media outreach, and media access. Of particular note is the role of culture, with numerous studies examining cultural values or dimensions, especially those by Geert Hofstede (2001). Scholars such as Sriramesh and Vercic (2009) examined these specific variables through contextualized regional and country descriptions of public relations practices.

Sriramesh and Vercic (2009) is by far one of the most influential books on global public relations. It uses a coherent framework in global theory of public relations that incorporates generic principles and specific applications. It examines the application of principles of public relations in over 30 countries or regions with different environmental variables. This book articulates a strong and consistent theoretical framework and applications of the framework. It also provides a solid knowledge base for practitioners who need to be aware of the global influences on public relations. Other major books focusing on contextualized regional/country descriptions using a cross-national approach are from the following authors: Culbertson and Chen (1996), Freitag and Stokes (2008), Sriramesh (2004), Srirmesh and Vercic (2012), Vilanilam (2011), Watson (2014).

It is worth noting that Srirmesh and Vercic (2012) offered a broad overview of the relationship between culture and public relations. In addition to examining public relations practice within specific countries such as New Zealand, China, Nigeria, Germany, the United Kingdom, and Mexico, the book also examines the concept of "culture," broadly defined, including such areas of culture as citizenship, cultural identity, critical-cultural theory, anthropology, professional culture, and occupational culture. Overall, it follows primarily the cross-cultural, comparative approach that is typical to books on global public relations.

However, the authors specifically examined culture in the *intercultural* sense in two chapters: One chapter examined the engagement of New Zealand organizations with indigenous peoples, and another chapter examined communication between U.S. military public affairs officers and Arab journalists.

Multicultural Approach

The *multicultural* approach focuses on the co-existence and representation of diverse cultures in the society, highlighting the importance of diversity in publics. This approach typically takes a critical perspective, focusing primarily on the concept of power. Books published in this category include Bardhan and Weaver (2010) and Curtin and Gaither (2007), among others.

One line of research under this approach examines the impact of global public relations on individuals and societies. Taylor (2000) and Taylor and Doerfel (2003) argued for the critical role of global public relations and development communication in nation-building efforts for a civil society. However, critical and postmodernist scholars have questioned such an impact. For example, Dutta-Bergman (2005) examined how public relations efforts in civil-society building across the world could be employed for imperialist invasions of Third World nations in the name of helping tear down the authoritarian governments of these nations and rebuilding new and democratic ones. Pal and Dutta (2008) further suggested the incorporation of a critical modernist perspective and the need for culture-centered public relations practices. Somerville, Hargie, Taylor, and Toledano (2016) further provided empirical research findings on public relations from various types of deeply divided societies across the world to give a voice to these marginalized societies.

Another line of research focuses on representation of various cultures and the importance of diversity. Studies have focused on demographic categories and diversity issues as manifested by differences in gender, race, and sexual orientation (e.g., Edwards & Hodges, 2011; Hon, 1995; Pompper, 2005; Tindall & Waters, 2012; Waymer, 2012).

Intercultural Interaction

The third line of research examines intercultural public relations focusing on exploring the processes of communication between two important players, publics and practitioners, as they cope with globalization in intercultural settings.

More individuals than ever are interacting with people from outside of their home countries, voluntarily or not. How organizations manage relationships with important *publics* has become an important topic for research. Ni (2009), and Ni and Wang (2011) examined relationship management with customers, local employees in multinational companies, and international students, respectively.

On the other hand, the intercultural competencies of *practitioners* become critical as they enter new cultural environments and build relationships with diverse publics. Practitioners should not only have knowledge about the contextualized environments, but also comprehensive competencies at trait-based, perceptual, behavioral, and culture-specific aspects as identified by Lustig and Koester (2009). Wang, Ni, and de la Flor's (2014) study findings indicate that these competencies significantly affect practitioners' relationship management with local community members of multinational companies.

Need for the Current Book

In summary, research following the cross-cultural approach focuses more on, and thus are delimited to, specific variables at a *macro* level, such as political system and other infrastructure, culture, and media environment. Many of these variables are beyond the direct control of typical practitioners at an individual level. In addition, most such research on cross-cultural comparison focuses primarily on the *knowledge* element of intercultural competencies of practitioners by discussing what these practitioners need to know about a particular country.

The intercultural approach, on the other hand, supplements the cross-cultural approach by delving into the delicate processes of the actual interaction between practitioners (and their organizations) and publics, as well as incorporating skill-based and behavior-based competencies (in addition to knowledge-based), in particular, the abilities to engage in interpersonal communication with diverse publics.

To supplement these existing books that shed light for public relations students and practitioners, this current book aims to provide a theory-driven, empirically tested framework that will guide practical solutions for effective intercultural public relations practice. Following an *intercultural approach* (i.e., how individuals and entities with dissimilar cultural identities interact and negotiate to solve problems and reach mutually satisfying outcomes), this book analyzes issues at interpersonal, intra-organizational, and organizational levels.

To our knowledge, this book is the first to use a coherent theoretical framework unifying public relations and intercultural communication theories and to examine actual intercultural interactions based on empirically tested studies.

Content of this Book

This book consists of two main parts: (1) theoretical foundations in public relations management, intercultural communication, and conflict management and negotiation; and (2) integrated processes in intercultural public relations ranging from interpersonal (competencies), intra-organizational (identification of publics, relationship management, and conflict management), to organizational

(organizational identity and culture) levels. The last chapter discusses new trends in intercultural public relations, especially the influences and challenges of social media.

Part I: Theoretical Foundations

Chapter 2: Foundational Theories in Public Relations Management

This chapter discusses key theories in public relations management, mainly following the behavioral, strategic management paradigm in public relations scholarship. Theories include the strategic management process of public relations, as well as critical elements in such a management process, which include identification of publics; development and identifying of messages, messengers, and channels; relationship management; and conflict management. Many public relations studies and theories in these areas are further detailed in later chapters that review the evolution and theoretical development in identifying publics (Chapter 6), relationship management (Chapter 7), and conflict management (Chapter 8) in intercultural settings.

Chapter 3: History and Foundational Theories of Intercultural Communication

This chapter discusses the history of intercultural communication, conceptualization of culture, and key concepts and key theories in intercultural communication. The chapter reviews various disciplines that started and heavily shaped the field, such as sociology, anthropology, linguistics, and naturalism. It then discusses the formal establishment of the field with the hallmark of the Foreign Service Institute. The chapter then delves into a philosophical discussion of the origin of culture and full conceptualization. After introducing other similar terms with intercultural communication, the chapter summarizes and critiques 13 of the most widely influential and tested intercultural communication theories. The chapter ends with a discussion on methodological issues and conclusion.

Chapter 4: Conflict Management and Negotiation

This chapter starts with the conceptualization of conflict because how conflict is defined and perceived decides how the involved parties manage the conflict. With a review of extant definitions, we provide a construct definition and discussion of the properties, antecedents, consequences, and constants of conflict. An example is discussed in depth to explicate the concept. The second part of this chapter reviews and critiques conflict management literature, with a focus on the two-dimensional conflict management model based on

Blake and Mouton's (1964) managerial grid. Based on the critique, we provide some suggestions for future research. The third part of the chapter focuses on the relationship between negotiation and conflict management, and provides a framework of public relations negotiation strategies.

This chapter is the last chapter setting the theoretical foundation in this book (Part I). It ends with an expanded model of intercultural public relations management, integrating major concepts in this book to provide a general framework for the readers. The chapters in the second part of this book then discuss each element of the model in more detail.

Part II: Intercultural Public Relations at Various Levels

Chapter 5: Interpersonal Level: Competencies and Practices

This chapter highlights key theories and concepts that can be used to theorize about the processes for strategic intercultural public relations management at the interpersonal level. This chapter starts by establishing a case for the importance of intercultural communication competencies from the perspective of any player in intercultural settings, both public relations practitioners and publics. The chapter then provides an overview of the various theoretical frameworks in intercultural communication competencies (ICC), followed by a discussion of ICC development for the practitioners and publics, respectively. For the practitioners, it is noted that such competencies involve multiple levels, going beyond the typical knowledge base required for these practitioners in intercultural settings. For the publics, the chapter provides various theoretical approaches in acculturation and adaptation to enhance the overall well-being of culturally diverse publics, such as ethnic minority publics and immigrants. The chapter discusses these publics' cultural adjustment and adaptation, as well as outcomes reflected in mental health, career advancement, and social support. The chapter then discusses a framework that incorporates past theories in training and competency building for both practitioners and publics. The discussion includes the current status, different approaches to competency building and training, strategies and methods, and evaluation of such training. The chapter ends with a brief conclusion on the implications of these theories for both scholarship and practice.

Chapter 6: Intra-Organizational Level: Identifying and Communicating with Publics

This chapter starts by explicating the relevance of identifying publics in different stages of the strategic management process of public relations programs. Meanwhile, it reviews different approaches to identifying publics, ranging from cross-situational to situational, with different typologies of publics presented. The chapter then draws in the content from previous chapters on the strategic management of public relations and discusses guidelines for identifying publics in different stages. Then it discusses main issues in identifying publics in intercultural settings, in particular, the challenges in the digital age, the various consequences of public formation, as well as the antecedents of public perceptions and formation. In the antecedents of public formation, we integrate the current literature by following a multilevel approach: micro-level influence, meso-level influence, and macro-level influence. The chapter then reviews literature on how cultural influences play a role in communicating with diverse publics. Finally, the chapter touches on the challenges of pigeonholing, whereby practitioners of specific cultural backgrounds are restricted to working with those perceived as being culturally similar to themselves.

Chapter 7: Intra-Organizational Level: Relationship Management

This chapter first reviews recent developments on relationship management research and then focuses more specifically on relationship management in intercultural settings. As discussed in an overview in Chapter 2, relationship management research has been developed as a three-stage model (J. Grunig & Huang, 2000): antecedents, maintenance strategies (more recently called cultivation strategies), and outcomes. After reviewing recent development in this literature in general and the specific work in intercultural relationship management, we revise and reformulate the model as a multi-level, multi-stage model.

The model consists of antecedents of relationships (organizational level and public level), process of relationship building (approaches and strategies), measurements of relationships (reliable and valid instruments), and outcomes of relationships (organization-centered and public-centered). We briefly review these components first, followed by more details for each stage. We then conclude with a revised theoretical framework for intercultural relationship management. In this new framework, each of these components involves factors unique to interaction with publics in intercultural settings.

Chapter 8: Intra-Organizational Level: Conflict Management and Negotiation

This chapter discusses the importance of conflict management and negotiation within an organization, because it poses a major challenge in intercultural public relations. After reviewing extant theoretical frameworks in public relations of conflict management, especially the models involving symmetrical communication, we propose a new model of intercultural conflict management that consists of three stages: pre-conflict, conflict, and post-conflict.

This model integrates theories reviewed in previous chapters that come from strategic management of public relations including (a) environmental scanning, (b) identifying publics, (c) relationship management, (d) conflict management, as well as those from intercultural communication including identity and identification.

The pre-conflict management approach and preparation prior to a conflict addresses both stakeholder engagement and practitioner competency and preparation. The conflict stage includes conflict assessment from multiple aspects, conflict management strategies in general, and negotiation strategies in particular. The post-conflict stage assesses the uses and effectiveness of conflict management strategies, the outcomes of the conflict, changes in identity and positions in both parties and their relationships; this stage also sets goals for the next stage. Based on the proposed model, we then review and integrate existing research and propose potential areas of research in intercultural settings.

Chapter 9: Organizational Level: Organizational Identity and Identification

This chapter reviews different perspectives on organizational identity, including identification *with* an organization and identity *of* an organization. It then discusses factors that may influence both members' identification with an organization and the different kinds of organizational identities. In particular, we review and integrate research that highlights the mutual influence of public relations and organizational identity. Chapters 3 and 5 consider the identity of and cultural influences on individuals as a part of an organizational public. At the same time, organizations also have unique features that influence how public relations is practiced. Chapter 9 thus focuses on organizational identity and how it influences the way public relations is practiced and perceived. We also acknowledge the substantial influence of organizational culture and societal culture but do not discuss these in this chapter because this topic has been heavily addressed in various books following the cross-cultural comparison approach, such as Bardhan and Weaver (2010), Sriramesh and Vercic (2009, 2012) and Vercic et al. (2015). Interested readers should refer to those books for more detailed information.

Chapter 10: Social Media

Given the growing importance of social media, it is fair to assume that social media affect identity development for publics, public relations practitioners, and organizations. The influence of social media touches almost all areas in public relations practice, ranging from environmental scanning, identifying publics, messaging strategies, and relationship management, to conflict management. This chapter starts with an overview of social media use in public relations, followed by a more detailed discussion on the effects of social media on individual and organizational identities, as well as how social media have changed the various areas of public relations management. It ends with an evaluation of social media use based on their different purposes and functions in intercultural public relations, and directions for future research.

Chapter 11: Conclusions

This chapter summarizes the main arguments and theoretical structures in the previous chapters and culminates with a discussion of the new model of intercultural public relations management. It then proposes directions for future research.

Overview of the Theoretical Structure in the Book

To provide an overview, this book synthesizes literature and theories from different fields and generates a theoretical structure of public relations practices in intercultural settings that are both public- and organization-centered.

Public-Centered

We examine the importance and strategies of identifying publics by looking into the antecedents to the formation and/or change of publics (Chapter 6). These antecedents include multilevel factors. At the micro level, publics' perceptions and communication behaviors are influenced by their individual cultural identity (Chapter 3) and personal life experiences (Chapter 5). At the meso level, publics' perceptions and communication behaviors are linked to organizational factors, such as how organizations manage relationships (organization–public relationships, Chapter 7) and conflicts with these publics (conflict management, Chapter 8). At the macro level, societal culture's role is linked to the formation of publics (Chapter 3 and Chapter 9).

Organization-Centered

Because this book adopts the strategic, managerial approach to public relations, we examine how different types of organizations can practice intercultural public relations in the most effective and ethical way. Adapting and expanding Kim and Ni's (2013) theoretical structure, this book makes an argument that, to achieve different goals in the two types of public relations problems, different strategies are needed.

In particular, the goal of organization-initiated public relations problems is to "activate" the publics, potentially changing them from latent publics to aware or even active publics. This is accomplished primarily through public relations in the more traditional sense such as messaging and persuasion (Chapter 2). On the other hand, the goal of public-initiated public relations problems is to "de-activate" the publics, potentially changing them from active, and usually angry, publics to aware or latent publics. This is accomplished primarily through relationship management and conflict management (Chapters 8 and 9) because messaging alone will not be sufficient or ethical. The publics cannot be simply persuaded if the organization does not engage in substantial, internal adjustment and change in terms of policies, procedures, and behaviors. This is also the essence of symmetrical communication.

References

Banks, S. (2000). *Multicultural public relations: A social-interpretive approach* (2nd ed.). Ames, IA: Iowa State University Press.

Bardhan, N., & Weaver, C. K. (2010). *Public relations in global cultural contexts: Multi-paradigmatic perspectives.* New York, NY: Routledge.

Blake, R. R., & Mouton, J. S. (1964). *The managerial grid.* Houston, TX: Gulf.

Culbertson, H. M., & Chen, N. (1996). *International public relations: A comparative analysis.* New York, NY: Routledge.

Curtin, P. A., & Gaither, T. K. (2007). *International public relations: Negotiating culture, identity, and power.* Thousand Oaks, CA: Sage.

Dutta-Bergman, M. J. (2005). Civil society and public relations: Not so civil after all. *Journal of Public Relations Research, 17,* 267–289. doi: 10.1207/ s1532754xjprr1703_3

Edwards, L., & Hodges, C. E. M. (Eds.) (2011). *Public relations, society and culture: Theoretical and empirical explorations.* New York, NY: Routledge.

Freitag, A. R., & Stokes, A. Q. (2008). *Global public relations: Spanning borders, spanning cultures.* New York, NY: Routledge.

Grunig, J. E., & Huang, Y. H. (2000). From organizational effectiveness to relationship indicators: Antecedents of relationships, public relations strategies, and relationship outcomes. In J. A. Ledingham & S. D. Bruning (Eds.), *Public relations as relationship management: A relational approach to the study and practice of public relations* (pp. 23–53). Mahwah, NJ: Erlbaum.

Grunig, L. A., Grunig, J. E., & Dozier, D. M. (2002). *Excellent public relations and effective organizations: A study of communication management in three countries.* Mahwah, NJ: Erlbaum.

Hofstede, G. (2001). *Culture's consequences: Comparing values, behaviors, institutions, and organizations across nations* (2nd ed.). Thousand Oaks, CA: Sage.

Hofstede, G., & Hofstede, G. J. (2005). *Cultures and organizations: Software of the mind* (2nd ed.). New York, NY: McGraw-Hill.

Hon, L. C. (1995). Toward a feminist theory of public relations. *Journal of Public Relations Research, 7,* 27–88. doi.org/10.1207/s1532754xjprr0701 03

Jain, R., DeMoya, M., & Molleda, J. C. (2014). State of international public relations research narrowing the knowledge gap about the practice across borders. *Public Relations Review, 40,* 595–597. doi: 10.1016/j.pubrev.2014.02.009

Kim, J.-N., & Ni, L. (2013). Two types of public relations problems and integrating formative and evaluative research: A review of research programs within the behavioral, strategic management paradigm. *Journal of Public Relations Research, 25,* 1–29. doi: 10.1080/1062726X.2012.723276

Lustig, M. W., & Koester, J. (2009). *Intercultural competence: Interpersonal communication across cultures*. Upper Saddle River, NJ: Pearson.

Ni, L. (2009). Strategic role of relationship building: Perceived links between employee–organization relationships and globalization strategies. *Journal of Public Relations Research, 21*, 100–120. doi: 10.1080/10627260802520512

Ni, L. (2013). Globalization and public relations. In Heath, R. L. (Ed.), *Encyclopedia of public relations* (2nd ed., pp. 395–396). Thousand Oaks, CA: Sage.

Ni, L., & Wang, Q. (2011). Anxiety and uncertainty management in an intercultural setting: The impact on organization–public relationships. *Journal of Public Relations Research, 23*, 269–301. doi: 10.1080/1062726X.2011.582205

Pal, M., & Dutta, M. J. (2008). Public relations in a global context: The relevance of critical modernism as a theoretical lens. *Journal of Public Relations Research, 20*, 159–179. doi: 10.1080/10627260801894280

Pompper, D. (2005). "Difference" in public relations research: A case for introducing critical race theory. *Journal of Public Relations Research, 17*, 139–169. doi: 10.1207/s1532754xjprr1702_5

Sha, B.-L. (1995). *Intercultural public relations: Exploring cultural identity as a means of segmenting publics*. Unpublished master's thesis, University of Maryland, College Park, MD.

Sha, B.-L. (2006). Cultural identity in the segmentation of publics: An emerging theory of intercultural public relations. *Journal of Public Relations Research, 18*, 45–65. doi: 10.1207/ s1532754xjprr1801_3

Singer, M. R. (1998). *Perception & identity in intercultural communication*. Yarmouth, MA: Intercultural Press.

Somerville, I., Hargie, O., Taylor, M., & Toledano, M. (Eds.). (2016). *International public relations: Perspectives from deeply divided societies*. New York: NY: Routledge.

Sriramesh, K. (2004). *Public relations in Asia*. Singapore: Thomson Asia Pte.

Sriramesh, K., & Vercic, D. (2009). *The global public relations handbook, revised and expanded edition: Theory, research, and practice* (2nd ed.). New York, NY: Routledge.

Srirmesh, K., & Vercic, D. (2012). *Culture and public relations: Links and implications*. New York, NY: Routledge.

Taylor, M. (2000). Toward a public relations approach to nation building. *Journal of Public Relations Research, 12*, 179–210. doi: 10.1207/S1532754XJPRR1202_3

Taylor, M., & Doerfel, M. L. (2003). Building interorganizational relationships that build nations. *Communication Research, 29*, 153–181. doi: 10.1111/j.1468-2958.2003.tb00835.x

Tindall, N. T. J., & Waters, R. D. (2012). Coming out to tell our stories: Using queer theory to understand the career experiences of gay men in public relations. *Journal of Public Relations Research, 24*, 451–475. doi: 10.1080/1062726X.2012.723279

Vercic, D., Zerfass, A., & Wiesenberg, M. (2015). Global public relations and communication management: A European perspective. *Public Relations Review, 41*, 785–793. doi: 10.1016/j.pubrev.2015.06

Vilanilam, J. V. (2011). *Public relations in India: New tasks and responsibilities*. Thousand Oaks, CA: Sage.

Wang, Q., Ni, L., &De la Flor, M. (2014). An intercultural competence model of strategic public relations management in the Peru mining industry context. *Journal of Public Relations Research, 26*, 1–22. doi: 10.1080/1062726X.2013.795864

Watson, T. (2014). *Asian perspectives on the development of public relations: Other voices*. New York, NY: Palgrave Macmillan.

Waymer, D. (Ed.) (2012). *Culture, social class, and race in public relations: Perspectives and applications*. Lanham, MD: Lexington Books.

PART I
Theoretical Foundations

2

FOUNDATIONAL THEORIES IN PUBLIC RELATIONS MANAGEMENT

This chapter reviews the key theories in public relations management that are relevant to the purpose of this book. This review is delimited to the behavioral, strategic management paradigm (L. Grunig, J. Grunig, & Dozier, 2002; J.-N. Kim & Ni, 2013) in public relations scholarship. The delimitation is set because we acknowledge that multiple complementary or competing theoretical perspectives exist in public relations scholarship. We do not attempt to claim the perspective introduced here is the only or the best approach. All perspectives can be used in different situations to tackle different problems.

This chapter starts with an overview of the strategic management process of public relations, followed by key theories in the specific areas of strategic management of public relations: environmental scanning, identification of strategic publics, development of messages and messengers/channels, relationship management, and conflict management. The chapter ends with an initial model of public relations management and an illustration of the model using a case campaign. The model will be expanded with each of the following chapters, and we present a new model of intercultural public relations management at the end of Chapter 4.

Strategic Management of Public Relations

The behavioral, strategic management approach to public relations has been primarily established and developed by James E. Grunig and his colleagues over the years, with a key milestone of the *IABC Excellence Study*. Funded by the International Association of Business Communicators (IABC) Research Foundation, the Excellence Study began in 1985. It was conducted in response to the IABC's call for proposals to answer two questions: How do public relations functions make organizations more effective (the effectiveness question), and how should public relations functions be organized to help achieve such effectiveness (the excellence question). Answers to these two main questions revealed (a) the mechanisms through which public relations adds value to organizations and to society, and (b) the generic principles of excellent public relations (see L. Grunig et al. [2002] for details about the research team and the three books resulting from the Excellence project). This section reviews research findings on these two main questions, followed by the role of public relations in the strategic management process, a key condition to public relations excellence.

The Effectiveness Question: Value of Public Relations

In order to show how public relations adds value to organizations and society, L. Grunig et al. (2002) began by examining what people mean by "effectiveness." After reviewing literature in sociology and business management, they identified four major approaches to organizational effectiveness. Each approach has its own strengths and weaknesses. The *goal-attainment* approach focuses on whether the organization is effective in achieving its goals. However, it is sometimes difficult to address the challenges of multiple, conflicting, and constantly changing goals. The *systems* approach evaluates effectiveness by whether an organization can survive in the environment through obtaining necessary resources. However, this approach has its own problems, including treating the environment as a vague term; the failure to differentiate between efficiency and effectiveness; and the focus on survival, which is an insufficient goal for an organization at times. The *strategic constituencies* approach focuses on more specific segments of the environment rather than the total environment, and identifies those segments that are most important for organizational survival and success. This approach can be problematic too because of the difficulty in determining the priority or "strategic-ness" of the constituencies. Finally, the *competing values* approach focuses on whether an organization can incorporate the competing values of its constituencies into organizational goals.

Based on the above, the Excellence team decided to combine the four major approaches. Researchers on the team concluded that organizations are effective when they choose and achieve *goals* that are important to their self-interest as well as to the interests of *strategic constituencies* in the *environment*—groups that might have *competing values* (J. Grunig, Ferrari, & Franc, 2009, p. 26). Linking this integrated view of organizational effectiveness to the public relations function, the value of public relations then lies in helping organizations become more effective by scanning the organizational environment; identifying strategic publics; reconciling organizational goals with the expectations of these publics; and building long-term, quality relationships with these publics to reduce costs and gain support. This chapter reviews each of these elements in the following sections.

Demonstrating the Value of Public Relations

After the value of public relations is established, the next challenge is demonstrating and measuring such value. Recognizing the difficulty in assigning direct, monetary value to public relations efforts, the Excellence team used an alternative measure of such value by using a cost-benefit technique called compensating variation (Ehling, 1992; L. Grunig et al., 2002). *Compensating variation* provides a way of transforming nonmonetary values, such as the value of good relationships, into monetary values. Essentially, the following two questions are asked: (a) for a program beneficiary, what amount of money is one willing to pay so as to be equally well off with the program or with the payment; and (b) for a person made worse off by a program, what amount of money is one willing to pay to eliminate the effects so as to be equally well off without the program or the payment. Although these are soft, comparative measures, they yielded strong statistical evidence of the value of public relations and have strong statistical correlations with the characteristics of excellent public relations. This then showed that an excellent public relations function contributes more value than less-excellent public relations (L. Grunig et al., 2002).

In recent years, however, more efforts have been made on demonstrating public relations value through relationships cultivated. Even though it is difficult or impossible to establish a monetary value for relationships created through the public relations function (for reasons, see L. Grunig et al., 2002; J. Grunig et al., 2009), it is possible to measure the quality of an organization's relationships with its publics (more in the "Relationship Management" section in this chapter, as well as Chapter 7). This thereby indirectly confirms that a public relations function has created value for an organization. In addition, public relations has value to society by encouraging organizations to practice social responsibility and helping reduce societal conflicts. Public relations achieves societal value by helping organizations develop quality relationships with their publics and pushing organizations to take into account both the interests of publics and their self-interests (J. Grunig et al., 2009, p. 30).

The Excellence Question: Generic Principles of Excellent Public Relations

The follow-up question then is how public relations should be practiced so that it adds value to organizations and society. Empirical research conducted in more than 300 companies extracted some generic principles of excellence in public relations. These principles describe the characteristics of excellent public relations at different levels (functional and program) and provide the internal and environmental contexts of an organization that increases the likelihood that the public relations function will be practiced in an excellent way (L. Grunig et al., 2002). These principles are summarized as follows.

Principles at the Functional Level

The public relations function should be configured in a way that leads to excellence in this performance. The characteristics include empowerment, roles, models, and the organization of the public relations function.

Empowerment of the Public Relations Function

Three principles advocate for the empowerment of the public relations function as a distinctive and strategic managerial function if it is to play a role in making organizations effective.

1. The senior public relations executive is involved with the strategic management processes of the organization, and communication programs are developed for strategic publics identified as a part of this strategic management process.
2. The senior public relations executive is a member of the dominant coalition of the organization, or the senior public relations executive has a direct reporting relationship to senior managers who are part of the dominant coalition.
3. Diversity is embodied in all public relations roles.

Public Relations Roles

Extensive research suggests four major roles that communicators play in organizations—the manager, senior adviser (also known as the communication liaison), technician, and media relations (for a review, see Dozier, 1992; Dozier & Broom; L. Grunig et al., 2002, ch. 6). The manager and technician roles are the most common of the four. Three principles about roles have been proposed and tested.

1. The public relations unit is headed by a manager rather than a technician.
2. The senior public relations executive or others in the public relations unit must have the knowledge needed for the manager role, or the communication function will not have the potential to become a managerial function.
3. Both men and women must have equal opportunities to occupy the managerial role in an excellent department.

The results of the Excellence study solidly supported the proposition that, for the senior communicator in a public relations department, the distinction between the manager and technician role is a core factor in distinguishing excellent from less-excellent departments. More important than any other variable, the availability of knowledge about performing a managerial role distinguishes excellent departments from less-excellent ones. However, results also showed the vital supporting role of technical expertise to the management role.

Public Relations Models and Dimensions

The *models of public relations* were introduced as a way of understanding and explaining the behavior of public relations practitioners (J. Grunig, 1976). Four models were originally proposed (J. Grunig & Hunt, 1984): the *press agentry* model (to get publicity in any way possible), the *public information* model (to offer objective information on the organization but not to volunteer negative information), the *two-way asymmetrical* model (to do research and listen to publics in an effort to determine how best to change the behavior of publics to benefit the organization), and the *two-way symmetrical* model (to do research to understand publics and to balance the interests of organizations with those of their publics).

Over the years, these public relations models have been researched and debated (for reviews see J. Grunig & L. Grunig, 1998; J. Grunig, 2001; L. Grunig et al., 2002, ch. 8). L. Grunig et al. (2002) summarized and concluded that the two-way symmetrical model still appears to be a normative ideal for public relations practice but is practiced in the real world as well. If public relations professionals have the knowledge of practicing the two-way symmetrical model and if society recognizes the value of public relations, these practitioners can use the power of their knowledge to advocate for a symmetrical approach to public relations. Two-way symmetrical public relations aims to balance the interests of the organization and its publics through research and communication to manage conflict and cultivate relationships with strategic publics. As a result, two-way symmetrical communication produces better long-term relationships with publics than the other models of public relations. Symmetrical practitioners therefore have *mixed motives*—they are loyal to both their employers and to the publics of their organizations. Three specific propositions were based on the symmetrical model:

1. The public relations department and the dominant coalition share the worldview that the communication department should reflect the two-way symmetrical, or mixed-motive, model of public relations.
2. Communication programs developed for specific publics are based on the two-way symmetrical, mixed-motive model.
3. The senior public relations executive or others in the public relations unit must have the knowledge needed for the two-way symmetrical model, or the communication function will not have the potential to practice that excellent model.

As a continuous development in theory and research, the Excellence project (L. Grunig et al., 2002) isolated three continuous variables or *dimensions* underlying the original four models. The first three dimensions were a continuum from a one-way to two-way *direction* of communication (i.e., whether communication is two-way in the sense that research is used to help organizations obtain feedback from the publics), a continuum from an asymmetrical to a symmetrical *purpose* of public relations, and two continua indicating the frequency of using mediated *techniques*, interpersonal techniques, or both, depending on the situation and public. The Excellence team also proposed, but did not measure or test, a fourth dimension that represented the extent to which public relations activities are *ethical*. These new dimensions seemed to explain why organizations with an excellent public relations function practiced the two-way symmetrical, two-way asymmetrical, and public information models at the same time. These organizations practiced these three models because they had a symmetrical purpose in mind, favored research (i.e., two-way communication), and used both mediated and interpersonal communication (J. Grunig et al., 2009). Excellent public relations can therefore be better described in terms of these underlying dimensions than in terms of the four discrete models themselves (more in Chapters 7 and 8).

Organization of the Public Relations Function

For public relations to be managed strategically and to serve a role in the overall strategic management of the organization, two theoretical principles were proposed and tested.

1. An organization must have an integrated communication function. An excellent public relations function integrates all public relations programs into a single department, or provides a mechanism for coordinating programs managed by different departments.
2. Public relations should be a management function separate from other functions. It should not be integrated into another department with any primary responsibility other than communication.

Principles at the Program Level

In addition to theorizing about and researching the characteristics of the overall public relations function, the Excellence study also examined ongoing programs that excellent communication departments design to cultivate relationships with their key publics, such as media relations, community relations, or employee relations. The results from the Excellence study provided strong support for the proposition that specific programs organized by excellent departments should be *managed strategically*, or are more likely to have strategic origins (i.e., programs designed to achieve strategic purposes) and less likely to have historical origins (i.e., programs designed that simply repeat what has been done in the past). For more information, see the section in this chapter on the management of public relations programs.

External Context for Excellence: Activism and the Environment

The Excellence study also examined characteristics of the organization and its environment to determine whether excellence in communication requires certain external and internal contexts. The Excellence theory predicted that, externally, *a turbulent, complex environment with pressure from activist groups* stimulates organizations to develop an excellent public relations function. Results confirmed that activism tended to push organizations toward excellent public relations.

Internal Context of Excellence

Organizational characteristics of internal structure, culture, internal system of communication, treatment of men and women, and power of the dominant coalition were reported to predict organizational behavior and public relations practice. The Excellence theory included five propositions regarding the organizational context for excellent public relations:

1. Participative rather than authoritarian organizational cultures.
2. A symmetrical system of internal communication.
3. Organic rather than mechanical structures.
4. Programs to equalize opportunities for men and women and for minorities.
5. High job satisfaction among employees.

Research results from the Excellence study demonstrated that excellent public relations will thrive most in an organization with an organic structure, participative culture, and a symmetrical system of communication, and one in which opportunities exist for women and racio-ethnic minorities. These conditions alone cannot produce excellent public relations, but they do provide a hospitable environment (L. Grunig et al., 2002).

The Role of Public Relations in Strategic Management

As recognized in the answer to the second question, how should public relations functions be organized to help achieve organizational effectiveness, public relations should participate in the strategic management of an organization, an essential condition for bringing excellence to public relations (J. Grunig &

Repper, 1992; L. Grunig et al., 2002). J. Grunig and Repper (1992) suggested a three-stage model for strategic management of public relations: stakeholder, public, and issues. L. Grunig et al. (2002) added the crisis stage as the fourth stage. The complete model of strategic management of public relations illustrates the connection between central concepts such as management decisions, stakeholders and publics, and relationship outcomes (p. 145).

Stakeholder Stage

In the *stakeholder stage*, behaviors of the organization or of a stakeholder have decisional or behavioral consequences on the other. Groups exist that have stakes needed by the organization to achieve its mission. Public relations practitioners should therefore perform environmental scanning (see more in the "Environmental Scanning" section in this chapter) to identify those stakeholders whose behaviors will influence the organization and who will be influenced by organizational behaviors. Practitioners should first make a list of people who are linked to the organization through (potential) consequences on each other, rank these stakeholders to indicate their impacts on the organization or the organization's impact on them, and then plan ongoing communication programs beginning with the most important stakeholders.

In the stakeholder stage, the concept of linkages (J. Grunig & Hunt, 1984) is commonly used. The four major types of linkages are enabling, functional, normative, and diffused. Enabling linkages provide the authority and control the resources that enable the organization to exist. *Functional* linkages provide inputs and take outputs. Input linkages include employees, unions, and suppliers, whereas output linkages include consumers and industrial purchasers. *Normative linkages* refer to those groups that face similar problems or share similar values, such as associations. *Diffused linkages* are those that cannot clearly be identified by membership, but when the organization has done something that creates consequences these linkages can organize to do something against the organization.

Public Stage

In the *public stage*, groups find that they can use their stakes to push for changes in the performance of the targeted organization or industry; these groups form to exercise their influence. As organizations enter into the public stage, the consequences that organizations and stakeholders have on each other may become a problem; in other words, a public arises as it finds certain consequences to be problematic. In most cases, publics approach organizations hoping to get organizational acknowledgement of their concerns and proactive corrections to the problem.

In this stage, practitioners need to identify and segment publics to increase the possibility of achieving communication goals with these publics. Specifically, practitioners are advised to use focus groups to involve publics in the decision-making process. The situational theory of publics (cf. J. Grunig, 1997) has been used extensively in this stage to strategically identify publics. The common types of publics include hot-issue, single-issue, all-issue, and apathetic publics. Regarding the evolution of different stages of publics for the same situation, publics can be classified into nonpublics, latent, aware, and active publics (more in the section "Identification of Publics" and Chapter 6).

We note that, in current public relations literature and practice, the relationship and distinction between a "stakeholder" and "public" is not always clear. Sometimes these two terms are used interchangeably. As seen in the brief introduction here and more in Chapter 6, the concepts of "stakeholder" and "public" are differentiated in three ways: type of connection with an organization, level of activeness, and composition of the entity. First, a stakeholder is defined purely from an organizational standpoint. If an individual has a stake in an organization (i.e., his/her behaviors will influence the organization or the behaviors of the organization will influence him/her), then he/she is a stakeholder. On the other hand, a public may or may not have a direct relationship with an organization. Second, a stakeholder is less active than a public in most cases. The public, especially aware and active publics or publics that are defined by issues (hot-issue, single-issue, all-issue), are typically active and engage with an organization in various ways. However, the latent public is similar to stakeholders. Third, a stakeholder is an individual, whereas a public is a collective group of individuals.

Issues Stage

Finally, in the *issues stage*, publics arise and make issues out of problems that they believe need to be resolved in their interest. Practitioners should segment publics, use mediated and interpersonal communication, and engage in negotiation and conflict management (see more in the next sections "Relationship Management" and "Conflict Management," as well as Chapters 7 and 8). If the issues are not handled well, they can evolve into crises.

Regardless of the stage of strategic management of public relations, the use of research is essential. The two types of research—formative and evaluative research—can be used at both organizational level and program level. At the organizational level, formative research involves environmental scanning, and evaluative research involves both short-term and long-term outcome indicators (e.g., types of relationships and relationship outcomes).

Strategic Management of Public Relations Programs

At a program level, public relations should be managed strategically as well. This strategic management process is commonly known as the four-stage process of RPIE (Research, Planning, Implementation, and Evaluation) (see Broom & Sha, 2013). This section provides a brief overview of this management process.

Research

Any public relations program starts with research to identify the problem, key forces or constituencies in the organizational environment, and important stakeholders involved in the situation. Based on these goals, the research is done to understand (a) the situation around a particular problem or opportunity, (b) the organization, and (c) the publics. Three deliverables are produced accordingly after the research process: a situational analysis, a problem statement, and identification of publics.

A *problem statement* is used to describe the current situation in specific and measurable terms. It does not imply solution or place blame. The *situational analysis* contextualizes the problem statement and involves both positive and negative factors or forces in the internal and external environments of the organization. An example of analysis of internal factors is the communication audit and an example for that of external factors is a stakeholder analysis. Ultimately a *SWOT analysis* should be generated that synthesizes the internal strengths (S) and weaknesses (W), as well as external opportunities (O) and threats (T) surrounding this issue. Environmental scanning can be used to generate this situational analysis. Finally, the *identification of stakeholders*, who they are and how they are involved, is a critical part where practitioners use theories and best practices to understand stakeholders that are strategic to the organization and relevant to the particular situation.

Planning

Based on the findings from the first stage of research, a public relations program enters the planning stage where a program goal statement, target publics, specific objectives for the target publics, action strategy and tactics, and communication strategy and tactics are developed.

First, the *goal statement* is derived from the problem statement developed in the research stage. Moving from "what is the problem now," or "where we are now," the public relations program needs to specify "where we want to be" after the program implementation.

Then based on the stakeholder analysis developed in the research stage, more focused segmentation of strategic publics is conducted. Among all stakeholders, selected target publics for the particular public relations programs are identified, segmented, and analyzed. Based on the overall goal statement, each target public needs to have specific objectives in terms of their changes in knowledge, attitude, and behavior desired by the organization.

After target publics and objectives are determined, the program team needs to plan for corresponding program strategy and tactics that can be used to achieve these specific objectives, and ultimately the overall goal. There are two types of strategy and tactics: action and communication, which need to be implemented in the next stage.

Implementation

During this third stage, a public relations program is implemented (Broom & Sha, 2013). The different action strategy and tactics, as well as communication strategy and tactics, are utilized.

The *action strategy* directly addresses the source of the initial problem. It requires internal adjustment and adaption, especially with regard to internal policies, procedures, products, services, and behaviors.

The *communication strategy*, on the other hand, comes after the action strategy. Any actions taken to address the problem need to be communicated to the public. There are two parts to the communication strategy: messaging strategy (the content of communication) and the message delivery strategy (channels of communication). See more in the section "Developing Messages" in this chapter.

Evaluation

After a public relations program is conducted, its effectiveness is assessed to discover what has worked, what has not, and what lessons have been learned for future program planning. Evaluation of a public relations program typically includes three levels: preparation, implementation, and impact. The *preparation level* evaluates how well the inputs of the program have been prepared. The *implementation level* evaluates how well the outputs of the program have been produced and executed. The *impact level* evaluates how well the program has generated intended outcomes or effects on the publics. See Broom and Sha (2013) for details.

At the preparation level, evaluation needs to be done on three elements: the adequacy of *background* information, the organization and appropriateness of the message *content*, activity/event, and the *technical and production values* of the messages and events produced.

At the implementation level, evaluation needs to be done on the *distribution* (the number of messages distributed to the media and the public and the events designed); the *placement* of messages (the number of messages placed in the media and the number of events produced); the *potential audience* (the number of people potentially exposed to messages and events); and the *attentive audience* (the number of people who attend to messages or attend events).

At the impact level, evaluation needs to be done on the *knowledge* gain (the number of people who learn the message content); *opinion* change (the number of people who form or change feelings); *attitude* change (the number of people who form or change dispositions); *behavior* change (the number of people who act as desired); *repeated behavior* (the number of people who continue desired behavior); and *social and cultural change* (the long-term changes in society).

Having summarized the key theoretical structure and findings in the overall behavioral management approach to public relations as well as the strategic management of specific public relations programs, we continue with theories in the main theoretical components to the strategic management approach:

environmental scanning, identification of strategic publics, development of messages and messengers/channels, relationship management, and conflict management.

Note that the following sections discuss theoretical frameworks in accordance with the four stages of the program management process: environmental scanning is useful in the research stage; identification of publics is useful in the planning stage; and development of messages, messengers/channels, and relationship management are useful in the implementation stage. The evaluation stage does not have a separate detailed section but is included in the overall, integrated model of public relations practices in the "Model of Public Relations Practice" section. We then use a case on countering violent extremism that the first author conducted with her students to illustrate this overall public relations program management process.

This book then continues to revise and expand this model of public relations management in the following chapters, with the goal of generating a new model that integrates important theoretical aspects in intercultural public relations. For the overall, expanded model, please see the end of Chapter 4.

Environmental Scanning

Environmental scanning is a major part of the strategic management of public relations because it is closely related to business strategy. *Environmental scanning* is defined as "a methodology for coping with external competitive, social, economic, and technical issues that may be difficult to observe or diagnose but that cannot be ignored and will not go away" (Stoffels, 1994, p. 1). Together with the strategy of identifying publics, environmental scanning can play an important role in public relations practice.

The function of environmental scanning is to identify emerging situations, trends, threats, and opportunities in society, particularly those that may be difficult for the organization to absorb or turn to its advantage, but that may critically influence the organization's growth and success.

Environmental scanning can take place at multiple levels, ranging from low-level observation for learning purposes, to high-level prediction or synthesis, as the organization seeks to integrate signals of future happenings into a meaningful model for strategy development. The use of environmental scanning is not without criticism. Some have felt that the scanning results could be subject to biased interpretation, the organization's preoccupation with reactive and defensive strategy, excessive input or signals, and narrowly selected scenarios (Stoffels, 1994).

Despite such criticism, environmental scanning has proven to be valuable. This function identifies the segment of an organization's strategic management activities that require a view outside the organization's boundaries. By identifying emerging trends, companies develop and modify strategies to meet changing external circumstances and learn to increase the responsiveness and adaptability of organizational decision-making.

Stoffels (1994) provided the following guidelines for a scanning strategy. It starts with identifying the environmental focal zone (EFZ), which includes five dimensions (operational, financial, technological, competitive, and stakeholders) that influence the organization directly through task environment and indirectly through the remote environment. Then, the scanning range settings should be determined. An organization needs to study improbable events with very high impacts, and examine the plausibility range (seek high-payoff events from probable, possible, and improbable environment), time range, and geography range.

Such environmental information could be collected using different formats. Organizations need to decide on the intensity of information collection, such as the continuity of scanning with such questions: Is scanning to be done at an irregular, regular, or continuous rate? What are the methods of scanning? How formal should the scanning effort be? This could range from informal observation, conditioned observation, informal search, to formal search. Organizations also need to determine the specific sources monitored (Stoffels, 1994, p. 108), as well as other factors such as scanning input processing methods and managing and communicating with the scanning system.

Based on some foundational works in environmental scanning, more efforts have been made to build this practice into the strategic management of public relations. Sung (2007), for example, identified key steps in environmental scanning with the goal of scenario building that helps organizations better cope with emerging environmental forces in politics, economy, society, and technology. Major steps in such scenario building include task analysis, environmental influence analysis, issue selection and analysis, key uncertainty identification, key information on the publics, scenario plot and component identification, scenario development and interpretation, final decision on scenarios, and consequence analysis and strategies development.

Identification of Publics

Identification of publics is a key component of environmental scanning, as it focuses on understanding and identifying important segments of people in the social environment. Its importance has produced a plethora of research. In particular, the *situational theory of publics* (see J. Grunig, 1997; J. Grunig & Hunt, 1984) has been developed and used extensively over the years.

Consisting of mainly three independent variables and two dependent variables, the situational theory is considered one of the most useful theories for understanding why publics communicate and when they are most likely to do so (Aldoory & Sha, 2007). The three independent variables include *problem recognition*, or the extent to which "people detect that something should be done about a situation and stop to think about what to do" (J. Grunig, 1997, p. 10); *constraint recognition*, the extent to which people perceive that some constraints prevent them from doing anything about the situation; and *level of involvement*, the extent to which people feel connected to the situation.

These three variables have repeatedly been shown to affect whether and to what extent an individual engages in communication behaviors, as reflected in the two dependent variables: *information seeking* (actively searching for information) and *information processing* (processing of information that is available). This theory has been applied and tested in different contexts (see J. Grunig, 1997 for a review). It has also been extended with studies about antecedents of variables (Aldoory, 2001; Aldoory & Sha, 2007; Sha, 2006), as well as in different cultural contexts (Sriramesh, Moghan, & Wei, 2007; Tkalac, 2007).

J.-N. Kim and J. Grunig (2011) developed a more generalized situational theory, the situational theory of problem solving (STOPS). The theory refines and expands the way for identifying publics for research and practice. Some of the main changes are described below.

First, STOPS adds a new dependent variable: *communicative action in problem solving* (CAPS), as its dependent variable (J.-N. Kim, J. Grunig, & Ni, 2010). CAPS consists of four sub-variables: *information forwarding, sharing, forefending,* and *permitting*—in addition to the two dependent variables of the situational theory of publics, information seeking and information attending (originally termed information processing). CAPS therefore expands the scope of communication behaviors from information taking to information giving and information selecting.

In addition, to explain communicative action, STOPS refines the independent variables of the situational theory of publics. Notably, problem recognition and referent criterion have been redefined, and involvement has been renamed. Problem recognition is now conceptualized as a purely perceptual dimension and defined as "one's perception that something is missing and that there is no immediately applicable solution to it" (J.-N. Kim & J. Grunig, 2011, p. 12). The other part of "stop to think about what to do" about a problematic situation in the original definition of problem recognition is conceptually under a separate, motivational dimension. The new motivational variable (situational motivation) mediates the effects of antecedent perceptual variables on communicative behaviors.

STOPS has new implications for defining and identifying publics. It expands the dynamic and interactive nature of a public by adding the sharing and selecting of information from publics, in addition to the consumption of information in the original situational theory. Therefore, STOPS can better represent the nature of a public and the process of communication. The new features are even more important in intercultural settings because information exchange is a delicate but essential process for resolving problems.

Segmentation of Publics

Understanding and identifying publics leads to better segmentation of publics for strategic communication management. When defining any public relations problem, communicators need to map out the subsegments in the population. In the process, they need to take into account constraints in material and time resources or constraints from the lack of problem recognition of latent or nonpublics.

Researchers and practitioners can benefit from the variety of segmentation methods and taxonomies of publics that capture the different aspects of public profiles (J.-N. Kim, Ni, & Sha, 2008). Several taxonomical frames of public segmentation have been proposed, such as J. Grunig and Hunt's (1984) within-an-issue typology of publics (active, aware, latent, and nonpublic), J. Grunig's (1997) across-issues typology (all-issue, apathetic, hot-issue, and single-issue public), and Hallahan's (2000) typology based on knowledge and involvement (high knowledge/low involvement, high knowledge/high involvement, low knowledge/low involvement, low knowledge/high involvement). Ni and J.-N. Kim (2009) later proposed additional segmentation of "aware" and "active" publics into eight types of subgroups using three problem-solving characteristics of a public: *history*, *activeness* and *openness to approaches* (see more in Chapter 6).

After reviewing the strategic management of public relations, starting with environmental scanning in general and identification of publics in particular, the next question naturally is what to do with these environmental factors and diverse publics. J. Grunig (1993) identified two types of relationships: symbolic relationships and behavioral relationships. Similarly, Broom and Sha (2013) proposed the communication strategies and action strategies in the RPIE management process of public relations programs. Thus, two different but related routes to reach out to these publics most effectively include *messaging* (symbolic) and *relationships* (substantial and behavioral). The challenges for any communicator include both designing and implementing the most appropriate messages to the publics (through the most appropriate channels) and building quality relationships with these publics. The latter route in many cases calls for organizational adjustment internally (i.e., changes to the organization's own behaviors or actions). The next two sections review research in both routes: messaging and relationship management.

Development of Messages and Choice of Media/Channels

Strategic message development is focused on producing messages highly appealing and tailored to the identified publics. Extant research has explored several key areas of messaging, including message design, dissemination channels or media, and implementation. However, most research has pointed to an overarching communication framework based on the traditional commu-nication model with special focus on the sender, receiver, and message. Not much research has been done to examine how different types of publics iden-tified (i.e., active vs. passive) should be reached using different messages and through different channels.

This section reviews these main areas of research mostly taken from scholarly literature in persuasion, compliance gaining, and public relations. According to Broom and Sha (2013), public relations programs should follow the seven Cs of communication:

1. *Credibility*: The sender should show credibility to the messaging by having competency and expertise to gain trust from the audience.
2. *Context*: Communication must fit with the realities of its environment. Messages need to be consistent with actions or organizational behaviors.
3. *Content*: The message must have meaning and relevance for the receiver.
4. *Clarity*: The message must be put in simple terms and should convey the same meanings as understood by both the sender and the receiver.
5. *Continuity and consistency*: Information needs to be repeated and reiterated to achieve understanding. Such repetition should be consistent among dif-ferent iterations.
6. *Channels*: Senders should use established channels of communication that are used and trusted by receivers.
7. *Capability of audience*: Communication is most effective when it requires the least effort on the part of the recipient.

Based on the seven Cs, messaging strategies can be broken down into five categories: the sender (Credibility), audience or receiver (Capability of audi-ence), the messaging (Content, Clarity, Continuity and consistency), the channels (Channels), and the social and cultural environment (Context).

Sender or Messenger

Several major patterns have been found in public relations research on what kinds of senders or organizations tend to be perceived as credible. In crisis situations, the public prefers to have messengers from an organization that are culturally similar to themselves (Heath, Lee, & Ni, 2009), and the sender should bear the characteristics of transparency and authenticity (Men & Tsai, 2015).

In addition, Rogers' (1983) theory of innovation diffusion helps commu-nicators locate different segments in the general population in terms of their likelihood to adopt a new product or idea. Rogers differentiated individuals into five clusters: innovators, early adopters, early majority, late majority, and laggards. A two-step flow model is proposed based on this differentiation and argues for the need for identifying and using opinion leaders to serve as messengers in this context (Broom & Sha, 2013).

Audience

In the field of public relations, more research is needed that examines what messages/communication strategies work best for different types of publics, because the fundamental rationale for segmenting and identifying publics is to use more tailored messages to appeal to these different publics. Taken from persuasion research, some key differences in publics can be identified through differences in their involvement, affect, motivation behind attitudes, and previous attitudes on an issue (e.g., Pfau & Wan, 2006). Some public relations research has touched upon the variables in the situational theory of publics (e.g., Werder, 2005). This section first reviews persuasion research, followed by more specific exploration in the field of public relations.

Involvement

The Elaboration Likelihood Model (ELM) and Heuristic and Systematic Model (HSM) are two theories that focus on the relationship between characteristics of individuals and their preferred information behaviors, and consequently, attitude change. These two models state that, upon receiving a message, high-involvement people follow central and systematic routes of information processing, which require effort and attention to message content. Low-involvement people follow peripheral and heuristic routes of information processing, which require less effort. The latter tend to pay attention to peripheral cues in messages, such as packaging, popularity of spokesperson, authority, length, and other factors. Representative heuristic refers to the fact that people associate a member of the category as representative of the whole category. This stems from a false belief in homogenous categories.

These two theories give insight on how the audience processes messages. Audience characteristics help to determine whether the nature of the sender/source or the content of the message itself will be more effective. Having this information about audiences can help organizations develop messages that will be more effective in persuading their audience.

However, these theories have limitations. They do not explain how the act of persuasion affects impression formation. Different paths, level of involvement with the issue, and content in the message may interact with each other to form different lasting impressions overall. HSM does not explain the specific motivation for being persuaded. It only serves as a simple cognitive guide to how message processing occurs. These theories also assume that message processing takes place only in two routes and exclude the possibility that a route between the two may exist (Pfau & Wan, 2006).

Affect

Affect refers to subjective emotional experience. Using affect can help design messages with different emotional appeals to different audiences. However, the use of affect in messaging is limited because of the arbitrary nature of emotion, different ways through which different emotions may be elicited, and different variability in emotional vulnerability among publics (Pfau & Wan, 2006).

Strategies of using affect in messaging include the following: directly eliciting affect in the receiver, associating a corporation or a product with positive affect, using classical conditioning; and using associations with positive events and causes (e.g., Coca-Cola commercials with polar bears; Michelin Tires' use of babies; see Pfau & Wan, 2006).

Motivation for Attitudes

Knowledge of the specific motivations behind manifest attitudes is essential to the understanding of these attitudes and communication's influence on them. The functional theory (e.g., Katz, 1960) identified different functions of attitudes, or why people hold certain attitudes. These functions include utilitarian (to maximize benefits and minimize penalties), value expressive (to express attitudes and give a sense of self and a signal to others who we are), knowledge-based (to clarify and simplify events for people), and ego-defensive (to protect people's self-images).

The functional theory places emphasis on the motivation behind attitudes. It is to be noted that the core values of people from different cultures may differ, which leads to the formation of different motivations and different attitudes. The limitations of this theory lie in the difficulty of operationalizing the functions served by attitudes. In addition, attitudes serve different functions for different people, as well as serving multiple functions for a single person.

Prior Attitudes

Inoculation theory (e.g., Papageorgis & McGuire, 1961) aims to explain resistance to influence and change. Acknowledging that different publics have different attitudes about an issue prior to certain communications, public relations practitioners need to address the fact that challenges to these existing attitudes may threaten the individual and can create different levels of motivation to increase these individuals' attitude against such proposed change.

In designing messages, refutational defense is superior to supportive defense in protecting attitudes. There are two ingredients in inoculation: Threat and refutational preemption (counter arguing). This has application as a proactive approach in crisis communication. It can be used to soften the impact of crisis and to establish a base of goodwill to offset crisis (Pfau & Wan, 2006).

Public Relations: Fit Between Messaging Strategies and Publics' Characteristics

In public relations research, Smith (1993) first applied psychological type theory to persuasion and message effectiveness. Smith developed an instrument to measure inherent message characteristics that connect to information gathering and decision-making of individuals. Results show that messages that exhibit the characteristics of receivers' own psychological type are preferred.

Other studies have examined the relationship between overall public relations strategies and attributes of publics. Werder (2005) examined the influence of the independent variables in the situational theory of publics and goal compatibility on the use of different public relations strategies (informative, facilitative, persuasive, and cooperative problem solving). The study found that the perceived attributes of publics significantly influenced the public relations strategy used by organizations. Further, attributes of publics and goal compatibility significantly predicted strategy effectiveness.

A more direct exploration of the influence of message strategies on different types of publics as reflected in the situational theory of publics was done in two of Anderson's (1995, 2009) studies on drunken driving. These studies used constraint recognition as a dependent variable. Experiments were conducted to see what kinds of persuasive mechanisms could best enhance self-efficacy in dissuading one's friends from drunken driving. Anderson (2009) tested how constraints could be removed, or self-efficacy enhanced, through two forms of symbolic modeling (behavioral and verbal) and verbal persuasion. Results showed that behavioral and verbal modeling created greater perceived self-efficacy and behavioral intentions than did verbal persuasion.

Werder (2006) went a step further and examined the influence of public relations strategies on other attributes of publics, including both independent and dependent variables in the situational theory of publics. Using experimental methods, this study found that the levels of problem recognition and involvement were indeed influenced by various public relations strategies (informative, facilitative, persuasive, and cooperative problem solving). It also found that involvement and goal compatibility were the strongest predictors of information seeking.

Some studies are focused on message design and effectiveness in crisis contexts. For example, S. Kim and K.-H. Sung (2014) examined the differences between the base crisis-response strategy (i.e., instructing and adjusting information) and reputation management crisis-response strategies as recommended by the situational crisis communication theory (SCCT) in terms of generating positive responses from the public. The study found that the latter was no more effective than the former, thereby providing little support for SCCT recommendations.

Messaging

Messages can be constructed using different strategies. Compliance gaining strategies (see Broom & Sha, 2013) can be used for public relations campaigns. They include foucr major strategies: sanction strategies (offering reward and punishment), altruism strategies (promoting action through considering other's, either the sender's or a third party's well-being, emotional satisfaction), argument strategies (providing pros and cons and using rational argument to make direct request or hinted request), and circumvention (using deceit or exaggeration, often through misleading promises or threats, and is usually unethical).

Framing is also a major part of messaging. Hallahan's (1999) seven models of framing include situations, attributions, choices, actions, issues, responsibility, and news.

Newsworthiness refers to constructing a message to gain attention from news media. It helps diffuse a public relations program's messaging to the media, and in turn, to a large audience. Message newsworthiness centers on six criteria: impact (or the number of people affected, seriousness of consequence, immediacy), proximity (distance and local connection), timeliness (perishability and currency of the information), prominence (involving something or someone recognizable and well known), novelty (involving elements that are unusual, bizarre, deviant, or offbeat), and conflict (involving opposing sides such as strikes, fights, disputes, war, crime, politics, and sports).

Channels and Media

This area of research examines the best and most strategic use of message dissemination channels to achieve objectives. It is generally acknowledged that both interpersonal and mediated channels are important. The medium theory (e.g., McLuhan, 1964) examines how different types of media/mediums influence people differently. It looks at television, print messages, radio, public address, and interpersonal communication. In relation to ELM and HSM, it seems that television tends to elicit the peripheral or heuristic path. TV messages are related to affect because it has more intimate relational messages and emphasis on communicator expressiveness. The medium theory could help public relations practitioners use different types of mediums to get maximum effectiveness for their messages.

Hallahan (2010) developed a five-category integrated model for media: public, interactive, controlled, event/group, and one-on-one (p. 626). *Public* media represent all channels owned by and operated by third-party media organizations. Its main uses are building awareness and public agenda setting, and its key challenge is capturing audience attention. *Interactive* media allow people to communicate with organizations electronically. Its main uses are handling queries and sharing information, and its key challenges are availability and accessibility. *Controlled* media represent all categories of media that are physically produced and delivered to the recipient by the sponsor. Its key challenges are distribution and design of messages. It can be used for promotion and providing detailed information. *Events* are mainly used for motivation and reinforcement of beliefs and values, but face the challenges of attendance and atmosphere. Finally, *one-on-one* communication is best used to obtain commitments and problem management, but faces the challenges of empowerment and personal dynamics.

Avery (2010) linked the situational theory of publics to message reception and channel selection. Arguing that key variables of the situational theory of publics may be moderated by broader variables such as demographic and contextual factors in the consumption of health information, Avery found that involvement and demographics played key moderating roles in audience preferences of channels. Specifically, those with high health involvement were more likely to use active media channels such as newspapers and magazines. The author thus advocated for receiver-based studies in public relations.

Channel and media choices are often studied in crisis or risk communication contexts. For example, Liu, Jin, and Austin (2013) examined the social-mediated crisis communication (SMCC) model to understand why and how publics communicate about crises. Specifically, the study focused on how the source and form of the initial crisis information that publics are exposed to affect their crisis communication. They found that traditional media, compared to other media forms, exerted a stronger influence on how publics communicate about crises. More recently, Liu et al. (2017) examined how visuals influence public response to disaster information and argued that visuals such as maps could help personalize a risk situation such as a disaster. They found that maps only marginally improved message understanding. However, message comprehension was a key component in compliance to risk messages and consequently information sharing behavior.

Interactivity as a delivery approach and its effect on different publics has also been examined (Lee & Park, 2013; Sung & S. Kim, 2014). Interactivity refers to the frequency and engagement level with which an organization responds to the publics' comments (Lee & Park, 2013). Lee and Park (2013) assessed website interactivity and how it influenced perceptions of relationship management and reputation. They found that regardless of familiarity with the company, higher interactivity was related to perceptions of better relationship quality in terms of trustworthiness, commitment, control mutuality and communal relationships, and higher satisfaction. K.-H. Sung and S. Kim (2014) examined the effect of organizations' interpersonal approaches to communication as shown in non-promotional messages and high interactivity in social networking sites (SNSs). Findings indicated that the publics that perceived SNSs more as a personal space considered corporate activities on those platforms more negatively, but when the organization was highly interactive and employed nonpromotional messages, these publics showed a more positive attitude. In addition, organizations' higher interactivity was related to more positive evaluations of those organizations.

Based on the research reviewed above, it appears that public media are best used for information exposure, controlled media for information processing, and interactive media for information seeking. However, more research is needed in this area. For example, with increasingly diversified publics and uses of different types of media, future research may explore and theorize the connections between media types and the identification/segmentation of publics. The main research question is, what types of media best suit what types of publics, with what outcomes (e.g., short-term objectives such as knowledge, attitude, and behavioral changes, as opposed to long-term objectives such as relationship building and reputation)?

Social and Cultural Environments

All the previously discussed factors such as audiences, messengers, messaging, and channels, are heavily influenced by social and cultural environments. Paying attention to the contexts of messages and to the social and cultural environments of the communication is key to messaging efforts in intercultural settings. The influences of culture and identity play significant roles on how the same messages, messengers, and channels can be interpreted differently. Other chapters in this book discuss in more detail such influences, including how audiences or publics should be identified, and how relationships and conflicts should be managed.

Relationship Management

This section reviews research on relationship management (see a focused discussion in Chapter 7). Since Ferguson's (1984) call for a shift in focus of public relations research to relationships, much research has been conducted to answer the call. The fundamental premise of the behavioral, strategic management approach to public relations is that the value of public relations lies in the relationships an organization develops with its publics.

Earlier research on relationship management explicated the concept of relationship and developed its operational definition (model of relationships consisting of antecedents, concepts, and consequences; see Broom, Casey, & Ritchey, 2000; types of relationships including professional, personal, and community, Ledingham & Bruning, 2000). Later, J. Grunig and Huang (2000) developed a three-stage model of relationship management that is widely used today. That model includes the antecedents, maintenance strategies (more recently called cultivation strategies), and relational outcomes. Hung (2005) further explored types of relationships. Measures for the quality of relationships were also developed (see Hon & J. Grunig, 1999; Huang, 2001).

Hon and J. Grunig (1999) identified four quality dimensions of relationships between organizations and publics. *Trust* refers to "one's confidence in the other party and the willingness to open oneself to the other party" (p. 19);

control mutuality refers to the "degree to which partners agree about which of them should decide relationship goals and behavioral routines" (Stafford & Canary, 1991, p. 224), *relational satisfaction* is the degree to which both parties are satisfied with the relationship, and *relational commitment* is a desire to maintain a relationship because it is valued (Hon & J. Grunig, 1999).

Two types of relationships are also distinguished (Hon & J. Grunig, 1999). *Exchange relationships* exist when different parties in the relationship do things for each other for instrumental reasons: They are getting something out of the relationship or have gotten something out of it in the past. *Communal relationships* exist when parties do things for each other out of genuine concern for the other's well-being.

Researchers have explored the three stages of relationship management, including antecedents and mediators of relationships (H.-S. Kim, 2007), relationship cultivation strategies (Rhee, 2007), and outcomes of relationships (e.g., measurement of the quality of relationships, Huang, 2001; and types of relationships, Hung, 2005). Some studies have also explored the contribution of relationships to organizational effectiveness as reflected in organizational reputation (Yang, 2007) and achieving organizational strategies (Ni, 2006, 2009).

However, more studies are needed to examine exactly how public relations practitioners can and should engage in the efforts of relationship building and cultivation. Ni and Wang (2011) explored how organizations should utilize relationship cultivation strategies to manage the anxiety and uncertainty of publics, and how such an effort leads to quality relationships. Following the studies on community relations (e.g., Rhee, 2007), employee relations (e.g., H.-S. Kim, 2007), and student–university relations (e.g., Ki & Hon, 2007), more research has been done to examine the relationship between management processes and outcomes in different contexts or situations, or with different stakeholders (see Chapter 7 for more details).

Based on the literature, we argue for an updated model that consists of antecedents of relationships (organizational level and public level), the process of relationship building (approaches and strategies), measurements of relationships, and outcomes of relationships (organization-centered and public-centered).

Research on the *antecedents* of relationship management used to focus on the situations through which organizations and their publics may interact with each other. Recently, some studies have examined patterns for when and why organizations and publics will enter a relationship. From the organizational side, Cardwell, Williams, and Pyle (2017) found that internal relationship dynamics promote relationship building with publics. From the public's side, Bortree (2015) found that the publics' motivation to volunteer helps relationship building with the organization. Unique to intercultural settings, both parties' (publics or stakeholders and public relations practitioners) intercultural communication competencies also play a key role in how organizations and publics enter a relationship (Wang, Ni, & De la Flor, 2014).

In the *process* of managing relationships, different approaches to communication exist (e.g., cultural, symmetrical, and interactive/two-way), as well as different strategies for the messengers, messaging, and channels. In particular, incorporation of culture and cultural factors in relationship management has been reflected in recent research, especially in the process of relationship management. For example, Hung-Baesecke and Chen (2015) studied how relationship cultivation strategies can incorporate traditional Chinese value orientations; and Y. Kim and J. Yang (2015) examined how the concept of Chemyon plays a role in relationship management and conflict management in Korea. A new framework of engaging with intercultural publics or stakeholders has also been proposed and tested in several recent studies (see Ni et al., 2016; Ni, De la Flor, Romero, & Wang, 2017).

Research in the third stage of the original relationship management model was initially called OPR (organization–public relationship) outcomes. We argue that these outcomes consist of two related but different aspects: measurement and assessment of relationships, and consequences of relationships. For *measurements*, the issues have been focused on identifying multiple types and the quality of organization–public relationships (e.g., Hung, 2005; Waters & Bortree, 2012; personal network added by Jo, 2006, and emotions added by Muskat, 2014). More recent studies have started to examine alternative dimensions of OPR measurements such as distrust in particular and negative dimensions of OPR as a whole (e.g., Kang & Park, 2017).

Consequences or outcomes of relationship management can be divided into organization-centered and public-centered. The organization-centered outcomes have focused on either reducing negative impact (e.g., conflict management and crisis management) or increasing positive impact through a wide range of perceptual, attitudinal, communicative, and behavioral outcomes desired by organizations in different sectors such as business, non-profits, and political organizations. They include reputation (e.g., J. Grunig & Hung-Baesecke, 2015; S. Yang & Cha, 2015) and favorable behaviors from different publics such as employees' voluntary information behaviors (e.g., J.-N. Kim, Park, Krishna, & Martino, 2015). Studies on intercultural public relations have focused on public-centered outcomes, or outcomes that matter to the publics or stakeholders themselves (e.g., Ni et al., 2016). These public-centered outcomes include community empowerment, either health empowerment or identity development (see more in Chapter 7).

Conflict Management

The issues stage in the strategic management process is where publics arise and pursue an issue with an organization. At this point, conflict management and negotiation with these publics is critical and typically requires the use of two-way and symmetrical communication. In negotiation, both mediated and interpersonal two-way symmetrical communication are important, although negotiation typically relies more on interpersonal communication (L. Grunig et al., 2002).

Current theoretical frameworks and relevant research on conflict management in the public relations context are primarily built upon the two-way symmetrical model of public relations and conflict management theory. Conflict management theories have conceptualized and assessed different conflict management strategies such as contending (contention), collaboration (cooperation), avoiding, compromise, and accommodation (e.g., Pruitt & Rubin, 1986). Many classic books and articles from business negotiation and conflict management have also provided theoretical structure and practical applications to conflict management in public relations. The following sections review some of the classic texts (see a detailed discussion in Chapter 4).

Principled Negotiation and Unconditionally Constructive

Many researchers have examined models for maintaining good relations with an opponent without necessarily yielding on the issues at stake (Fisher & Brown, 1988; Fisher & Ury, 1983).

For example, Fisher and Ury (1983) proposed a negotiation strategy called "best alternative to a negotiated agreement." BATNA is adopted when parties fail to reach agreement and is usually settled with the status quo; that is, the situation that would have been obtained if negotiation had never taken place. Being unconditionally constructive (see Fisher & Brown, 1988) refers to following the guidelines that will benefit both the relationship and the party using the principles, regardless of whether the other party reciprocates or not.

Mutual-Gains Approach

Susskind and Field (1996) proposed a mutual-gains approach to conflict management. One key premise in this approach is the authors' belief that anger is a defensive response to pain or the threat of pain, whether it is real or perceived. Therefore, these authors warned against labeling one's opponents as "irrational." Doing so limits a person's ability to absorb new information, discounts plausible arguments or evidence that requires a change to his/her mind, and exacerbates "irrational" anger by implying that the actor is the only one who is rational.

Conflict management strategies may vary, but share the six principles of the mutual-gains approach outlined in this book (Susskind & Field, 1996):

1. Acknowledge the concerns of the other side and try to look at the issue from the standpoint of others.
2. Encourage joint fact-finding.
3. Offer contingent commitments to minimize negative impacts if they do occur; and promise to compensate knowable but unintended negative impacts.
4. Accept responsibility, admit mistakes, and share power.
5. Act in a trustworthy fashion at all times.
6. Focus on building long-term relationships.

Plowman and colleagues (Plowman, 2007; Plowman et al., 1995) have applied and adapted these theories and principles to the organizational level in the public relations context. Based on the literature in conflict management and business negotiation, Plowman et al. (1995) identified a continuum of conflict management strategies ranging from asymmetrical to symmetrical: contention, avoidance, compromise, accommodation, cooperation plus being unconditionally constructive, and win/win or no deal.

It is also worth noting that *the contingency theory* developed by Cameron and colleagues specified many contextual factors facing any organization as it deals with conflicts (Cancel, Cameron, Sallot, & Mitrook, 1997). The contingency theory states that two-way communication can be considered as a continuum between pure advocacy and pure accommodation. In this view, multiple internal and external factors influence the way organizations communicate with their publics. The goal is to capture dynamics in organizational stances and decisions on public relations strategies along the advocacy-accommodation continuum.

Model of Public Relations Practice

Summarizing the major public relations theories following the behavioral, strategic management approach, we identify the following model (J.-N. Kim & Ni, 2013) that can be used to integrate various theories and adopted in general public relations practice.

Integrated Model for Public Relations Management

J.-N. Kim and Ni (2013) provided a model of strategic management of public relations based on two types of public relations problems (Figure 2.1).

In this review of program and advancement of theory development for public relations, the authors aimed to answer three questions:

1. How to diagnose and classify the types of public relations problems?
2. How to choose segmentation theories that are relevant to the given problems?

3. How to choose communication theories and variables that offer the most appropriate nonfinancial metrics for assessing the success of strategies and tactics chosen for the given problem-solving context? (J.-N. Kim & Ni, 2013, p. 2)

Types of Problems

The two types of problems proposed by J.-N. Kim and Ni (2013) are public-initiated public relations problems (PPRPs) and organization-initiated public relations problems (OPRPs). PPRPs generally come from publics sensing a problem in organizational decisions or actions. They are often controversial and policy/issue-related. They begin in the public stage in the strategic management of public relations (Grunig & Repper, 1992).

Because these problems begin with problem recognition when active publics arise, the goal of public relations programs for this type of problem is to deactivate the public types (i.e., turn from active to passive). To do that, the programs need to decrease stakeholders' and publics' problem perceptions, motivations, and actions as these can create problems for the organization that hinder its effectiveness. These problems:

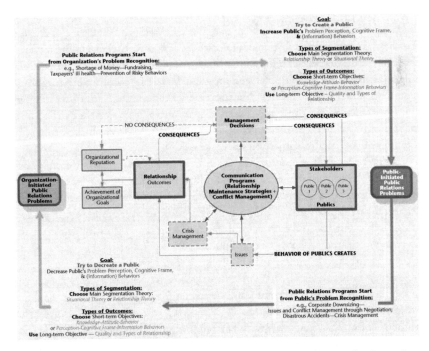

FIGURE 2.1   A Taxonomy of Types of Public Relations Problems in the Strategic Management Context

Source: J.-N. Kim and Ni (2013). Reproduced with permission of Taylor & Francis Group, Philadelphia, PA.

require the use of public relations programs and managerial interventions that directly address the issues at hand, then change publics who may be active or angry about the issues into publics who are satisfied with the solution of these problems.

(J.-N. Kim & Ni, 2013, p. 5)

On the other hand, organization-initiated public relations problems (OPRPs) come from an organization sensing potential problems affecting the publics' or the organization's own interests. They include more routine public relations activities such as publicity and promotion or awareness building. These programs need to begin by considering the state of the relations between publics and the organization.

Because OPRPs begin from the organization's problem recognition when they "encounter problems that prevent the accomplishment of their mission" (J.-N. Kim & Ni, 2013, p. 5), organizations attempt to "create" a public about this problem by turning them from latent into aware or active. To do that, the programs need to increase stakeholders' or publics' problem perception, introduce a new cognitive frame, and foster information behaviors at various levels.

Types of Segmentation Methods

As a part of strategic management of public relations, understanding organizational environments and segmenting strategic publics are important components of any public relations program because "constructing solutions requires segmentation of an organization's environment and problem-solving contexts—identifying the critical segments in an organization's environment that are affected by the problem and that can facilitate or prevent the problem-solving process" (J.-N. Kim & Ni, 2013, p. 6).

In this process, the situational theory of publics is typically used. At the same time, while traditionally relationship theory has been used mostly at the evaluation stage of a public relations program, where the quality of organization–public relationships are used to measure the outcome of a program, J.-N. Kim and Ni's (2013) model argued that relationship theory can be used also at the research or planning stage to segment publics.

On the other hand, relationship theory typically helps determine the effectiveness of public relations. Relationship quality is a cumulative indicator of program effectiveness because it includes past experiences and present interactions. However, in the Kim and Ni (2013) model, it can serve as another way to segment publics by predicting what publics will be supportive or opposed to organizational goals.

In addition to the four relationship quality indicators (i.e., trust, control mutuality, satisfaction, and commitment) and two types of relationships (exchange and communal), another two types of relationships need to be distinguished. *Behavioral or experiential relationships* stem "from direct inter-actions," whereas *reputational relationships* are those formed "through media exposure or witnessing from people with behavioral relationships" (J.-N. Kim & Ni, 2013, p. xx).

Combining the segmentation and relationship theories can provide a more comprehensive picture and analysis of the environment of an organization and its strategic publics.

Types of Outcomes

Public relations is usually evaluated by both process and outcome measures. Process evaluation assesses outputs (materials that have been produced) or the immediate results of a public relations program. Outcome evaluation focuses on the impact that the public relations program has created, or the differences made on the publics. No outcome objective can be achieved without accom-plishing the process objective, but outcome objectives in the end show if the program has had its intended impact.

Two foundational theories can help outcome evaluation: theory of persuasion and theory of problem solving. According to the theory of persuasion, the impact of a public relations program on the publics can be measured through the pub-lics' changes in knowledge, attitude, and behavior (KAB), whereas in the theory of problem solving, the impact on publics can be measured through the changes in perception, cognitive frame, and information behaviors (PCI) (J.-N. Kim & Ni, 2013). Taken as a whole, completing these short-term objectives (i.e., KAB and PCI) contributes to the development of relationships, which serve as the long-term goal of an organization. Evaluating both long-term and short-term objectives is important for effective strategic management of public relations.

To synthesize, for both public-initiated problems (PPRPs) and organization-initiated problems (OPRPs), a public relations program could do any of the fol-lowing: using the situational theory to segment publics and persuasion theories for message design and evaluation, using relationship theory to segment pub-lics and persuasion theories for message design and evaluation, using situational theory to segment publics and problem-solving theories for message design and evaluation, or using relationship theory to segment publics and problem-solving theories for message design and evaluation.

Finally, the overall worldview or direction of an organization influences the general approach to public relations. The organizations taking primarily a symmetrical communication approach would give the same weight to both the organization's and public's interests. In that case, for public-initiated public rela-tions problems, they are likely to look for mutually beneficial ways to negotiate and find potential for conflict resolution. For organization-initiated public rela-tions problems, they are likely to look for ways to assist and facilitate a public's voluntary problem-solving process and to improve resources for these publics.

The organizations taking primarily an asymmetrical communication worldview are likely to give more weight to either their own interests or the public's interests. For public-initiated public relations problems, organizations may look for ways to improve persuasion effectiveness so they can better change the knowledge, attitudes, and behaviors of their publics. For organization-initiated public relations problems, they may look for ways to educate and reform the behaviors of publics.

Both approaches may be needed for different purposes and in different situations. Having a comprehensive and thorough understanding of theories is important for practical uses. Sometimes it is effective to combine theories together for application to public relations practice.

Case Illustration of the Strategic Management Model of Public Relations: Countering Violent Extremism

Background and Research

The first author led a public relations campaign conducted by students at the University of Houston (UH) in the spring of 2017. This campaign won third place in a national competition on social media campaigns aiming at countering violent extremism. The competition was sponsored by the U.S. Department of Homeland Security (DHS) and Facebook, and organized by Edventure Partners. The overall goal of the competition was to have "university students develop and execute campaigns and social media strategies against extremism that are credible, authentic, and believable to their peers and resonate within their communities" (University of Houston Campaign, 2017).

Based on theoretical foundation and best practices in the strategic management of public relations, the UH campaign is used here to illustrate this model. In particular, the campaign identified target audience and appropriate objectives based on the two types of public relations problems, PPRPs and OPRPs (cf. -N. Kim & Ni, 2013), utilized the theories in segmentation of publics (J. Grunig, 1997; J.-N. Kim & Grunig, 2011) as the basis of the formative research on the target audiences, developed strategies in both messaging and communication channels to address key findings in the audience research, and conducted evaluations of the campaign based on (a) program effectiveness (knowledge, attitude, and behavior), (b) situational perceptions of publics (problem recognition, involvement recognition, and constraint recognition), and (c) communication behaviors (information giving, information taking, and information selection).

To review, for organization-initiated public relations problems (OPRPs) where the goal is to "activate" publics to make them more communicatively active, the strategies lie in motivating them to enhance their awareness, attitude, and behavior; messaging is key in the process. Whereas for public-initiated public relations problems (PPRPs), where the goal is to "de-activate" the publics by removing the root cause of the problem, relationship management and conflict management are key. In this process, face-to-face interaction and perspective taking are more critical than planning messages only.

The Countering Violent Extremism (CVE) campaign has suggested different types of campaign strategies: upstream vs. downstream (Reynolds & Tuck, 2016). The upstream campaign is similar to organization-initiated public relations problems and the downstream is similar to public-initiated public relations problems. In the efforts to counter terrorism and violent extremism, two different types of publics can be targeted: the at-risk youth (people who are vulnerable to radicalization efforts of terrorist groups) and the general youth population who are not yet aware of what they can do to counter violent extremism.

These two groups of publics need to be addressed using different types of strategies. For the at-risk youth, more relationship management and face-to-face interaction will be needed to make them feel connected and have a sense of belonging and community, and thus prevent them from being marginalized, and, as a result, recruited by terrorist groups. In other words, the root cause of the "problem" they have in life needs to be reduced or eliminated, and their involvement in radicalization reduced or eliminated, so that they are "de-activated" to a point where their communication activeness about potentially joining terrorist groups is reduced or eliminated. They can then switch to other problems in their lives and mentally leave the original problem state.

On the other hand, the general youth population who remain silent because they are not fully aware of what they can do to counter violent extremism need to be "activated." They need to recognize the problem more fully, feel more involved personally with this problem, and build more self-efficacy so that they perceive fewer obstacles and feel more confident about their ability to make a difference in this process. This current campaign has tackled this OPRP by targeting the silent youth population, or the upstream approach.

Specifically, both primary and secondary research were conducted. Primary research included qualitative in-depth interviews and quantitative surveys with both target audience members and qualitative interviews with experts (religious and community leaders, homeland security experts, media professionals, and academics). Secondary research was done to examine existing studies and literature on countering violent extremism.

Planning

Mission and Main Campaign Goal

The goal of this campaign was to counter violent extremism by thinking in "non-extremes": Giving voice to the silent majority to address the perceived polarization in opinions on Muslim immigrants.

Audience/Publics

Based on the overall goal and the type of problem to tackle, the campaign chose the silent majority youth group as the target audience. This choice of target audience was based on three factors: recommendations from experts from DHS, community leaders, and media professionals; the critical importance to break the silence among this particular group; and easy access to this group due to student peer influence on campus.

The audience somewhat recognized the problem in the current divide on opinions regarding Muslim immigration; they somewhat felt involved but needed more "triggering events" to make it an issue that they personally cared about; and they felt constrained in their ability to do anything about it because of their lack of knowledge, lack of time, and fear or concern over social repercussions of speaking up (University of Houston Campaign, 2017).

Objectives

To achieve the overall campaign goal, objectives were generated for the audience to both provide directions for the campaign and also guide the evaluation of the campaign. Three different sets of objectives were generated and later evaluated using different types of metrics.

1. K.A.B. objectives:

   a. *Knowledge objective*: to be more aware of the issue of Muslim immigration and extreme opinions.
   b. *Attitude objective*: to feel more comfortable voicing opinions about Muslim immigration.
   c. *Behavioral objective*: to take actions to learn more about Muslim immigration and try perspective taking to make informed decisions.

2. Perceptual objectives:

   a. *Problem recognition*: to recognize that individual voices are being silenced by extreme opinions, especially around this topic.
   b. *Involvement recognition*: to have individuals start feeling personally involved in speaking up against extreme opinions.
   c. *Constraint recognition*: to minimize people's constraints by providing them with a safe space to voice their opinions.

3. Communication activeness objectives:

   a. *Information giving*: to motivate people to share with others the information they learned from the campaign.
   b. *Information taking*: to motivate individuals to search for and process information related to Muslim immigration.

Implementation

Campaign Strategies

The campaign developed a range of strategies (both messaging and channels) in response to the formative (pre-campaign) research on the audience as well as the suggestions from expert interviewees to change all three perceptional variables.

Strategies Based on Formative Research on Target Audience

First of all, in terms of communication *channels*, the campaign made sure to include both interpersonal (face-to-face) and mediated communication. For interpersonal communication, we planned and implemented an on-campus event where 175 people attended. For mediated communication, the campaign developed a website and a social media plan with three platforms (Facebook, Twitter, and Instagram) to reach the target audience. On these platforms, both one-way information dissemination (sharing fact-based information about CVE to inform the public) and two-way communication were used to engage with the audience and invite comments and questions. The mediated communication was also used to promote the face-to-face event as well as two follow-up Facebook live sessions with experts. So it was a mixture of both communication channels (mediated and interpersonal).

In terms of developing and implementing *messaging* strategies, the campaign made sure to effectively utilize the formative research on the publics.

To increase problem recognition, the attention-getting strategy was used of inviting a prominent set of panelists who were from diverse backgrounds and who shared different perspectives on this issue. They included representatives from law enforcement agencies such as the Federal Bureau of Investigation (FBI) and Department of Homeland Security (DHS), religious leaders in the Islam and Christian communities, and media professionals in both the industry and academia. The involvement of a Congresswoman and her remarks at the beginning of the event furthered added to the arousal of people's interest and problem recognition.

To increase involvement recognition, the campaign team engaged with the audience during the event by asking questions such as, "have you . . ." This way, the audience felt immediately more connected to the issue and to everyone else attending, and that they did not feel they were the only ones facing these problems.

To decrease constraint recognition, the three different types of constraints through the formative research on our audience were recognized: the lack of knowledge and information to form or express any opinion, the lack of time and energy to devote to this issue, and the fear/concern about social repercussions if one expressed his/her opinion in public. To address each of these three constraints, the following strategies were used:

1. To address the lack of knowledge, the campaign provided fact-based, research-oriented information on the website, which was also promoted through social media.
2. To address the lack of time, the campaign designed action pledge items that did not require excessive efforts, for example, reading a book about the Islamic faith.
3. To address the fear/concern about social repercussions, the campaign designed action pledge items that included "refraining from labeling some-one who has a different opinion than you."

Tactics

The specific communication tactics included the following. The channels were a combination of online and offline platforms and a face-to-face event. Using a media mix proved to be effective in reaching, engaging, and ultimately un-silencing the silent audience. The website acted as a "hub," a place that provided educational and other valuable resources. Facebook was the primary social media platform, which was used to promote the website and encourage audience participation through shares and comments. Twitter, Instagram, and Snapchat served as supporting platforms that pointed back to Facebook and website content.

Tactics also included the face-to-face event with experts from diverse back-grounds as well as two Facebook live interviews as post-event follow up tactics.

Evaluation: Metrics, Methods, and Results

Finally, the evaluation of these public relations efforts was conducted based on the type of problem tackled in this campaign and the goals. Different applicable criteria were chosen to assess the three sets of objectives. All theoretical and practical best practices for campaign evaluation indicated two different types of metrics: outputs and outcomes.

Outputs

Outputs referred to what were produced and the attention received during the campaign. In this campaign, different social media platforms generated nearly 35,000 impressions, 1,000 engagements, and over 2,000 website views. The campaign also received market-wide coverage from media outlets such as Univision, KHOU, Houston Public Media, and others.

Outcomes

Outcomes are the actual impact of the campaign on the target audience. In the current campaign, given the target audience and the specific objectives determined earlier, outcomes were assessed through the changes in perceptions, knowledge, attitude, behaviors, and communication activeness.

Real impact was made on these areas. Research found an increase in the audience's recognition that polarized opinions were a problem, increased their personal involvement in the issue, and increased level of feeling as though they could make a difference in addressing this issue. They also exhibited higher level of knowledge of different topics such as the Islamic faith, the travel ban and violent extremism; higher level of willingness to speak up in public and with friends regarding Muslim immigration; and more commitment to action, such as having conversations with others who disagreed and refraining from labeling others.

In terms of communication activeness, participants became more likely to inform others about Muslim immigration, join conversions about Muslim immigration, and search for information on Muslim immigration. They were also more likely to pay attention to issues in the news, get information from a variety of sources, and pay attention to reputation and credibility of the sources.

Expanded Model

J.-N. Kim and Ni (2013) identified some trends in the future development of the strategic management approach. First, more emphasis should be placed on behavioral and communicative efforts. As opposed to the symbolic, interpretive paradigm of public relations that relies on messaging to change or negotiate publics' interpretations of organizations' behaviors, the behavioral, strategic paradigm considers communication as dialogue and interaction, bridging the gap between an organization and its publics. This paradigm provides management with information from publics to help the organization make more responsible decisions.

Second, public relations should be institutionalized from a buffering to a bridging function. A buffering function mainly uses favorable impressions to buffer the organization from the environment (against harm), whereas bridging functions to decrease gaps in interests and stances and to increase connections by communicating interactively and proactively.

To modify this model further, in this book, we argue that for organization-initiated public relations problems (OPRPs) where the goal is to "activate" publics and make them more communicatively active, the strategies lie in motivating them to enhance their awareness, attitude, and behavior, and messaging is key in the process. Whereas for public-initiated public relations problems (PPRPs) where the goal is to "de-activate" the publics by removing the root cause of the problem, relationship management and conflict management are key. In this process, face-to-face interaction and perspective taking will be more critical than planning messages only.

J.-N. Kim and Ni (2013) also suggested that more adaptive management structures and strategies should be implemented for digitalization and virtualization. The current trend in technology development may favor such an approach even more because of the dissolution of the "illusion of control," i.e., organizations can no longer control the media, information, or messages and hide things from the public. These trends are all the more critical in today's intercultural settings where misunderstandings are ubiquitous and digital communication can play a crucial role in it (see more in Chapter 10).

Integrating the foundational theories in public relations and the recent model of public relations practice, the authors of this text propose a new framework that is generally applicable in the strategic management of public relations (see Figure 2.2).

To give a brief overview of this model, research is first conducted to identify the type of public relations problem, that is, organization-initiated public relations problems (OPRPs) or public-initiated public relations problems (PPRPs), as well as research on the organization and the publics. In the planning stage, the goal for the public relations program is determined (i.e., to "activate" publics and make them more communicatively active for OPRPs or to "de-activate" the publics by removing the root cause of the problem for PPRPs). The objectives for different publics are then determined based on these goals. These objectives go beyond the traditional knowledge, attitude, and behavioral objectives to include also situational perceptions, communicative activeness, and organization–public relationships. In the implementation stage, again, different types of strategies are used to motivate publics to enhance their awareness, attitude, and behavior, through messaging or communication strategies in the case of OPRPs, and relationship management and conflict management through face-to-face interaction and perspective taking in the case of PPRPs. Finally, in the evaluation stage, the strategies are assessed with the consideration of both the outputs and outcomes as specified in the planning stage.

Later in the book, after reviewing and integrating research in intercultural communication and conflict management and negotiation, we propose a new, revised model of strategic intercultural public relations management at the end of Chapter 4, which marks the end of Part I of this book on theoretical foundations. In Part II, we then discuss how that model and related theories need to be incorporated and adapted in settings where intercultural differences exist.

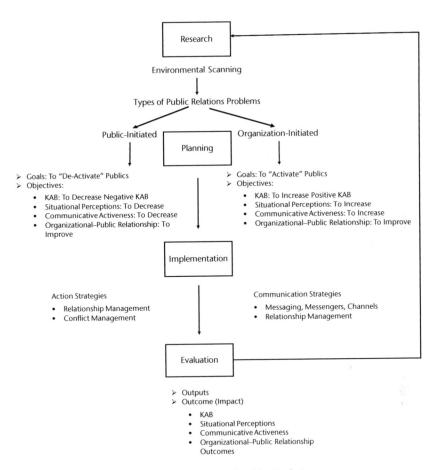

FIGURE 2.2 Strategic Management Model of Public Relations

Those chapters include intercultural communication competence and training, identifying publics, relationship management, conflict management, and organizational culture and identity.

References

Aldoory, L. (2001). Making health communications meaningful for women: Factors that influence involvement. *Journal of Public Relations Research, 13,* 163–185.

Aldoory, L., & Sha, B.-L. (2007). The situational theory of publics: Practical applications, methodological challenges, and theoretical horizons. In E. L. Toth (Ed.), *The future of excellence in public relations and communication management: Challenges for the next generation* (pp. 339–355). Mahwah, NJ: Erlbaum.

Anderson, R. B. (1995). Cognitive appraisal of performance capability in the prevention of drunken driving: A test of self-efficacy theory. *Journal of Public Relations Research, 7,* 205–229. doi: 10.1207/s1532754xjprr0703_03

Anderson, R. B. (2009). Comparison of indirect sources of efficacy information in pretesting messages for campaigns to prevent drunken driving. *Journal of Public Relations Research, 21,* 428–454. doi: 10.1080/1062726090296636

Avery, E. (2010). Contextual and audience moderators of channel selection and message reception of public health information in routine and crisis situations. *Journal of Public Relations Research, 22,* 378–403. doi: 10.1080/10627261003801404

Bortree, D. S. (2015). Motivations of publics: The power of antecedents in the volunteer–nonprofit organization relationship. In E.-J. Ki, J.-N. Kim, & J. A. Ledingham (Eds.), *Public relations as relationship management: A relational approach to the study and practice of public relations* (2nd ed., pp. 144–158). New York, NY: Routledge.

Broom, G. M., & Sha, B.-L. (2013). *Cutlip and Center's effective public relations* (11th ed.). Upper Saddle River, NJ: Pearson.

Broom, G. M., Casey, S., & Ritchey, J. (2000). Concepts and theory of organization–public relationships. In J. A. Ledingham & S. D. Bruning (Eds.), *Public relations as relationship management: A relational approach to the study and practice of public relations* (pp. 3–22). Mahwah, NJ: Erlbaum.

Cancel, A. E., Cameron, G. T., Sallot, L. M., & Mitrook, M. A. (1997). It depends: A contingency theory of accommodation in public relations. *Journal of Public Relations Research, 9,* 31–63. doi: 10.1207/s1532754xjprr0901_02

Cardwell, L. A., Williams, S., & Pyle, A. (2017). Corporate public relations dynamics: Internal vs. external stakeholders and the role of the practitioner. *Public Relations Review, 43,* 152–162. doi: 10.1016/j.pubrev.2016.11.004

Dozier, D. M. (1992). The organizational roles of communications and public relations practitioners. In J. E. Grunig (Ed.), *Excellence in public relations and communication management* (pp. 327–355). Hillsdale, NJ: Erlbaum.

Dozier, D. M., & Broom, G. M. (2006). The centrality of practitioner roles to public relations theory. In C. H. Botan & V. Hazelton (Eds.), *Public relations theory II* (pp. 120–148). Thousand Oaks, CA: Sage.

Ehling, W. P. (1992). Estimating the value of public relations and communication to an organization. In J. E. Grunig (Ed.), *Excellence in public relations and communication management* (pp. 617–638). Hillsdale, NJ: Erlbaum.

Ferguson, M. A. (1984, August). *Building theory in public relations: Interorganizational relationships.* Paper presented at the annual convention of the Association for Education in Journalism and Mass Communication, Gainesville, FL.

Fisher, R., & Brown, S. (1988). *Getting together: Building a relationship that gets to yes.* Boston, MA: Houghton Mifflin.

Fisher, R., & Ury, W. (1983). *Getting to yes: Negotiating agreement without giving in.* New York, NY: Penguin.

Grunig, J. E. (1976). Organizations and public relations: Testing a communication theory. *Journalism Monographs, 46,* 1–59.

Grunig, J. E. (1993). Image and substance: From symbolic to behavioral relationships. *Public Relations Review, 19,* 121–139. doi: 10.1016/0363-8111(93)90003-U

Grunig, J. E. (1997). A situational theory of publics: Conceptual history, recent challenges and new research. In D. Moss, T. MacManus, & D. Vercic (Eds.), *Public relations research: An international perspective* (pp. 3–48). London: International Thomson Business Press.

Grunig, J. E. (2001). Two-way symmetrical public relations: Past, present, and future. In R. L. Heath (Ed.), *Handbook of public relations* (pp. 11–30). Thousand Oaks, CA: Sage.

Grunig, J. E., & Grunig, L. A. (1998). The relationship between public relations and marketing in excellent organizations: Evidence from the IABC study. *Journal of Marketing Communications, 4*, 141–162. doi: 10.1080/135272698345816

Grunig, J. E., & Huang, Y. H. (2000). From organizational effectiveness to relationship indicators: Antecedents of relationships, public relations strategies, and relationship outcomes. In J. A. Ledingham & S. D. Bruning (Eds.), *Public relations as relationship management: A relational approach to the study and practice of public relations* (pp. 23–53). Mahwah, NJ: Erlbaum.

Grunig, J. E., & Hung-Baesecke, C.-J. F. (2015). The effect of relationships on reputation and reputation on relationships: A cognitive, behavioral study. In E.-J. Ki, J.-N. Kim, & J. A. Ledingham (Eds.), *Public relations as relationship management: A relational approach to the study and practice of public relations* (2nd ed., pp. 63–113). New York, NY: Routledge.

Grunig, J. E., & Hunt, T. (1984). *Managing public relations*. New York, NY: Holt, Rinehart & Winston.

Grunig, J. E., & Repper, F. C. (1992). Strategic management, publics, and issues. In J. E. Grunig (Ed.), *Excellence in public relations and communication management* (pp. 31–64). Hillsdale, NJ: Erlbaum.

Grunig, J. E., Ferrari, M. A., & Franc, A. F. (2009). *Relações públicas: Teoria, contexto e relacionamentos (Public relations: Theory, context, and relationships)* São Paulo, Brazil: Difusao Editora.

Grunig, L. A., Grunig, J. E., & Dozier, D. M. (2002). *Excellent public relations and effective organizations: A study of communication management in three countries*. Mahwah, NJ: Erlbaum.

Hallahan, K. (1999). Seven models of framing: Implications for public relations. *Journal of Public Relations Research, 11*, 205–242. doi: 10.1207/s1532754xjprr1103_02

Hallahan, K. (2000). Inactive publics: The forgotten publics in public relations. *Public Relations Review, 26*, 499–515. doi: 10.1016/S0363-8111(00)00061-8

Hallahan, K. (2010). Public relations media. In R. L. Heath (Ed.), *The Sage handbook of public relations* (2nd ed., pp. 623–641). Thousand Oaks, CA: Sage.

Huang, Y.-H. (2001). Values of public relations: Effects on organization–public relationships mediating conflict resolution. *Journal of Public Relations Research, 13*, 265–301. doi: 10.1207/S1532754XJPRR1304_01

Hung, C.-J. F. (2005). Exploring types of organization–public relationships and their implications for relationship management in public relations. *Journal of Public Relations Research, 17*, 393–426.

Hung-Baesecke, C.-J. F., & Chen, Y.-R. R. (2015). Factoring culture into relationship management theory: Cultivation strategies and traditional Chinese value orientations. In E.-J. Ki, J.-N. Kim, & J. A. Ledingham (Eds.), *Public relations as relationship management: A relational approach to the study and practice of public relations* (2nd ed., pp. 217–239). New York, NY: Routledge.

Heath, R. L., Lee, J., &Ni, L. (2009). Crisis and risk approaches to emergency management planning and communication: The role of similarity and sensitivity. *Journal of Public Relations Research, 21*, 123–141. doi: 10.1080/10627260802557415

Hon, L. C., & Grunig, J. E. (1999). *Guidelines for measuring relationships in public relations*. Gainesville, FL: The Institute for Public Relations. Commission on PR Measurement and Evaluation.

Jo, S. (2006). Measurement of organization–public relationships: Validation of measurement using a manufacturer–retailer relationship. *Journal of Public Relations Research*, *18*, 225–248. doi: 10.1207/s1532754xjprr1803_2

Kang, M., & Park, Y. E. (2017). Exploring trust and distrust as conceptually and empirically distinct constructs: Association with symmetrical communication and public engagement across four pairings of trust and distrust. *Journal of Public Relations Research*, *29*, 114–135. doi: 10.1080/1062726X.2017.1337579

Katz, D. (1960). The functional approach to the study of attitudes. *Public Opinion Quarterly*, *24*, 163–204.

Ki, E.-J., & Hon, L. C. (2007). Testing the linkages among the organization–public relationship and attitude and behavioral intentions. *Journal of Public Relations Research*, *19*, 1–23. doi: 10.1207/s1532754xjprr1901_1

Kim, H.-S. (2007). A multilevel study of antecedents and a mediator of employee–organization relationships. *Journal of Public Relations Research*, *19*, 167–197. doi: 10.1080/10627260701290695

Kim, J.-N., & Grunig, J. E. (2011). Problem solving and communicative action: A situational theory of problem solving. *Journal of Communication*, *61*, 120–149. doi: 10.1111/j.1460-2466.2010.01529.x

Kim, J.-N., & Ni, L. (2013). Two types of public relations problems and integrating formative and evaluative research: A review of research programs within the behavioral, strategic management paradigm. *Journal of Public Relations Research*, *25*, 1–29. doi: 10.1080/1062726X.2012.723276

Kim, J.-N., Grunig, J. E., & Ni, L. (2010). Reconceptualizing public's communicative action: Acquisition, selection, and transmission of information in problematic situations. *International Journal of Strategic Communication*, *4*, 126–154. doi: 10.1080/15531181003701913

Kim, J.-N., Ni. L., & Sha, B.-L. (2008). Breaking down the stakeholder environment: Explicating approaches to the segmentation of publics for public relations research. *Journalism and Mass Communication Quarterly*, *85*, 751–768. doi: 10.1177/107769900808500403

Kim, J.-N., Park, S., Krishna, A., & Martino, V. (2015). Risk management through employees: Testing employees' voluntary scouting and corporate readiness for cyber risks. In E.-J. Ki, J.-N. Kim, & J. A. Ledingham (Eds.), *Public relations as relationship management: A relational approach to the study and practice of public relations* (2nd ed., pp. 199–214). New York, NY: Routledge.

Kim, S., & Sung, K. H. (2014). Revising the effectiveness of base crisis response strategies in comparison of reputation management crisis responses. *Journal of Public Relations Research*, *26*, 62–78. doi: 10.1080/10627726X.2013.795867

Kim, Y., & Yang, J. (2015). Chemyon, relationship building, and conflicts. In E.-J. Ki, J.-N. Kim, & J. A. Ledingham (Eds.), *Public relations as relationship management: A relational approach to the study and practice of public relations* (2nd ed., pp. 240–257). New York, NY: Routledge.

Ledingham, J. A., & Bruning, S. D. (Eds.) (2000). *Public relations as relationship management: A relational approach to the study and practice of public relations*. Mahwah, NJ: Erlbaum.

Lee, H., & Park, H. (2013). Testing the impact of message interactivity on relationship management and organizational reputation. *Journal of Public Relations Research, 25,* 188–206. doi: 10.1080/1062726X.2013.739103

Liu, B. F., Jin, Y., & Austin, L. L. (2013). The tendency to tell: Understanding publics' communicative responses to crisis information form and source. *Journal of Public Relations Research, 25,* 51–67. doi: 10.1080/1062726X.2013.739101

Liu, B. F., Wood, M. M., Egnoto, M., Bean, H., Sutton, J., Mileti, D., & Madden, S. (2017). Is a picture worth a thousand words? The effects of maps and warning messages on how publics respond to disaster information. *Public Relations Review, 43,* 493–506. doi: 10.1016/j.pubrev.2017.04.004

McLuhan, M. (1964). *Understanding media: The extensions of man.* New York, NY: McGraw-Hill.

Men, L. R., & Tsai, W. S. (2015). Infusing social media with humanity: Corporate character, public engagement, and relational outcomes. *Public Relations Review, 41,* 395–403. doi: 10.1016/j.pubrev.2015.02.005

Muskat, B. (2014). Emotions in organization–public relationships: Proposing a new determinant. *Public Relations Review, 40,* 832–834. doi: 10.1016/j.pubrev.2014.06.004

Ni, L. (2006). Relationships as organizational resources: Examining public relations impact through its connection with organizational strategies. *Public Relations Review, 32,* 276–281.

Ni, L. (2009). Strategic role of relationship building: Perceived links between employee–organization relationships and globalization strategies. *Journal of Public Relations Research, 21,* 100–120. doi: 10.1080/1062726X.2013.795864

Ni, L., & Kim, J.-N. (2009). Classifying publics: Communication behaviors and problem-solving characteristics in controversial issues. *International Journal of Strategic Communication, 3,* 217–241. doi: 10.1080/15531180903221261

Ni, L., & Wang, Q. (2011). Anxiety and uncertainty management in an intercultural Setting: The impact on organization–public relationships. *Journal of Public Relations Research, 23,* 269–301. doi: 10.1080/1062726X.2011.582205

Ni, L., Cui, Y., Xiao, Z., Lu, Q., Gor, B., & Ji, B. (2016). *The role of stakeholder engagement in the context of community health: A qualitative study on strategic communication and community empowerment.* Paper presented at the 2016 International Communication Association Conference in Fukuoka, Japan.

Ni, L., De la Flor, Romero, B., & Wang, Q. (March, 2017). *Community engagement and public health: A qualitative study of strategic communication of Hispanic community organizations.* Paper accepted at International Public Relations Research Conference, Orlando, FL.Papageorgis, D., & McGuire, W. J. (1961). The generality of immunity to persuasion produced by pre-exposure to weakened counterarguments. *Journal of Abnormal and Social Psychology, 62,* 475–481.

Pfau, M., & Wan, H.-H. (2006). Persuasion: An intrinsic function of public relations. In C. H. Botan, & V. Hazelton (Eds.), *Public relations theory II* (pp. 88–119). Thousand Oaks, CA: Sage.

Plowman, K. D. (2007). Public relations, conflict resolution, and mediation. In E. L. Toth (Ed.), *The future of excellence in public relations and communication management: Challenges for the next generation* (pp. 85–102). Mahwah, NJ: Erlbaum.

Plowman, K. D., ReVelle, C., Meirovich, S., Pien, M., Stemple, R., Sheng, V., & Fay, K. (1995). Walgreens: A case study in health care issues and conflict resolution. *Journal of Public Relations Research*, 7, 231–258. doi: 10.1207/ s1532754xjprr0704_01

Pruitt, D. G., & Rubin, J. Z. (1986). *Social conflict: Escalation, impasse, and resolution.* Reading, MA: Addision-Wesley.

Rhee, Y. (2007). Interpersonal communication as an element of symmetrical public relations: A case study. In E. L. Toth (Ed.), *The future of excellence in public relations and communication management: Challenges for the next generation* (pp. 103–117). Mahwah, NJ: Erlbaum.

Reynolds, L., & Tuck, H. (2016, November). *The counter-narrative monitoring & evaluation handbook* [e-handbook]. Retrieved from the Institute for Strategic Dialogue website: www.isdglobal.org/wp-content/uploads/2017/06/CN-Monitoring-and-EvaluationHandbook.pdf

Rogers, E. M. (1983). *Diffusion of innovations* (3rd ed.). New York, NY: Free Press of Glencoe.

Sha, B.-L. (2006). Cultural identity in the segmentation of publics: An emerging theory of intercultural public relations. *Journal of Public Relations Research*, 18, 45–65. doi: 10.1207/ s1532754xjprr1801_3

Smith, R. D. (1993). Psychological type and public relations: Theory, research, and applications. *Journal of Public Relations Research*, 5, 177–199. doi: 10.1207/ s1532754xjprr0503_02

Sriramesh, K., Moghan, S., & Lim, K.-W. (2007). The situational theory of publics in a different cultural setting: Consumer publics in Singapore. *Journal of Public Relations Research*, 19, 307–332. doi: 10.1080/10627260701402424

Stafford, L., & Canary, D. J. (1991). Maintenance strategies and romantic relationship type, gender, and relational 725 characteristics. *Journal of Social and Personal Relationships*, 8, 217–242. doi: 10.1177/0265407591082004

Stoffels, J. (1994). *Strategic issues management.* Thousand Oaks, CA: Sage.

Sung, K.-H., & Kim, S. (2014). I want to be your friend: The effects of organizations' interpersonal approaches on social networking sites. *Journal of Public Relations Research*, 26, 235–255. doi: 10.1080/1062726X.2014.908718

Sung, M.-J. (2007). Toward a model of scenario building from a public relations perspective. In E. L. Toth (Ed.), *The future of excellence in public relations and communication management: Challenges for the next generation* (pp. 173–197). Mahwah, NJ: Erlbaum.

Susskind, L., & Field, P. (1996). *Dealing with an angry public.* New York, NY: Free Press.

Tkalac, A. (2007). The application of situational theory in Croatia. In E. L. Toth (Ed.), *The future of excellence in public relations and communication management: Challenges for the next generation* (pp. 527–543). Mahwah, NJ: Erlbaum.

University of Houston Campaign (2017). Retrieved from www.dropbox.com/ s/3fwddxh230rmqa6/S17_P2P_DHS_3rd.pdf?dl=0 on https://edventurepartners. com/wordpress/wp-content/uploads/2017/08/Univ_Houston_OneSheet.pdf

Wang, Q., Ni, L., & De la Flor, M. (2014). An intercultural competence model of strategic public relations management in the Peru mining industry context. *Journal of Public Relations Research*, 26, 1–22. doi: 10.1080/1062726X.2013.795864

Waters, R. D., & Bortree, D. S. (2012). Advancing relationship management theory: Mapping the continuum of relationship types. *Public Relations Review*, 38, 123–127. doi: 10.1016/j.pubrev.2011.08.018

Werder, K. P. (2005). An empirical analysis of the influence of perceived attributes of publics on public relations strategy use and effectiveness. *Journal of Public Relations Research*, 17, 217–266. doi: 10.1207/s1532754xjprr1703_2

Werder, K. P. (2006). Responding to activism: An experimental analysis of public relations strategy influence on attributes of publics. *Journal of Public Relations Research, 18,* 335–356. doi: 10.1207/s1532754xjprr1804_3

Yang, S.-U. (2007). An integrated model for organization–public relational outcomes, organizational reputation, and their antecedents. *Journal of Public Relations Research, 19,* 91–121. doi: 10.1080/10627260701290612

Yang, S.-U., & Cha, H. (2015). A framework linking organization–public relationships and organizational reputations in public relations management. In E.-J. Ki, J.-N. Kim, & J. A. Ledingham (Eds.), *Public relations as relationship management: A relational approach to the study and practice of public relations* (2nd ed., pp. 114–129). New York, NY: Routledge.

3

HISTORY AND FOUNDATIONAL THEORIES OF INTERCULTURAL COMMUNICATION

Culture is like a map. . . . If you know a culture, you will know your way around in the life of a society.

(C. Kluckhohn, 1949/2017, p. 54)

Cultural exchanges and encounters trace back to the beginning of human history when family-based tribes engaged in trading, collaborating, competing for resources, or wars. The earliest record showed that sophisticated cultural artifact production appeared 50,000 years ago, when ancient humans experienced an abrupt transformation from stone culture to modern human culture (Klein & Edgar, 2002). At the time, ancient people produced painting, complicated tools for fishing and building, and symbolic group behaviors such as rituals and ceremonies (Klein & Edgar, 2002). Despite earlier human group communication, modern intercultural communication research received its major influence from the time of colonialism, which brought a big move of global cultures.

Although most intercultural communication scholars consider the establishment of the Foreign Service Institute (FSI) in the United States after the Second World War as the beginning of intercultural communication, these scholars also acknowledge the earlier influence from various disciplines behind this establishment, especially anthropology, naturalism, sociology, psychology, and linguistics (e.g., Martin, Nakayama, & Carbough, 2012; Rogers, 1994; Rogers & Hart, 2002; Sadri & Flammia, 2011; Sharifian & Jamarani, 2013). In the following section, we review key scholars in these various fields who contributed to modern intercultural communication research. The goal is to help readers understand the historical influence of today's intercultural communication research. Knowing why and how the field started and what ideological and philosophical systems are behind it enables interested researchers to assess its general framework. Globally, with the issues of immigration, political divisions, activist movements around ethnic and racial inequalities, and other group-related issues, understanding the history and various disciplinary inputs of intercultural communication may shed light on new theoretical and research directions.

Part I: History of Intercultural Communication

Roots in Anthropology, Naturalism, and Linguistics

Communication refers to the process whereby people collectively create and transmit meaning through the exchange of verbal and nonverbal messages in a particular context (Oetzel, 2009, p. 11). *Intercultural communication* refers to social interactions between culturally dissimilar individuals or groups (Oetzel, 2009). Sharifian and Jamarani (2013) traced the start of research in intercultural communication to several anthropologists and linguists who were foundational in linking language, cognition, and culture together, such as Wilhelm von Humboldt, Franz Boas, Edward Sapir, and Benjamin Whorf. Martin et al. (2012) added that the works of Charles Darwin, Sigmund Freud, and Karl Marx significantly propelled the research in intercultural communication, and that the works of early 20th century anthropologists such as Margaret Mead and Clyde Kluckhohn started the research in the effects of culture on personality, which laid a direct foundation for scholarship on intercultural communication. Other intercultural communication scholars such as Rogers and Hart (2002) support these traces of lineage. In the following paragraphs, we connect these foundational works in chronological order.

Humboldt (1767–1835) was a Prussian philosopher, linguist, educator, and diplomat. He is credited to be the first linguist who considered languages to be rule-governed systems and that these different systems influence how different groups of people view the world. As a multilingual person, Humboldt noted that cultural groups differ in representing observations and experiences through symbolic systems. The differences go beyond the sounds or oral symbols, but demonstrate different views of the same phenomenon. Therefore, Humboldt argued, how a group of people assign meanings to words, sentences, and larger-form linguist expressions reflect how this group perceive the outer world (Freund, 2017). Humboldt termed the relationship between the linguistic expressions and the view of the world as the *inner form of a language*. This idea is similar to the linguistic worldview fully developed a century later and well known as the Sapir-Whorf hypothesis (Freund, 2017).

By the mid-19th century, Europe had successfully colonized Asia, Africa, and the Americas. This historical climate brought a large scale of cultural encounters. Meanwhile, Charles Darwin published his *Origin of Species* in 1859, which by the 1870s had been accepted almost as fact by the scientific community and the general public. His later publications of *The Descent of Man* (1871) and *The Expressions of the Emotions in Man and Animals* (1872) greatly influenced Sir Herbert Spencer, Lewis Henry Morgan, Edward Burnett Tylor, Karl Marx, and Friedrich Engels (Rogers & Hart, 2002; Winthrop, 1991). These scholars exerted great influence in promoting an evolutionary perspective on various humanities disciplines and a naturalist approach in methodology (i.e., exploring and understanding the objective phenomena through finding the cause-effect laws, also called *covering laws*; see Papineau, 2007).

Herbert Spencer was an enthusiastic supporter of Darwinism. In the 1900s, he was the most prominent advocate of *social Darwinism* and proposed a theory of sociocultural revolution, the essence of which is the social survival of the fittest and social evolution through competition (Stewart, 2011). Although his influence faded later, social Darwinism gained popularity and still has influence today (McKinnon, 2010). Spencer's other influence on the humanities research field is through his promulgation of the principle of evolution in the natural sciences and human sciences. His evolutionary principle is similar to Auguste Comte's positivism that insists on the universality of natural laws and valid knowledge only through empirical testing. The evolution principle differs from Comte's positivism in that, whereas Comte argued for the unity of scientific truth, Spencer postulated that all natural laws would be reduced to one law, the principle of evolution, which governs all object movement, organic or inorganic (McKinnon, 2010).

Anthropologists Lewis Morgan and Edward Tylor independently developed *cultural evolutionary theories* based on the Darwinian model. The basic premise is that cultures, just like species, evolve from simplicity into complexity, and generally go through three stages: savagery, barbarism, and civilization. Whereas Tylor argued that all cultures had the potential to reach civilization because of similar mental compositions, Morgan argued for the different developments based on each culture's use of technology and evolvement of social rituals and units, such as marriage, family, and political organizations (Winthrop, 1991).

Karl Marx and Friedrich Engels came to a highly similar idea at almost the same time as Morgan and Tylor. Marx and Engels' *social evolution theory* was based on Darwin's evolution theory as well, but with a strong focus on the economic dynamics between the social institutions such as monogamy, private property, the state, and the exploitation of the working classes. Their postulation was that communism would eventually bring human beings back to the communism of the primitive society (Winthrop, 1991).

Anthropologist Franz Boas criticized cultural revolutionary models because they represented highly ethnocentric approaches (the tendency to judge other cultures by one's own cultural standards), lacked empirical data, and supported the erroneous premise that it was a universal law that all cultures would go through the same hierarchical evolutionary steps. Out of these criticisms, Boas formulated a new basic tenet of anthropology, which developed in intercultural communication research later—*cultural relativism* (i.e., the degree to which a cultural practice is not judged by the standards of another culture; Rogers & Hart, 2002).

Boas' student, Edward Sapir, together with his own student, Benjamin Whorf, formally advanced the notion of cultural relativism and the relationship between language and perception into the Sapir-Whorf *linguistic relativity hypothesis*, the notion that language influences perceptions and hence behavior. The weaker form of the hypothesis states that language and perceptions are related, and the stronger form states that language determines the perception of the world (Sharifian & Jamarani, 2013).

Two other students of Boas, Ruth Benedict and Margaret Mead, were credited to have contributed to the development of culture and personality (Winthrop, 1991). Benedict conducted field studies in American Indian, Asian, and European cultures and argued for cultural relativism rather than cultural determinism: Cultures are products of human groups; different patterns are found in different cultural groups. Mead's works contributed to the cross-cultural comparisons of gender roles and child upbringing (R. Levine, 1982; Winthrop, 1991). Benedict's and Mead's works helped the development of intercultural communication research by promoting racial equality, gender equality, and the study of nonverbal communication (Rogers & Hart, 2002).

Another key influencer in the field of culture and personality was Sigmund Freud (Rogers & Hart, 2002). The concept of unconsciousness in his psychoanalytic theory shaped the research in the unconscious influence of cultural values on personality and behavior. R. Levine (1982) maintained that the field of culture and personality was an intersection of Sigmund Freud's psychoanalysis and anthropology.

To summarize, the major influence on intercultural communication from the 1800s and early 1900s is trifold. First, the evolutionary perspective was used to understand cultures both within and between. On one hand, a culture is postulated to evolve from simplicity to complexity and promote the survival of the fittest. On the other hand, natural selection exists between cultures too. The colonialism where in a relatively more "civilized" cultural system dominates its less "civilized" counterpart appeared to be a natural outcome of evolution. This evolutionary perspective is seen in today's international communication and development communication research (concepts defined later in this chapter), where certain cultural or political standards in more economically advanced countries are imposed on less economically advanced countries (e.g., democracy, human rights, etc.)

Second, the evolutionist perspective, anthropological approach, and Marxism greatly influenced the three major paradigms of intercultural communication research: post-positivist, interpretivist, and critical. Spencer's evolution principle and Compte positivism, with later critiques from 20th-century philosophers such as Karl Popper (1935/1959) and Thomas Kuhn (1962), laid the foundation of the post-positivist paradigm. The anthropological research methods such as ethnography and field observations contributed to the interpretivist paradigm, and Marxist philosophy contributed greatly to the critical paradigm.

Finally, the linguistic research tradition to the culture was foundational to theory development in culture, personality, cognition, and communication behavior. The anthropological and evolutionary approaches also contributed to the study of nonverbal communication and cross-cultural value and behavior comparisons. We hope this brief sketch helps readers gain a glimpse of the hidden influences from centuries ago behind the intercultural communication field today. Next, we review the formal establishment of intercultural communication as a discipline.

Establishment of Intercultural Communication Research Efforts

Despite the various influences described above, most scholars consider the establishment of the Foreign Service Institute (FSI) after the Second World War as the beginning of intercultural communication research (Leeds-Hurwitz, 1990; Martin et al., 2012; Rogers, 1994; Rogers & Hart, 2002; Sadri & Flammia, 2011; Sharifian & Jamarani, 2013). After the Second World War, the United States built a foreign aid program, called the Marshall Program, to help rebuild Europe. The program was named after George Marshall, U.S. Secretary of State. The motivation was to create a strong relationship with European allies and to repel communism. Later, President Truman expanded the program to developing countries in Asia, Latin America, and Africa. The focus was shifted to development issues such as poverty, education, gender inequality, environment, and health and medical impediments, such as infant mortality, maternal mortality, and reproductive health and contraceptive use. To execute this grand program, the U.S. Congress and the Department of State established FSI to train overseas personnel (Rogers & Hart, 2002). Prominent scholars such as Edward T. Hall (anthropologist and cross-cultural researcher), Ray Birdwhistell (anthropologist and nonverbal communication expert), George Trager (linguist), and Charles Hockett (linguist) were hired to train workers going overseas. Much of these scholars' research, publications, and approaches are credited as the foundation of intercultural communication research.

Among them, Edward Hall was the most prominent and is widely considered the founding father of intercultural communication. He applied his life experience in foreign countries and with the Hopi and Navajo tribes in the U.S., as well as his doctoral anthropology training at Columbia University, to train the expatriates. His books, *The Silent Language* (1959), *The Hidden Dimension* (1966), and *Beyond Culture* (1976), were among the most-read books by intercultural communication scholars. He coined the terms *proxemics*, the use of space; the linear view of time (*monochronic*) and the cyclic view of time (*polychronic*), and *high and low context*. These terms were used to compare different cultures (i.e., cross-cultural communication research), and inspired researchers to uncover other hidden concepts that help understand different cultures. At FSI, Hall taught the trainees that classroom teaching would differ from actual interactions; therefore, they should gain a solid understanding of culture through cultural encounters, and pay attention to the moment-to-moment interactions with people in the specific culture (Leeds-Hurwitz, 1990; Martin et al., 2012; Sadri & Flammia, 2011).

Ray Birdwhistell was also an anthropologist. He is known to have coined the term *kinesics*. He was a key figure in theorizing and researching nonverbal communication. He also emphasized the importance of meaning-making in messages by intersecting the communication context, such as time, location, occasion, historical events, and relationship between interactants. He famously estimated that "probably no more than 30 to 35 percent of the social meaning of a conversation or a social interaction is carried by the words" (Birdwhistell, 1970, p. 158). To study nonverbal communication, he recorded people's nonverbal communication in various social interactions, observed and coded their body movements, and inferred meanings and their relationships with the specific communication contexts. He argued that the meanings of body languages are culture specific, and that body languages have their own unique "grammars." Although Paul Ekman later refuted this claim by demonstrating universally recognized emotions through facial expressions (McDermott, 1980), cross-cultural communication comparisons in nonverbal communication bring a new understanding of potential cultural clashes due to lack of awareness in meanings attached to behavior.

George Leonard Trager was a linguist and colleague of Sapir and Whorf. He approached linguistics from an anthropologist's perspective. His job at the FSI was to train U.S. workers going abroad to understand paralanguage. Paralanguage refers to "no-speech" sounds and other vocal expressions when people speak, also known as *vocalics* (Trager, 1961, p. 17). Trager developed a typology of paralanguage that included vocal characterizers, vocal qualifiers, vocal segregation, and vocalizations. Examples for vocal qualifiers include "pitch range, pitch control, rhythm control, and tempo" (p. 18). Vocalics remains an important nonverbal category in intercultural communication as well.

Charles Hockett was an anthropologist and linguist, also a colleague of Sapir and Whorf. He was a structuralist linguist, who summarized 13 design features of language and compared these features against animal sounds.

Although historical events, the development of media, and international programs such as the Marshall Program propelled intercultural communication research, the work of the leading scholars at FSI still credited directly the literature from about a century before. For example, Hall's works on ethology and nonverbal communication showed influence from Darwin's book, *The Expressions of the Emotions in Man and Animals*; and he used Freud's psychoanalysis to show that sometimes people are unaware of their personality or cultural roots (Rogers & Hart, 2002).

The major criticism of the Marshall Program was its post-colonialist influence on other countries, especially so-called developing countries. With its humanitarian programs came ideological paradigms (Martin et al., 2012). For example, medical interventions could interfere with local people's beliefs in health maintenance; contraceptive use could violate a religion's basic principles; human rights are defined and interpreted differently in different historical and cultural contexts. The U.S. ideological system may pose different standards among an autonomous people consciously or unconsciously (Martin et al., 2012). As a result, international communication and development communication attracted scholars to address these and other problems.

International communication refers to the study of communication between culturally dissimilar countries linked by mass-mediated communication (Rogers & Hart, 2002). The central focus was on the examination of information flow between countries through mass media channels such as TV, radio, movies, and prints. Research is also done to compare mass media systems across countries. International communication research addresses post-colonialism through understanding the effects of one country's media products and channels on the other (Rogers & Hart, 2002).

More akin to the post-colonialism issues than international communication research is the area of *development communication* research, which refers to "the study of social changes brought about by the application of communication research, theory, and technologies to bring about development" (Rogers & Hart, 2002, p. 9). The term "development" contains the meanings of desirable advancement in social and material capital and wide participation of a social movement. The advancement can be in "improved nutrition, family planning, better health, higher literacy, and improved agricultural production" and "by the means of more effective communication" (pp. 9–10). Many indigenous scholars objected to the standards of "development." After all, what one nation considers desirable may not fare well in another nation. Thus, the critical approach began to gain popularity in analyzing media imperialism and post-colonialism (Martin & Nakayama, 2017; Rogers & Hart, 2002).

Among the various perspectives that FSI proposed, the cross-cultural comparisons and hidden dimensions that drive different perceptions and behaviors received the most attention in intercultural and cross-cultural communication research. In the 1960s, communication scholars began to organize classes, write papers, and conduct research around Hall's paradigm. Intercultural communication programs proliferated in the 1970s and 1980s. William Starosta was the first Ph.D. in an intercultural communication program endowed by Indiana University in 1975. Samovar and Porter's *Intercultural Communication: A Reader* (1972) was among the first published textbooks in the area (Rogers & Hart, 2002). Further, the start of the following institutions and journals pioneered the formal professional outlets for research in intercultural communication:

In 1974, the Speech Communication Association (SCA), now the NCA [National Communication Association of the United States], published the first *International and Intercultural Communication Annual*, edited by Fredrick Casmir (1974). In 1977, the *International Journal of Intercultural Relations*, edited by Daniel Landis, began publication, and the first edition of *The Handbook of Intercultural Communication* appeared in 1978 (Asante, Newmark, & Blake, 1979). *The Howard Journal of Communication*, edited by Starosta, was established to provide a qualitative outlet for ICC [intercultural communication] scholars.

(Rogers & Hart, 2002, p. 4)

In 1970, the Intercultural Communication Division (later the Intercultural and Development Communication Division) was established in the International Communication Association. In 1975, the Intercultural Communication Division was established in the then-SCA. Main research topics during this time included the "sojourning process, assimilation versus cultural maintenance, prejudice and discrimination, ethnocentrism versus cultural relativism, nonverbal communication, uncertainty in initial contact among strangers, and collectivism versus individualism" (Rogers & Hart, 2002, p. 5).

So far, we have reviewed the history and establishment of the intercultural communication field. Since its establishment, the field has witnessed flourishing theory development in the 1980s to 2000s. The remaining part of this chapter is focused on the conceptualization of culture, introduction of other related terms, and introduction to the main theories in the field. The chapter closes with reflections and directions for the future.

Part II: Key Concepts and Theories in Intercultural Communication

Origin of Culture and Philosophical Definitions

Although most standard definitions of culture in the current intercultural communication field describe the major components such as customs and traditions that distinguish one group from another (e.g., Hall, 1976; Hofstede, 2001; Ting-Toomey & Takai, 2006), we deem it important to include some discussions on the origin of culture (e.g., Becker, 1971; Róheim, 1943). The purpose of this inclusion is consistent with what we indicate in the beginning of the chapter: To promote new, creative thinking about intercultural communication, it is necessary to step out of what is described and presented in the current field and to delve into the questions that started and shaped the field.

In his book, *The Origin and Function of Culture*, Róheim (1943, pp. 36–37) argued that culture originates from the resistance of leaving infancy behind:

The life of an infant consists in a series of frustrations which commence with birth. He has to bear the loss of intrauterine happiness; he learns what it means to desire something without receiving it. He can tolerate suspense. At this juncture the road is bifurcated. One road is determined by the substitute objects which the infant finds in his own body. The other road is extrovert, it finds substitutes in environment; the clutching becomes a seeking.

As babies grow up, they experience continual loss from being taken care of, learn to tolerate others, endure all kinds of unsatisfied desires, and even live through suffering. In such situations, seeking internal consolation is insufficient. Instead, building external alliances with others becomes a much stronger buffer against the anxiety and bitterness of life. Thus, culture is formed: "The great danger against which mankind has evolved culture is that of object loss, of being left alone in the dark" (Róheim, 1943, p. 77). Culture comprises "defense systems against anxiety" (p. 81), and "civilization is a series of institutions evolved for the sake of security" (p. 84). In other words, Róheim's definition of culture can be expressed as follows (as cited in Becker, 1971, p. 146): "Culture is a composition of the 'mechanisms of defense of an infant afraid of being alone in the dark'."

Building on Róheim's argument, Becker (1971) pointed out that humans' utmost fear is death. Because humans are the only known species to think symbolically and know their mortality, this knowledge brings anxiety and potentially, despair. To defend against this anxiety, humans rely on each other and their ability to codify a symbolic system to attach meanings to life. With this common goal, a group of people living in proximity starts establishing a system of meanings through symbolic interactions. Becker (1971, p. 79) stated:

> Culture is a structure of rules, customs, and ideas, which serve as a vehicle for heroism. It is a logical extension of the early ego development, and the need for self esteem. The task for the ego is to navigate in its world without anxiety, and it does this by learning to choose actions that are satisfying and bring praise instead of blame. Only in this way can it earn the vital self-esteem that is a buffer against anxiety. Culture provides just those rules and customs, goals of conduct that place right actions automatically at the individual's disposal.

The establishment of ego and culture reflects individual-level and group-level systems to defend humans' deepest anxiety. Culture provides rules and customs for forming and understanding status and role for each person. In this way, others become predictable, and the self can act flexibly according to the heroic qualities one desires. In other words, life becomes an acting procedure with plots and predictable lines of each other's. Although the actors try their best to make this abstract, made-up hero system meaningful, deep down "the network of codified meanings and perceptions . . . are in large part arbitrary and fictional" (Becker, 1971, pp. 126–127). This is why a cultural group's biggest threat is abnormality. People who do not act normally—do not follow norms—threaten the meanings established in the cultural system. Therefore, they are ostracized or put away for medical treatment. In the same vein, a cultural member or a cultural system feels significantly challenged when encountering a different culture. The realization that another group of people who live under different rules and systems can live just as "normally" or functionally reminds them of the arbitrary nature of their own cultural system and hence, the fabricated nature of the system against death. Thus, Becker (1971, p. 148) defined culture as follows: "A culture reflects the particular style that a society adopts to deny despair, the particular ways it lies to itself about the nature of reality." Becker then offered other ways humans search for individuality and freedom from anxiety, such as religion, science, and democracy.

Finally, Becker (1971, p. 113) argued for human universality across cultures: "Men everywhere have the same possibilities of experience, . . . and even if you can never actually feel and see as another, you can understand strange premises and see sympathetically why people do not act as we do." Becker listed six universal human problems (p. 118):

1. What is the relation of man to nature?
2. What are the innate predispositions of men?
3. What types of personality are most valued? What statuses and hierarchy are preferred?
4. What are the modes of relating to others? What roles do people perform in social web?
5. In what kind of space-time dimension does human action take place? What is the relation of past, present, and future?
6. What is the hierarchy of power in nature and society?

These questions were echoed in other scholarly works such as F. Kluckhohn and Strodtbeck's (1961) value orientation theory. The answering of these questions helps develop value dimensions that can be used to compare across cultures (e.g., Hofstede's cultural dimension theory, 1980). We will discuss these theories later in the chapter.

Although Becker's (1971) conclusion is somewhat pessimistic about the nature of culture and its function to save humans from a helpless situation, culture is no coincidence. A cultural system evolves to form a stronghold for its members. Culture cultivates and protects its members from falling into the abyss of feeling meaningless in life. However, being too absorbed in the cultural system could enslave individuals from living out their own identities. Thus, it is beneficial to be in contact with various cultural groups and members, so that an individual can learn to live a balanced life between following group norms and personal interpretations of life.

Now that we have discussed the origin of culture from a philosophical perspective, let us examine traditional definitions of culture and its components that distinguish one group from another. These definitions help a systematic view of main concepts key to any culture.

Normative Definitions of Culture

Clyde Kluckhohn was an anthropologist but contributed tremendously to intercultural communication research. He defined culture as follows (1949/2017, p. 6): "The total lifeway of people, the social legacy the individual acquires from his group, . . . that part of the environment that is the creation of man, . . . and a way of thinking, feeling, believing." C. Kluckhohn (1949/2017) discussed characteristics of culture such as its acquisition nature, dynamism, relatively stable structure, explicit and implicit elements, and functionality for individuals to use to "adjust both to the external environment and to other men" (p. 11). He and his colleague Alfred Kroeber reviewed 164 definitions of culture and concluded that no all-inclusive definition should be used to define culture, because it would become undistinguishable from the concept of society. Instead, the definition should be focused on cognitive and symbolic features, with its unique components, structural relations between these components, and patterns (Kroeber & C. Kluckhohn, 1952). This demarcation for the conceptualization fares especially well in intercultural communication research because communication scholars study cognitive, social interactional, and symbolic natures of human behavior. Below, we review three of the most widely used definitions of culture, from Geert Hofstede (1980, 2001; Hofstede & Hofstede, 2005), Edward T. Hall (1976), and Stella Ting-Toomey and her colleagues (Ting-Toomey & Takai, 2006; Oetzel, 2009). These definitions capture the communication perspective on culture and provide succinct yet sufficient discussions on the concept.

Hofstede and Hofstede (2005, p. 4) defined culture as follows: "The collective mental programming of the mind that distinguishes the members of one group or category of people from others." Hofstede and Hofstede (2005) used computer programs to analogize human groups' unique patterns of cognition, emotion, and behavior. They also disclaimed that, unlike computer programs, people are only partially programmed by their cultures and still have the ability to think, feel, or act creatively and differently from cultural patterns. Hofstede and Hofstede (2005) proposed three components of an individual's mental programming: personality (individual-specific characteristics consisting of inheritance and social acquisition), culture (group-specific cultural programming), and human nature (universal and inherited) (p. 4). Hofstede and Hofstede's definition succinctly depicted the relationship between individuals and their cultures. Ting-Toomey and Takai's (2006) definition below lists key components in the mental programming Hofstede and Hofstede described.

Ting-Toomey and Takai (2006, p. 691) defined culture as follows:

> A learned system of meanings that fosters a particular sense of shared identity-hood and community-hood among its group members. It is a complex frame of reference that consists of a pattern of traditions, beliefs, values, norms, symbols, and meanings that are shared to varying degrees by interacting members of an identity group.

In this definition, the first sentence expresses the acquired nature of culture through social interaction, shared experience, shared meanings, shared identities, and sense of belonging to a group. In the second sentence, the six components describe a culture from unobservable depth to observable embodiment. *Traditions* are "rituals and ceremonies that mark important times in the year, developmental points in life, and relationships," and *beliefs* are "cognitive assumptions that members of a culture hold on to, often without questioning" (Oetzel, 2009, pp. 4–5). *Values* are judgmental meanings associated to a phenomenon about whether it is right and wrong, good or bad, desirable or undesirable. *Norms* are rules about behavioral correctness, often implicit. These four components tend to be acquired from a young age, instilled without discussion. *Symbols* are "signs, artifacts, or words that stand for something other than themselves and which represent something meaningful for members of a culture," and *meanings* are "the objective and subjective interpretations that members of a culture hold about the symbols" (p. 6). These two categories are more observable, verbally and behaviorally exchanged in social interactions.

In Ting-Toomey and Takai's (2006) definition, communication is the soul of culture. Learning of any of the cultural elements can only happen through social interaction; being labeled as a cultural member requires communicating with other members; not communicating or participating in the culture marginalizes or isolates a person; and active individual communication can shape a culture. Hall (1959, p. 169) famously said, "Culture is communication and communication is culture."

Hall (1976) further discussed culture with a focus on its hidden influence on its members. Specifically, he emphasized the unconscious transference from cultural values to human behavior. He used monochronic versus polychronic time as an example. Whereas those who are taught by their culture to be monochronic (doing one thing at a time) emphasize scheduling, segmentation, and promptness, those who are polychronic (doing several things at a time) emphasize involvement of people and completion of transactions. However, without communication, this cultural meaning is hidden, and clashes may happen between a monochronic person and a polychronic person.

In addition, Hall (1976) discussed culture as one form of human extension, meaning that because of humans' limitation as organisms and ability of invention, they build external materials and social resources to help overcome life hindrances and gain control over situations. This idea is similar to McLuhan's (1964) idea that mediums are extensions of humans. McLuhan compared different mediums of communication (e.g., spoken words, written words, printed words, roadmaps, photographs, telephones, radio, television, movies, and so on) and analogized mediums with languages, because mediums have their own systems, grammars, intentions, and effects. McLuhan (1964, 1967) predicted that electronic media would have control over people because of their own system characteristics. In the same manner, Hall (1976) warned people to be aware of "extension transference," which means that once people begin to evolve their extensions, they are trapped in a web such that they begin to lose control over what they have created (p. 180). The extensions may lead to the loss of functions in related human parts, most importantly, creativity. Consequently, humans lose confidence and feel powerless when they have little control over situations and have to depend on external inter-ference. In sum, Hall (1976) advocated the study of hidden power of a culture, especially its implicit effects on people during intercultural encounters.

Connecting the manifest and implicit components of culture, Trompenaars and Hampden-Turner (1998) described culture as containing an explicit, exter-nal layer such as artifacts and products, a middle layer containing norms and values, and an implicit, internal layer containing basic "assumptions about exist-ence" (p. 23). Sometimes an iceberg analogy is used to describe these elements as well. For example, Oetzel (2009) illustrated an iceberg to represent culture, with the observable tip including artifacts, symbols, language, and behavior. Right below the surface level are meanings, followed by norms, then beliefs, and deep down, values (p. 11).

Synthesizing the different conceptualizations of culture, we offer this definition for use in this book:

> A culture is a system of meanings shared and continuously created among a specific group of people, whereby the meanings are created through symbolic social interactions and defined by an interface of dialectic sym-bolic elements: static and dynamic, explicit and implicit, creative and restrictive, and individual and collective.

We hope that the above discussion on the concept of culture can help readers see the multifaceted nature of culture. How culture should be conceptualized depends on what kind of research is to be conducted. For example, if one wants to study why so much hatred and fear exists between ethnic groups or between countries that hold drastically different ideologies, one may look into Róheim's (1943) and Becker's (1971) conceptualizations of culture. If one wants to examine the culture-general and culture-specific domains of individual behavior (e.g., comparing a communication phenomenon across cultures), Hofstede's (1980, 2001) definition is helpful. If the research interest is to explore a new cultural group (e.g., the culture of Instagram users), Ting-Toomey and Takai's (2006) definition with its detailed explanation on cultural components is highly useful. If the research topic is on how a cultural phenomenon goes beyond control and negatively affects cultural members (e.g., increased social media use and reduced social interactions), Hall's (1976) and McLuhan's (1964, 1967) works can help. Certainly, a researcher can combine various conceptualization frameworks to develop his or her own definitions of culture. The fluidity and comprehensiveness of the concept allow creative use of it.

Key Concepts Related to Intercultural Communication

In this section, we provide definitions of other concepts that are related to intercultural communication. First, *cross-cultural communication* refers to the comparison and contrast of a communication phenomenon across different cultures (Oetzel, 2009). An example is the study of interactive constraints among different cultures (M. Kim, 2005). Cross-cultural communication is most prone to be confused with *intercultural communication*, which refers to the study of social interactions between or among culturally dissimilar individuals or groups (Oetzel, 2009). However, some research falls in between. For example, Y. Kim's (1988) cross-cultural adaptation theory was named as if it were a theory in cross-cultural communication, but it examines how a person who migrates to a new culture adapts to the new host culture. This theory was included in Gudykunst and Mody's (2002) *Handbook of International and Intercultural Communication Theory* as an intercultural communication theory, but it can be used in cross-cultural communication research, such as when two cultural value systems are compared among adapting individuals, or in intercultural communication research when social interactions between adapting individuals and host members are studied.

Intracultural (interracial, interethnic, co-cultural) communication refers to the study of communication between smaller units of cultural groups that belong to a dominant culture. An example is the study of interracial marriages within the United States (Oetzel, 2009). *Multicultural communication* has been used rarely but is worth mentioning because it is related to multiculturalism, a term that is used increasingly nowadays. The meaning of multiculturalism contains a spectrum from something similar to *diversity*, a neutral term that describes the composition of people who identify themselves or are identified with different group affiliations (Oetzel, McDermott, Torres, & Sanchez, 2012), to *multiculturalism*, a term that contains critical connotations and meanings to support the rights of minority group identities (Spencer, 1994). Spencer (1994) defined multiculturalism as "a specific aspect of the broader movement of 'political correctness,' which is itself a product of the dynamics of the collective construction and reconstruction of identity in America" (p. 548). An example of using the word "multicultural" as "diversified" is seen in Van der Zee and Van Oudenhoven's (2000) research, which developed and tested a "multicultural personality questionnaire" to study what variables compose communication competence in a diversified workplace (p. 291).

Examples of using "multicultural" as including both neutral and critical elements are seen in articles by Tanno and Jandt (1993–1994) and by Fine (1991). Tanno and Jandt (1993–1994) advocated the use of multicultural communication as a term that "serves an inclusive function, since it subsumes all the communicative acts previously defined as occurring in intercultural, cross-cultural, and international contexts" (p. 37). Fine (1991) discussed the lack of multicultural communication research in multicultural workplaces. She approached the topic through a critical perspective and called for the "assumption of difference" rather than "assumption of homogeneity" (p. 263). Thus, "multicultural" here contains the meaning of both diversity and perceived inequality of different cultural groups. Finally, multiculturalism is clearly used as a critical research term in Spencer's (1994) article, where Spencer discussed how multiculturalism is related to identity politics through a historical development perspective in the United States.

Another term related to intercultural communication is *globalization*, which refers to "the increasing interconnectedness of people and places as a result of changes in communication technologies, communication, and migration patterns which cause political, economic, and cultural convergence" (Oetzel, 2009, p. 16). The term has roots in Marshall McLuhan's phrase, *global village*. In his book, McLuhan (1964) analyzed a great number of mediums of communication. His famous saying, "The medium is the message," means that each medium has its unique effects and is used purposefully by the message sender. One of the most important arguments is that medium has a superseding order: Spoken words are to be superseded by manuscripts, which are to be superseded by print media, and finally by electronic media. Through each superseding, people's information becomes less idiosyncratic and fragmented, but more collective and unified. Eventually, when electronics replace print media, the world becomes "a computer, an electronic brain, exactly as an infantile piece of science fiction" (McLuhan, 1962, p. 32). McLuhan (1962), decades before the social media boom, predicted that the collective identity will eventually bring people together as in a tribe and the new society will become a global village. This concept of togetherness is also called *cultural convergence*.

Related with the terms globalization and convergence are *divergence* and *digital gap*. Divergence is the opposite of convergence, meaning that cultural groups will become increasingly different and ideologies discrepant (Nisbett, 2003). Digital gap describes the phenomenon that people who have resources to media will become increasingly connected, whereas those without these resources will become increasingly disconnected (Martin & Nakayama, 2017).

From an ethical perspective, *cultural universalism/relativism, moral inclusion/exclusion*, and *social justice* are often studied in intercultural communication, because when culturally dissimilar individuals and groups interact, many clashes occur due to different yet implicit value systems. Without mindful thinking and cultural training, such clashes can cause significant damage to communication and relationship building. Cultural universalism refers to the use of one set of value systems to judge human behaviors, whereas cultural relativism refers to the use of different sets of value systems to make such judgments (Oetzel, 2009). Moral inclusion refers to treating all humans equally, with the same kind and level of acceptance, esteem, and dignity, whereas moral exclusion refers to not treating some people with the same standards of respect or dignity because they do not deserve it (Oetzel, 2009). For example, a society may offer murderers and thieves equal protection under the law to the extent it embraces a morally inclusive position. Finally, social justice "is a philosophical stance that emphasizes fair distribution of wealth, power, and income across cultures" (Oetzel, 2009, p. 20).

The study of culture and communication cannot be complete without an understanding of *identities*, because any cultural component becomes influential in human societies only through individual members who acquire them. In essence, an *identity* is a person's concept of self in its entirety, which directs the person's cognitive, emotive, and behavioral manifestations. Identity has been defined with different emphases in different theories. The first emphasis is on the content of self-concept itself. For example, Yep (1998) defined identity as "a 'person's conception of self within a particular social, geographical, cultural, and political context' . . . In other words, identity is a sense of self or who we are in a specific situation" (p. 57). Markus and Kitayama (1991) used self-construal to describe the concept of self, which refers to a person's entire system of self-related concepts that defines, assesses, expresses, and regulates his or her behavior. It functions as a mediating agent between cultural values and individual cognition, emotion, and behavior.

The second emphasis is on the social, relational, and interactional aspects of self-concept. Ting-Toomey (2005a) defined identity as a reflective and derivative concept of "self-conception or self-image" based on the interaction with one's main social and cultural groups (p. 212). Tajfel and Turner (1979) defined identity as a person's concept of self based on the myriad social groups with which he or she self-identifies and is externally identified by others. Turner, Hogg, Oakes, Reicher, and Wetherell (1987) defined self-identity as a reflective product based on one's interactions with other social interactants. This perspective is similar to the social constructivist perspective (e.g., Goffman, 1959) that the concept of self-identity is a social product of symbolic interactions throughout a person's life. However, self-identity in general has both implicit and explicit relations with the social and cultural environments in which it is formed. For example, a cultural identity is based on the cultural groups one identifies with, but at the same time, it refers to a self-claimed image specific to a given situation, tantamount to the concept of *face* (Imahori & Cupach, 2005). With its multidimensional characteristics, *identity* is a fluid concept and can be studied with different foci depending on the researcher's topic of interest.

Oetzel (2009) summarized seven characteristics of identity:

1. *Multifaceted*: Identity contains multiple dimensions. Imagine drawing a pie chart with different sizes of slices to represent different facets of self. The results will show what essential roles and what importance is given to these roles. Kanagawa, Cross, and Markus (2001) asked participants to respond to the "Who am I?" question multiple times, and the results demonstrated myriad self-concepts with finite themes.

2. *Social and personal*: Whereas social identity depicts what group people feel a belonging to, personal identity depicts people's self-perceived uniqueness.

3. *Strength and salience*: Whereas strength refers to the perceived "degree of importance of a particular identity," salience refers to the aspect of identity that stands out in a particular situation (Oetzel, 2009, p. 59).

4. *Stable and fluid*: Each identity has core and unchanging components as well as flexible and adaptive components. This can be used to assess what are malleable aspects of identity in different life stages or environments.

5. *Avowed and ascribed*: Avowed identity refers to a voluntary, self-perceived, and self-claimed identity. Ascribed identity refers to an assigned, other-perceived, and other–imposed identity.

6. *Passing and outing*: Whereas passing refers to a decision and process to behave like and associate with a more powerful and prestigious group, outing refers to a decision and process to behave like a less prestigious and accepted group.

7. *Performance and expression*: Both terms mean that people use various verbal and nonverbal messages to claim publicly their selected identity facets, such as the use of clothing items, hairstyles, and particular speech styles. Expression is focused more on revealing the self-perceived "true" self with an emphasis on what the inner self thinks and feels, whereas performance is focused more on showing the emphasized facets of self-claimed identity to educate others. Although the two are often embodied together, expression is more internally driven and performance is more externally driven.

Finally, Oetzel (2009) also summarized Phinney's (1993) general model of cultural identity development, Helms' (1993) minority group model of cultural identity development, and Hardiman's (1994) majority group model of cultural identity development. The models are described below.

1. General model of cultural identity development (Phinney, 1993, as cited in Oetzel, 2009):

   a. *Unexamined cultural identity phase*: Individuals are not aware of cultural differences; the stage usually lasts in childhood.

   b. *Cultural identity search phase*: Individuals become aware of cultural differences and start seeking information about their own cultural groups and other cultural groups to gain a deeper understanding of their own identities. This phase is usually triggered by a problematic cultural encounter or experience.

   c. *Cultural identity achievement phase*: The stage in which individuals "have reached a sense of clarity and confidence about their identities" (p. 67).

2. Minority group model of cultural identity development (Helms, 1993, as cited in Oetzel, 2009)

   a. *Pre-encounter phase*: This phase is similar to the unexamined stage above, where individuals (often still in childhood) have not realized their minority group identity. They automatically subscribe to the majority cultural identity through various institutions.

   b. *Encounter phase*: An awareness of their minority group identity when individuals encounter a triggering event, typically discriminatory and negative. Individuals realize that they do not pass as a majority group member and start seeking information to gain better understanding about their minority group identity.

   c. *Immersion-emersion phase*: Minority group individuals start embracing their minority identities and rejecting the majority cultural identities, because they typically find more acceptance and security in their minority group. They emerge with strong identifications and expressions as a minority group member.

   d. *Internalization-commitment phase*: Individuals gain clarity and confidence in their minority cultural identities, but they have also developed better understanding of other cultural groups, including the majority cultural group. They can respect other cultural groups and handle discrimination with more constructive methods.

3. Majority group model of cultural identity development (Hardiman, 1994, as cited in Oetzel, 2006):

   a. *Unexamined cultural identity phase*: This phase is similar to the unexamined phase in the general model above.

   b. *Acceptance phase*: Individuals form a privileged ideology without realization of any problem. The ideology may be with or without intentional choice, and they accept that minority groups need help and should be assimilated into the majority culture. The conduct of maintaining the privilege can vary from showing distance to minority group members to expressing racism.

c. *Resistance phase*: Majority group members realize the problems with their own group and shift the blame from minority groups to the majority group. They may distance themselves from other majority group members, associate with minority group members, and even express identities of minority groups to show resistance to the mainstream culture.

d. *Redefinition phase*: Majority group members gain a relatively clear and confident cultural identity. Although aware of privileges and biases of their own group, they accept themselves being in the majority group, seeing its positive sides and feeling at ease to be a member.

e. *Integration phase*: Majority group members embrace their cultural identities comprehensively, and they respect and appreciate other cultural groups.

The key concepts reviewed in this section relate to intercultural communication to various extents. These and other important concepts in the field are described in detail in the following section, where the most prominent theories in intercultural communication are introduced.

Key Intercultural Communication Theories

After the formal establishment of the intercultural communication discipline in the 1960s, the field received its first big wave in theory development in the 1980s to 2000s. Below we will discuss the theories most widely received and tested in five categories. The first two theories are focused on culture-level value orientations: value orientations theory and cultural dimensions theory. The next three theories bridge cultural values to individual behavior through a mediating variable: self-construal. These are self-construal theory, face-negotiation theory, and interactive constraints theory. The third category includes three theories that examine intercultural interaction situations: expectancy violation theory, anxiety and uncertainty management theory, and communication accommodation theory. The fourth category contains one theory, cross–cultural adaptation theory, which examines migrants' cultural adaptation experience. The last category contains four identity theories: identity negotiation theory, social identity theory, cultural identity theory, and identity management theory. In discussing identity negotiation theory, relational dialectics theory and acculturation strategies theory are briefly discussed also.

Value Orientations Theory

First, we come back to Clyde Kluckhohn, anthropologist and social theorist. Together with his wife, Dr. Florence Kluckhohn, and colleague, Fred Strodtbeck, they developed value orientations theory. Although not as influential as Hofstede's (1980) cultural dimensions theory, F. Kluckhohn and Strodtbeck's (1961) value orientations theory greatly contributed to the cross-cultural research in an emic versus etic lens. The *emic* approach emphasizes cultural insiders' views and experiences, whereas the *etic* approach emphasizes cultural outsiders' (e.g., researchers') observations and interpretations of cultural insiders' activities (Pike, 1967). F. Kluckhohn and Strodtbeck's theory proposed five value orientation questions that can be used to understand any human cultural group. Then they tested these value orientations among five communities in a southwestern region in the United States. Thus, their research represents a collection of emic data with an etic examination.

The five value orientation questions are as follows:

1. What is human nature (good, evil, or a mixture)?
2. What is the relationship between humans, nature, and the supernatural (domination, submission, or stewardship)?
3. What is the concept of time and where is the focus (past, present, or future)?
4. What motivates human behavior, being (expressing internal self), being-in-becoming (personal growth), or achieving (obtaining external materials and power)?
5. What is the nature of human relations, lineal (hierarchical), collateral (equal), or varied based on individual merits (equity-driven)?

F. Kluckhohn and Strodtbeck (1961) argued that although cultures vary in myriad aspects, answers to these questions reveal each culture's worldview. Knowing the answers to these questions tells the essential value systems of a culture and helps predict collective behavioral orientations in general. These scholars also created culture-specific measures and developed group profiles for their samples. Similar research methods were used later in cultural dimensions development by scholars such as Hofstede (1980), Schwartz (1999), and Trompenaars and Hampden-Turner (1998).

Cultural Dimensions Theory

Hofstede's Cultural Dimensions

Geert Hofstede, a Dutch social psychologist and former IBM employee, is one of the most prominent researchers in cross-cultural psychology and communication research. Oyserman, Coon, and Kemmelmeier (2002) stated, "Hofstede's model was important because it organized cultural differences into overarching patterns, which facilitated comparative research and launched a rapidly expanding body of cultural and cross-cultural research in the ensuing 20 years" (p. 3). Because of Hofstede's works, the concept of individualism-collectivism is not only widely examined in research, but also well known among training practitioners of cross-cultural workers and even laypeople. In this section, we place similar scholarly works with Hofstede's together, so that readers may have a general list of cultural dimensions that have been used in cross-cultural and intercultural communication research. In general, a *cultural dimension* represents a value construct bracketed in a continuum, with each polar end representing the opposite end value of this construct. For example, a cultural dimension of masculinity-femininity is a construct that measures to what degree a culture values competitiveness, assertion, and general toughness, as compared with nurturing, cooperation, and general tenderness (Hofstede & Hofstede, 2005). Cultural dimensions theory holds the following assumptions (Hall, 1959; Hofstede, 1980):

1. Cultural universals exist.
2. People's scores vary in magnitude along a value dimension.
3. Cultures can be located along a value dimension based on the group's average score.
4. Ecological fallacy should be avoided (i.e., a cultural group's average score on a dimension does not represent a cultural group member's individual score).

In the 1970s, Hofstede collected over 116,000 surveys from IBM employees across more than 40 countries and regions. The multinational company work environment provided naturally comparable sampling pools. Hofstede (1980) asked questions about values and organizational behaviors. He generalized four dimensions. The first dimension is *power distance*, defined as "the extent to which the less powerful members of institutions and organizations within a country expect and accept that power is distributed unequally" (Hofstede & Hofstede, 2005, p. 46). *Individualism-collectivism* was originally one dimension that describes the extent to which individuals connect with their groups (Hofstede, 1980). Although this dimension attracted the most attention and examination in studies, it had not been generally supported (see Oyserman et al.'s meta-analysis on the dimension, 2002). Most research suggested that individualism and collectivism are not bipolar ends of each other and that each concept contains a universe of sub-concepts of its own (Oyserman et al., 2002). Thus, Hofstede and Hofstede (2005, p. 76) redefined individualism and collectivism as follows:

> *Individualism* pertains to societies in which the ties between individuals are loose: everyone is expected to look after himself or herself and his or her immediate family. *Collectivism* as its opposite pertains to societies in which people from birth onward are integrated into strong, cohesive ingroups, which throughout people's lifetimes continue to protect them in exchange for unquestioning loyalty.

These definitions maintain that individualism and collectivism are opposite values of each other, but the definitions did add more and differing categories of lower-level indicators than the previous version.

The third dimension is *masculinity-femininity*. Hofstede and Hofstede (2005) stated that the name of this dimension was selected because this was the only dimension on which men and women scored significantly differently. They defined this dimension as follows:

> A society is called *masculine* when emotional gender roles are clearly distinct: men are supposed to be assertive, tough, and focused on material success, whereas women are supposed to be more modest, tender, and concerned with the quality of life. A society is called *feminine* when emotional gender roles overlap: both men and women are supposed to be more modest, tender, and concerned with the quality of life.
>
> *(Hofstede & Hofstede, 2005, p. 120)*

The fourth dimension is *uncertainty avoidance*, which is defined as the extent to which cultural members "feel threatened by ambiguous or unknown situations" (Hofstede & Hofstede, 2005, p. 166). High uncertainty avoidance cultures tend to have clear rules and regulations, prefer direct communication, and confrontational conflict management styles, whereas low uncertainty avoidance cultures tend to hold relative rules based on situations, prefer indirect communication, and non-confrontational management styles (Oetzel, 2009).

The fifth dimension, *long- vs. short-term orientation*, was added later, after Geert Hofstede's colleague Michael Bond (1992; also see Hofstede & Bond, 1988) discovered this new dimension among Hong Kong employees. Geert Hofstede adopted this dimension in his cultural dimensions theory, and it is defined as follows:

> *Long-term orientation* stands for the fostering of virtues oriented toward future rewards—in particular, perseverance and thrift. Its opposite pole, *short-term orientation*, stands for the fostering of virtues related to the past and present—in particular, respect for tradition, preservation of "face," and fulfilling social obligations.
>
> *(Hofstede & Hofstede, 2005, p. 210)*

Hofstede's (1980) research dominated intercultural and cross-cultural communication research for two decades. Power distance was the most confirmed dimension; individualism was much better confirmed than was collectivism; uncertainty avoidance and masculinity-femininity received mixed results; and long- or short-term orientation received the least attention and confirmation (e.g., Merritt, 2000; Oyserman et al., 2002; Trompenaars & Hampden-Turner, 1998). Hofstede's cultural dimensions theory has inspired the development of other cultural dimensions and theories (e.g., self-construal theory, Markus & Kitayama, 1991). This theory has also been widely used in public relations research to examine how public relations is practiced in different parts of the world.

Trompenaars and Hampden-Turner's Cultural Dimensions

Trompenaars and Hampden-Turner (1998) examined culture in the organizational context. They defined culture as the ways different groups of people solve problems and approach dilemmas. Influenced by F. Kluckhohn and Strodtbeck (1961), they aimed to develop universal dimensions to compare among cultures. They gathered data in over a decade and collected more than 30,000 surveys from managers in 28 countries. The survey included hypothetical dilemmas and asked respondents to choose between two opposite value or behavioral tendencies (some scenarios included an option of middle ground). Results revealed seven dimensions. Trompenaars and Hampden-Turner (1998) grouped them into three categories.

1. Attitude to human relations

    a. *Universalism versus particularism*: Whereas universalism means that the same standards should apply invariably to people, particularism means that standards should be applied flexibly based on relationships and circumstances.

    b. *Individualism versus communitarianism*: This dimension is similar to Hofstede's (1980) individualism–collectivism, and asks whether people regard themselves more as independent and autonomous individuals or interdependent members of groups.

    c. *Neutral versus emotional*: The dimension on one end is marked by neutral, objective, detached social interactions, and on the other end, by social interactions with open and unrestricted emotional expressions.

    d. *Diffuse vs. specific*: This dimension measures to what extent a person should dive into a business relationship as a "whole person, . . . with a real and personal contact," versus maintaining only "a specific relationship prescribed by a contract" (p. 9).

    e. *Achievement versus ascription*: This dimension measures to what extent an individual should be judged by external accomplishments through personal efforts, or by the social status and network he/she is born with and other internal attributes such as age, appearance, and gender.

2. Attitude to time

    a. *Time orientation*: This dimension assesses a cultural group's general attitude toward time: Is time sequential or synchronous (i.e., linear or repetitive and cyclical)? What is the relationship and relative importance between past, present, and future?

3. Relation to nature

    a. *Internal or external control:* This dimension assesses a cultural group's attitude toward the relationship between humans and nature. Whereas internal control means that humans control and dominate nature and that individuals have control over their own fates, external control means that humans should adapt to nature as part of it, and that others and external environment have control over individuals' fates.

Trompenaars and Hampden-Turner's (1998) cultural dimensions extend and complement F. Kluckhohn and Strodtbeck's (1961) and Hofstede's (1980) dimensions, and more importantly, the methodology exemplifies how cultural dimensions theory can be adapted with different research purposes and samples.

Schwartz's Cultural Dimensions (1999)

Schwartz (1999) indicated that Hofstede's (1980) dimensions were significant, but lacked data from Central and Eastern European countries, which were influenced by communism and could contain considerably different value systems from the United States and Western Europe. He theorized three dimensions and spent six years (1988–1993) to collect survey data from more than 35,000 participants in 49 nations. The three dimensions received general support through multidimensional scaling.

1. *Conservatism versus intellectual and affective autonomy:* This dimension depicts that on one end, a culture promotes conservatism, "a cultural emphasis on maintenance of the status quo, propriety, and restraint of actions or inclinations that might disrupt the solidary group or the traditional order (social order, respect for tradition, family security, wisdom)" (p. 27). On the other end, a culture promotes intellectual autonomy (the freedom to pursue knowledge due to personal curiosity or self-fulfillment) and affective autonomy (the freedom to pursue positive and pleasurable life experiences).

2. *Hierarchy versus egalitarianism:* This dimension is similar to Hofstede's (1980) power distance, but puts more emphasis on social responsibilities, social justice, and policy making. It refers to "a cultural emphasis on the legitimacy of an unequal distribution of power, roles and resources (social power, authority, humility, wealth)" (p. 27).

3. *Mastery versus harmony:* This dimension contains similar values as Trompenaars and Hampden-Turner's (1998) internal versus external control dimension. Whereas mastery refers to active efforts to control one's own fate through assertion, competition, accomplishments, and control over the environment, harmony refers to active efforts to fit in and get along with others and the environment.

Schwartz's (1999) cultural dimensions complement the other cultural dimensions. However, his dimensional perspective was focused more on societal than on symbolic facets of culture.

Hall's (1976) Cultural Dimension

The last cultural dimension that we want to add here is Hall's (1976) *high versus low context*. Although Hall did not explicitly label this concept as a cultural dimension, he did compare cultures along a spectrum that varied from low context, where meanings are contained mainly in messages and the speaker bears the responsibility to clarify the meanings intended, to high context, where meanings are contained more in the contextual cues than in the actual messages and the listener bears the responsibility to interpret the meanings as intended. This dimension is highly relevant to intercultural communication because its emphasis is on the communication elements.

Although cultural dimensions theory inspired much research and was well received in the practical field, such as in cultural training programs, it faces challenges in construct and measurement validity, ecological fallacy issues, and lack of explanatory power. Take the most researched dimension, individualism-collectivism (IC), for example. Oyserman et al. (2002) conducted a meta-analysis of the empirical research of IC in influencing communication behavior, and found that first, IC was not reflected by Western and Eastern cultures as Hofstede and others (e.g., Triandis, 1995) previously found. For example, the Japanese are not more individualist than North Americans.

Also, mixed results were found for collectivism. Fiske (2002) argued that intrinsic problems existed not just in the operationalization of IC, but in the conceptualization as well. Most researchers have treated IC as static and invariant. However, both individualism and collectivism should include unique subsets that could vary in different contexts. For instance, Gudykunst (2002) argued that IC should only be used to study ingroup–outgroup communication, and people's groups vary in strength, length, and rank order. Treating collectivism without distinguishing among ingroups is conceptually problematic. To fix the problem, researchers have advised reconceptualization of the construct (e.g., Fiske, 2002; Oyserman et al., 2002; Triandis, 1995). Triandis and Gelfand (1998), for instance, developed horizontal and vertical IC, which was focused on the equal (horizontal) or hierarchical (vertical) nature of individualism and collectivism. This way, individualism can be further distinguished between being equity-based and equality-based, and collectivism can be further distinguished between being hierarchical and communal.

Ecological fallacy refers to the erroneous assumption that the characteristics found at a collective level apply to all individuals of that group (Hofstede, 2001; Oetzel, 2009). Cultural dimensions theory uses scores of countries along dimensions to compare national-level cultural characteristics. When individual behavior is of interest and participants of a country are assumed to have a certain cultural value score represented by their country of residence, ecological fallacy occurs. To fix the problem, individual-level measurements should be created and validated, and individual data should be collected on the value dimension of interest (Markus & Kitayama, 1991).

Finally, although cultural dimensions help understand value orientations among different cultures, they cannot offer explanations for such variations. On the construct level, research should develop construct space to find its sub-components. Typology development is one way to construct such a space. For example, Oyserman et al. (2002) found that "individualism domain" contained seven sub-concepts: independence, individual goals, competition, uniqueness, privacy, self-knowledge, and direct communication; and "collectivism domain" contained eight sub-concepts: relatedness, belonging, duty, harmony, advice, context, hierarchy, and teamwork (p. 9). Examination of these sub-concepts with various samples and contexts through qualitative research such as in-depth interviews and field observations may help researchers uncover the sources of the importance placed on these values.

Moreover, cultural values should also be measured on individual levels, especially when the research goal is to explain and predict individual communication behavior. Hofstede (1980, 2001) forewarned the occurrence of ecological fallacy in using his cultural dimensions. Oetzel (2009) distinguished between subjective (personal absorption of cultural values) and normative culture (general cultural value). By measuring individual cultural values and connecting them with individual behavior, researchers bring the unit of observation and unit of analysis to the individual level, and can build theoretical models to explain and predict behavior. In fact, the three theories below all brought in individualism-collectivism, conceptualizing and measuring this dimension at the individual level: self-construal theory, face-negotiation theory, and interactive constraints theory. All three theories added an individual-level mediator, self-construal, to bridge the cultural-level values to individual behavior.

Self-Construal Theory

The self-construal model was developed by Markus and Kitayama (1991) and is rooted in cross-cultural psychology. In the decade after its introduction, the model gained a position almost as important as individualism-collectivism in intercultural communication research (Gudykunst et al., 1996; T. Levine et al., 2003; Matsumoto & Yoo, 2006). The popularity of the self-construal model in communication was no coincidence. Although originally developed in the field of psychology, the model was able to address communication issues. To fully explicate how the self-construal model was used in communication research, the rest of the paragraphs in this section are ordered as follows. First, the concept of self-construal is introduced. Second, the link from self-construal to outcome variables (including communication variables) are discussed. Third, major theories in the intercultural communication field related to self-construal are discussed. Fourth, Singelis and Brown's (1995) study is used as an example. Finally, the overall evaluation of the theory is discussed.

Markus and Kitayama (1991) developed the concept of self-construal to address the ecological fallacy issue related with cultural dimensions theory. Specifically, they proposed self-construal as a mediator between cultural values and individual cognition, emotion, and behavior. *Self-construal* is defined as a repertoire of self-related schemata that evaluate, organize, and regulate people's behavior. It is the totality of self-schemata (Markus & Kitayama, 1991).

Culture shapes self-construal through the socialization process and its institutions such as family, school, and government. Markus and Kitayama (1991) argued that individualism and collectivism (IC) greatly influence people's self-construals. Individualist cultures tend to foster their members to develop a bounded, unitary, and relatively stable self, defined as *an independent self-construal*. People with independent self-construals emphasize (a) internal abilities, thoughts, and feelings; (b) uniqueness of self and self-expression; (c) personal attributes and goals; and (d) direct communication (also see Singelis, 1994). Their concerns about others and the environment are less important than their concerns for self. Others are not totally dismissed, but are used primarily to validate one's own attributes. The environment ought to be manipulated and controlled to fulfill personal goals and preferences. An *interdependent self-construal*, on the other hand, is defined as a flexible and variable self that connects to others and the environment closely. An interdependent self emphasizes (a) external and public self-expression, (b) belonging to and fitting in, (c) occupying appropriate space and engaging in appropriate behavior, and (d) indirect communication (Markus & Kitayama, 1991; Singelis, 1994). This type of self-construal is fostered by collectivism.

Markus and Kitayama argued that roles of others and the environment are core to differentiate between the two types of self-construals. Not for a validation purpose as an independent self-construal does, an interdependent self-construal embraces others in its formation. An independent self-construal resembles a cell living with other cells in an environment. Despite the material exchanges with the others and the context, the cell remains its unity. The context provides a background of the living space. An interdependent self resembles a cell that is always tightly surrounded by its closely related cells (ingroup). It sees itself as part of a whole, without which it is no longer meaningful. Further, an interdependent self-construal believes that the substance of the context is the same with itself. Thus, the context should never be dismissed. In sum, the core difference between independent and interdependent self-construals is how one considers his or her relationship with the environment and "self-in-relation-to-other" (Markus & Kitayama, 1991).

Markus and Kitayama (1991, 1998) argued that independent and inter-dependent self-construals are the overarching schemata of self-system. The consequences were addressed from three aspects: cognition, emotion, and motivation. First, to learn how people assimilate, evaluate, and organize information, researchers should know how people perceive it, what they pay attention to, and what they are sensitive to. Markus and Kitayama (1991) sum-marized earlier research on cross-country comparisons (especially Japan and the United States) and concluded that people with interdependent self-construals perceive more connections between people and between people and their environment, and they are more sensitive and attentive to others' needs than are those with independent self-construals.

Second, self-construal affects how people experience emotions. Markus and Kitayama (1991) specified two types of emotions: ego-focused and other-focused. Ego-focused emotions center on expressing one's internal feelings. Other-focused emotions center on the estimated responses of others. For exam-ple, anger and frustration are ego-focused emotions, but shame and guilt are other-focused emotions. Matsumoto, Kudoh, Scherer, and Wallbott (1988) found that, at a general level, U.S. Americans reported experiencing longer and more intense emotions than did the Japanese. Matsumoto et al. reasoned that the Americans emphasize self-expression and the need to be attended to, whereas the Japanese emphasize appropriateness and harmony. Last, self-construal affects motivations. Independent and interdependent self-construals are motivated by different goals (Markus & Kitayama, 1991). Whereas independent self-construals are motivated more by personal achievements, one's own status, and the need to control, interdependent self-construals are motivated more by group goals, ingroup status, and social expectations.

The self-construal model received immediate attention and was tested in empirical research. The concept of self-construal was also added in several extant theories (e.g., Ting-Toomey's face-negotiation theory and M. Kim's interactive constraints theory, introduced later in this chapter). Below we dis-cuss one sample study that assessed the model in intercultural communication.

Singelis and Brown (1995) applied the model in communication. They hypothesized that collectivism would negatively predict independent self-construal but positively predict interdependent self-construal, and that independent self-construal would negatively, whereas interdependent self-construal positively, predict attribution to context, receiver orientation, and indirect communication. The hypothesis received mixed results. First, col-lectivism did positively predict interdependent self-construal and negatively predict independent self-construal. Second, interdependent self-construal did positively, predict attribution to context and indirect communication, but not receiver orientation. However, independent self-construal failed to predict any of the three dependent variables. The authors concluded that independent and interdependent self-construals are not opposite concepts of each other, but rather, related, with different communication behavior (similar to Gudykunst et al.'s argument, 1996). Several scholars criticized the study because no direct link was included from culture to behavior, and thus, excluded the test of a partially mediated model (e.g., Gudykunst et al., 1996; Oetzel, 1998).

For the general model assessment, empirical studies have not lent strong support. More often than not, the links from IC to self-construals are not supported. For example, Gudykunst et al. (1996) used samples from the United States, Australia (both individualist), Japan, and Korea (both collectivist), and found that the Japanese were higher in independent self-construal and lower in interdependence than were the Australians. In addition, various researchers have found that independent and interdependent self-construals co-exist in any culture (Bontempo, 1993; Singelis, 1994; Singelis & Brown, 1995; Triandis & Singelis, 1998; Yamada & Singelis, 1999). Yamada and Singelis (1999) proposed a model that treats the two types of self-construals as two orthogonal dimensions producing four combinations: biculturals (high in both self-construals), independents (high in independent and low in interdependent self-construal), interdependents (high in interdependent and low in independent self-construal), and marginalized (low in both self-construals). T. Levine et al. (2003) conducted a meta-analysis on self-construal research and provided five criticisms: (a) inconsistent findings, (b) unsupported priming effect for interdependent self-construal, (c) a Western bias of the concept, (d) scale invalidity, and (e) over-simplification of the model.

Despite the criticisms of the theory, the self-construal model is still merited for its added explanatory power from cultural values to communication behavior. Future research should consider reconceptualizing self-construal and include more influencing concepts than mere IC. For intercultural communication research, a conceptual space with a typology can be developed for each self-construal, and the sub-concepts may link to various communication behaviors.

Face-Negotiation Theory

Ting-Toomey's (1988, 2005b; Ting-Toomey & Kurogi, 1998) face-negotiation theory (FNT) was rooted in cultural dimensions theory, conflict management styles research (e.g., Blake & Mouton, 1964; see a review in Chapter 4 of this book), Goffman's (1952) concept of face, and Brown and Levinson's (1978) politeness theory. FNT examines how individualism–collectivism (IC) and power distance predict individuals' self-construals, which in turn predict face-concerns, which in turn predict conflict management styles. Note that Ting-Toomey's (1988) original theory did not contain self-construals. The basic assumptions are: (a) People try to maintain face in all human interactions, (b) face is vulnerable in influence situations where identities are challenged,

(c) IC affects self- and other-face maintenance, (d) IC influences autonomy and approval facework, (e) power distance affects power resources (personal or positional power), (f) power distance affects horizontal vs. vertical facework, and (g) underlying contextual conditions such as relational intimacy and issue of conflict affect facework (Ting-Toomey, 1988).

Ting-Toomey and Kurogi (1998) defined *face* as a person's claim of "favorable social self-worth" that s/he wants others to see (p. 187). It is both an identity-based and a relational concept. In a conflict situation, people have concerns for self-face, other-face, and mutual-face. Because a conflict situation is face-threatening, facework is needed. *Facework* refers to a cluster of communication behaviors that one uses to maintain one's own face and to support or threaten the other's face (Brown & Levinson, 1978; Ting-Toomey & Kurogi, 1998). Facework can be researched at both the strategic level and the tactic level.

In a conflict situation, culture influences facework both directly and indirectly. On one hand, culture shapes individuals' facework, such as how one sees needs of facework in various social interactions and what appropriate communication behavior carries out facework. Brown and Levinson (1978) suggested two types of facework: preventive and restorative. *Preventive facework strategies* refer to behaviors to prevent future occurrences of face damage. *Restorative facework strategies* are behaviors to repair lost face or reestablish one's claimed image after face has been threatened. Ting-Toomey and Kurogi proposed that individualists tend to use more restorative strategies whereas collectivists use more preventive strategies. Moreover, individualists tend to use more direct, self-face enhancing and face-threatening strategies (dominating), yet collectivists tend to use indirect, other-enhancing, and mutual-face strategies (avoiding, obliging, and compromising) (Ting-Toomey & Kurogi, 1998). Individualists and collectivists equally value integrating across situations (Cai & Fink, 2002).

On the other hand, culture influences facework indirectly, mediated by self-construal and face concerns. Specifically, individualism predicts independent self-construal, which in turn predicts high self-face concern; collectivism predicts interdependent self-face construal, which in turn predicts high other-face and mutual-face concern. Whereas high self-face concern predicts the use of dominating, high other-face concern predicts the use of avoiding, obliging, and compromising. High mutual face-concern predicts integrating.

Most empirical research has supported FNT. Ting-Toomey, Oetzel, and Yee-Jung (2001) found that independent self-construals predicted more dominating and solution-oriented strategies than did interdependent self-construals and ambivalent self-construal (low on both self-construals). Interdependent self-construals predicted more use of avoiding and third-party mediation. Biconstruals (high on both self-construals) used the widest range of strategies from dominating, compromising, integrating, to emotional appeal. Ambivalents preferred avoiding and third-party mediation. Similar results were reported in cross-cultural communication research (e.g., see Ting-Toomey & Oetzel, 2002, for a review).

Interactive Constraints Theory

M. Kim's (1994) interactive constraints theory (also called conversational constraints theory) was similarly rooted as Ting-Toomey's (1988) FNT. M. Kim (1994, 2005) focused on request situations and theorized the relationships between high- and low-context communication, self-construal, face concerns, and interactive constraints. M. Kim (1994) borrowed Brown and Levinson's (1978) conceptualization of face in politeness theory. Brown and Levinson (1978) discussed four types of face. *One's own negative face* refers to a person's need for autonomy, whereas *one's own positive face* refers to the person's need for inclusion and approval. *Other negative face* refers to the awareness of the other's need for autonomy, whereas *other positive face* refers to the awareness of the other's need for inclusion and approval.

M. Kim (1994) argued that five interactive constraints are most important in regulating people's strategies and tactics used in communication: *concern for message clarity, concern for effectiveness, concern for not being negatively evaluated, concern for not imposing upon the other,* and *concern for not hurting the other's feelings.* She hypothesized that high individualism would predict high self-face concern, and thus high concerns for the first three interactive constraints and low concerns for the latter two constraints; high collectivism would predict high other-face concern, and thus low concerns for the first three constraints and high concern for the latter two.

M. Kim (1994) tested the theory using Korean, Hawaiian, and mainland U.S. samples. Results supported the hypothesized predictions on concerns for message clarity, not imposing, and not hurting the other's face. Concerns for effectiveness and not being negatively evaluated had similar importance for individualists as for collectivists.

M. Kim (2005) updated the theory by adding self-construal. Three constraints were tested: concern for clarity, concern for not being negatively evaluated, and concern for not hurting the other's face. M. Kim (2005) hypothesized that independent self-construal would positively predict the first two concerns but interdependent self-construal would positively predict the third. Using Hawaiian students as a sample, all the hypotheses were supported. M. Kim (2005) concluded that self-construal predicts communication behavior better than the cultural group one belongs to. Although this theory has not been widely used, its focus on interactive constraints exemplifies how cultural values can be linked to communication behavior.

Expectancy Violation Theory

Another intercultural communication theory that focuses on interaction is expectancy violation theory (EVT). EVT was first proposed as a theory on nonverbal communication. Specifically, it explained what would happen when the expected proximity was violated (Burgoon, 1978). Later it was expanded to include both verbal and nonverbal communication (Burgoon, 1992, 1993). More recently, it has been extended to an intercultural communication context. In essence, the original theory contains six key concepts, some of which have sub-concepts. We will introduce the original theory first, and then discuss its adapted version for intercultural communication research.

First, *communication expectancy* refers to anticipated communication behavior due to its consistent occurrence (Burgoon & Hubbard, 2005; Burgoon & Walther, 1990). The expectancy comes both from normative patterns adhered to the type of social interactional context and from personal communication styles known by the other. When personal knowledge is low, people tend to depend on socially normative and stereotypic information to form expectancy. Expectancies can be *predictive* and *prescriptive*. Predictive expectancy is based on frequency and refers to what is expected to happen, and prescriptive expectancy is based on desirability and refers to what is hoped to happen. People's expectancies are formed based on the characteristics of communicator, relationship, and context (Burgoon & Hubbard, 2005).

Second, *expectancy violation* refers to communication behavior that the message receiver classifies as sufficiently violating the range of communication expectancy (Burgoon & Hubbard, 2005). Third, the violation arouses attention and activates *an appraisal process*, which contains two elements: meaning-making (or interpretation) and evaluation. Fourth, the outcome of the appraisal process is the *behavior and violation valence*, which refers to the value given to the violation. It can be positive, negative, or ambiguous. Fifth, an important moderating concept is *communicator valence*, also called *communicator reward value*, which describes the attractiveness, familiarity, and desirability of the violator. In EVT and its empirical tests, communicator valence appears to be a game changer: Whenever a desirable person violates an expectancy, even negatively by objective standards, the violation is considered positive or at least not as damaging as when an undesirable person does the violation. In fact, almost any violation from people with negative communicator valence is considered negative. Because of its importance in the theory, this concept has been operationalized with different variables and measurements. Examples include "physical attractiveness, task expertise and knowledge, socioeconomic status, an authoritative demeanor, giving positive or negative feedback, possession of appealing personal attributes, similarity, familiarity, and status equality" (Burgoon & Hubbard, 2005, p. 155).

Finally, the *effects of violation* include the receiver's immediate communication response, communication outcomes, and relational outcomes. Whereas positive violations lead to positive effects and negative violations lead to negative outcomes, ambiguous violations are again swayed heavily by communicator valence.

In intercultural communication, each of these concepts can be examined through a cultural lens. First, cultural values influence the formation, format, and content of expectancies. Burgoon and Hubbard (2005, p. 151) stated:

The content of each culture's interactional expectancies will vary substantially along such cultural dimensions as collectivism-individualism,
uncertainty avoidance, power distance, masculinity-femininity, ascription
versus achievement orientation, time and activity orientation, universalism-
particularism, degree of face-concern, and high- versus low-context
communication.

These cultural value orientations influence how members of a culture form
expectancies and perceive violations. Also, communicator valence may vary
greatly from culture to culture. However, Burgoon and Hubbard (2005) sur-
mised that human universality might exist so that culture-general expectancies,
communicator valence, and behavior and violation valence would be discovered.

In an intercultural communication context, communicators tend to have
low socially normative and low personal knowledge. This lack of knowledge
leads to the expectancy on "whatever outgroup the individual appears to most
closely resemble. To the extent that expectancies are linked to outgroup stereotypes, they may also be more negatively valenced than expectancies for those
from familiar or similar cultural backgrounds" (Burgoon & Hubbard, 2005,
p. 153). In other words, people are prone to placing negative communicator
valence on someone from a different culture.

Nonetheless, all is not lost. Burgoon and Hubbard (2005) argued that frequent contact with other cultures and increased personal contact would enhance
a person's culture-specific knowledge, and a shift would occur from heavy reliance on stereotypic data to psychological and individual data. Further, because
of cultural unfamiliarity, many violations are categorized as ambiguous violation. How does ambiguous violation affect communication outcomes in an
intercultural communication context? What elements are most influential in
the appraisal process? What can be done to sway people from depending on
stereotypic data to mindfully focusing on useful data? These and other questions await answers in future research. Burgoon and Hubbard (2005) discussed
the importance of understanding anxiety and uncertainty in helping understand expectancy violation in intercultural communication. We will discuss
Gudykunst's (2005a, 2005b) theory on this issue next.

Anxiety and Uncertainty Management Theory

Gudykunst's (1985, 2005a, 2005b) anxiety and uncertainty management theory
(AUM) combines covering law and human interaction perspectives. It states
that intercultural communication competence is based on successful management of anxiety and uncertainty. The theory can be used by two interactants in
intercultural communication from both sides. For example, in an intercultural
encounter of an immigrant and a host-country member, AUM can be used to
explain what causes a host-country member's anxiety and uncertainty, and how

the mindful management of these two elements leads to effective communication. Meanwhile, AUM can be used to explain what causes the immigrant's anxiety and uncertainty, and how mindful management leads to effective communication in the interaction, and over the long term, intercultural adjustment. Thus, AUM is focused on the competence-related, short- and long-term communication outcomes, such as intercultural communication effectiveness and intercultural adjustment. Although the model for the "stranger would be a mirror image of the ingroup member," Gudykunst provides two versions of the theory (2005a, 2005b) to depict a host member's and a stranger's psychological processes. Most elements in the model are the same. We discuss these elements and the models below. (Note that a *stranger* in AUM refers to a person who comes to a host culture from a different cultural group.)

The two central concepts are uncertainty and anxiety. *Uncertainty* refers to the lack of confidence in making attributions or predictions about others or the environment. Through uncertainty reduction, an individual's capacity to demystify and predict the interactant's behaviors increases (Gudykunst & Hammer, 1988). This capacity is labeled as *attributional confidence*. Whereas uncertainty is cognitive, *anxiety* is an affective concept that describes the apprehension of possible negative outcomes (Gudykunst & Hammer, 1988). *Uncertainty management* is the active reduction of uncertainty and increase of attributional confidence, and *anxiety management* is the active control and reduction of apprehension. Uncertainty management and anxiety management are labeled as "basic causes" of effective communication (Gudykunst, 2005a, p. 292) and intercultural adjustment (Gudykunst, 2005b, p. 426)

In the version that explains the host member's psychological process, effective communication is the outcome of successful anxiety and uncertainty management. *Effective communication* refers to the overlapping of the meanings between a receiver and a sender (Gudykunst, 2005a). In the version that explains the stranger's psychological process, intercultural adjustment is the outcome of successful anxiety and uncertainty management. *Intercultural adjustment* refers to "a process involving feeling comfortable in the host culture, as well as communicating effectively and engaging in socially appropriate behavior with host nationals" (Gudykunst, 2005b, p. 425).

In both versions, mindfulness is the moderator between the basic causes and communication outcomes. *Mindfulness* is defined as the creation of new categories in schemas and acceptance of new information (Langer, 1989; Gudykunst, 2005a, 2005b). Langer argued that people could choose to mindfully react to the environment so that they can gain control over it rather than unconsciously or subconsciously submit to it. She used the Birdman of Alcatraz as an example to show how a person can change the perceived superior–subordinate relationship between the context and the individual by being mindful. Gudykunst (2005a, 2005b) used mindfulness in the same way. He argued that individuals are not mere passive creatures and determined by socialization and contexts.

Instead, they can actively choose to interpret the environment and the other with non-stereotypic and insightful information, become competent communicators, and achieve satisfactory communication outcomes.

Finally, Gudykunst (2005a) proposed seven "superficial causes" of uncertainty and anxiety in the host member's model (p. 292). He added an eighth cause in the stranger's model (p. 426). These causes are listed below:

1. *Self-concept*: Knowledge about oneself that includes personal, social, and collective identities.
2. *Motivation to interact*: Needs for predictability, group inclusion, and self-concept maintenance.
3. *Reactions to the other interactant*: The extent to which a person can empathize with the other, tolerate ambiguity, and be flexible in receiving others.
4. *Social categorization of the other interactant*: Placement of the other in social groups from one's own frames of reference, which result in positive or negative expectancies, perceived personal similarities, and perceived group differences.
5. *Situational processes*: Perception of the interaction situation that includes ingroup power, cooperative tasks, and presence of other ingroup and outgroup members.
6. *Connection with the other interactant*: Levels of attraction to strangers, interdependence with strangers, and quality and quantity of contact.
7. *Ethicalness of interactions*: Maintenance of personal dignity, moral inclusiveness, and respect for strangers.
8. *Condition in host culture*: Perceived receptivity of the host culture, encouragement of cultural pluralism, and levels of discrimination against strangers. (This cause only applies to the model for the stranger's psychological process).

Thus, both versions of the model have the superficial causes as independent variables, anxiety management and uncertainty management as mediators, communication effectiveness (Model 1) or intercultural adjustment (Model 2) as outcome variables, and mindfulness as the moderator between the mediators and the outcomes.

The concepts of anxiety and uncertainty have been well received in intercultural communication research, especially in the intercultural communication competence domain (e.g., Ni & Wang, 2011). However, anxiety appears to be a less effective mediator than uncertainty in empirical research (Wang, Ni, & de la Flor, 2014). Further, although the model provides a comprehensive list of superficial causes, they can hardly be operationalized in one study. Future research may consider adapting the components of the model based on the research purpose. For example, if the research focus is to help enhance a host environment's receptivity, the last four superficial causes can be emphasized. If the research focus is on how mindfulness moderates AUM on effective communication, then the study can focus on the relationships between anxiety and uncertainty management, mindfulness, and effective communication. If the focus is on the effect of AUM on long-term intercultural adjustment, then a developmental perspective can be added to the model, such as the changes in different stages of adjustment depicted in the U-curve sojourner adjustment model (see Gullahorn & Gullahorn, 1963).

Communication Accommodation Theory

Howard Giles, a social psychologist, first developed a speech accommodation theory in the 1970s. The theory explains the code-switching phenomenon, or why people change their speech styles in social interactions. Giles and colleagues (1987) expanded the theory from a pure examination of speech styles to the inclusion of both verbal and nonverbal communication changes in social interaction, and they labeled the theory *communication accommodation theory* (or CAT; Giles, Mulac, Bradac, & Johnson, 1987). Later, the theory started to focus on intergroup communication and has also become an intercultural communication theory (Gallois & Giles, 1998). Gallois, Ogay, and Giles (2005, p. 122) stated: "In our view, CAT is a theory of both intergroup and interpersonal communication, invoking the dual importance of both factors in predicting and understanding intergroup interactions . . . As such, intercultural encounters provide the richest basis for understanding the theory." The theory sets any social interaction in *a socio-historical context*, characteristic of intergroup history, interpersonal history, and societal/cultural norms and values (Gallois et al., 2005, p. 135). It proposes that when two people enter into an interaction, both bear with them their *initial orientations*—frames of reference and personal traits. When both exit the interaction, they form *evaluations* and *future intentions*—valences and plans about future communication and relationships with the other and the other's group. The essence of the theory is in the *immediate interaction* that leads to different exit outcomes.

During the interaction, both parties form a "*psychological accommodative stance*, which influences the accommodative and nonaccommodative strategies they adopt" (Gallois et al., 2005, p. 135). Based on each point of interaction, both parties adjust their *behavior tactics* (the small units of verbal and nonverbal communication), which affect each other's *perceptions and attributions* (attaching meanings, forming attitudes, and inferring motives). In this process, people may adapt their behavior using *convergence*, an accommodative communication strategy that makes them adopt more similar communication to each other. They may also adapt their behavior using *divergence*, a nonaccommodative strategy to make them more dissimilar to each other, or *maintenance*, a nonaccommodative, non-adaptive behavior to maintain their original communication styles (Gallois et al., 2005). Two questions arise at this point: (a) What causes accommodative or nonaccommodative strategies? (b) What are the consequences of these strategies?

Regarding the first question, one obvious answer is a person's repertoire of strategies (Gallois et al., 2005). Some people may have more capacity, knowledge, and skill to accommodate than others. Other reasons for convergence include seeking approval, need for cognitive organization, and affective display. Divergence can be motivated by the facilitation of comprehension (e.g., a foreigner's use of accent to cue the other to slow down), information eliciting (e.g., a patient–therapist situation), and identity maintenance (e.g., a police officer's accentuation of power in an interrogation). Gallois et al. (2005) indicated that maintenance of a social identity is a major motivation of nonaccommodative behavior.

Regarding the second question, people who converge are generally more positively evaluated, better received, and more likely to be invited to future interactions than are those who diverge. The messages of those who converge and the group they are identified with tend to be positively regarded as well. People who use divergence or maintenance tend to receive negative outcomes in all these aspects. However, opposite outcomes can occur in some cases too (Gallois et al., 2005). For example, insincere convergence or giving up one's social identity to fit in may cause negative perceptions, and insistence on personal style without becoming a chameleon may win the trust of others. Future research should continue to explore the cognitive, emotive, and situational causes of accommodative and nonaccommodative strategies, different tactics to carry out such strategies, and the effects of such strategies over the long term.

Cross-Cultural Adaptation Theory

Y. Kim's (2005) cross-cultural adaptation theory, also called a stress–adaptation-growth model, used an open systems approach, which analogizes an individual's migration and adaptation to a new culture as an organism's migration to a new ecological environment. This migration breaks the organism's equilibrium established in its home habitat. The survival instinct forces the organism to strive to reach and maintain a new equilibrium. In the cross-cultural context, this organism is labeled as a *stranger*, who can be a short-term sojourner, a long-term immigrant, a refugee, or a person acquainted with one cultural environment entering another cultural environment (e.g., a high school student entering a college). The "integration-disintegration-reintegration" process (Jourard, 1974, as cited in Y. Kim, 2005, p. 384) the organism experiences to reach a new equilibrium is *adaptation*, a process through which the stranger "strives to establish and maintain a relatively stable, reciprocal, and functional relationship with the environment" (Y. Kim, 2005, p. 380).

A unit of adaptation process is described as follows (Y. Kim, 2005). (Note that the adaptation goes through uncountable such units.) When the stranger comes to the new culture, a *deviation* (an encounter differently interpreted from the home culture) may become a *stressor*, if it causes psychological *stress* ("a state of disequilibrium, manifested in emotional 'lows' of uncertainty, confusion, and anxiety," p. 383). Overcoming the initial psychological resistance and driven by survival instinct, the stranger stops and seeks a solution. In this process, certain kinds and levels of *acculturation* (acquiring some elements of the new culture) and *deculturation* (unlearning some elements of the old culture) occur until the problem is solved, which leads to a new point of equilibrium (*growth*) (Y. Kim, 2005). This "draw back to leap" model (p. 384) is labeled as a *stress-adaptation-growth* model.

The ideal outcome of the adaptation process is *intercultural transformation*, and an *intercultural identity* with the components of individualization and universalization. Intercultural transformation is an outcome reflecting psychological and functional fitness, including such indicators as satisfactory income and workplace status, "life satisfaction, positive feelings, sense of belonging, and greater congruence in subjective meaning systems" (Y. Kim, 2005, p. 391). Emergent intercultural identity is another outcome of a new self-understanding after tearing one's self apart and putting it back together again. Not everyone adapts. Some people may become negative and dysfunctional. An intercultural identity is marked by newly gained *individualization*, a self-hood with "a clearer self-definition and definition of the other that reflects a capacity to see the connectedness of oneself to humanity without being restricted by categories of social grouping" (p. 392). It is also marked by *universalization*, cognition of "the oneness and unity of humanity" and ability to "locate the points of consent and complementarity beyond points of difference and contention" (p. 392). In other words, an identity with individualization and universalization enables one to view himself or herself as a unique being associated with other unique beings within humanity, equally and freely with much cultural knowledge but without its constraints.

Other concepts that are proposed to affect adaptation include the following:

1. *Predisposition*: Preparedness and ethnic proximity (similarity and compatibility).
2. *Personality*: Openness, strength, and positivity.
3. *Host communication competence*: culture-specific language and culture (cognitive); motivational capacity to regulate emotions, open up, participate, and enjoy the new culture (affective); and capacity to express and enact (behavioral).
4. *Channels and receiver:*
   a. *Host social communication*: Interpersonal interactions and mass media with host culture. Whereas the former facilitates the sense of belonging, the latter facilitates the attainment of environment information.
   b. *Ethnic social communication*: Interpersonal interactions and mass media with ethnic culture. Moderate amount of use facilitates, yet excessive amount hinders, adaptation.

5. *Environment:* Receptivity, conformity pressure, and ethnic group strength. These factors define how friendly the host environment is. *Receptivity* refers to the extent to which the host culture provides access to immigrants and makes it open to receive immigrants' cultures. *Conformity pressure* refers to the extent to which the host culture expects the immigrants to conform and assimilate, instead of bringing their own cultures to enrich the host culture. *Ethnic group strength* refers to the extent to which the host culture promotes "institutional completeness" (facilitation of an ethnic group to build its own institutions to serve its members' needs autonomously) and "ethnolinguistic vitality" (empowerment of an ethnic group to behave competently and independently through political, economic, and geographic facilitations; Y. Kim, 2005, p. 388).

The theory contains a full range of concepts that examine intercultural adaptations as processes in a system. Depending on the topics of interest, researchers can focus on different concepts to explore the adaptation phenomenon.

Identity Negotiation Theory

Ting-Toomey's (1993, 2005a) identity negotiation theory is focused on explaining how people negotiate their cultural and ethnic identities in intercultural interactions. She distinguished between social and personal identities, as well as between cultural and ethnic identities. First, *identity* is defined as "the reflective self-conception or self-image that we each derive from our family, gender, cultural, ethnic, and individual socialization process" (Ting-Toomey, 2005a, p. 212). Whereas *social identity* encloses self-concepts based on socialization processes such as gender identity, age identity, disability identity, and professional identity, *personal identity* encloses the "unique attributes that we associate with our individuated self in comparison to those of others" (p. 215). Ting-Toomey (2005a) emphasized the importance of family and gender socialization in identity formation because most value systems are fostered through the family a person belongs to, and the gender group assigned to.

Second, cultural and ethnic identities are formed through a young age as well. *Cultural identity* refers to the "emotional significance we attach to our sense of belonging or affiliation with the larger culture" (Ting-Toomey, 2005a, p. 214). *Ethnic identity* refers to the emotional significance and affinity with ancestral lineage. Both identities can be further measured for their value content and identity salience. *Value content* refers to the moral standards and importance people use to make judgments. *Identity salience* refers to the perceived strength and affinity of an identity. Ethnic identity salience also has the implicit meanings of loyalty and subjective perception of belongingness.

Ting-Toomey (2005a) argued that what is essential in intercultural communication is the reflexive identity negotiation process. In particular, *identity negotiation* refers to "a transactional interaction process whereby individuals in an intercultural situation attempt to assert, define, modify, challenge, and/or support their own and others' desired self-image" (p. 217). Ting-Toomey proposed ten core assumptions. Assumption 1 states that personal, cultural, and ethnic identities are formed via symbolic interactions. Assumptions 2–7 discuss people's negotiation and management of the following five sets of dialectics in intercultural communication (pp. 218–219):

1. Identity security vs. identity vulnerability
2. Identity inclusion vs. identity differentiation
3. Identity predictability vs. identity unpredictability
4. Identity connection vs. identity autonomy
5. Identity consistency vs. identity change.

Assumption 8 states that cultural, personal, and situational variables influence the meanings of the above dialectics. Assumption 9 states that competent communicators integrate their own and others' identities in different levels. Assumption 10 states that "satisfactory identity negotiation outcome include the feelings of being understood, respected, and affirmatively valued" (p. 218).

Ting-Toomey (2005a) also developed a typology based on the intersection of cultural identity salience and ethnic identity salience. Strong salience in both leads to *bicultural identity*, whereas weak salience in both leads to *marginal identity*. Strong cultural identity salience and weak ethnic identity salience lead to *assimilated identity*. Strong ethnic identity salience and weak cultural identity salience lead to *ethnic-oriented identity*. Finally, competence-based variables such as identity knowledge, mindfulness, and identity negotiation skills influence identity negotiation outcomes.

One of the strengths as well as the weaknesses is the complexity of the theory. Ting-Toomey's (2005a) model is based in Baxter's (1988) *relational dialectic theory* and Berry's (1997) *acculturation strategy model*. Baxter (1988) proposed that relational partners need to manage between competing discourses. Internally, they need to manage connection vs. autonomy, predictability vs. novelty, and openness vs. closedness. Externally, they need to manage inclusion vs. seclusion, conventionality vs. uniqueness, and revelation vs. concealment. The outcomes influence the partners' relational quality and self-identity. Ting-Toomey's model is focused on intercultural communication, and provides a unique perspective for interactants to consider the expression and negotiation of their own and the other party's identities on different levels, as well as the consequences on their relationship.

Berry's (1997) acculturation model discussed how people manage their home cultural values and host cultural values when entering a new culture. Strategies to integrate both cultural values are called *bicultural*. Strategies to maintain home cultural values and reject host cultural values are called *traditional*. Strategies to embrace host cultural values and give up home cultural values are called *assimilated*. Not accepting either is called *marginalized*. Ting-Toomey's (2005a) model used cultural identity salience and ethnic identity salience and came to a similar typology. The model can be particularly useful to study intragroup communication, where people need to balance their ethnic identity and cultural identity.

However, the weakness of Ting-Toomey's theory is also in its complexity. It combines a rhetorical and social scientific approach in the same theory, rendering it challenging for empirical assessment. Like AUM, this theory can be tested partially based on research interests.

Social Identity Theory

Tajfel and Turner's (1979) social identity theory is also named "an integrative theory of intergroup conflict" (p. 33), because the theory was initially developed to understand intergroup conflict. Tajfel and Turner critiqued the two dominant trends of studying intergroup relations back in the 1960s and 1970s. One was focused on individuals' internal motivations and psychological processes during interpersonal interactions. The other was focused on the "real conflicts of group interests" that arise from intergroup competition for scarce resources and incompatible interests, and thus put external, objective social conditions as the causes of intergroup conflict (p. 33). Tajfel and Turner indicated that social identity theory was developed to provide a detailed analysis of the social psychology of group identities, ingroup cohesions, and intergroup relations during social conflict.

The theory started off by describing an interpersonal and intergroup behavior continuum. At one end of the continuum, interpersonal interactions are completely focused on individual characteristics and interpersonal relations regardless of what social categories the interactants belong to. This end represents *interpersonal interaction*. At the other end, the interactions occur fully based on the interactants' awareness and interpretations of each other's group memberships. This end represents *intergroup interaction*. Tajfel and Turner (1979) argued that although institutionalized and resources-based intergroup conflict can promote more intergroup behavior, people's psychological recognition of different group memberships is often enough to promote such behavior; Tajfel and Turner cited Sherif's (1967) study as an example, in which participants in a field experiment gave up their preliminary friendship easily when they were told that they would be assigned to competing groups.

Further, Tajfel and Turner (1979) proposed a pair of variables that reflect people's subjective social realities that influence interpersonal–intergroup behavior: social mobility vs. social change. *Social mobility* refers to the belief that the society is flexible enough that a person who is unsatisfied with one group membership can become a member of another group, through effort and other means. On the contrary, *social change* refers to the belief that the society is so rigid that group membership is rarely changeable; a person unsatisfied with his or her group membership can hardly move to another group through any means, and such group membership is often "underprivileged, or stigmatized" (p. 35). To change group membership and associated meanings, drastic social change such as revolution must occur.

The belief system of social mobility versus social change has three key consequences. First, it affects interpersonal–intergroup behavior in the way that, when interacting with someone from a different group, those who believe in social mobility tend to display more interpersonal behavior and develop interpersonal relationships, whereas those who believe in social change tend to display more intergroup behavior and treat the other as a stereotypical member of the other group. Second, it affects the intensity of intergroup conflict: Those who believe in social mobility perceive intergroup conflict as more solvable through dialogue, yet those who believe in social change perceive intergroup conflict as less solvable and rooted in the unfair distribution of resources. Third, those who believe in social mobility have less ingroup membership loyalty, less ingroup positivity, less ethnocentrism, less endorsement of the concept of "us" versus "them," and more acceptance of ingroup derogation, than those who believe in social change (Tajfel & Turner, 1979).

Another social condition that influences the intensity of intergroup conflict is *social comparison*. When a group does not perceive a "range of meaningful comparisons" with another group, its members tend not to engage in social conflict (Tajfel & Turner, 1979, p. 37). However, when the underprivileged group begins to build positive ingroup attitudes and experience awakening, they may develop new goals and stir social change (Tajfel & Turner, 1979).

After analyzing social conditions underlying social conflicts, Tajfel and Turner (1979) described the importance of self-categorization into social groups, or a person's *social identity*: "It consists of those aspects of an individual's self-image that derive from the social categories to which he perceives himself as belonging" (p. 40). A *social group* refers to a collective of people who perceive that they belong to the same social category and share the same socioemotional elements. A person's self-identity is defined both by his or her perceived social identity and by the members of the social groups he or she subscribes to.

Tajfel and Turner (1979) proposed the following hypotheses in the social identity theory:

1. People act to maintain a positive social identity.
2. The positivity of social identity is based on the perception that, through comparison, one's ingroup is positively different from the relevant outgroups.
3. The lack of positivity in social identity leads to a person's decision to either leave the current ingroup or do something to enhance the ingroup's positive identity.

Thus, social identity theory explains the origin of intergroup conflict: the maintenance of superiority of one's own ingroup over a socially comparable outgroup. Tajfel and Turner (1979) contended that intergroup conflict can be either resource-based and tangible or relation-based and intangible. Moreover, when one perceives the lack of superiority of social identity, he or she either strives to move to a more positively perceived group (when social mobility is perceived), or to use two other ways to change the situation. First, *social creativity* can be used to redefine the situation, such as comparing with the outgroup on new dimensions, reassigning values of comparison to enhance one's ingroup's scoring, and finding new groups to compare against. Second, *social competition* can be used to overthrow the hierarchy of the groups so that they can become the privileged or superior group rather than their competing group; in this case, strong enmity and social conflict arise.

In sum, social identity theory contains three major elements that describe ingroup–outgroup relations or any intragroup–intergroup behavior: "social categorization, self-evaluation through social identity, and intergroup social comparison" (Tajfel & Turner, 1979, p. 46). It defines the conduit of intergroup conflict through a social psychological perspective, and was foundational to myriad other communication theories in cultural identities.

Cultural Identity Theory

Collier and Thomas (1988) first developed cultural identity theory (CIT) to compare cultural competencies (within a group) and intercultural competencies (between groups). They were interested to find out whether people behave differently in order to be competent with an *insider*—one with same the ethnic identification, and with an *outsider*—one not identified as being in the same ethnic group. In its original version, *culture* was defined as "a historically transmitted system of symbols, meanings, and norms" that uniquely distinguishes one group of people from other groups (Collier, 2005, p. 236). *Identity* refers to one's self-conception. *Cultural identity* refers to an identity based on the process of identification with a specific cultural group (Collier & Thomas, 1988).

Similar to Tajfel and Turner's (1979) concept of social identity, cultural identity is a multidimensional concept because a person often subscribes to various cultural groups. The difference lies in that cultural identity is more focused on the influence of cultural elements. For example, a person's cultural identification can be an intersection of gender, race, ethnicity, political affiliation, age group, and the like. *Cultural identification* involves a complex process that continues evolving, being negotiated, being influenced, and influencing. Ethnic cultural identity is similar to cultural identity because it is a self-categorization product, but different from cultural identity because it emphasizes "multivocality" that an ethnic person may want to stress to distinguish from a mainstream culture. *Ethnic cultural identity* is defined as "a 'problematic event' that was situated and negotiated in social interaction" (Collier, 2005, p. 241). This definition is given because an ethnic identity tends to be labeled, defined, and interpreted differently by an insider than by an outsider, and a person who endorses a strong ethnic identity in a specific situation bears the burden to express and negotiate his or her specific identity characteristics.

The original CIT was developed to understand the process of cultural identity formation through social interactions. Collier and Thomas (1988) proposed seven properties of cultural identities:

1. Cultural identities are formed when a person shows patterned behavior under the influence of myriad cultural groups that he or she endorses, such as national, gender-based, political, ethnic, and so on.
2. A person perceives a different level of *salience*—the most prominent aspects— of his or her cultural identities in different communication situations.
3. Cultural identities "vary in *scope*, referring to how widely held and generalizable they are" (Collier, 2005, p. 240).
4. Cultural identities are developed through both *avowal* (the self-conception a person claims and embraces on his or her own) and *ascription* (the "self-identity" viewed and imposed upon one by others). Avowed and ascribed aspects may overlap, but often have discrepancies that cause tension and conflict.
5. The avowed and ascribed cultural identities vary in *intensity*—the enactment of chosen aspects of an identity—depending on the communication context that includes time, location, topic, relationship, etc.
6. Cultural identities have both stable and changeable elements over time and across places.
7. Cultural identities "have both content and relational aspects" that can be especially important in intercultural relationship development (Collier, 2005, p. 240). These aspects come from social interaction experience and thus are socially constructed (Collier & Thomas, 1988).

The key concepts and propositions of CIT show that the original form of the theory was interpretivist with the main goal to understand and apply to specific cultural groups. The theory was also built in social constructivism. However, facing criticisms that the theory did not consider any privileges and was built upon "equal agency across individuals," Collier (2005) reflected upon her academic and personal growth and extensive research experience, and decided to incorporate the critical perspective into the theory (p. 240). She stated, "My goal is to live, work, and have my conduct reflect what Yep . . . calls the embodiment of social justice: ethics and progressive social change" (p. 238). Accordingly, her conceptualizations of *culture* and *cultural identification* were both transformed. She stated,

> I am now exploring a conception of *cultures* as a combination of contextual identifications, representations, and relationships; a position along a path that provides an orientation for speaking, acting, and producing; a view of the past and the histories; and a contingent and changing direction of movement of the present and future. *Cultural identifications* are shared locations and orientations evidenced in a variety of communication forms, including conduct of groups of people, discourse in public texts, mediated forms, artistic expressions, commodities and products, and individual accounts and ascriptions about group conduct.
>
> *(Collier, 2005, p. 237, emphases added)*

With this perspective change, Collier (2005) clarified that CIT should be understood and applied with the consideration of historical, political, and social positions. She provided five new suggestions in the continued refinement of the theory. First, theorize with a personal and "intimate engagement" (p. 241). Second, theorize with an emphasis on uncovering biases and privileges. Third, expand the view of culture. Fourth, be open-minded and examine various theoretical and paradigmatic perspectives. Fifth, pay attention to the positioning and mutual influences of "researchers, respondents, and audiences" (p. 242) so that multivocality is allowed in theory development and application.

Collier (2005) used data to demonstrate how a combination of interpretivist and critical perspectives gave more power to the theory. The revised version of CIT provides a larger scope and more content for researchers with different scholarly orientations.

Identity Management Theory

Cupach and Imahori (1993) developed identity management theory (IMT) in the domain of intercultural communication competence (ICC). The focus was on interpersonal relationships in intercultural encounters. Cupach and Imahori (1993) started off discussing three levels of ICC: culture-general, culture-specific, and culture-synergistic. *Culture-general ICC* refers to the ability to conduct effective (i.e., goal-attaining) and appropriate (i.e., considered normatively polite) social interactions. *Culture-specific ICC* refers to the knowledge of a specific culture and ability to behave effectively and appropriately in that specific culture. *Culture-synergistic ICC* refers to the ability to develop a synergistic relationship with an individual from a specific culture and to facilitate identity negotiation in this relationship.

IMT relied on concepts from Ting-Toomey's (1988) identity negotiation theory, Collier and Thomas' (1988) cultural identity theory, Goffman's face theory (1959), and Brown and Levinson's (1978) politeness theory. Specifically, *identity* is defined as "self-conception—one's theory of oneself" (Cupach & Imohari, 1993, p. 113) and formed based on "self-categorization into social groups" and specific social roles (Imohari & Cupach, 2005, p. 197). Thus, an identity contains multiple sub-identities, including *relational identity*, which is defined by a specific social relationship. *Cultural identity* refers to "the identification with and perceived acceptance into a group that has shared systems of symbols and meanings as well as norms/rules for conduct" (Collier & Thomas, 1988, p. 113). IMT is mostly focused on cultural and relational identities.

Borrowing Collier and Thomas' (1988) cultural identity theory, Imahori and Cupach (2005) used three dimensions to describe an identity. *Scope* refers to the range of characteristics an identity can take. Depending on the type of identity under examination, identity can vary as widely as all shared identities among a cultural group, or as narrowly as defined by a special relationship, such as within a spousal relationship. *Salience* refers to the perceived importance of certain aspects of an identity. *Intensity* refers to the activation and enactment of chosen aspects of an identity. Whereas scope is relatively stable, salience and intensity vary greatly depending on given situations (Imahori & Cupach, 2005). For example, although the scope of a wife's identity is relatively stable in a marriage, the nurturing aspect of identity such as empathy, caring, and patience may be particularly salient when the husband is in deep need of support.

Imohari and Cupach (2005) maintained that identity salience greatly affects whether a social interaction is interpersonal, intracultural, or intercultural. An interaction is *interpersonal* if the focused social exchanges are based on individual and relational characteristics, *intracultural* if the focus is on cultural but similar characteristics, and *intercultural* if the focus is on cultural and different characteristics. Take an interethnic couple's discussion on their children's religious education for an example. The interaction can be interpersonal if the discussion is mainly about parental decision-making, intracultural if both agree on the same religious views, and intercultural if the couple disagrees on which ethnic group-based school the children should go to. In this example, a spousal identity, a shared religious identity, and differentiated ethnic identities all become salient and, thus, influence to what extent the interaction is interpersonal, intracultural, or intercultural.

Finally, IMT incorporates the concept of *face*, or the "socially situated identity" (Imahori & Cupach, 2005, p. 198), as well as the concepts of positive face, negative face, self-face, other-face, and facework. (Refer to interactive constraints theory covered earlier in this chapter for definitions.) Skills in facework are used to reflect communication competence in IMT.

Imahori and Cupach (2005) laid out the following propositions regarding identity management in a complex interaction that involves interpersonal, intracultural, and intercultural communication:

1. In identity management, four problematics are potential: *identity freezing* (locked in the other's group identity without recognizing individual characteristics, threatening to the other's negative face); *non-supportive problematic* (focusing only on individual characteristics and ignoring group identity, threatening to the other's positive face); *self-other face dialectic* (choosing to support one's own or the other's face); and *positive-negative face dialectic* (choosing to make the other feel included or autonomous).

2. Three interdependent and cyclical phases happen in identity management. *Trial* refers to the early interaction stage where interactants experiment on bringing out different salient aspects of each other's identities and try to establish appropriate boundaries for each other's identities. Any or all four of potential problematics outlined in Proposition 1 can form a barrier. *Enmeshment* refers to the stage after trial, if the interactants have established sufficient commonalities and decide to pursue a relationship. In this stage, convergence of symbols, rules, and frameworks for interpretation occur so that the interactants can form a unique relational cultural frame to understand each other. *Renegotiation* is the third stage, in which the interactants can discuss cultural differences and problematics to formulate a positive relationship. Cultural differences become integral, instead of problematic, to the relationship.

3. Identity management in problematics and phases becomes cyclical when interactants discover new aspects of cultural identities of each other and have to go back to earlier phases to reach later phases.

Although the theory is considered too optimistic (see Abrams, O'Connor, & Giles, 2002), it provides an intercultural perspective on interpersonal relationship development. It has also received empirical support regarding its various sub-components of the propositions (Imohari & Cupach, 2005).

Methodological Considerations

In this chapter, we started with the historical roots of intercultural communication, then we discussed culture and other related concepts both philosophically and normatively. Finally, we dived into the key theories in the intercultural communication field. Through this journey, we hope that the readers have gained a relatively comprehensive understanding of the field and have become excited to theorize or apply the concepts and theories in their own research or practical contexts. Below, we will discuss some methodological issues in intercultural communication research.

First, intercultural and cross-cultural communication research has to deal with an intrinsic validity issue. Specifically, how do we know that we are studying what we want to study in different cultures? In other words, how can we know that the observed differences are caused by the same etic concepts and conceptual relations we have proposed? Brislin (1989) argued that conceptual and linguistic equivalences are hard to establish across cultures. Although back-translation and decentering are often used to solve the linguistic equivalence problem (see Brislin, 1989; van de Vijver & Leung, 1997), the procedures are too complicated to use. *Back-translation* is the procedure where one bilingual expert translates the messages into another language, another bilingual expert translates the version back to the original language, and then the two translators discuss and compare differences and decide on the final version. *Decentering* refers to the procedure in which a translator translates a set of messages with relatively great change in another language instead of the word-for-word or stilted translation. Decentering aims to gain a natural sense in another language and reach equivalence in meanings. The benefit of it is that it removes any influence of the original culture and makes the study idiosyncratic for another culture (Brislin, 1989). The down side is that because the translation depends on the expertise and personal input of the translator, subjectivity and bias can become issues. Thus, back-translation and decentering should be used side by side so that both language comparability and accuracy in the meanings can be achieved.

Another solution is to use collaborative research across cultures, especially inviting researchers from local cultures to join the research team to develop the research (Brislin, 1989; Johnson & Tuttle, 1989). The collaboration can facilitate the use of back-translation and decentering techniques. It can also help establish other equivalences crucial in intercultural and communication research. Gudykunst (2002), Leung (1988), and van de Vijver and Leung (1997) discussed non-equivalence and ecological fallacy issues. Van de Vijver and Leung (1997) proposed six equivalences in intercultural and cross-cultural research that should be aimed for.

1. *Functional equivalence*: Observed differences are from the same reasons.
2. *Construct equivalence*: The meanings of a concept are the same across cultures.
3. *Measurement equivalence*: Same aspects of the constructs are measured.
4. *Scalar/metric equivalence*: Scores on the scale report the same amounts of difference.
5. *Language equivalence*: Similar meanings should be contained in the study instructions and items.
6. *Samples equivalence*: Study samples should be comparable to exclude rival hypotheses.

Van de Vijver and Leung (1997) further added that researchers should be clear about levels of analysis so that they would not make ecological errors. Ecological error refers to the mistake that is made to infer relationships among objects at one level based on the discovery of the relationships at another level. For example, group behavior code is sometimes used to predict individual behavior. Without appropriate rationale, such a prediction is ecologically problematic.

Second, a related issue is about the use of emic and etic approaches (Pike, 1967). *Emic* research refers to the studies done within a system, whereas *etic* research refers to the studies done outside the system. In intercultural and cross-cultural communication research, the problem of imposed etic phenomenon exists (Berry, 1989). *Imposed etic approach* means that the researcher conceptualizes and operationalizes constructs and develops conceptual relations between constructs in one culture, tests the model in its original culture and then in another culture with mere translation (if a different language is spoken), and finally compares the results. The problem with the approach is the intrinsic ethnocentric values embedded in the original model and the potential lack of equivalence in any or all aspects that Van de Vijver and Leung (1997) discussed. Thus, the entire study could be invalid. Nonetheless, much cross-cultural research still uses the imposed etic approach (Berry, 1989).

Berry (1989) proposed the *derived etic* method to solve the problem. Specifically, researchers should develop an emic concept, use it as an imposed etic concept in another culture, develop a new emic concept in this culture, and compare the two emic concepts. The commonality will be used to form the content of the new derived etic concept, and the differences will be used in etic–emic comparison research. For example, *filial piety* is a unique concept in Chinese culture based in Confucianism, which refers to children's unconditional submission, respect, and support of parents in both materials and spirit. If the researcher wants to conduct a cross-cultural comparison in U.S. culture, the closest concepts might include submission to parents as authority, caretaking, respect, and support to parents. With these sub-components, filial piety becomes a derived etic concept and can be studied in U.S. culture. The common components represent the etic aspects, and the different components should be researched in the etic–emic comparison. Certainly, the label can be changed too, based on the rationale or research findings to best represent a concept recognizable in both cultures.

Finally, van de Vijver and Leung (1997) discussed sampling of culture. A random sample refers to a random acquisition of cultures around the world, which is unrealistic. Convenience sampling is to use cultures that researchers are in or familiar with. Although it is time and money saving, such sampling does not contribute much to theorization and generalization. System sampling is proposed as a better choice because cultures are chosen based on certain theorized dimensions. At least two cultures should be used to represent one cluster along one dimension. More cultures should be used to form clusters when multiple dimensions are compared. For example, Oetzel et al. (2001) clustered Japan and China together to represent Eastern culture, and Germany and the United States together to represent Western culture, in examining face negotiation theory. If the theoretical relations proposed in face-negotiation theory hold in this cross-cultural examination, the empirical support is considerably stronger than the results from comparing two cultures from convenience sampling. If the relations varied among the four cultures, the specific emic aspects can be further explored to refine the theory in future research.

Conclusion

Both Hall's (1976) and Becker's (1971) views on culture suggest that people tend to hold on to their cultural values as if holding on to the truth. Intercultural encounters provide us an opportunity to escape from this delusion, and to rediscover ourselves, others, human relations, and human relations with the universe. We are neither more sane nor more insane than others. We can choose to follow either artificially fabricated norms due to fear and anxiety, and insist on the differences between "us" versus "them," or embrace the uniquely autonomous yet connected identities of "us" all together.

References

Abrams, J., O'Connor, J., & Giles, H. (2002). Identity and intergroup communication. In W. B. Gudykunst & B. Mody (Eds.), *Handbook of international and intercultural communication* (2nd ed., pp. 225–240). Thousand Oaks, CA: Sage.

Asante, M. K., Newmark, E., & Blake, C. A. (Eds.). (1979). *The handbook of intercultural communication*. Beverly Hills, CA: Sage.

Baxter, L. A. (1988). A dialectical perspective of communication strategies in relationship development. In S. Duck. (Ed.), *Handbook of personal relationships* (pp. 257–273). New York, NY: Wiley.

Becker, E. (1971). *The birth and death of meaning: An interdisciplinary perspective on the problem of man*. New York, NY: The Free Press.

Berry, J. W. (1989). Imposed etics-emics-derived etics: The operationalization of compelling idea. *International Journal of Psychology, 24,* 721–735. doi: 10.1080/00207598908247841

Berry, J. W. (1997). Immigration, acculturation, and adaptation. *Applied Psychology, 46,* 5–68. doi: 10.1111/j.1464-0597.1997.tb01087.x

Birdwhistell, R. L. (1970). *Kinesics and context: Essays on body motion communication*. Philadelphia, PA: University of Pennsylvania Press.

Blake, R. R., & Mouton, J. S. (1964). *The managerial grid*. Houston, TX: Gulf.

Bond, M. H. (1992). The process of enhancing cross-cultural competence in Hong Kong organizations. *International Journal of Intercultural Relations, 16,* 395–412.

Bontempo, R. (1993). Translation fidelity of psychological scales. *Journal of Cross-Cultural Psychology, 24,* 149–166. doi: 10.1177/0022022193242002

Brislin, R. W. (1989). Comparative research methodology: Cross-cultural studies. *International Journal of Psychology, 11,* 215–229.

Brown, P., & Levinson, S. (1978). Universals in language usage: Politeness phenomena. In E. Goody (Ed.), *Questions and politeness: Strategies in social interaction* (pp. 56–310). Cambridge, UK: Cambridge University Press.

Brown, P., & Levinson, S. (1987). *Politeness: Some universals in language usage.* Cambridge, UK: Cambridge University Press.

Burgoon, J. K. (1978). A communication model of personal space violations: Explication and an initial test. *Human Communication Research, 4,* 129–142.

Burgoon, J. K. (1992). Applying a comparative approach to nonverbal expectancy violation theory. In J. Blumler, K. E., Rosengren, & J. M. McLeod (Eds.), *Comparatively speaking* (pp. 53–69). Newbury Park, CA: Sage.

Burgoon, J. K. (1993). Interpersonal expectations, expectancy violations, and emotional communication. *Journal of Language and Social Psychology, 12,* 30–48. doi: 10.1177/0261927X93121003

Burgoon, J. K., & Hubbard, A. S. E. (2005). Cross-cultural and intercultural applications of expectancy violation theory and interaction adaptation theory. In W. B. Gudykunst (Ed.), *Theorizing about intercultural communication* (pp. 149–171). Thousand Oaks, CA: Sage.

Burgoon, J. K., & Walther, J. B. (1990). Nonverbal expectancies and evaluative consequences of violations. *Human Communication Research, 17,* 232–265. doi: doi. org/10.1111/j.1468-2958.1990.tb00232.x

Cai, D. A., & Fink, E. L. (2002). Conflict style differences between individualists and collectivists. *Communication Monographs, 69,* 67–87. http://dx.doi.org/10.1080/03637750216536

Casmir, F. S. (Ed.). (1974). *The international and intercultural communication annual, 1.* New York, NY: Speech Communication Association.

Collier, M. J. (2005). Theorizing cultural identifications. In W. B. Gudykunst (Ed.), *Theorizing about intercultural communication* (pp. 235–256). Thousand Oaks, CA: Sage.

Collier, M. J., & Thomas, M. (1988). Cultural identity: An interpretive perspective. In Y. Y. Kim and W. B. Gudykunst (Eds.), *Theories in intercultural communication* (pp. 99–120). Thousand Oaks, CA: Sage.

Cupach, W. R., & Imahori, T. T. (1993). Identity management theory: Communication competence in intercultural episodes and relationships. In R. L. Wiseman, & J. Koester (Eds.), *Intercultural communication competence* (pp. 112–131). Newbury Park, CA: Sage.

Fine, M. G. (1991). New voices in the workplace: Research directions in multicultural communication. *Journal of Business Communication, 23,* 259–275.

Fiske, A. P. (2002). Using individualism and collectivism to compare cultures: A critique of the validity and measurement of the constructs: Comment on Oyserman et al. (2002). *Psychological Bulletin, 128,* 78–88. doi: 10.1037/0033-2909.128.1.78

Freund, M. (2017). Wilhelm von Humboldt. In M. Cameron, B. Hill, & R. J. Stainton (Eds.), *Sourcebook in the history of philosophy of language: Primary source texts from the pre-Socratics to Mill* (pp. 963–1028). Cham, Switzerland: Springer International.

Gallois, C., & Giles, H. (1998). Accommodating mutual influence in intergroup encounters. In M. T. Palmer & G. A. Barnett (Eds.), *Mutual influence in interpersonal communication: Theory and research in cognition, affect and behavior* (Vol. Progress in Communication Sciences, pp. 135–162). Stamford, UK: Ablex.

Gallois, C., Ogay, T., & Giles, H. (2005). Communication accommodation theory: A look back and a look ahead. In W. B. Gudykunst (Ed.), *Theorizing about intercultural communication* (pp. 121–148). Thousand Oaks, CA: Sage.

Giles, H., Mulac, A., Bradac, J. J., & Johnson, P. (1987). Speech accommodation theory: The first decade and beyond. In M. L. McLaughlin (Ed.), *Communication yearbook* (Vol. 10, pp. 13–48). Newbury Park, CA: Sage.

Goffman, E. (1952). On cooling the mark out: Some aspects of adaptation to failure. *Psychiatry, 15*, 451–463.

Goffman, E. (1959). *The presentation of self in everyday life.* New York, NY: Doubleday.

Gudykunst, W. B. (1985). A model of uncertainty reduction in intercultural encounters. *Journal of Language and Social Psychology, 4*, 79–98.

Gudykunst, W. B. (2002). Issues in cross-cultural communication research. In W. B. Gudykunst & B. Mody (Eds.), *Handbook of international and intercultural communication* (2nd ed., pp. 165–177). Thousand Oaks, CA: Sage.

Gudykunst, W. B. (2005a). An anxiety/uncertainty management (AUM) theory of effective communication: Making the mesh of the net finer. In W. B. Gudykunst (Ed.), *Theorizing about intercultural communication* (pp. 281–322). Thousand Oaks, CA: Sage.

Gudykunst, W. B. (2005b). An anxiety/uncertainty management (AUM) theory of strangers' intercultural adjustment. In W. B. Gudykunst (Ed.), *Theorizing about intercultural communication* (pp. 419–457). Thousand Oaks, CA: Sage.

Gudykunst, W. B., & Hammer, M. R. (1988). Strangers and hosts: An extension of uncertainty reduction theory to intercultural adaptation. In Y. Y. Kim & W. B. Gudykunst (Eds.), *Cross-cultural adaptation* (pp. 106–139). Newbury Park, CA: Sage.

Gudykunst, W. B., & Mody, B. (Eds.) (2002). *Handbook of international and intercultural communication* (2nd ed.). Thousand Oaks, CA: Sage.

Gudykunst, W. B., Matsumoto, Y., Ting-Toomey, S., Nishida, T., Kim, K. S., & Heyman, S. (1996). The influence of cultural individualism-collectivism, self-construals, and individual values on communication styles across cultures. *Human Communication Research, 22*, 510–543. doi: 10.1111/j.1468-2958.1996.tb00377.x

Gullahorn, J., & Gullahorn, J. (1963). An extension of the *U*-curve hypothesis. *Journal of Social Issues, 19*, 33–47. doi: 10.1111/j.1540-4560.1963.tb00447.x

Hall, E. (1959). *The silent language.* New York, NY: Doubleday.

Hall, E. (1966). *The hidden dimension.* New York, NY: Anchor.

Hall, E. (1976). *Beyond culture.* New York, NY: Anchor.

Helms, J. (1993). Introduction: Review of racial identity terminology. In J. Helms (Ed.), *Black and white racial identity: Theory, research, and practice* (pp. 3–8). Westport, CT: Praeger

Hardiman, R. (1994). White racial identity development in the United States. In E. P. Salett & D. R. Koslow (Eds.), *Race, ethnicity and self: Identity in the multicultural perspective* (pp. 117–142). Washington, DC: National Multicultural Institute.

Hofstede, G. (1980). *Culture's consequences: International differences in work-related values.* Beverly Hills, CA: Sage.

Hofstede, G. (2001). *Culture's consequences: Comparing values, behaviors, institutions and organizations across nations* (2nd ed.). Thousand Oaks, CA: Sage.

Hofstede, G., & Bond, M. H. (1988). The Confucius connection: From cultural roots to economic growth. *Organizational Dynamics, 16*, 4–21.

Hofstede, G., & Hofstede, G. J. (2005). *Cultures and organizations: Software of the mind* (2nd ed.). New York, NY: McGraw-Hill.

Imohari, T. T., & Cupach, W. R. (2005). Identity management theory: Facework in intercultural relationships. In W. B. Gudykunst (Ed.), *Theorizing about intercultural communication* (pp. 195–210). Thousand Oaks, CA: Sage.

Johnson, J. D., & Tuttle, F. (1989). Problems in intercultural research. In M. K. Asante & W. B. Gudykunst (Eds.), *Handbook of international and intercultural communication* (pp. 461–483). Newbury Park, CA: Sage.

Kanagawa, C., Cross, S. E., & Markus, H. R. (2001). "Who am I?" The cultural psychology of the conceptual self. *Personality and Social Psychology Bulletin, 27*, 90–103. doi: 10.1177/0146167201271008

Kim, M.-S. (1994). Cross-cultural comparisons of the perceived importance of conversational constraints. *Human Communication Research, 21*, 128–151. doi: 10.1111/j.1468-2958.1994.tb00343.x

Kim, M.-S. (2005). Culture-based conversational constraints theory: individual- and cultural-level analyses. In W. B. Gudykunst (Ed.), *Theorizing about intercultural communication* (pp. 93–117). Thousand Oaks, CA: Sage.

Kim, Y. Y. (1988). *Communication and cross-cultural adaptation: An integrative approach*. Avon, UK: Multilingual Matters.

Kim, Y. Y. (2005). Adapting to a new culture: An integrative communication theory. In W. B. Gudykunst (Ed.), *Theorizing about intercultural communication* (pp. 375–400). Thousand Oaks, CA: Sage.

Klein, R. G., & Edgar, B. (2002). *The dawn of human culture: A bold new theory on what sparked the "Big Bang" of human consciousness*. New York, NY: Wiley.

Kluckhohn, C. (1949/2017). *Mirror for man: The relation of anthropology to modern life*. New York, NY: McGraw-Hill.

Kluckhohn, F. R., & Strodtbeck, F. L. (1961). *Variations in value orientations*. Evanston, IL: Row, Peterson.

Kroeber, A. L., & Kluckhohn, C. (1952). *Culture: A critical review of concepts and definitions*. Cambridge, MA: Peabody Museum.

Kuhn, T. (1962). *The structure of scientific revolutions* (2nd ed.). Chicago, IL: University of Chicago Press. Retrieved from https://projektintegracija.pravo.hr/_download/repository/Kuhn_Structure_of_Scientific_Revolutions.pdf

Langer, E. (1989). *Mindfulness*. Reading, MA: Addison-Wesley.

Leeds-Hurwitz, W. L. (1990). Notes on the history of intercultural communication: The Foreign Service Institute and the mandate of intercultural training. *Quarterly Journal of Speech, 76*, 262–281.

Leung, K. (1988). Some determinants of conflict avoidance. *Journal of Cross-Cultural Psychology, 19*, 125–136.

Levine, R. A. (1982). *Culture, behavior, and personality*. New York, NY: Aldine.

Levine, T. R., Bresnahan, M. J., Park, H. S., Lapinski, M. K., Wittenbaum, G. M., Shearman, S. M., Lee, S. Y., Chung, D., & Ohashi, R. (2003). Self-construal scales lack validity. *Human Communication Research, 29*, 210–252. doi: 10.1111/j.1468-2958.2003.tb00837.x

McDermott, R. (1980). Profile: Ray L. Birdwhistell. *The Kinesics Report, 2*(3), 1–16.

McKinnon, A. M. (2010). Energy and society: Herbert Spencer's "energetic sociology" of social evolution and beyond. *Journal of Classical Sociology, 10*, 439–455. doi: 10.1177/1468795X10385184

McLuhan, M. (1962). *The Gutenberg galaxy: The making of a typographic man*. Toronto, Canada: University of Toronto Press.

McLuhan, M. (1964). *Understanding media: The extensions of man*. Cambridge, MA: The MIT Press.

McLuhan, M. (1967). *The medium is the message: An inventory of effects*. New York, NY: Penguin.

Markus, H. R., & Kitayama, S. (1991). Culture and the self: Implications for cognition, emotion, and motivation. *Psychological Review, 98*, 224–253. doi: 10.1037/0033-295X.98.2.224

Markus, H. R., & Kitayama, S. (1998). The cultural psychology of personality. *Journal of Cross-Cultural Psychology, 29*, 63–87. doi: 10.1177/0022022198291004

Martin, J. N., & Nakayama, T. K. (2017). *Intercultural communication in contexts* (7th ed.). New York, NY: McGraw-Hill.

Martin, J. N., Nakayama, T. K., & Carbaugh, D. (2012). The history and development of the study of intercultural communication and applied linguistics. In J. Jackson (Ed.), *The Routledge handbook of language and intercultural communication* (pp. 17–37). New York, NY: Routledge.

Matsumoto, D., & Yoo, S. H. (2006). Toward a new generation of cross-cultural research. *Perspectives on Psychological Science, 1*, 234–250. doi: 10.1111/j.1745-6916.2006.00014.x

Matsumoto, D., Kudoh, T., Scherer, K., & Wallbott, H. (1988). Antecedents of and reactions to emotions in the United States and Japan. *Journal of Cross-Cultural Psychology, 19*, 267–286.

Merritt, A. C. (2000). Culture in the cockpit: Do Hofstede's dimensions replicate? *Journal of Cross-Cultural Psychology, 31*, 283–301. doi: 10.1177/0022022100031003001

Ni, L., & Wang, Q. (2011). Anxiety and uncertainty management in an intercultural setting: The impact on organization–public relationships. *Journal of Public Relations Research, 23*, 269–301. doi: 10.1080/ 1062726X.2011.582205

Nisbett, R. E. (2003). *The geography of thought: How Asians and Westerners think differently . . . and why*. New York, NY: Free Press.

Oetzel, J. G. (1998). The effects of self-construals and ethnicity on self-reported conflict styles. *Communication Reports, 11*, 133–144.

Oetzel, J. G. (2009). *Intercultural communication: A layered approach*. New York, NY: Vango.

Oetzel, J. G., McDermott, V. M., Torres, A., & Sanchez, C. (2012). The impact of individual differences and group diversity on group interaction climate and satisfaction: A test of the effective intercultural workgroup communication theory. *Journal of International and Intercultural Communication, 5*, 144–167. doi: 10.1080/17513057.2011.640754

Oetzel, J. G., Ting-Toomey, S., Masumoto, T., Yokochi, Y., Pan, X., Takai, J., & Wilcox, W. (2001). Face and facework in conflict: A cross-cultural comparison of China, German, Japan, and the United States. *Communication Monograph, 68*, 235–258. doi: 10.1080/03637750128061

Oyserman, D., Coon, H. M., & Kemmelmeier, M. (2002). Rethinking individualism and collectivism: Evaluation of theoretical assumptions and meta-analyses. *Psychological Bulletin, 128*, 3–72. doi: 10.1037//0033-2909.128.1.3

Papineau, D. (2007). Naturalism. In *Stanford Encyclopedia of Philosophy*. Retrieved from https://plato.stanford.edu/entries/naturalism.

Phinney, J. S. (1993). A three-stage model of ethnic identity development in adolescence. In M. E. Bernal & G. Knight (Eds.), *Ethnic identity* (pp. 61–79). Albany, NY: State University of New York Press.

Pike, K. L. (Ed.) (1967). *Language in relation to a unified theory of structure of human behavior* (2nd ed.). The Hague, Netherlands: Mouton.

Popper, K. (1959). *The logic of scientific discovery.* (K. Popper Trans.). London, England: Hutchinson. (Original work published 1935)

Rogers, E. M. (1994). *A history of communication study: A biographical approach.* New York, NY: The Free Press.

Rogers, E. M., & Hart, W. B. (2002). The histories of intercultural, international, and development communication. In W. B. Gudykunst & B. Moody (Eds.), *Handbook of international and intercultural communication* (2nd ed., pp. 1–18). Thousand Oaks, CA: Sage.

Róheim, G. (1943). The origin and function of culture. *Nervous and Mental Disease Monographs Series, 69,* 3–107.

Sadri, H. A., & Flammia, M. (2011). *Intercultural communication: A new approach to international relations and global challenges.* New York, NY: Continuum.

Samovar, L. A., & Porter, R. E. (1972). *Intercultural communication: A reader.* Belmont, CA: Wadsworth.

Schwartz, S. H., (1999). A theory of cultural values and some implications for work. *Applied Psychology: An International Review, 48,* 23–47. doi: 10.1111/j.1464-0597.1999.tb00047.x

Sharifian, F., & Jamarani, M. (2013). Language and intercultural communication: From the old era to the new one. In F. Sharifian & M. Jamarani (Eds.), *Language and intercultural communication in the new era* (pp. 1–19). New York, NY: Routledge.

Sherif, M. (1967). *Social interaction: Process and products.* Oxford, England: Aldine.

Singelis, T. M. (1994). The measurement of independent and interdependent self-construals. *Personality and Social Psychology Bulletin, 20,* 580–591. http://dx.doi.org/10.1177/0146167294205014

Singelis, T. M., & Brown, W. J. (1995). Culture, self, and collectivist communication: Linking culture to individual behavior. *Human Communication Research, 21,* 354–389. doi: 10.1111/j.1468-2958.1995.tb00351.x

Spencer, M. E. (1994). Multiculturalism, "political correctness," and the politics of identity. *Sociological Forum, 9,* 547–567.

Stewart, I. (2011). Commandeering time: The ideological status of time in the social Darwinism of Herbert Spencer. *Australian Journal of Politics and History, 57,* 389–402. doi: 10.1111/j.1467-8497.2011.01604.x

Tajfel, H., & Turner, J. C. (1979). An integrative theory of intergroup conflict. In W. G. Austin & S. Worchel (Eds.), *The social psychology of intergroup relations* (pp. 33–37). Monterey, CA: Brooks/Cole.

Tanno, D. V., & Jandt, F. E. (1994). Redefining the "other" in multicultural research. *The Howard Journal of Communications, 5,* 36–45.

Ting-Toomey, S. (1988). Intercultural conflict styles: A face-negotiation theory. In Y. Y. Kim & W. Gudykunst (Eds.), *Theories in intercultural communication* (pp. 213–235). Newbury Park, CA: Sage.

Ting-Toomey, S. (1993). Communicative resourcefulness: An identity negotiation perspective. In R. L. Wiseman & J. Koester (Eds.), *Intercultural communication competence.* Newbury Park, CA: Sage.

Ting-Toomey, S. (2005a). Identity negotiation theory: Crossing cultural boundaries. In W. B. Gudykunst (Ed.), *Theorizing about intercultural communication* (pp. 211–233). Thousand Oaks, CA: Sage.

Ting-Toomey, S. (2005b). The matrix of face: An updated face-negotiation theory. In W. B. Gudykunst (Ed.), *Theorizing about intercultural communication* (pp. 71–92). Thousand Oaks, CA: Sage.

Ting-Toomey, S., & Kurogi, A. (1998). Facework competence in intercultural conflict: An updated face-negotiation theory. *International Journal of Intercultural Relations, 22*, 187–225. doi: 10.1016/S0147-1767(98)00004-2

Ting-Toomey, S., & Oetzel, J. G. (2002). Cross-cultural face concerns and conflict styles: Current status and future directions. In W. B. Gudykunst & B. Mody (Eds.), *Handbook of international and intercultural communication* (2nd ed., pp. 143–163). Thousand Oaks, CA: Sage.

Ting-Toomey, S., & Takai, J. (2006). Explaining intercultural conflict: Promising approaches and future directions. In J. G. Oetzel & S. Ting-Toomey (Eds.), *The Sage handbook of conflict communication* (pp. 691–723). Thousand Oaks, CA: Sage.

Ting-Toomey, S., Oetzel, J. G., & Yee-Jung, K. (2001). Self-construal types and conflict management styles. *Communication Reports, 14*, 87–104.

Trager, G. L. (1961). The typology of paralanguage. *Anthropological Linguistics, 3*, 17–21.

Triandis, H. C. (1995). *Individualism and collectivism*. Boulder, CO: Westmore.

Triandis, H. C., & Gelfand, M. J. (1998). Covering measurement of horizontal and vertical individualism and collectivism. *Journal of Personality and Social Psychology, 74*, 118–128. doi: 10.1037/0022-3514.74.1.118

Triandis, H. C., & Singelis, T. M. (1998). Training to recognize individual differences in collectivism and individualism within culture. *International Journal of Intercultural Relations, 22*, 35–47.

Trompenaars, F., & Hampden-Turner, C. (1998). *Riding the waves of culture: Understanding cultural diversity in global business* (2nd ed.). New York, NY: McGraw-Hill.

Turner, J. C., Hogg, M. A., Oakes, P. J., Reicher, S. D., & Wetherell, M. S. (1987). *Rediscovering the social group: A self-categorization theory*. Cambridge, MA: Blackwell.

Van de Vijver, F., & Leung, K. (1997). *Methods and data analysis for cross-cultural research*. Newbury Park, CA: Sage.

Van der Zee, K. I., & Van Oudenhoven, J. P. (2000). The multicultural personality questionnaire: A multidimensional instrument of multicultural effectiveness. *European Journal of Personality, 14*, 291–309.

Wang, Q., Ni, L., & De la Flor, M. (2014). An intercultural competence model of strategic public relations management in the Peru mining industry context. *Journal of Public Relations Research, 26*, 1–22. doi: 10.1080/1062726X.2013.795864

Winthrop, R. H. (1991). *Dictionary of concepts in cultural anthropology*. New York, NY: Greenwood Press.

Yamada, A. M., & Singelis, T. M. (1999). Biculturalism and self-construal. *International Journal of Intercultural Relations, 23*, 697–709.

Yep, G. A. (1998). My three cultures: Navigating the multicultural identity landscape. In J. N. Martin, T. K. Nakayama, & L. A. Flores (Eds.). *Readings in cultural contexts* (pp. 79–85). Mountain View, CA: Mayfield.

4

CONFLICT MANAGEMENT AND NEGOTIATION

This chapter discusses conflict management and negotiation processes in intercultural contexts. The chapter conceptualizes conflict and reviews conflict management literature. It then discusses a goals approach to conflict management research. Negotiation is then defined and discussed in its relation with conflict management literature, and information management between intercultural parties within public relations context is analyzed and related with negotiation outcomes. The chapter ends with a revised theoretical framework specific to intercultural public relations conflict management and negotiations.

In the *Oxford Dictionary*, the word origin of *conflict* is *confligere*: "Con" means together and "fligere" means to strike; thus, conflict originally meant to strike together. When a conflict occurs, what is the sensible and appropriate response? The initial academic research in conflict in the early 20th century by Western scholars emphasized its competitive aspect and thus, striking back, or using competitive acts, was proposed to lead to productivity and desirable outcomes (Deutsch, 2002). Deutsch contended that this focus largely resulted from a superficial and vulgarized comprehension of the writings of the three giants, Darwin, Freud, and Marx, combined with the then-existing social conditions:

> The intellectual atmosphere prevalent during the period when social psychology began to emerge contributed to viewing conflict from the perspective of "competitive struggle." Social conditions too—the intense competition among businesses and among nations, the devastation of the First World War, the economic depression of the 1920s and 1930s, the rise of Nazism and other totalitarian systems—reinforced this perspective.

> *(p. 308)*

Kurt Lewin (1935) and his student Morton Deutsch (1973) were among the early most important social psychologists who criticized the reduction of the concept of conflict to competition. Instead, they theoretically proposed and empirically tested both the cooperative and competitive natures of conflict. Conflict research in the fields of business management and communication has benefited by adopting this perspective, witnessing a blossoming of research being focused on identifying problem solving and integrative conflict management strategies (e.g., Blake & Mouton, 1964; Pruitt & Rubin, 1987; Putnam & Wilson, 1982; Ting-Toomey & Oetzel, 2001). Before we explore further into the competitive and cooperative natures of conflict and the conflict management literature, let us first take a look at what conflict is.

Defining Conflict

Defining conflict may be more important than it appears to be. Dean Tjosvold, a student of Morton Deutsch and proliferate researcher and practitioner in the cross-cultural business management field, lamented the deficient attention paid to the definition of conflict (Tjosvold, 2006). He argued that because of its practical use, conflict management research not only signifies itself in academia, but is most avidly consumed by practitioners and other non-academic people as well. How academicians define conflict notably influences people's perceptions of it and the ways to deal with it. Reviewing literature, Tjosvold found that conflict had been defined with a negative undertone, implying destruction and negative emotional arousals. He reviewed predominant research from the 1950s to 1980s and concluded that conflict was defined as to happen between interdependent, mixed-motive relational parties who have opposing interests or goal incompatibility. It is often associated with resource scarcity and accompanied by negative emotions such as frustration (Tjosvold, 2006).

Tjosvold (1998, 2006) critiqued that these previous definitions are not realistic, because not all conflicts are based on opposing interests or incompatible goals. Whether the interests or goals are opposing is an empirical question; only the involved party could answer it. Thus, any incompatibility can be rather subjective than objective. He further argued that such definitions made conflict management difficult because they prime the involved parties with the competitive and destructive perception of the conflict from the beginning, and hence, render potential positive outcomes impossible. Last but not least, these definitions have confused *conflict* with *competition*, which is defined as opposing goals (Deutsch, 1973; Tjosvold, 2006).

Tjosvold (2006) advocated Deutsch's definition of conflict: "incompatible activities" (p. 90; also see Deutsch, 1973, p. 10). This definition neutralizes conflict and could include various types of conflict, those caused by incompatible goals such as two employees' competition for an award or relatively compatible goals such as two employees' different proposals on a project to benefit the company. This definition also allows conflict to be treated constructively.

Although Tjosvold's (2006) proposal is appealing and inspiring, we have found a few questions unanswered. First, apparently unnoticed by Tjosvold, the definition of conflict in the five groups of later researchers (1990s and 2000s) that he reviewed all added the word *perceived* or its variant to the earlier definitions (Table 4.1). The word "perceived" is too important to ignore because defining conflict as based on perceived opposing goals or interests already opens a window for constructive outcomes. Perception does not equal reality. Defining conflict as a perception means that the reality may not be that way. If perceptions change, the views of the phenomenon change. Therefore, the later researchers' reconceptualization of conflict as a perception should be fully credited.

Moreover, Deutsch's (1973) definition of conflict—incompatible activities—does not sufficiently capture the characteristics of conflict. Miscommunication, disagreements, and debates may all demonstrate incompatible activities. A demarcation is needed: At what point can we say that incompatible activities reflect conflict? People who behave differently can be labeled as *different*. They may not experience a conflict until they start speaking or acting. Even as they speak or act, they may not experience a conflict until their information exchange intensifies their attitudes. They may then have a *debate*. Only when they feel certain outcomes or changes of status will happen because of these differences, such as a breaking of rules, a fight, a flight, a relational damage, or positively, a change of policy, an advancement of relationship (e.g., a dating couple's first fight), etc., can their communication (or lack of it) be labeled as conflict.

TABLE 4.1 Excerpts of Conflict Definitions

Authors	*Definition of conflict*
Rubin, Pruitt, and S. H. Kim (1994)	"perceived divergence of interest, or a belief that the parties' current aspirations cannot be achieved simultaneously" (p. 5)
Lewicki, Saunders, and Minton (1997)	"the interaction of interdependent people who perceived incompatible goals and interference from each other in achieving those goals" (p. 15)
Barki and Hartwick (2004)	"a dynamic process that occurs between interdependent parties as they experience negative emotional reactions to perceived disagreements and interference with the attainment of their goals" (p. 234)
Jehn and Bendersky (2003)	"perceived incompatibilities or discrepant views among the parties involved" (p. 189)
De Dreu, Harinck, and Van Vianen, (1999)	"the tension an individual or group experiences because of perceived differences between him or herself and another individual or group" (p. 369)

Source: summary of content from Tjosvold (2006, p. 89).

At this point, two more questions must be carefully considered before a satisfactory definition of conflict is given. First, do negative emotional arousals demarcate conflict from other similar concepts such as disagreement or argument? Second, which is a more precise description of conflict, incompatible activities or incompatible goals?

Regarding the first question, affect-negative and affect-neutral definitions have both been used in defining conflict. In the examples of definitions given in Table 4.1, Barki and Hartwick (2004) specifically used negative emotions to qualify perceived disagreements. Similarly, Ting-Toomey (1985) viewed conflict as an emotion-laden dissonance between interdependent parties caused by incompatible goals, values, and ideas. Other researchers defined conflict more broadly and did not qualify conflict with emotional arousals (e.g., Lewicki et al., 1997; Rubin et al., 1994). Some researchers criticized reducing conflict to agonistic interaction behaviors (e.g., Messman & Canary, 1998). Mooney, Holahan, and Amason (2007) specifically distinguished and tested the relationship between task-induced (cognitive) and emotion-laden (affective) conflicts in the workplace. Tjosvold (1998, 2006) argued that constructive conflict is only possible when people no longer perceive conflict as a negative occurrence to begin with. Thus, emotional arousals should not be considered as an essential characteristic of conflict.

Indeed, conflict research can benefit from not treating conflict as an affective concept. On one hand, we agree with Tjosvold (1998) that conflict management research aims to help people solve conflict satisfactorily and thus a neutral meaning applied to conflict is more consistent with the research purpose. On the other hand, whether emotions and what kinds of emotions (e.g., negative or positive) are aroused in a conflict is more of an empirical question than an answer. For example, anger and fear could be experienced in a conflict (e.g., Roloff & Ifert, 2000). Information exchange induced by some conflict episodes could arouse relief, excitement, and an increased level of trust. Based on Baxter and Bullis's (1986) turning points analysis, a dating couple's first fight could elicit positive outcomes and closer affect.

Regarding the second question, whether incompatible goals or incompatible activities better define conflict, we believe that a combination of both should provide the most precise definition. As we argued earlier, the phrase "incompatible activities" itself can hardly distinguish conflict from other similar concepts of disagreeing activities. However, the phrase "incompatible goals" is not precise either. Extensive research has found that conflict situations typically stimulate multiple goals in social actors (e.g., Afifi & Guerrero, 2000; Roloff & Ifert, 2000; Wilson, Aleman, & Leatham, 1998). Very likely the social actors involved in a conflict have some compatible goals and some incompatible goals. Which goals should we use to judge whether a conflict occurs? What if 90% of goals are compatible whereas 10% are not, or 70% to 30%? Certain qualifications about the incompatible activities and goals are needed to make the definition precise.

Moreover, when people have incompatible goals or different views, a conflict may not occur unless they start interacting and perceive interference from each other. For example, a religious wife and an agnostic husband may not consider their religious differences as "conflict" until they start teaching beliefs to their child. In other words, some verbal or nonverbal acts must be present to elicit a conflict. Rubin and Levinger (1995) maintained that resource scarcity, ideological differences, and different understandings of roles in a relationship could all cause conflict. Importantly, people often misconstrue conflict. A procedural conflict reflects fundamental ideological differences. For example, a couple's disagreement on how a bill is paid may reflect their fundamental differences in perceiving money or other possessions (Rubin & Levinger, 1995). Therefore, goals and acts are both indispensible elements in conceptualizing conflict.

Based on the above reflections, we propose the following definition of conflict: *Conflict refers to perceived incompatible verbal or nonverbal activities between interdependent parties in achieving salient goals; it is prone to arouse emotional responses.* This definition describes six properties of conflict:

1. Perceived interdependence with the other party.
2. Perceived incompatibility of one's own salient goals with the other's salient goals.
3. Perceived incompatibility of verbal and nonverbal activities.
4. These activities are often (although not always) goal-oriented, or intentional communicative acts.
5. These activities are prone to arouse intense emotions.
6. These activities may evolve based on the dynamics of the encounter.

Wang, Fink, and Cai (2012) discussed the differences between incompatibility of goals and incompatibility of activities: Whereas "incompatibility of goals relates to the conflict of interests that causes disagreement between the parties, incompatibility of actions refers to the behaviors that are used to manage the disagreement" (p. 224). These two properties help define the essence of conflict in terms of the central issue. We added the word "salient" to address the most important goal that involved parties perceive. The conflict and communication literature has well established that conflict situations often involve multiple goals (e.g., Putnam, 2006; Tjosvold, 2006). Dillard's (2015) goals–plans-action theory well conceptualized primary and secondary goals. Thus, it is necessary to use the most important, or salient, goal(s) to understand the nature and intensity of the conflict.

Further, Wang et al. (2012) defined interdependence as "the relational ties that cause incompatible goals and actions to become issues that need to be managed or resolved. Furthermore, interdependence shapes how these issues will be handled" (p. 224). This property defines the essential parties that are influenced by the central issue and explains to what degree they are motivated to engage in the conflict. For example, an inter-religious marital couple tends to have higher interdependence, urgency, and motivation in resolving their conflicts in teaching their children belief-related issues than two professors who have distinctive religious beliefs in teaching their students. Exploration of the nature of incompatibilities in goals and activities as well as the nature of interdependence helps establish the anatomy of a conflict.

The last three properties are often present, but less essential than the first three properties. In most conflict and communication literature, including what has been reviewed in this chapter, researchers have used words such as interests, goals, motives, concerns, motivations, etc., to describe *what* is incompatible in a conflict (refer to Table 4.1). However, theoretical frameworks have only been robust with the terminology of *goals* in the conflict and communication literature (e.g., Putnam & Wilson, 1982; Schrader & Dillard, 1998; Wang et al., 2012; Wilson, 1990). Therefore, we continue using goals as the central term that covers the initiative components involved in a conflict. A *goal* is defined as the end goal to be achieved through social interactions (Dillard, Segrin, & Harden, 1989).

A disclaimer is that, although goals are often behind behaviors, rarely have conflict and conflict management been described as certainly intentional. Sillars and Wilmot (1994) stated that "much conflict behavior is experienced as 'just happening'" (p. 164). Conflict behavior resembles other social interactions; its purposefulness varies in a spectrum from low to high. Although parties involved in the conflict may or may not perceive or admit them, outsiders, especially neutral researchers, therapists, or mediators, may have a more advantaged angle to detangle deeper motivational drives under each conflict. As Sillars and Wilmot (1994) maintained, researchers of conflict and communication often aim to help resolve conflict and reach satisfactory outcomes for both parties, and we consider the understanding of the goals behind activities involved in conflict useful, even in the conflicts that "just happened," and essential, in those that are constructed and managed strategically.

Properties 5 and 6 describe the emotional arousals and escalation-proneness of conflict. Unlike other types of social interactions that are mostly governed by courtesy and mutually role-supportive rules (e.g., Goffman, 1959), conflict communication involves intrinsically incompatible sides of ideas and expressions. Thus, emotional arousal manifests, although not always, but often. The emotions frequently associated with conflict are negative emotions such as anger, anxiety, and fear. Anger and anxiety tend to occur in goal-incongruent situations (Lazarus & Lazarus, 1994), as does fear (Roloff & Cloven, 1990; Saarni, Mumme, & Campos, 1997; Sorenson, Morse, & Savage, 1999). The heightened emotional arousals and escalating behaviors during the conflict not only may cause both parties to accumulate more conflict issues that may evolve from the original conflict issue, but also may contribute to long-term, serial conflict and hurtful feelings. For example, when unsolvable family conflict endures, individuals tend to withdraw from conflict situations, internalize fear, and adopt self-protective behavior (Crokenberg & Langrock, 2001; Saarni et al., 1997). Below is an example that shows how the definition can be used to understand whether a phenomenon is a conflict and what related concepts are important in understanding it.

The recent phenomenon of "taking the knee" in the National Football League (NFL) during the U.S. national anthem playing has caught wide attention. Colin Kaepernick with the San Francisco 49ers first started this act in 2016 to protest police brutality toward "black people and people of color" (Wyche, 2016). Some NFL players followed suit, but the act caught nationwide attention and more than 200 NFL players sat or knelt after President Trump called for the firing of the kneeling athletes at a rally in Huntsville, Alabama, on September 22, 2017. The nation was divided on this protest. The polls varied by their political leaning, but most news agencies reported somewhere around 50%. For instance, CNN reported that 49% of U.S. Americans considered the protest wrong (Agiesta, 2017), and U.S. News reported that 58% proposed that "professional athletes should be required to stand during the national anthem at sporting events" (Walsh, 2017). Is this phenomenon a conflict? Let's analyze it with the definition.

First, the proponents of "taking the knee" (including kneeling athletes) and the opponents had incompatible goals. President Trump was an example of the opponent side. Whereas the kneeling athletes' goal was to protest against police violence toward certain ethnic groups, Trump's goal was to maintain the proper flag and anthem code and their patriotic meanings. Arguably, both parties also had the common goal to bring more harmony to U.S. society. Whereas Kaepernick and his proponents took the knee during the playing of the national anthem to carry out their protesting goal, Trump and his proponents used disagreeing language and behavior, as well as following the flag code, to carry out their goals to show patriotism. Thus, incompatible goals and activities are both present. Second, the proponents and opponents had interdependence—both groups shared the same national flag and anthem, and mostly were citizens of the same country. The interdependence can be further explored in their role relationships, such as democratically elected president and citizens, famous football athletes and fans, etc.

Now, let's examine at what point a conflict came into being. Before anybody protested the kneeling act, no incompatible activities had been performed. However, any opponent who responded with either verbal or nonverbal messages began a conflict. In this instance, President Trump's speech was an example. At the rally, he said, "Wouldn't you love to see one of these NFL owners, when somebody disrespects our flag, to say, 'Get that son of a (expletive) off the field right now. Out. He's fired. He's fired!'" (Tsuji, 2017). These words indicated the perceived incompatibility of showing or not showing respect—mainly nonverbally in this case—during the playing of the national anthem; and more important, the incompatible goals that drove these different behaviors and remarks. Thus, a conflict became present. In Pondy's (1967) term, this was the "manifest conflict" stage.

In addition, the interpersonal conflict between the kneeling athletes and Trump quickly escalated into a national level. At this point, a related but new conflict was formed. For those who agreed with President Trump, the meanings contained in his message were considered to be an appropriate response. For those who disagreed with part or all of the meanings that Trump's message contained, the conflict was escalated. For example, Trump's message contained at least three meanings: taking the knee disrespected the flag, those athletes should be fired, and they deserved foul language. More nuanced meanings can be inferred, but are omitted here to focus on the discussion of the concept. When both groups started expressing their opinions via social media and other platforms, more and different incompatible goals and activities from the original conflict encounter were demonstrated. For example, nonverbal behaviors such as locked arms among the athletes and sitting during the national anthem appeared; some members of the audience booed and walked out of the stadium when the athletes knelt, and some returned their tickets. Thus, new conflicts about whether players should obey the flag code, whether using foul language was presidential, whether protests should be given at appropriate times and locations, and so on, became the central issues.

Further, intense emotions were reflected from kneeling athletes' behaviors and remarks in their interviews, President Trump's speeches and tweets, and other proponents' and opponents' behaviors and social media messages. The fact that Trump used foul language could imply dissatisfaction, defiance, or anger. Emotional tension was more evident in the new conflict as discussed above. Kaepernick's words showed his frustration and indignation in his interview (Wyche, 2016). Right after the president's speech, a wave of kneeling occurred not only among NFL players, but also among those with other vocations. A wave of Trump-supporting verbal and nonverbal manifestations occurred in various public spheres as well. Both groups used intensified language and actions to display their emotions. As often seen in protests, positive emotions from proponents and negative emotions from opponents were both highly augmented, sometimes to such dangerous degrees that physical violence and even fatal clashes occurred.

The last note about understanding conflict is to also examine its antecedents, consequences, and potential constants. Pondy (1967, pp. 298–299) stated:

> The term "conflict" has been used at one time or another in the literature to describe: (1) antecedent conditions (for example, scarcity of resources, policy differences) of conflictful behavior, (2) affective states (e.g., stress, tension, hostility, anxiety, etc.) of the individuals involved, (3) cognitive states of individuals, i.e., their perception or awareness of conflictful situations, and (4) conflictful behavior, ranging from

passive resistance to overt aggression. Attempts to decide which of these classes—conditions, attitude, cognition, or behavior—is really conflict is likely to result in an empty controversy. The problem is not to choose among these alternative conceptual definitions, since each may be a relevant stage in the development of a conflict episode, but to try to clarify their relationships.

Pondy also added a fifth stage, conflict aftermath, to make the picture complete. Whereas we agree with his argument that all five stages are relevant to the conceptualization of conflict, it is important to distinguish the concept itself from its antecedents, consequences, and influential constants: Knowing antecedents help analyze the causes of a conflict, knowing consequences help analyze the effects of social actors' communicative acts during the conflict, and knowing constants help understand what personal and environmental factors shape the dynamics in the conflict. Below is a list of potential antecedents, consequences, and constants. This list is generated based on the extant literature that has examined conflict from different angles, as Pondy (1967) summarized above (e.g., Pruitt & Rubin, 1987; Sillars & Wilmot, 1994; Thomas, 1976; Thompson, 1998; Ting-Toomey, 1985).

Antecedents of conflict:

1. Prior relationship between the two parties.
2. Previous incompatibilities in goals and activities related to the issue.

Consequences of conflict:

1. *Relational outcomes*: Perceived interdependence is likely to be moved to a new state, such as relational enhancement or deterioration.
2. *Issue outcomes*: Perceived incompatibility is likely to move to a new state (e.g., resolved, escalated, de-escalated, etc.).
3. *Individual attitudinal outcomes*: Both parties' attitudes are likely to move to a new state because of emotional arousals during the conflict.
4. *Longitudinal outcomes*: It is prone to become an antecedent of future conflicts.

Potential constants that influence conflict:

1. Conflict management style and other personality-related variables (e.g., temper).
2. External influences, including other people, time, location, etc.
3. Relational history.
4. Investment in the issue of the conflict (e.g., one-time or serial).

The condensed meanings of a conflict from the list above mostly surround effective or ineffective communicative acts to manage *a conflict issue* and the *relationship* of the two parties. When the acts are consciously motivated to achieve a goal, we can use the term, *strategy*, to describe the acts. Admittedly, it is not uncommon for people to handle conflict with impulsive, non-rational verbal and nonverbal acts, especially if their emotions dominate the communication process. Because our goal is to develop effective, appropriate, and satisfactory conflict management models for the readers, we follow the majority conflict management research that is based in the rational, conscious framework (e.g., Sillars & Wilmot, 1994). The following section discusses conflict management literature.

Two-Dimensional Conflict Management Models

This body of literature is credited to Blake and Mouton (1964), who proposed the *managerial grid* to use two dimensions to predict conflict management styles by managers in organizations: the degree of concern for production and the degree of concern for people. When the degree of concern for production is high and for people is low, the manager is predicted to use *domination*, a strategy of acting like an authoritarian who tells the other party what to do and pushes his or her own way over the other party. When the degree of concern for production is low and for people is high, the manager is predicted to use *accommodation*, a strategy of giving in to satisfy the other party's needs (Blake & Mouton, 1964).

High concern on both dimensions predicts the use of *integration*, a strategy of maximizing gains by exploring both parties' needs to achieve an agreement beneficial to both. Low concern for both production and people predicts a manager's use of *avoidance*, a non-confrontational strategy of taking no action (Blake & Mouton, 1964). Later on, a fifth strategy, compromise, was added to the model: Moderate concern for both predicts the use of *compromise*, a strategy of finding concession or a common middle ground that both parties can accept (e.g., Thomas, 1976).

Blake and Mouton's (1964) managerial grid is the foundation of other two-dimensional models that predict conflict management behaviors. Later revisions of the grid have maintained the dimensional structure and the spatial positioning of the five conflict styles, but the labels of the two dimensions change (e.g., Oetzel & Ting-Toomey, 2003; Pruitt & Carnevale, 1993; Pruitt & Rubin, 1987; Thomas, 1976; Ting-Toomey, 1988; Ting-Toomey & Kurogi, 1998). For example, Thomas and Kilmann (1974) used cooperativeness-noncooperativeness (to satisfy the other's needs) and assertiveness-nonassertiveness (to satisfy one's own needs) as two dimensions to generate the space for five conflict management styles. Pruitt and Rubin (1987) reworked Blake and Mouton's (1964) managerial grid for the purpose of predicting negotiator's behaviors based on the negotiator's concern for self-outcomes and concern for the other's outcomes; again, a space of five conflict

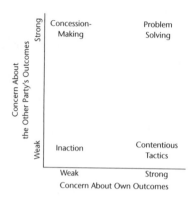

FIGURE 4.1 Dual Concern Model

Source: Carnevale and Pruitt (1992). Reproduced with permission of Annual Reviews, Palo Alto, CA.

styles was similarly proposed as in Blake and Mouton's managerial grid. Pruitt and Rubin's (1987) model is aptly referred to as *the dual-concern model* (also see Pruitt & Carnevale, 1993). Based on the model, Rahim (1983) developed an instrument, Rahim's Organizational Conflict Inventory-II (ROCI-II), to measure the likelihood of using each of the five strategies.

Evaluation and Extension of the Two-Dimensional Models in Communication

One of the most influential two-dimensional models in conflict communication research is Putnam and Wilson's (1982) version. They criticized that, as built in Blake and Mouton's (1964) grid model, most of the management models related the two-dimensional concerns with conflict management *styles*, instead of *strategies*. Various communication researchers (e.g., Putnam & Wilson, 1982; Sillars & Wilmot, 1994; Wang et al., 2012; Wilson, 2002) stressed the importance of differentiating between these two concepts. Wilson (2002) defined a strategy as "an abstract category of behaviors that share a common feature or quality and that appear to pursue a goal" (p. 27). Wang et al. (2012) stated that conflict management strategies are used to pursue goals arising from a conflict situation, whereas conflict management styles refer to the recurrent approach to the management of conflict across situations and are often related to personality. In other words, whereas strategies are more active and planned behaviors based on the specificities of a conflict situation, styles are more automatic and patterned behaviors (Putnam & Wilson, 1982). To approach conflict management from a perspective of strategic behavior, Putnam and Wilson developed an Organizational Communication Conflict Instrument (OCCI) to measure conflict management strategies. They found three general types: *integrative* (focusing on problem solving, collaboration, and open discussion), *distributive* (focusing on imposing, winning, competing, and attacking), and *nonconfrontational* (avoiding and accommodating).

Another well-known version of the two dimensional model for conflict management is face-negotiation theory. Ting-Toomey and Kurogi (1998) defined face as a person's claim of "favorable social self-worth" (p. 187) that the person wants others to see. People's face needs predict conflict strategies they would use (Ting-Toomey & Kurogi, 1998). Whereas high self-face concerns predicted domination, high other-face concerns predicted accommodation, avoidance, and to some degree, compromise (see Ting-Toomey, 1988; Ting-Toomey & Kurogi, 1998; Ting-Toomey & Oetzel, 2001).

Note that in both Putnam and Wilson's (1982) and Ting-Toomey and colleagues' versions, the two dimensions did not predict the five conflict management behaviors as Blake and Mouton's (1964) original model proposed. Instead, several strategies cluster together more than others. These empirical findings correspond with other studies that specifically evaluated the dual–concern model and their affiliated models (e.g., Cai & Fink, 2002; Sorenson et al., 1999; van de Vliert & Kabanoff, 1999; Wang et al., 2012). Whereas some supported the two-dimensional models (e.g., Ruble & Thomas, 1976), most did not.

Cai and Fink (2002) used multidimensional scaling to test whether the five conflict styles proposed in the two-dimensional model (e.g., Blake & Mouton, 1964) would indeed form a two-dimensional structure. The five conflict styles were measured by Rahim's (1983) Organizational Conflict Inventory II. Results did not support a two-dimensional structure. The first three dimensions explained 50% of the variance in the space formed by the five conflict styles, and the remaining dimensions explained the remaining 50% of the variance. Seven dimensions were found to explain more variance than a single measurement item (Cai & Fink, 2002). An important implication in this study is that multiple rather than two dimensions better explain the preferred use of conflict management strategies. Sorenson et al. (1999) found that, whereas high levels of self-concern predicted domination and high levels of other-concern predicted obliging, the levels of dual concern did not predict avoiding, compromising, and integrating as the two-dimensional models predicted.

Moreover, personality traits appear to influence conflict management styles more than concerns for the conflict issue. Rhoades and Carnevale (1999) studied how differently motivated people would respond to opponents with different conflict management behaviors. Results indicated that, in general, when faced with the opponents who used problem-solving strategies, people would match those strategies; when faced with those who used avoidance, people would call for action. Other matching behaviors also emerged. Friedman, Tidd, Currall, and Tsai (2000) found that, in the workplace, people who typically used integrative styles perceived less task or relational conflict, less domination from others, and less stress, whereas those who typically used domination styles perceived more task and relational conflict, more aggression from others, and more stress. These perceptions reinforced their preferred styles and formed a cycle. These studies suggest that other variables such as one's own and one's opponent's conflict management behaviors and cognitive perceptions may better predict a person's conflict management behavior in actual conflict communication than static, preset concerns proposed in the two-dimensional models.

Van de Vliert and Kabanoff (1999) further assessed two widely used instruments to measure the five conflict management styles, Thomas and Kilmann's (1974) MODE and Rahim's (1983) ROCI-II. Both instruments had moderate construct validity, and the five strategies' positioning did not match up to what the dual concern model prescribed. In MODE, domination and integration were not well distinguished, neither were avoidance and accommodation. ROCI-II did not discriminate between compromise and integration, neither between avoidance and accommodation. In MODE, integration was located far from compromise, accommodation, and avoidance; but the latter three were located close to each other. In ROCI-II, these four were closely clustered.

More recently, Wang et al. (2012) used a goals approach to examine strategic use of avoidance to manage conflict. They developed a typology of goals and a typology of conflict avoidance strategies. In addition, they also tested the relationships between the goals and the other four conflict management strategies in the traditional two-dimensional model: integration, compromise, accommodation, and domination. Unlike the traditional view that avoidance is simply nonaction (e.g., Putnam & Wilson, 1982) or withdrawal (Blake & Mouton, 1964, Pruitt & Rubin, 1987), Wang et al. argued that avoidance not only could be used strategically to manage conflict, but also consisted of a spectrum of meanings of its own: Whereas some avoidance strategies were used to escape from conflict, others were used functionally to support, to object, and even to aggress.

Wang et al.'s (2012) typology of goals included four orthogonal dimensions: socioemotional, instrumental, competitive, and cooperative. Although the original typology included nine types of goals, their results supported four distinctive types that affected conflict management strategies: enmity goals (competitive goals because of negative emotions to the other), task goals (competitive goals to assert one's own position for an instrumental outcome), support goals (cooperative goals because of positive emotions to the other), and utility goals (cooperative goals for instrumental gains).

Wang et al.'s (2012) typology of conflict avoidance strategies was based on the avoidance of person, issue, or both, immediately or long term. Avoidance strategies in the immediate conflict situation included withdrawal (stopping talking or leaving the scene), passive domination (stopping talking but carrying out one's position on the issue), and pretending (continued communication and dropping the issue). The other three avoidance strategies were long term: exit (giving up talking to the person and dropping the issue), outflanking (giving up talking to the person but carrying out one's position on the issue in other ways), and yielding (continued communication with the person and dropping the issue).

Using the goals approach, Wang et al. (2012) had three major findings. First, goals were most distinct between being collaborative and cooperative. Whereas both enmity and task goals (competitive goals) predicted the likelihood of domination, passive aggression, outflanking, and exit, both support and utility goals (cooperative goals) predicted pretending and yielding. Second, emotional negativity such as enmity goals decreased accommodation, compromise, and integration; instrumental needs such as utility goals increased compromise and integration. Third, most strategies clustered as Wilson and Putnam categorized to form three groups: integrative (integration, compromise, and accommodation), distributive (passive aggression, outflanking, exit, and domination), and nonaction (withdrawal).

Future Research on a Goals Approach to Conflict Management

Identity Goals

The evolution of the dual concern model and other two-dimensional models indicates that the goals-strategy approach appears to be most robust in theorizing communication behaviors in a conflict situation. Although Wang et al.'s (2012) theory was pioneering in linking goals to strategies in conflict management, their research was focused on interpersonal relations and the typology goal was developed based on the socioemotional and instrumental dimensions. An important type of goal, an identity goal, which is essential in many public relations contexts, was not included. Dillard et al. (1989) defined *identity goals* as the goals to maintain personal standards or moral standards. Dillard and his colleagues (e.g., Dillard et al., 1989; Dillard & Schrader, 1998; Shrader & Dillard, 1998) developed the goals-plans-action theory to explain influential communication. Therefore, they considered an identity goal as a secondary goal that affects the achievement of the primary goal. A primary goal "motivates planning and action, [and] explains what the interaction is about: It is what the actor is trying to accomplish" (Schrader & Dillard, 1998, p. 278). Secondary goals are generated by the primary goal, and they are defined as the goals to help the actor achieve the primary goals while attending to other features of the situation (Schrader & Dillard, 1998).

Whereas Wang et al.'s (2012) typology of goals covered most of the goal types in Dillard and colleagues' model, they left out the identity goal. This goal can be especially important in a public relations context because many conflicts between an organization and its publics do not just arise from resources or relationships, but from a threatened identity or moral standards as a group. For example, the "take the knee" example we used above to explain the term *conflict* implies ideological differences among different groups who feel involved in this issue. Most people may have felt various degrees of indignation not because of any material or relational outcomes, but because of their personal and moral standards that affected how they interpreted the meanings of the nonverbal communication of taking the knee and of standing and saluting the national flag during the anthem playing.

Here, moral standards are often related to what is good, desirable, and just, versus what is evil, undesirable, and unjust. Personal standards are more related to the unique individual's personality, idiosyncratic socialization, and other life experiences. For example, one veteran may consider the national anthem and flag to be symbolic of falling soldiers' brave battles. Thus, standing at the ceremony shows respect, commemoration, unity, and celebration of the peace of the nation. Another veteran may consider the same symbols as the American Dream, equality of all individuals, and freedom of pursuing happiness. While the first veteran may feel indignant toward anybody who does not stand for the national anthem playing and flag ascension, the second may feel equally angry toward perceived racial discrimination. Other people who feel emotional tension and need to act may yet have other moral and personal standards that are perceived to be violated. Therefore, we encourage future researchers to add identity goals in their efforts to understand conflict situations and communication behaviors.

Development of Tactics in Conflict Management Research

Future public relations researchers should also consider developing a taxonomy of conflict management tactics to help practitioners. Now that multiple goals and strategies are available for the readers to ruminate on, they provide a solid foundation to define a space of tactics to embody these concepts. Again, a *goal* is defined as a cognitively structured end that an actor seeks to achieve (Dillard et al., 1989). A *strategy* results from the attempt to achieve relevant goals (Schrader & Dillard, 1998), or a sequence of planned behaviors to actualize goals (Putnam & Jones, 1982). A *tactic* is a small unit of verbal and nonverbal communication that serves a strategy in handling different conflict situations (Putnam & Wilson, 1982). A taxonomy of tactics can be particularly useful in conflict management training programs.

Both deductive and inductive methods can be used in developing a taxonomy. Briefly, deductive methods involve developing parsimonious, exhaustive, and mutually exclusive conceptual dimensions to represent a construct space, whereas inductive methods involve uncovering themes that are comprehensive and robust in representing all collected data (see Bailey, 1994). In other words, a theoretical space is developed prior to data collection in deductive methods and generated after data collection in inductive methods. Wang et al.'s (2012) study used the deductive method in detail and demonstrated it via examples. They proposed goals applicable in most types of interpersonal conflict and empirically tested the typology by linking it to conflict management strategies. To develop the goal typology, they conceptualized *conflict*, developed theoretical dimensions of goals to manage conflict, and finally created a typology based on the dimensions.

A good number of researchers have used the inductive method to develop a taxonomy (e.g., Cody, Canary, & Smith, 1994; Dillard et al., 1989; Samp & Solomon, 1998). For example, Samp and Solomon's (1998) study represents a typical typology development through inductive goals. They asked 174 participants to write a recent problematic event, the subsequent conversations, and participants' intentions in the recalled conversations. Samp and Solomon's (1998) pilot study generated 76 goal-relevant statements. Then, 96 individuals from the same population as the pilot study sorted out seven themes (or seven types of conflict goals) from the 76 statements. Two coders re-sorted the statements, confirmed the seven themes, and named each type of goal.

Below is Sillars and Wilmot's (1994, pp. 166–167, table 6.1) taxonomy of conflict communication. It is based on a combination of inductive and deductive methods, because on one hand, it was developed based on the dimensions of directness and affect, and on the other hand, it was also based on data from their earlier research. The tactics are mainly verbal and vary in the spectrum from complete denial or avoidance of conflict to full confrontation. We hope it serves as an example and foundation for the future development of conflict management tactics in intercultural public relations contexts.

1. Denial and equivocation

   a. *Direct denial*: Explicit rejection of the existence of conflict.
   b. *Implicit denial*: Implicit rejection of the existence of conflict.
   c. *Evasive remarks*: Failure to admit or reject the existence of conflict after the other party asks about the conflict at hand.

2. Topic management

   a. *Topic shifts*: Changing the topic of conflict.
   b. *Topic avoidance*: Terminating the topic of conflict.

3. Noncommittal remarks

   a. *Noncommittal statement*: A message that pertains to the issue of conflict, but does not make a clear stand.
   b. *Noncommittal questions*: Questions relevant but not focused on the issue.

    c. *Abstract remarks*: Principle-based, hypothetical, non-concrete statements "that are not evasive remarks" (p. 166).

    d. *Procedural remarks*: General conversation rule-based remarks.

4. Irrelevant remarks

    a. *Joking or use of humor*: "friendly joking or laughter" (p. 166).

5. Conciliatory remarks

    a. *Supportive remarks*: Remarks to show support, acceptance, relational closeness, and other positive regard.

    b. *Concessions*: Showing willingness to change and considering acceptance of the other's stand.

    c. *Acceptance of responsibility*: Accepting one's own or shared responsibility for conflict.

6. Analytic remarks

    a. *Descriptive statements*: Non-evaluative description of acts in conflict.

    b. *Disclosive statements*: Non-evaluative description of ideas and feelings in conflict that the other cannot observe.

    c. *Qualifying statements*: Remarks to define the nature and characteristics of the conflict.

    d. *Soliciting disclosure*: Questions that ask about the ideas and feelings that the other has.

7. Confrontational remarks

    a. *Personal criticism*: Statements that criticize the other person's personality or communication.

    b. *Rejection*: Direct, hostile denial of the other person's description of an issue or a person.

    c. *Hostile imperatives*: Adversarial demands; threatening or blaming statements.

    d. *Hostile jokes*: Other-deprecating, sarcastic, humiliating humor use.

    e. *Hostile questions*: Questions to show enmity or insult.

    f. *Presumptive remarks*: Accusations that the other is responsible for any negative ideas and feelings although not admitted.

    g. *Denial of responsibility*: Statements to reject responsibility.

Thus far, we have discussed the concepts of conflict; conflict management styles and strategies; the relationships between goals, strategies, and tactics; the extant literature in conflict management; and recent theoretical framework of a goals approach. Next, we discuss negotiation and its relationship to conflict management in research.

Negotiation and Its Relation to Conflict Management

Definition and the Development of Negotiation in Communication

Although conflict management and negotiation are sometimes used interchangeably, these concepts are not the same. One of the popular anecdotes on this point is the tale of two sisters, who agree over the division of an orange between them (Fisher & Ury, 1981). Each would like the entire orange. The solution is to split it 50–50, which although is fair, it is not necessarily wise. One sister proceeds to peel the orange, discard the peel and eat her half of the fruit; the other peels the orange, discards the fruit, and uses her part of the peel to bake a cake. The key in any negotiation and conflict settlement is to understand each side's underlying interests, needs, and values instead of focusing on each side's positions. Whereas conflict management is focused more on understanding the conflict situation in terms of incompatible goals, activities, interdependent nature of the involved parties, and potential emotional arousal, negotiation is focused more on finding a solution that both parties can potentially accept.

Putnam and Roloff (1992) defined *negotiation* as "two or more interdependent parties who perceive incompatible goals and engage in social interaction to reach a mutually satisfactory outcome" (p. 3). This definition is similar to the definition of conflict, with the difference in the focal point on the last part, or the solution. To a certain degree, negotiation resembles conflict resolution more than conflict management. Conflict resolution aims to find a solution and usually implies the negativity of conflict, yet conflict management does not have this connotation. In fact, conflict in various situations can be positive or even encouraged. For example, task-oriented conflict is necessary and inevitable in the workplace, and when managed effectively (e.g., minimal negative emotional involvement), promotes productivity (Mooney et al., 2007). In close relationships, manifest conflict can initiate topic discussion and has more positive relational outcomes than does topic avoidance (Wang et al., 2012). Thus, negotiation should be treated as a distinctive concept, even though some strategies to manage conflict and negotiation overlap.

Negotiation is a special case of communication. Indeed, all negotiation can only happen through communication. Putnam and Wilson (1992) traced communication research in negotiation back to the 1960s, when game theory, influence communication, interpersonal communication and conflict, social conflicts, rhetoric with a focus on persuasion, and mediation began to flourish. Negotiation scholarship also crosses the literature in strategic thinking and decision-making in the fields of psychology and business management (Steptoe-Warren, Howat, & Hume, 2011). Nonetheless, the essence of negotiation is communication because only through verbal and nonverbal exchanges can agreements be reached (Bell, 1988). Also, negotiation is a distinctive type of communication; it uses persuasion with a goal of problem solving and expects bargaining (Putnam & Wilson, 1982).

Negotiation analysis has been distinguished among five types (Zartman, 1988; Putnam & Roloff, 1992). *Structural analysis* aims to analyze the relative positioning of the involved parties through a hierarchy and power lens. *Strategic analysis* is focused on the application of game theory in understanding perceived utilities, evaluation of choices, and decision-making. *Process analysis* is focused on the dynamics of giving and taking and their relationship with outcomes. *Behavioral analysis* centers on the negotiators, their personal traits and likes, and their communication behaviors. Last, *integrative analysis* is focused on the ongoing nature of negotiation and approaches negotiation through sequential stages and related events in each encounter. Communication scholars can apply different analytical approaches based on the context and type of negotiation of research interest.

Putnam and Roloff (1992) proposed that negotiation literature could be studied across different disciplines including "behavioral decision theory, economics, social psychology, sociology, political science, communication, anthropology, . . . marketing, and industrial relations" (p. 6). In international communication, developmental communication and international relations, negotiation at the state-level can also be approached through a communication perspective combined with appropriate negotiation analytical frameworks. Sometimes, interdisciplinary literature can be helpful in understanding a specific type of negotiation. For example, the 2017 social and mass media insult exchange between the North Korean leader, Kim Jong-un, who called President Trump a dotard, and President Trump, who called Kim a rocket man (Ramzy, 2017), can be analyzed through a rhetoric as well as international relations lens. The analysis can be focused on behavioral analysis because both leaders' personalities and backgrounds can shed light on their language choices, and on integrative analysis because the serial events prior to these direct mutual insults must be understood to solve the puzzle of why these two leaders use this type of "dialogue" and what goals they aim to achieve.

More recently, Putnam (2010) wrote a reflective piece on the negotiation literature in communication in the past half century. Her goal was to provide insights to promulgate positive negotiation processes and outcomes. First, she argued that people should treat differentiation constructively without bias. By understanding the opposing views and positions, the involved parties are able to develop the central issue to focus on and to reshape. Second, both parties should openly exchange information and pay special attention to what the other party omits; this way both can understand deep concerns of each other. Third, both parties should not try to smooth things out quickly and reach a premature closure. Fourth, both should agree to disagree with respect. Fifth, avoid labeling the issue under discussion as a "conflict" or other negative term. Sixth, engage in effective question development and joint storytelling. Seventh, learn non-adversarial conversational rituals. The central idea of these suggestions is to fully use the co-creative and negotiative nature of interpersonal communication. When people treat differences with respect instead of fear or antagonism, allow other- and mutual-gains, and adopt a relational building and collaborative attitude, mutually satisfactory negotiation is probable in most cases.

Other Key Terms in Negotiation Literature

Some other key terms are introduced here. *Issues and issue groups* are broad conflicts. Typically, parties need to reconceptualize the initial issues to reach some agreement. They typically need to negotiate an abstract formula of the overall agreement and then fill in the details (Carnevale & Pruitt, 1992). Topics under consideration in negotiation can usually be divided into one or more issues requiring separate decisions by the parties. When several issues are related, they are often discussed at the same time, in what can be called an "issue group."

Problems are more specific issues. *Position* refers to overt stances on issues. *Interests* are the underlying goals of an organization on which positions are based. *BATNA* (best alternative for a negotiated agreement) refers to an alternative better solution for an organization if no agreement results (Carnevale & Pruitt, 1992).

In the negotiation process, game theory and social exchange theory are important to consider. Carnevale and Pruitt (1992, p. 536) also discussed options, limits, and outcomes. *Options* are laid out at the beginning but can also be changed after creative thinking. In these options, utility is reflected (monetary value, level of happiness, etc.). *Limits* refer to the reservation prices (anything below will not concede). And *outcomes* may include: no agreement, victory for one party, simple compromise, or win–win (integrative agreement).

Both conflict management and negotiation can involve a third party. *Mediation* refers to the situation when a third party assists in discussion. *Arbitration* is used when a third party makes a binding decision (Carnevale & Pruitt, 1992, p. 532). Further, conflict management and negotiation, when going beyond the social interactional level, can escalate to *struggle*, which includes physical combat, wars of words, political contest, and taking unilateral advantage (Carnevale & Pruitt, 1992, p. 532). These three types (mediation, arbitration, and struggle) are used when dyadic communication between the involved parties is difficult, the trust level is low, the two parties are too proud or too angry, or the parties hold false belief (e.g., they can get more through struggle). Although mediation and arbitration can sometimes help involved parties reach a mutually perceived fair solution, struggle can endanger the relationship if no solution is found. It also can be expensive and risky (Carnevale & Pruitt, 1992, pp. 532–533).

Much negotiation research involves planning, strategic execution, and tactical execution. Wilson and Putnam (1990) discussed that in the planning of negotiation, a negotiator can develop three levels of goals: global, regional, and local. Wilson and Putnam (1990) defined *global goals* as the negotiators' plans of what to achieve overall (termed *final goals* in Donohue, 1990, and *consummate goals* in Benoit, 1990); the *regional goals* as the negotiators' plans of what to achieve in each encounter (*intermediate goals* in Donohue, 1990; and *contributory goals* in Benoit, 1990); and the *local goals* as the negotiators' plans of verbal tactics within each encounter. In each negotiation encounter, negotiators' local goals and tactics may be cooperative because these goals help regulate the exchange of information, the flow of conversation, and the maintenance of an amicable relationship. Negotiators' regional goals and strategies may be a combination of competitive and collaborative goals because gaining ground in each phase is important for the eventual outcome of the negotiation, but giving in to the other is also important to keep the conversation going. Negotiators' global goals and strategies may be instrumental if the main purpose of the negotiation is material benefit, such as in business negotiation. These goals and strategies may be socioemotional when the negotiation is mainly about emotional and relational outcomes, such as in divorce and custody negotiations. Thus, negotiation can also be studied with a goals–strategy–tactic approach similar to conflict management. The next section discusses a framework of negotiation strategies through a conflict management model.

Current Framework of Public Relations Negotiation Strategies

In the conflict management research, some researchers have specifically applied the two-dimensional models in negotiation (e.g., Carnevale & Pruitt, 1992; Thomas & Kilmann, 1974; Shell, 2001). They have examined determinants or sources of negotiation limits (including situation-based, person-based, and issue-based factors), used conflict management goals and styles in bargaining situations, and predicted negotiation outcomes. For example, based on Thomas and Kilmann's Instrument (TKI; 1974) to measure conflict management styles, Shell (2001) developed a Wharton–TKI bargaining style grid. Shell revised the original TKI into a personality assessment tool and applied it to various situations, such as negotiators' self-assessments, other-assessments, and team building. Below, we discuss Carnevale and Pruitt's (1992) negotiation frameworks based on Blake and Mouton's (1964) managerial grid. It was specifically adapted for negotiation and has been widely used (Bazerman, Curhan, Moore, & Valley, 2000). The model describes key concepts in the antecedents to negotiation, negotiation strategies, and negotiation outcomes.

Antecedents to Negotiation

Situation-Based Antecedents: Determinants or Sources of Limits

Most negotiators will place limits at the value of no agreement (will concede no lower than the best alternative to negotiated agreement or BATNA). Carnevale and Pruitt (1992) proposed ethical principles and principles of fairness in the process of negotiation, in particular:

1. *Equality*: Principles of equal division and equal concession.
2. *Fairness*: Gains proportional to the amount of work done.
3. *Shared principles*: Easiness to reach agreements.
4. *Different principles*: Difficulty to reach agreements; harder to solve than differences in pragmatics.
5. *Dissonance in principles*: Same principles but different interpretations, acceptance of different options.

These antecedents provide a sketch of socially expected ethical standards of negotiation. Two parties walk into a negotiation situation with the goal to reach a mutually agreeable and fair outcome. Although negotiations never lack for deceptions and information manipulation (Bazerman et al., 2000), negotiators, as social actors, understand the expected interaction rules and rituals in this type of social encounter. Although it is an earnest hope to work with those who share similar values and principles, people most often find others do not. Putnam (2010) argued that "scholars have long recognized that differentiation is fundamental to constructive conflict management" (p. 327). Contrary to the intuitive fear of differences, differentiation is linked to rewarding learning experience and "conflict transformation" (p. 327).

Further, these principles relate to the identity goals we have discussed earlier. Whereas equality and fairness represent universal moral standards in most cases, negotiators should also understand their own moral and personal standards and those of the other party. Most of the time, people behave without thinking about what standards or reasons guide their behavior. But when they feel frustrated or puzzled by others' responses, they should stop and think about the reasons that drive the awkwardness of their social interactions. The reasons may lie in their different principles, different interpretations of shared principles, or different means to achieve a shared goal.

Negotiator-Based Antecedents

In addition to the situational factors, the characteristics of negotiators themselves play a major role in the process. Carnevale and Pruitt (1992) distinguished between motivational and cognitive factors that affect negotiators. Negotiator goals predict their strategies, and their perception and information procedures predict negotiation outcomes. Carnevale and Pruitt described four mutually exclusive motivations: *individualistic* that indicate exclusive concern about one's own outcomes, *altruistic* which indicate exclusive concern about the other parties' outcomes, *cooperative* that include concern about both parties' outcomes, and *competitive* that show a desire to do better than the other party.

They argued that the individual orientation had appeared to be most researched in their time.

Carnevale and Pruitt (1992) also described two cognitive processes through which people process information: (a) heuristics and biases and (b) schematic information processing. Heuristics and biases are "mental shortcuts that provide erroneous judgments" (p. 554). *Heuristics*, or shortcuts and other simplifying strategies, include availability, representativeness, and anchoring and adjustment. Availability of information as a cue for judgments and representativeness ("making judgments on the basis of seemingly relevant characteristics that in fact belie the true state of affairs," p. 554) leads to too much reliance on historical analogies. *Anchoring and adjustment* is a simplifying strategy where "an arbitrarily chosen reference point has an inordinate influence on judgments" (p. 554). *Biases* tend to be present due to the framing of outcomes (gain vs. loss) and overconfidence.

Schematic information processing uses the "construction of organized knowledge structures that guide and potentially distort the acquisition, storage, and recall of information" (Carnevale & Pruitt, 1992, p. 554). Specifically, cognitive factors (perceptions of the other and of the situation) determine negotiation behaviors. Schemata influences information processing through the following (pp. 557–559):

1. *Selective attention and memory, which can perpetuate and exacerbate conflict*: Judgment of the same thing can be different.
2. *Fixed-pie perception*: Your win is my loss, zero sum or win/lose, false consensus effect, when we do not always share the same views or priorities.
3. *Illusory conflict*: When different parties want essentially the same thing regarding some issues ("common value issues") but do not realize it. This is also called "incompatibility error."
4. *Reactive devaluation*: Offers by opponents tend to be devalued
5. *Attribution and behavior*: Attributions negotiators make about the causes of behaviors influence reactions to those behaviors.
6. *Negotiation scripts*: Assumptions about certain procedures, guided by such scripts.
7. *Positive affect*: Tell jokes, to improve cooperation.

The negotiator-based antecedents show that without mindfulness, negotiators can easily fall into self-benefitting orientation with presumptive notions. The biased information process can lead to erroneous interpretation of the situation, the other, and potential outcomes. Moving beyond information processing, J.-N. Kim and Grunig's (2011) situational theory of problem solving proposed a more comprehensive model of information behaviors. When parties have heightened information selection, barring information that is not compatible with their previous or current beliefs, the conflict strategies adopted will be severely limited to those that are more combative. Negotiators bear the responsibility to constantly remind themselves to be mindful about taking mutual goals and perspectives into consideration, as well as reducing biases caused by perceptual traps.

Negotiation Strategies

Carnevale and Pruitt (1992) adapted the two-dimensional models in conflict management and proposed three negotiation strategies: concession-making (yielding), contending, and problem solving. For concession-making, an inverted U-shape relationship exists between the level of demand and the level of outcome. In other words, higher initial demands and slower concessions from either side make agreement less likely and less rapidly reached. Lower initial demands and faster concessions produce smaller outcomes for the party employing them and larger outcomes for the other party. It is somewhere in the middle, with moderate demands and moderate concessions, that produces better outcomes. Antecedents of concession-making include higher limits, aspirations (goals), time pressure, hostility, demands from one's own constituents, accountability, and constituent surveillance. Consequences or reactions to concession-making include matching and mismatching (Carnevale & Pruitt, 1992; Rhoades & Carnevale, 1999).

Contending is a "strategy aimed at pushing the other party in the direction of one's wishes" (Carnevale & Pruitt, 1992, p. 548). Contentious tactics include persuasive arguments (persuading the other party that concession-making is in his/her best interest), threats, and positional commitments (making the other party concede in order to reach some agreement). These tactics' effectiveness depends on the users' credibility as well as the likelihood that the other party can imitate these tactics. Antecedents of contending are related to those of concession-making in that the conditions that discourage concession-making tend to make people lean toward contending. An inverted U-shaped relationship may exist between power difference and contending: If the two parties have relatively equal power or highly unequal power, the parties are less likely to use contention. If a mild power difference exists, the more powerful party is more likely to use contention.

Problem solving aims at reaching a win–win solution (Carnevale & Pruitt, 1992, p. 551). This negotiation strategy is typically motivated by concerns for both one's own and the other's outcomes. Some main tactics include active listening, sharing one's own priorities, brainstorming for solutions, avoiding personal attacks, and putting oneself in the other's shoes (pp. 538, 552). In negotiation tasks that involve multiple issues, the following specific strategies can be used for potentially reaching win–win solutions: logrolling, where each party wins on the issues it finds important; expanding the pie; compensating the loser; cutting the losers' costs; and "bridging" that involves constructing new options that have not previously been considered. For the last strategy of bridging, the parties need to analyze interests, goals, values, and needs underlying each party's overt positions and reconceptualize the issue as achieving these underlying interests (Carnevale & Pruitt, 1992, p. 551).

To engage in problem solving, several factors need to be present. First, negotiators should be firm about their basic interests but flexible about the means to achieve these interests. Second, negotiators should be open to information exchange, especially their priorities or interests. Although some argue that unilateral disclosure can bring about danger, there is not adequate evidence. On the contrary, information sharing has been found to be closely related to positive negotiation outcomes (Cai, Wilson, & Drake, 2000). Openness and clear goals help build trust, which is key to using problem solving and finding win–win solutions.

Finally, Carnevale and Pruitt (1992) also proposed that when people have no interest in any gain, they will not be moved to negotiate, and hence, they will do nothing to approach the negotiation. This behavior is labeled as *inaction*.

Outcomes of Negotiation: Conflict Management Results

Carnevale and Pruitt (1992) identified the following main outcomes of negotiation. In Figure 4.2, the points correspond with the options available for settling an issue or issue group. Solid points represent issues known at the beginning of negotiation. Hollow points represent options that can be devised with some creative thinking. Axes represent utility to each party (i.e., monetary value, level of happiness). Dashed lines are the parties' limits ("reservation prices"). Ways in which negotiation can end include the following:

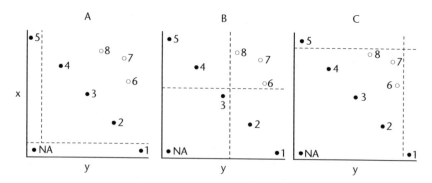

FIGURE 4.2 Three Contrasting Joint Utility Spaces

Source: Carnevale and Pruitt (1992). Reproduced with permission of Annual Reviews, Palo Alto, CA.

1. No agreement (i.e., point marked "NA").
2. Victory for one party (i.e., option 1 or 5).
3. Simple compromise (i.e., options 2, 3, or 4).
4. Win–win (i.e., options 6, 7, or 8).

Figure 4.2a shows a situation where both parties' limits are relatively low. Therefore several known alternatives are viable. Figure 4.2b on the other hand shows a situation where the limits are much higher, such that the obvious options are not viable. However, there is still some room for flexibility and creativity to reach win–win options. Figure 4.2c shows a situation where the parties' limits are so high that there are no viable options.

From the discussion of conflict management and negotiation, it is clear that successful negotiation must involve deliberate consideration of both parties' gains, willingness for information exchange, and minimal use of coercion when power play is not the dominant motivation. Putnam (2010) states that "negotiators should redefine issues, reframe conflict situations, and develop collective sense making to generate creative ways to transform disputes rather than to settle for easy compromises" (p. 333). To be a competent negotiator means to be a competent communicator. The essential beauty of communication is its co-creative power. When two people start talking, they form a new reality in every moment if they are willing to do it mindfully. No solution is the best solution. Negotiator perceptions decide what is "the best," and this best outcome cannot exist in one party's mind's eye. Rather, the solution is "the best" when the confirmation comes from the other and from outsiders. Therefore, satisfactory negotiation outcomes can never be a one-sided determination.

Expanded Model of Intercultural Public Relations Management

For collaboration among organizations and publics, there needs to be structured systems, processes, and rules set up for two-way symmetrical activities. Current frameworks of public relations negotiation strategies include the use of theory of principled negotiation (Fisher & Ury, 1983); being unconditionally constructive, which is a normative strategy (Fisher & Brown, 1989); and win–win negotiating (Jandt & Gillette, 1985; Susskind & Field, 1996).

Integrating different theories and stages of management, a new, expanded model of public relations conflict management in intercultural settings is proposed in Chapter 8.

Chapters 2, 3, and 4 have reviewed and integrated foundational theories in public relations management, intercultural communication, and conflict management and negotiation. Integrating different theories and stages of public relations management, a new, expanded model of public relations management

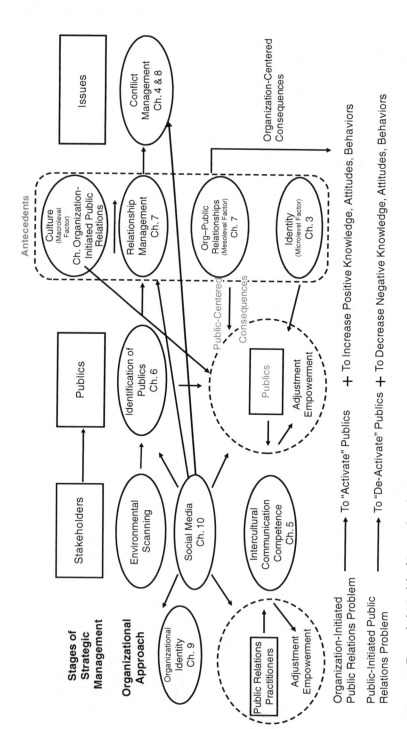

FIGURE 4.3 Expanded Model of Intercultural Public Relations Management

in intercultural settings is proposed. The following section explains the different elements, focusing on organization and public, respectively. The chapters in Part II of this book then discuss key elements in this model.

Organization-Focused Elements

Because this book adopts the strategic, managerial approach to public relations, we examine how different kinds of organizations can practice intercultural public relations in the most effective and ethical way. To illustrate this overall framework, we start with the strategic management process of public relations (see Figure 4.3, top). As the stages move from stakeholders, to publics, to issues, organizations need to respond using different strategies ranging from environmental scanning, identification of publics, relationship management, and conflict management.

Adapting and expanding the theoretical structure in J.-N. Kim and Ni (2013), this book further argues that, to achieve the different goals in the two types of public relations problem, different strategies will be needed. In particular, the goal of organization-initiated public relations problems is to "activate" the publics, from latent to aware or even active publics. This is accomplished primarily through public relations in the more traditional sense, i.e., messaging and persuasion (Chapter 2). On the other hand, the goal of public-initiated public relations problems is to "de-activate" the publics, from active (and usually angry) to aware or latent publics. This is accomplished primarily through relationship management and conflict management (Chapters 8 and 9) because messaging alone will not be sufficient or ethical. The publics cannot simply be persuaded if the organization does not engage in substantial, internal adjustment and change in terms of policies, procedures, and behaviors. This is also the essence of symmetrical communication.

Meanwhile, relationship management and conflict management have consequences for an organization both in terms of the traditional objectives of knowledge, attitude, and behavior, and also the communicative activeness of publics (see Figure 4.3, bottom).

Public-Focused Elements

However, at the same time, we argue that publics themselves need to take a central stage in intercultural public relations (see the dotted lines in the middle of Figure 4.3). Publics' own perceptions and communication behaviors are influenced by multiple levels of factors, many of which are not under the control of any organization. At the micro level, publics' perceptions and communication behaviors are influenced by their individual cultural identity (Chapter 3) and personal life experiences (Chapter 5), among other things. At the meso level, publics' perceptions and communication behaviors may be influenced by organizational factors, such as how organizations manage the relationships with these publics (organization–public relationships, Chapter 7), as well as how they manage conflicts with them (conflict management, Chapter 8). At the macro level, societal cultures including cultural dimensions (Chapter 3 and Chapter 9), among other things, may play a role in the formation of publics.

Highlighted in Figure 4.3 is the proactive nature of publics, who do not necessarily exist when in relation to a particular organization. Such independence from organizations is demonstrated, when the publics themselves need to adjust to a new cultural environment and build their own competencies (Chapter 5); when they can be empowered to communicate about issues that are important to them (Chapter 7), as well as when they perceive and manage a conflict not because they have a particular relationship with an organization, but because of their own values and identities (Chapter 8).

Finally, social media is increasingly playing an important role in any area of public relations. In our framework, social media plays a role in both the public and the organization. It influences the multiple antecedents of public formation, the identities of publics in particular, and their adjustment and empowerment. Social media also influences the organizational side in all areas, ranging from various organizational approaches to strategic management, and the maintenance and negotiation of organizational identity itself.

References

Afifi, W. A., & Guerrero, L. K. (2000). Conflict management through avoidance: Withholding complaints, suppressing arguments, and declaring topics taboo. In S. Petronio (Ed.), *Balancing the secrets of private disclosures* (pp. 165–179). Mahwah, NJ: Erlbaum.

Agiesta, J. (2017, September 30). CNN poll: Americans split on anthem protests. *CNN*. Retrieved from www.cnn.com/2017/09/29/politics/national-anthem-nfl-cnn-poll/index.html

Bailey, K. D. (1994). *Typologies and taxonomies: An introduction to classification techniques.* Thousand Oaks, CA: Sage.

Barki, H., & Hartwick, J. (2004). Conceptualizing the construct of interpersonal conflict. *International Journal of Conflict Management, 15,* 216–244. doi: 0.1108/eb022913

Baxter, L., & Bullis, C. (1986). Turning points in developing romantic relationships. *Human Communication Research, 12,* 469–493. doi: 10.1111/j.1468-2958.1986. tb00088.x

Bazerman, M. H., Curhan, J. R., Moore, D. A., & Valley, K. L. (2000). Negotiation. *Annual Review of Psychology, 51,* 279–314. doi: 10.1146/annurev.psych.51.1.279

Bell, D. V. J. (1988). Political linguistics and international negotiation. *Negotiation Journal, 4,* 233–246.

Benoit, P. J. (1990). The structure of interaction goals. In J. A. Anderson (Ed.), *Communication yearbook* (Vol. 13, pp. 407–416). Newbury Park, CA: Sage.

Blake, R. R., & Mouton, J. S. (1964). *The managerial grid.* Houston, TX: Gulf.

Cai, D. A., & Fink, E. L. (2002). Conflict style differences between individualists and collectivists. *Communication Monographs, 69,* 67–87. doi:10.1080/03637750216536

Cai, D. A., Wilson, S. R., & Drake, L. E. (2000). Culture in the context of intercultural negotiation: Individualism–collectivism and paths to integrative agreements. *Human Communication Research, 26*, 591–617.

Carnevale, P. J., & Pruitt, D. G. (1992). Negotiation and mediation. *Annual Review of Psychology, 43*, 531–582.

Cody, M. J., Canary, D. J., & Smith, S. W. (1994). Compliance-gaining goals: An inductive analysis of actors' goal types, strategies, and successes. In J. Daly & J. Wiemann (Eds.), *Communicating strategically: Strategies in interpersonal communication* (pp. 33–90). Hillsdale, NJ: Erlbaum.

Crokenberg, S., & Langrock, A. (2001). The role of specific emotions in children's responses to interparental conflict: A test of the model. *Journal of Family Psychology, 15*, 163–183.

De Dreu, C. K. W., Harinck, F., & Van Vianen, A. E. M. (1999). Conflict and performance in groups and organizations. In C. L. Cooper & I. Robertson (Eds.), *International review of industrial and organizational psychology* (Vol. 14, pp. 369–414). Indianapolis, IN: Wiley.

Deutsch, M. (1973). *The resolution of conflict.* New Haven, CT: Yale University Press.

Deutsch, M. (2002). Social psychology's contribution to the study of conflict resolution. *Negotiation Journal, 18*, 307–320. doi: 10.1023/A:1021041903956

Dillard, J. P. (2015). Goals–plans–action theory of message production: Making influence messages. In D. O. Braithwaite & P. Schrodt (Eds.), *Engaging theories in interpersonal communication: Multiple perspectives* (2nd ed., pp. 63–74). Los Angeles, CA: Sage.

Dillard, J. P., & Schrader, D. C. (1998). Reply: On the utility of the goals–plans–action sequence. *Communication Studies, 49*, 300–304. doi:10.1080/10510979809368540

Dillard, J. P., Segrin, C., & Harden, J. M. (1989). Primary and secondary goals in the production of interpersonal influence messages. *Communications Monographs, 56*, 19–38. doi: 10.1080/03637758909390247

Donohue, W. A. (1990). Interaction goals in negotiation: A critique. Commentary on Wilson and Putnam. In J. A. Anderson (Ed.), *Communication yearbook* (Vol. 13, pp. 417–427). Newbury Park, CA: Sage.

Jandt, F. E., & Gillette, P. J. (1985). *Win–win negotiating: Turning conflict into agreement.* New York, NY: Wiley.

Fisher, R., & Brown, S. (1989). *Getting together: Building relationships as we negotiate.* New York, NY: Penguin.

Fisher, R., & Ury, W. (1981). *Getting to yes: Negotiating agreement without giving in.* New York, NY: Penguin.

Friedman, R. A. Tidd, S. T., Currall, S. C., & Tsai, J. C. (2000). What goes around comes around: The impact of personal conflict style on work conflict and stress. *International Journal of Conflict Management, 11*, 32–55. doi: 10.1108/eb022834

Goffman, E. (1959). *The presentation of self in everyday life.* New York, NY: Doubleday.

Jehn, K. A., & Bendersky, C. (2003). Intragroup conflict in organizations: A contingency perspective on the conflict–outcome relationship. *Research in Organizational Behavior, 25*, 187–242. doi: 10.1016/S0191-3085(03)25005-X

Kim, J.-N., & Grunig, J. E. (2011). Problem-solving and communicative action: A situational theory of problem solving. *Journal of Communication, 61*, 120–149. doi: 10.1111/j.1460-2466.2010.01529.x.

Kim, J.-N., & Ni, L. (2013). Two types of public relations problems and integrating formative and evaluative research: A review of research programs within the behavioral, strategic management paradigm. *Journal of Public Relations Research, 25*, 1–29. doi: 10.1080/1062726X.2012.723276

Lazarus, R., & Lazarus, B. (1994). *Passion and reason: Making sense of our emotions.* New York, NY: Oxford University Press.

Lewicki, R., Saunders, D. M., & Minton, J. M. (1997). *Essentials of negotiation.* Chicago, IL: Irwin.

Lewin (1935). *A dynamic theory of personality.* New York, NY: McGraw-Hill.

Messman, S. J., & Canary, D. J. (1998). Patterns of conflict in personal relationships. In B. H. Spitzberg & W. R. Cupach (Eds.), *The dark side of close relationships* (pp. 121–149). Mahwah, NJ: Erlbaum.

Mooney, A. C., Holahan, P. J., & Amason, A. C. (2007). Don't take it personally: Exploring cognitive conflict as a mediator of affective conflict. *Journal of Management Studies, 44,* 733–758. doi:10.1111/j.1467-6486.2006.00674.x

Oetzel, J. G., & Ting-Toomey, S. (2003). Face concerns in interpersonal conflict: A cross-cultural empirical test of the face negotiation theory. *Communication Research, 30,* 599–624. doi :10.1177/0093650203257841

Pondy, L. R. (1967). Organizational conflict: Concepts and models. *Administrative Science Quarterly, 12,* 296–320.

Pruitt, D. G., & Carnevale, P. J. (1993). *Negotiation in social conflict.* Pacific Grove, CA: Brooks/Cole.

Pruitt, D. G., & Rubin, J. Z. (1987). *Social conflict: Escalation, stalemate, and settlement.* New York, NY: Random House.

Putnam, L. L. (2006). Definitions and approaches to conflict and communication. In Oetzel, J. O. & S. Ting-Toomey (Eds.), *The Sage handbook of conflict communication: Integrating theory, research, and practice* (pp. 1–32). Thousand Oaks, CA: Sage.

Putnam, L. L. (2010). Communication as changing the negotiation game. *Journal of Applied Communication Research, 38,* 325–335. doi: 10.1080/00909882.2010.513999

Putnam, L. L., & Jones, T. S. (1982). Reciprocity in negotiations: An analysis of bargaining interaction. *Communication Monographs, 49,* 171–191.

Putnam, L. L., & Roloff, M. E. (1992). Communication perspectives on negotiation. In L. L. Putnam & M. E. Roloff (Eds.), *Communication and negotiation* (pp. 1–17). Newbury Park, CA: Sage.

Putnam, L. L., & Wilson, C. E. (1982). Communicative strategies in organizational conflicts: Reliability and validity of a measurement scale. In M. Burgoon (Ed.), *Communication yearbook* (Vol. 6, pp. 629–652). Newbury Park, CA: Sage.

Rahim, M. A. (1983). *Rahim organizational conflict inventories: Professional manual.* Palo Alto, CA: Consulting Psychologists Press.

Ramzy, A. (2017, September 22). Kim Jong-un called Trump a "dotard." What does that even mean? *New York Times.* Retrieved from www.nytimes.com/2017/09/22/world/asia/trump-north-korea-dotard.html

Rhoades, J. A., & Carnevale, P. J. (1999). The behavioral context of strategic choice in negotiation: A test of dual concern model. *Journal of Applied Social Psychology, 29,* 1777–1802.

Roloff, M. E., & Cloven, D. H. (1990). The chilling effect in interpersonal relationships: The reluctance to speak one's mind. In D. D. Cahn (Ed.), *Intimates in conflict: A communication perspective* (pp. 49–76). Hillsdale, NJ: Erlbaum.

Roloff, M. E., & Ifert, D. E. (2000). Conflict management through avoidance: Withholding complaints, suppressing arguments, and declaring topics taboo. In S. Petronio (Ed.), *Balancing the secrets of private disclosures* (pp. 151–163). Mahwah, NJ: Erlbaum.

Rubin, J. Z., & Levinger, G. (1995). Levels of analysis: In search of generalizable knowledge. In B. B. Bunker & J. Z. Rubin (Eds.), *Conflict, cooperation, and justice: Essays inspired by the work of Morton Deutsch* (The Jossey-Bass management series and The Jossey-Bass conflict resolution series, pp. 13–38). San Francisco, CA: Jossey-Bass.

Rubin, J. Z., Pruitt, D. G., & Kim, S. H. (1994). *Social conflict: Escalation, stalemate, and settlement* (2nd ed.). New York, NY: McGraw-Hill.

Ruble, T. L., & Thomas, K. W. (1976). Support for a two-dimensional model of conflict behavior. *Organizational Behavior and Human Performance, 16*, 143–155.

Saarni, C., Mumme, D., & Campos, J. J. (1997). Emotional development: Action, communication, and understanding. In W. Damon (Series Ed.) & N. Eisenberg (Vol. Ed.), *Handbook of child psychology: Vol. 3. Social, emotional, and personality development* (pp. 237–309). New York: Wiley.

Samp, J. A., & Solomon, D. H. (1998). Communicative responses to problematic events in close relationships I. *Communication Research, 25*, 65–95.

Schrader, D. C., & Dillard, J. P. (1998). Goal structures and interpersonal influences. *Communication Studies, 49*, 276–293. doi: 10.1080/10510979809368538

Shell, G. R. (2001). Teaching ideas: Bargaining styles and negotiation: The Thomas–Kilmann conflict mode instrument in negotiation training. *Negotiation Journal, 17*, 155–174. doi: 10.1111/j.1571-9979.2001.tb00233.x

Sillars, A. L., & Wilmot, W. W. (1994). Communication strategies in conflict and mediation. In A. J. Daly & J. M. Wiemann (Eds.), *Strategic interpersonal communication* (pp. 163–190). Hillsdale, NJ: Lawrence.

Sorenson, R. L., Morse, E. A., & Savage, G. T. (1999). What motivates choice of conflict strategies? *International Journal of Conflict Management, 10*, 25–44. doi: 10.1108/eb022817

Steptoe-Warren, G., Howat, D., & Hume, I. (2011). Strategic thinking and decision-making: A literature review. *Journal of Strategy and Management, 4*, 238–250. doi: 10.1108/17554251111152261

Susskind, L., & Field, P. (1996). *Dealing with an angry public: The mutual gains approach to resolving disputes.* New York, NY: The Free Press.

Thomas, K. W. (1976). Conflict and conflict management. In M. D. Dunnette (Ed.), *Handbook of industrial and organizational psychology* (pp. 889–935). Chicago: Rand-McNally.

Thomas, K. W., & Kilmann, R. H. (1974). *Thomas–Kilmann Conflict MODE Instrument.* Tuxedo, NY: Xicom.

Thompson, R. A. (1998). Early sociopersonality development. In W. Damon (Series Ed.) & N. Eisenberg (Vol. Ed.), *The handbook of child psychology: Vol. 3. Social, emotional, and personality development* (pp. 25–104). New York, NY: Wiley.

Ting-Toomey, S. (1985). Toward a theory of conflict and culture. In W. B. Gudykunst, L. P. Stewart, & S. Ting-Toomey (Eds.), *Communication, culture, and organizational processes* (pp. 71–86). Beverly Hills, CA: Sage.

Ting-Toomey, S. (1988). Intercultural conflict styles: A face negotiation theory. In Y. Y. Kim & W. B. Gudykunst (Eds.), *Theories in intercultural communication* (pp. 213–238). Newbury Park, CA: Sage.

Ting-Toomey, S., & Kurogi, A. (1998). Facework competence in intercultural conflict: An updated face-negotiation theory. *International Journal of Intercultural Relations, 22*, 187–226.

Ting-Toomey, S., & Oetzel, J. G. (2001). *Managing intercultural conflict effectively.* Thousand Oaks, CA: Sage.

Tjosvold, D. (1998). Cooperative and competitive goal approach to conflict: Accomplishments and challenges. *Applied Psychology, 47,* 285–313. doi: 10.1111/j.1464-0597.1998.tb00025.x

Tjosvold, D. (2006). Defining conflict and making choices about its management: Lighting the dark side of organizational life. *International Journal of Conflict Management, 17,* 87–95.

Tsuji, A. (2017, September 22). President Trump says NFL players who protest anthem should be fired. *USA Today.* Retrieved from http://ftw.usatoday.com/2017/09/donald-trump-nfl-anthem-protest-alabama-rally-video-quotes-kneeling-fired-soft-concussion

Van de Vliert, E., & Kabanoff, B. (1990). Toward theory-based measures of conflict management. *Academy of Management Journal, 33,* 199–209.

Walsh, K. T. (2017, September 27). Poll: Majority doesn't think NFL players should be punished for anthem protests; Poll finds most would prefer players stand when the national anthem is played. *U.S. News.* Retrieved from www.usnews.com/news/ken-walshs-washington/articles/2017-09-27/poll-majority-doesnt-think-nfl-players-should-be-punished-for-anthem-protests

Wang, Q., Fink, E. L., & Cai, D. A. (2012). The effect of conflict goals on avoidance strategies: What does not communicating communicate? *Human Communication Research, 38,* 222–252. doi: 10.1111/j.1468-2958.2011.01421.x

Wilson, S. R. (1990). Development and test of a cognitive rules model of interaction goals. *Communication Monographs, 57,* 81–103. doi: 10.1080/03637759009376188

Wilson, S. R. (2002). *Seeking and resisting compliance: Why people say what they do when trying to influence others.* Thousand Oaks, CA: Sage.

Wilson, S. R., & Putnam, L. L. (1990). Interaction goals in negotiation. In J. A. Anderson (Ed.), *Communication yearbook* (Vol. 13, pp. 374–406). Newbury Park, CA: Sage.

Wilson, S. R., Aleman, C. G., & Leatham, G. (1998). Identity implications of influence goals: A revised analysis of face-threatening acts and application to seeking compliance with same-sex friends. *Human Communication Research, 25,* 64–96. doi: 0.1111/j.1468-2958.1998.tb00437.x

Wyche, S. (2016, August 27). Colin Kaepernick explains why he sat during national anthem. *NFL News.* Retrieved from www.nfl.com/news/story/0ap3000000691077/article/colin-kaepernick-explains-why-he-sat-during-national-anthem

Zartman, I. W. (1988). Common elements in the analysis of the negotiation process. *Negotiation Journal, 4,* 31–43.

PART II

Intercultural Public Relations at Various Levels

5

INTERPERSONAL LEVEL

Competencies and Practices

This chapter highlights key theories and concepts that can be used to theorize about the processes for strategic intercultural public relations management at the interpersonal level. The chapter starts by establishing a case for the importance of intercultural communication competencies from the perspective of any player in intercultural settings, both public relations practitioners and publics. The chapter then provides an overview of the various theoretical frameworks in intercultural communication competencies (ICC), followed by a discussion of ICC development for public relations practitioners and publics, respectively. For practitioners, it is noted that such competencies involve multiple levels, going beyond the typical knowledge base required for those practicing in intercultural settings. For publics, the chapter follows with a discussion of various theoretical approaches in acculturation and adaptation to enhance the overall well-being of culturally diverse publics such as ethnic minority publics and immigrants. The chapter discusses these publics' cultural adjustments and adaptations, as well as outcomes reflected in mental health, career advancement, and social support. The chapter ends with discussing and providing a framework for theories in training and competency building for both practitioners and publics. This discussion includes current status of training, different approaches to competency building and training, strategies and methods, and evaluation of such training. The chapter ends with a brief conclusion on the implications of these theories for both scholarship and practice.

Importance of Intercultural Communication Competencies

A rise in international businesses and mergers has created the need for intercultural training. Companies used to mistakenly assume that employees who performed well in their home countries would also perform well abroad (e.g., Rost-Roth, 2007). Nowadays, the need for internationalization and intercultural training is not only evident in cases of traveling and working abroad, but also in increasingly diversified workplaces.

As outlined in previous chapters, the strategic management of public relations involves the process of how to identify, interact with, and manage relationships with publics. In today's globalized world, these publics tend to come from diverse cultural backgrounds both at home and abroad, adding more challenges to public relations. An understanding and appreciation of cultural differences that lead to effective communication with multicultural, multi-faith, and multi-ethnic publics are essential for the modern-day public relations practitioner.

For public relations *practitioners*, having intercultural communication competency is increasingly important regardless of whether they are entering a new culture to interact with publics of a different cultural background, or whether they are themselves minority practitioners who face implicit or explicit biases from others in their own working environment.

At the same time, organizations are facing increasingly diversified *publics* in terms of cultural manifestations such as race and ethnicity, gender, country of origin, religion, and sexual orientation. When these minority cultural group members enter a new culture, be it a new country, a new community (either physical or virtual), or an organization (their employer or a university), they face acculturation challenges and have to learn to adjust. In this process, their intercultural communication competency can be a crucial factor in how they adjust, as reflected in various outcomes such as mental health, financial stability, social integration, and political engagement (see Jimenez, 2011).

Theoretical Frameworks of Intercultural Communication Competencies

Multiple perspectives and approaches exist with regard to theorizing about intercultural communication competencies. One of the common themes in defining intercultural communication competencies includes two aspects: attention to one's own goal and attention to the relationship one is in. This is reflected in multiple researchers' definitions. Spitzberg (2000) presented a systems model and defined *intercultural communication competence* (ICC) as "an impression that behavior is appropriate and effective in a given context" (p. 375). Similarly, Lustig and Koester (2009) defined ICC as an individual's ability to conduct contextually and relationally appropriate communication that facilitates their goal attainment when interacting with a culturally different individual or group. Imahori and Cupach (2005) argued that the culture-general definition of ICC refers to the ability to behave effectively (i.e., achieve personal goals) and appropriately (i.e., treat others politely). They contended that these could be universal standards for intercultural communication competency.

Further, from a communication perspective in the context of intercultural adjustment, Y. Kim (2005) defined *host communication competence* as a visitor's or migrant's ability to decode (i.e., receiving and processing information) and encode (i.e., designing and executing "mental plans in initiating or responding to messages") "appropriately and effectively" in the host culture (p. 385).

Intercultural communication competency is a multi-domain, multi-level concept. A culture-general approach focuses on culturally universal standards. Certain personality traits and communication features are applicable across different cultures. On the other hand, a culture-specific approach is also applicable to ICC, because different cultures have different expectations regarding what communicative behaviors are considered effective and socially appropriate (Imahori & Cupach, 2005).

Imahori and Cupach (2005) also suggested a third, culture-synergistic definition for ICC. This approach focuses on the fact that relational partners are able to negotiate their own idiosyncratic ways of behaving competently within their relationship. This relationally negotiated competence reflects a synergy between the partners' distinct cultural expectations for competence.

Intercultural communication competency has also been examined in its different dimensions. Spitzberg (2000) distinguished among (a) individual-level ICC, which is composed of personality traits and communication skills; (b) episodic ICC, which is the ability to facilitate "competence interaction" of all conversing co-actors; and (c) relational ICC, which is the ability to develop, maintain, or restore a mutually satisfying relationship (p. 376). Y. Kim (2005) broke down host communication competence into three aspects: cognitive (knowledge of host language and culture); affective (motivational capacity, openness and willingness to learn and participate, and "emotional sensibilities in their experience of beauty, fun, joy, as well as despair, anger, and the like" p. 385); and operational (expression and enactment). Although this definition covers the "three commonly recognized categories" (p. 385), some of these elements in communication competence conceptually overlap with Y. Kim's (2005) discussion of *predisposition* (conditions prior to emigration) such as personality (e.g., openness) and preparedness (e.g., knowledge of language and culture).

Similarly, Lustig and Koester (2009) proposed four approaches to the study of ICC. The *trait* approach identifies personality characteristics that "allow a person to avoid failure and achieve success in intercultural encounters" (p. 64). The *perceptual* approach aims to uncover an individual's ability to manage psychological distress (e.g., Abe & Wiseman, 1983). The *behavioral* approach focuses on assessing communication acts in intercultural interactions (e.g., Martin & Hammer, 1989). The *culture-specific* approach describes a person's ability assessed within a specific culture.

Further, in discussing identity, Ting-Toomey (2005) identified different components, criteria, and outcomes for identity negotiation competence. The components include knowledge (matching cultural value issues with identity-related behaviors, e.g., focusing on process-oriented, relationship-based assumptions when communicating with collectivists and focusing on outcome-oriented, instrumental result-based assumptions when communicating with individualists); mindfulness (the readiness to shift frames of reference, motivation to use new categories to understand, and preparedness to experiment) as opposed to mindlessness (focusing on the familiar frames of reference, old categories, and customary ways of doing things); and identity negotiation skills (such as mindful listening, and identity validation—recognize, respond, and accept as real, p. 227).

Among these different levels or aspects of ICC, Van der Zee and van Oudenhoven's (2000, 2001) work seems to capture trait-level (cf. Lustig & Koester, 2009) or affective (cf. Y. Kim, 2005) intercultural competence. In particular, they developed a five-factor multicultural personality model to assess employees' intercultural competence in a workplace environment. *Cultural empathy* refers to "the capacity to clearly project an interest in others, as well as to obtain and to reflect a reasonably complete and accurate sense of another's thoughts, feelings, and/or experiences" (van der Zee & van Oudenhoven, 2000, p. 293). *Open-mindedness* refers to an open and unprejudiced attitude toward outgroup members and toward different cultural norms and values. *Flexibility* reflects a person's ability to switch from one set of strategies to another based on specific individuals and situations. *Emotional stability* refers to the ability to remain calm and regulate emotions in various situations. Finally, *social initiative* refers to the inclination to take active initiatives to approach social situations.

Gudykunst's (2005) *anxiety and uncertainty management* (AUM) theory has also been identified as an ICC theory because it is focused on cognitive and affective management to reach effective communication in an intercultural setting (Wiseman, 2002). AUM connects the perceptual and enactment levels (behavioral level, per Lustig & Koester, 2009; or operational, per Y. Kim, 2005) of competency. AUM discusses the ability to manage psychological distress in intercultural encounters through the management of uncertainty (i.e., the lack of confidence in making attributions or predictions about others or the environment) and anxiety (i.e., the apprehension of possible negative outcomes, per Gudykunst & Hammer, 1988), which facilitate *effective communication* and *intercultural adjustment* when the immigrant feels emotionally stable, psychologically satisfied, socially appropriate, and communicatively capable (Gudykunst, 2005). See Chapter 3 for more on AUM theory.

In the field of public relations, Sha and Ford (2007) highlighted the importance of multicultural competence that included the following factors identified by Sheng (1995): self-awareness, multicultural relational skills, multicultural sensitivity, and managerial skills. Self-awareness means that practitioners need to be aware of the influence of their own cultural backgrounds on their perspectives and decisions. Multicultural relational skills are the ability to communicate with people from different cultures. Multicultural sensitivity means to be sensitive to cultural subtexts and concerns; sensitivity could be enhanced through education and personal experience. Finally, managerial skills are needed to design multicultural public relations programs that are free from interference from other organizational functions.

Integrating these different but related conceptualizations of competence, we argue that a person's intercultural communication competence can consist of three categories: culture-general, culture-specific, and enactment.

Culture-general competence refers to the ability to behave effectively (i.e., achieve personal goals) and appropriately (i.e., treat others politely). It indicates predisposition (Y. Kim, 2005) and is typically affective. It can include personality traits such as openness (Y. Kim, 2005; van der Zee & van Oudenhoven, 2000), resilience (strength and positivity in Y. Kim, 2005; flexibility in van der Zee & van Oudenhoven, 2000), proactivity (motivation and willingness in Y. Kim, 2005), empathy, emotional stability (van der Zee & van Oudenhoven, 2000), mindfulness (Ting-Toomey, 2005), and self-awareness (Sha & Ford, 2007). Taken from a systems approach, these general traits apply to a human's adaptation in *any* new environment.

Culture-specific competence refers to the preparedness specific to a new cultural environment, in particular the cognitive knowledge about different expectations in specific cultures regarding what communicative behaviors are considered effective and socially appropriate. This competence includes multicultural relational skills and sensitivity (cf. Sha & Ford, 2007) and can be acquired through formal and informal learning of the host's language and culture (including history, politics, economy, cultural values and practices, etc.). This acquisition can help reduce uncertainty and anxiety (cf. Gudykunst, 2005).

Enactment competence is an independent category, which can be influenced by and reinforce the other two competence types. It is typically operational, behavioral, and culture-synergistic. It describes the capacity of encoding a message and performing an act through appropriate verbal and nonverbal communication, consistent with Y. Kim's (2005) expression and enactment, Lustig and Koester's (2009) behavioral competence, Gudykunst's (2005) effective communication, and van der Zee and van Oudenhoven's (2000) social initiative.

Competency and Adaptation in Intercultural Public Relations: Practitioners

Public relations practitioners are interacting with increasingly diverse publics, both at home and abroad. The practitioners entering a new cultural environment face at least two levels of challenges. First, the practitioners need to adapt to a new environment or, in the case of minority practitioners, to multiple new environments both internal and external. Some practitioners may be considered as outsiders even within their organizations. In this process, these practitioners will need to adapt and form a new, fluid identity.

Second, externally, these practitioners need to interact with culturally diverse publics, and thus have to have an in-depth understanding of the challenges, dynamics, and outcomes of these publics' identity development. Such an understanding is essential in helping practitioners better engage and build relationships with organizational publics.

A rich body of literature exists on public relations practitioner education and career development, but not much information can be found on how to develop their intercultural competency and sensitivity, especially facing challenges both internally and externally.

Practitioners Interacting with Culturally Diverse Publics

Culture-General Competency

Some competency factors are universal regardless of which culture a public relations practitioner enters. At the organizational level, we need to explore how a practitioner entering a new cultural environment can adapt to the environment as well as to the publics so as to better build relationships with these publics, thereby achieving organizational goals. Given the constant conflicts and disagreements among different cultural groups in today's globalized world, the crucial role of two-way and symmetrical communication in public relations excellence should be recognized. This type of public relations practice aims at a genuine understanding of and adjustment to diverse publics, and thus makes it possible to acquire culture-specific knowledge. Research is particularly helpful in examining how practitioners develop the skill set needed to symmetrically communicate with diverse publics that have vastly different perspectives and interests.

Ni, Wang, and de la Flor (2015) studied the relationship between ICC levels and public relations practice preferences. They used a sample of public relations students, i.e., future practitioners, and found that the students' ICC levels were closely related to their preferred public relations practices. The three intercultural communication competence variables examined in this study were cultural empathy, open-mindedness, and flexibility. The four public relations practices included two-way, symmetrical, conserving and ethical communication. Together, the ICC variables significantly predicted the preferred use of all four public relations practices. Each ICC variable had a positive direct effect on symmetrical and ethical public relations practices. Empathy and flexibility each had a positive direct effect on two-way and conservation public relations practices.

Aiming to examine current practitioners' competency, Wang, Ni, and de la Flor (2014) explored a mediated ICC model for public relations practitioners in the context of the Peru mining industry. Results suggested that cultural empathy, open-mindedness, and flexibility (trait-level ICC) differently affected anxiety and uncertainty management (mediating variables; perceptual-level

ICC) and preferred public relations practices (outcome variables). Trait-level ICC showed significant direct and indirect effects on preferred public relations practices. Specifically, cultural empathy stood out as the critical competence trait: High empathy both reduced anxiety and uncertainty, as well as predicted symmetrical communication. Flexibility and open-mindedness played opposite roles in uncertainty and anxiety reduction: Flexibility reduced anxiety but not uncertainty, whereas open-mindedness reduced uncertainty but not anxiety. Such distress reduction enhanced the use of symmetrical and two-way public relations. Finally, symmetrical communication and lowered anxiety increased practitioners' perceptions of trust and control mutuality in the relationships their organizations had with the publics.

Culture-Specific Competency

Our current framework considers culture-specific competency to be multi-level. It can include macro-level knowledge about different countries and cultures; meso-level understanding of group dynamics, organization–public relationships, or organizational culture (Chapters 7 and 9); and micro-level knowledge about diverse publics themselves (Chapter 6).

The macro-level domain, i.e., societal knowledge of the culture-specific competency, has been explored extensively in current public relations research. The works by Sriramesh and colleagues (Sriramesh, 2004; Srirmesh & Vercic, 2009, 2012) have provided a vast body of research on the different areas of the world. Numerous other studies have also examined cultural values or dimensions, following primarily the framework of Hofstede (2001) through contextualized regional and country descriptions of public relations practices. In particular, such work has examined different political systems, economic systems, economic development levels, activism levels, media systems, and cultural values across different countries. They also have consolidated these culture-specific factors into specific variables that can influence public relations practices: *infrastructure* (political system, level of economic development, level of activism, and legal system); *culture* (societal and corporate); and *media environment* (media control, media outreach, and media access).

In addition to such macro-level, societal knowledge about each individual country or culture, knowing the identities, communication patterns, and formation of publics among different cultural groups at the micro level is also critical to building culture-specific competency. Chapter 6 details the process of identifying publics to examine the formation of publics, whereas this chapter only focuses on theories that shed light on building intercultural competence through communication in intercultural settings.

Co-cultural theory (Orbe & Spellers, 2005) is used to examine the interactions among under-represented or marginalized group members and dominant cultural group members. To reaffirm, culture is used here in a broad sense.

Cultural differences based on ethnicity, religion, gender, sexual orientation, disability, and socioeconomic status are all considered and can have different levels of salience. As Orbe and Spellers (2005) mentioned, co-cultural communication can happen when under-represented members perceive cultural differences as salient during any given interaction. An example they gave was an African American woman with a disability interacting with an able-bodied African American woman.

According to co-cultural theory, six interrelated factors influence the communication process among under-represented cultural groups and dominant groups. These factors are preferred outcomes (or the desired effect of an interaction); field of experience (sum of one's lived experiences, especially past interactions with dominant group members); abilities (physical and psychological limitations or ability to enact different practices); situational context (particular set of circumstances for interacting); perceived costs and rewards (gains and losses associated with different communication practices); and communication approach (speech style with a focus on confrontational level and type).

In particular, *preferred outcomes* include three main types: assimilation (to fit in to the dominant society through eliminating cultural differences or any unique characteristics of oneself), accommodation (to "transform existing dominant structures" by keeping some cultural uniqueness of everyone), and separation (to only form social communities with one's own co-cultural group and reject any bonding with the dominant groups; Orbe & Spellers, 2005, p. 175).

Communication approaches include nonassertive (nonconfrontational and putting the needs of others before one's own), aggressive (putting self needs before the needs of others), and assertive (a balance between the first two, "self-enhancing and expressive communication that takes into account the needs of both self and others") (Orbe & Spellers, 2005, p. 179).

Based on the three preferred outcomes (separation, accommodation, and assimilation) and three communication approaches (nonassertive, assertive, aggressive), nine main co-cultural orientations were identified (Orbe & Spellers, 2005, p. 176). These include nonassertive assimilation, assertive assimilation, aggressive assimilation, nonassertive accommodation, assertive accommodation, aggressive accommodation, nonassertive separation, assertive separation, and aggressive separation. Different examples for practices under each of the nine orientations were provided (see Table 5.1).

Orbe and Spellers (2005) used the typology above and explored how African American professional women negotiated their aesthetic representations in dominant-culture organizations. The authors identified three communication orientations: *nonassertive assimilation* where these women often dress more formally than needed to avoid reinforcing certain negative stereotypes, *assertive accommodation* where they often educate others in the organization about their hairstyles and other communicative acts, and *assertive assimilation* where they downplay aesthetic differences between dominant and subordinate groups by

TABLE 5.1 Co-Cultural Orientation

		Preferred outcome		
		Separation	Accommodation	Assimilation
Communication approach	Nonassertive	Nonassertive separation orientation	Nonassertive accommodation orientation	Nonassertive assimilation orientation
	Assertive	Assertive separation orientation	Assertive accommodation orientation	Assertive assimilation orientation
	Aggressive	Aggressive separation orientation	Aggressive accommodation orientation	Aggressive assimilation orientation

Source: Orbe and Spellers (2005). Reproduced with permission of Sage, Thousand Oaks, CA.

changing their hairstyle or clothing to blend in. These analyses showed how African American professional women navigate the organizational settings where they are considered as "outsiders within" (p. 182).

For public relations practitioners, learning how to manage situations to reach publics becomes a challenge, as well as how to improve interethnic communication between an organization and its publics. This co-cultural perspective can be used to gain a greater knowledge and understanding of diverse publics. It has been used in group counseling of inner-city youth and in a Civil Rights Health project that helped increase the ways community members discussed their experiences with civil rights issues (Orbe & Spellers, 2005).

When doing research on diverse publics, public relations practitioners need to consider the implications of the co-cultural theory for publics. Among the six factors identified, practitioners need to identify how they may use any or a combination of the factors to approach publics with varying types of co-cultural communication practices/strategies in varying stages of adaptation. They also should consider how publics may be formed and identified along with these six factors, what kinds of publics tend to grow out of one or more combinations of these factors, and essentially how to make sure the voices of marginalized publics are heard.

Enactment Competence

Enactment competence can be measured by the outcome of an intercultural interaction between a public relations practitioner and an organizational public. In the context of public relations research, this is seldom examined, perhaps because most of such interactions are not conducted just between individual practitioners and publics, but at an organizational level. Future research can explore this area at an interpersonal level.

Minority Public Relations Practitioners

The discussion in the previous section about competence applies to any public relations practitioners with the need to interact with publics different from themselves. However, minority practitioners face an additional layer of complexity in the sense that they themselves are often considered as outsiders even within an organization because of their marginalized position. The following discussion addresses this additional challenge and how minority practitioners can adapt effectively through competency building.

Current Research on Addressing Challenges for Minority Practitioners

Minority public relations practitioners themselves face implicit and explicit discrimination. Much literature has documented the struggle of female practitioners, ethnic minority practitioners (especially African American practitioners), and more recently LGBT practitioners (e.g., Hon, 1995; Pompper, 2005; Tindall & Waters, 2012). More studies are needed to examine how these minority public relations practitioners are doing in terms of their health, work–life balance, identity development, and career advancement.

These diversity issues for practitioners in public relations have been discussed extensively, with recommendations for individual-level changes, organizational/structural changes, and societal changes. For example, Hon (1995) identified the need for society to change perceptions about gender roles and proposed policy-level changes such as flexible work time for female practitioners. More recently, Tindall and Waters (2012) advocated for an increased awareness of the gay community, reduction of stereotypes, and adopting diversity-friendly policies.

In addition to these structural changes, what minority practitioners themselves can do at the personal level is also important. Most of the individual-level changes recommended in the current literature are focused on enhancing education and qualifications, getting more managerial experience and expertise, enhancing leadership skills, and proving the practitioners' worth to an organization and gaining power (see Hon, 1995; Pompper, 2005; Tindall & Waters, 2012).

In addition to these strategies specific to minority practitioners, some general strategies that can be used by *any* practitioner to gain more power and reduce marginalization at the organizational level are beneficial for minority practitioners to learn. For example, to gain *formal power*, the Excellence study served as one of the first that suggested multiple ways for public relations practitioners to gain access to the dominant coalition: use of two-way symmetrical communication, extensive use of research, and strategic (as opposed to operational) decision-making. Other scholars have proposed related strategies, such as the use of program research (Dozier, 1988); mixed-motive conflict resolution; short-term and long-term usage of negotiation tactics (Plowman, 1998); cyber-bridging, or how to connect with or influence the dominant coalition using information from the Internet (Kornegay & Grunig, 1998) for conducting environmental scanning and informal and evaluation research; and playing an advising or counseling role, especially as ethical conscience (Bowen, 2008).

As Dozier (1988) pointed out, authority or official position is not the only way to gain power and influence. People low in the organizational hierarchy can gain *informal* power in different ways. O'Neil (2003) suggested the tactic of coalition to persuade the dominant coalition and gain influence. In particular, O'Neil's (2003) study found that it is the quality of time, not the amount of time, that practitioners spend with the dominant coalition during counseling sessions that helps practitioners build quality relationships and gain influence. Aiming to identify the factors that contribute to the organizational influence of corporate public relations practitioners, Neill's (2014) study found four such variables: perceptions of value, enactment of the managerial role, reporting relationship, and years of professional experience. The upward influence tactics of rationality, assertiveness, coalition, and ingratiation also contributed to practitioners' organizational influence. Neill (2014) also emphasized the need to know "how and why coalitions are formed, particularly specific accounts of times when public relations practitioners engaged them and who they recruited as allies" (p. 599). Kanihan, Hansen, Blair, Shore, and Myers (2011) found four attributes of informal power that differentiate communications managers who are in the dominant coalition from those who are not: reciprocal trust, strategic business decision-making, social inclusion, and communication expertise. All these strategies can be helpful for minority practitioners as well.

Gaining Intercultural Communication Competence for Minority Practitioners

Although useful, these recommendations in the current research lack a communication and competence perspective: How can minority practitioners use communication to gain more recognition in the organization? We examine here how minority practitioners can build intercultural communication competencies in their efforts to adapt to and gain acceptance in an organization and in the profession. In particular, we apply Orbe and Spellers' (2005) co-cultural theory to analyze the interaction between minority public relations practitioners and the dominant cultural group in an organization.

Integrating this six-factor communicative perspective with current public relations literature on diversity, we propose a framework of building competence and improving adaptation that includes three main categories: preparation (field of experience and abilities), anticipation (preferred outcomes and perceived costs and rewards), and implementation (situational context and communication approach).

When minority practitioners need to adjust to their work environment or professional environment, they can work on improving in all three categories. They can enhance their field of experience and abilities by obtaining more education and training, as well as requesting more work assignments in the particular field.

They may plan for their communication with co-workers, supervisors, clients, and professional colleagues by assessing the ultimate goal, as well as the costs and rewards of each communication interaction. Finally, they should adjust their communication approach by taking into consideration the situational contexts.

Orbe and Spellers' (2005) theory can be used to explore issues of assimilation, access to opportunity, and career advancement of minority practitioners. It provides a tool for helping these practitioners better assess and perhaps adjust their communicative actions in an organizational setting and better develop their competency from a communication point of view. Meanwhile, the integration of the six factors is flexible. Minority practitioners may change their strategies based on the co-actor's traits, the relationship between the co-actors, and the interaction situation.

Parker (2002) examined how African American women senior executives within dominant-culture organizations use strategic communication to negotiate identity in workplace interactions. When interacting in two salient interaction contexts, with white male colleagues and with African American coworkers and clients, these women used direct, indirect, and avoidance strategies to adapt, resist, or transform perceived challenges in such interactions. Not much research along this line has been conducted in public relations practice. It should be a future direction for research to further our understanding of the lived professional experiences of minority public relations practitioners.

We note that the discussion in the following section of competency and adaptation for members of diverse publics also applies to minority public relations practitioners. It should be referred to when understanding minority practitioners. This is because these particular practitioners play a dual role; they are themselves the marginalized internal public of a dominant culture group. They need to go through the same process when struggling to adapt to an organization and gaining intercultural communication competence.

Competency and Adaptation in Intercultural Public Relations: Diverse Publics

This section discusses the competency of diverse publics, i.e., minority cultural group members based on countries of origin (immigrants, expatriates), race and ethnicity, gender, sexual orientation, disability, and socioeconomic status. Most of the extant diversity studies on publics in public relations literature follow a critical cultural approach. Because this book does not focus on that particular approach, those studies are not reviewed extensively here. Instead, this book adapts theories in intercultural communication and the strategic management approach to public relations.

This section aims at exploring the challenges encountered by diverse groups, their learning process of how to identify their own competence to handle stressors from various sources, and how they can achieve optimum adaptation and identity building, if at all. For culturally diverse publics, the outcome of their adaptation can be reflected in similar aspects, including health, career advancement, identity development, and political engagement. These outcomes are discussed below in the context of immigrants, but keep in mind that the same framework applies to any group that enters a new cultural environment and has to go through some kind of adjustment and adaptation. Thus, the discussion in this section also applies to minority public relations practitioners, as noted above.

Challenges to Intercultural Communication Competence

According to the integrative communication theory of adaptation (Y. Kim, 2005), *adaptation* is a process through which immigrants "strive to establish and maintain a relatively stable, reciprocal, and functional relationship with the environment" (p. 380). In this process, they experience challenges to their cross-cultural competence, changes in the communication environment, and changes in affiliations with different cultures or individuals, all of which influence their development of a more resilient identity or the lack thereof.

When immigrants come to a new culture, a *deviation* (an encounter differently interpreted from the home culture) may become a *stressor* if it causes psychological *stress* ("a state of disequilibrium, manifested in emotional 'lows' of uncertainty, confusion, and anxiety," Y. Kim, 2005, p. 383). Overcoming the initial psychological resistance and driven by survival instinct, immigrants achieve certain kinds and levels of *acculturation* (acquiring some elements of the new culture) and *deculturation* (unlearning some elements of the old culture, Y. Kim, 2005).

From a communication perspective, an immigrant has a relatively well enculturated self and homeostasis within his or her original culture (Y. Kim, 2005). Decoding (interpreting) and encoding (expressing) messages are acquired competencies in the home culture. In the host culture (where they have moved to), however, the immigrant's decoding and encoding skills are both challenged. Familiar signs are often to be decoded differently, not to mention unfamiliar signs, and encoding becomes effortful, even straining, with the new linguistic and cultural system requirements (Y. Kim, 2005; Oberg, 1960). In other words, the immigrant experiences a loss of communication competence.

Examining immigrants' culture-general, culture-specific, and enactment competencies may help identify different kinds of stressors and coping strategies (or lack thereof), as well as facilitate training and competence building. For example, whereas some immigrants are well prepared in culture-specific competence, they may not possess culture-general competence traits. Or they have learned and trained on both competencies at school but still have limited enactment experience. Thus, knowing what kinds of situations become stressors helps facilitate the search for corresponding coping strategies. Granted, all the competencies embody and are perceived and assessed through social interactions, or the first-hand organism–environment contact in an open systems perspective (Y. Kim, 2005). Competence, communication, and adaptation form a dynamic cycle with each other as the organism keeps growing in the environment.

Outcomes of Adaptation

When adapting to a new cultural environment, different levels of intercultural communication competency, coupled with other internal and external factors, influence the outcomes of adaption, particularly in the form of identity development and acculturation.

Ting-Toomey (2005) identified different criteria and outcomes for identity negotiation competence. Similar to intercultural communication competence, the criteria of identity negotiation competence includes appropriate, effective, and satisfactory management of desired shared identity meanings and shared identity goals in an intercultural episode.

The focus of these outcomes is placed on identity satisfaction, or the feelings of being understood (not necessarily agreement but empathetic emotional impact); being respected (deemed legitimate, credible, being on an equal footing with members of other groups through collaborative and respectful dialogue); as well as being affirmatively valued (or positively endorsed, feeling worthwhile through confirming communication) (Ting-Toomey, 2005).

Overall, outcomes of adaption are reflected in acculturation and identity development. Acculturation has evolved from a unidimensional to a bidimensional construct (Rudmin, 2009; Salant & Lauderdale, 2003), and more recently, a multidimensional construct (Schwartz, Unger, Zamboanga, & Szapocznik, 2010). The *unidimensional* perspective (e.g., Gordon, 1964) takes the retention of the home culture and the adoption of the host culture as the opposing ends of the same continuum. Unsubscribing to the home culture is proposed to occur while acquiring the host culture is occurring. The *bidimensional* perspective takes acculturation and deculturation as orthogonal processes, occurring independently and resulting in four outcomes: *integration* (little deculturation and much acculturation), *assimilation* (much deculturation and much acculturation), *separation* (little deculturation and little acculturation), and *marginalization* (much deculturation and little acculturation) (Berry, 1997).

Schwartz et al. (2010) proposed a *multidimensional* model that includes three independent dimensions: behavioral acculturation (cultural practices), value acculturation (cultural values), and identity-based acculturation (cultural identifications). *Behavioral acculturation* includes changes in language use, media preferences, social affiliations, and cultural norms. *Value acculturation* refers to changes in belief systems, which may be culture-general (e.g., self-achievement) or culture-specific (e.g., communalism in African descent contexts and familism in Hispanic contexts; see Schwartz et al., 2010). *Identity-based acculturation* refers to the newly formed attachments to various cultural groups and the positive esteem derived from such attachments.

During acculturation, immigrants experience at least two identity formation processes: ethnic identity and U.S. American identity. Acculturation can be considered an accumulative decision-making process on what to do with the two cultural systems externally and internally. For example, biculturalism may take two forms: keeping the two cultures separate as pluralistic and situation-dependent, or synthesizing the two cultures into a singular system, consistent and situational invariant. One immigrant may imitate host member behavior without adopting the relevant value, whereas another may behave like host members because of wholehearted adoption of the relevant values. The adaptation outcome may culminate in the immigrant's internal question: Who do I want to be (or passively, can I be) in this culture eventually?

Schwartz et al. (2010) argued that, compared with the separationist approach, "blended" integration shows an immigrant's ability to activate appropriate cultural schemata in any given situation and thus leads to high self-esteem and low psychological stress. Y. Kim's (2005) concept of *intercultural identity* overlaps with Schwartz et al.'s concepts of value acculturation and identity acculturation. Intercultural identity is an outcome from "a continuous search for authenticity in self and others across group boundaries," through which "the original cultural identity begins to lose its distinctiveness and rigidity while an expanded and more flexible definition of self emerges" (Y. Kim, 2005, pp. 391–392). This redefinition of self is a healthy view of "who I am" in terms of its connection with various groups and independence from any of these groups; it fits Schwartz et al.'s (2010) conception of a combination of culture-general and culture-specific self (value acculturation), and of a positive view of self, freely associated with both ethnic and host groups (identity acculturation).

In the frameworks above, an immigrant's adaptation outcomes include both outward and inward expressions of the new identity in the host environment. In other words, one's adaptation outcome encloses both external and internal elements. Whereas outward elements can be reflected through external criteria such as income and workplace positions, internal adaptation success pertains to the immigrant's own evaluations and feelings. The internal struggles tend to be unexpressed and only fathomable through immigrants' own meaning-making.

Identity acculturation is the ultimate outcome of acculturation (Schwartz et al., 2010). Y. Kim (2005) used *intercultural transformation* to refer to a person's identity change after successful adaptation, characteristic of mental health and of unrestricted and unbounded identity by specific cultures (Y. Kim, 2005). Although ideally a transformed intercultural identity should bear both *individualization* elements, where a clear, stable, and confident self-concept in its own boundary and connection with others is built, and *universalization* elements, where the self-concept flies above the cultures and freely adopts any value as situation fits (Y. Kim, 2005), most adapting individuals find themselves oscillating between struggles, successes, confusion, and attempts for clarification.

Outcomes of adaptation have been examined in a few public relations studies. Jang and H. Kim (2013) conducted ten in-depth interviews and two focus groups to examine how young Korean Americans perceived cultural identity, utilized social capital, and identified conflicts that arose between themselves and their significant others, particularly focusing on how they integrated Korean and American cultures. The findings revealed that young Korean Americans had multifaceted, situational identities, which went beyond existing cultural stereotypes and maximized their religious-based social capital and human capital; and they experience a varying range of cultural tensions and conflicts in social settings. Therefore, Jang and H. Kim (2013) proposed situational cultural identity as a new category of intercultural public relations.

Ni, Wang, and Gogate (under review) conducted a study that contributes to identity research in intercultural public relations by focusing on the intercultural identity development of immigrant professionals (IPs), a special public that composes the U.S. labor force. The study examined the process of intercultural identity development through IPs' stress, adaptation, and intercultural communication competence, as well as the outcomes of such identity development. Some 23 interviews with Indian IPs in a major southern cosmopolitan area revealed three types of stressors: insufficiency in culture-specific knowledge and skills, ineffective expression, and imbalance in home and host social communication. Adaptation responses included active language- and culture-learning, perspective-taking, compromising, ignoring, passive acceptance, and active initiating and participating in social interactions. Further, IPs demonstrated three major types of intercultural identities: integrated with both cultures, non-integrated (leaning more toward either home or host culture), and ambivalent (rootless and uncertain about what culture to teach their children). In the context of intercultural identity development, the concepts of avowed and ascribed identities become even more nuanced.

Bernstein and Norwood (2008) examined ethnic differences in public participation through two key factors of conflict communication styles and sense of community. The study addressed these two factors as predictors of community meeting attendance by two ethnic minority groups—African Americans and Korean Americans. Overall, the findings supported the argument that ethnic differences in both conflict communication and sense of neighborhood or community were related to individuals' intent to attend a community meeting. These findings highlighted the importance of cultural sensitivity to ethnic differences in public meetings and suggested recommendations for facilitation of meeting processes.

Competent adaptation at both an individual level and a community level is particularly important, because when people feel acceptance and belonging, they are motivated to integrate and help their community develop. If they do not perceive themselves as being capable of becoming a community member, they may live distressfully or develop antisocial behavior, which may range from isolation to extreme violence. An example of the identity development of marginalized publics lies in the countering of violent extremism efforts. These publics, both immigrant and domestic, are vulnerable to radicalization efforts.

For newer immigrants (i.e., first- and second-generation), raising a sense of belonging to a specific community can be challenging because they have two different, and oftentimes conflicting, narratives of allegiance. One consists of mainstream institutions represented by host members, mass media, and social media, and the other by ethnic group members and ethnic media. Whereas ethnic group association can be comforting and help immigrants feel a sense of bonding, only a moderate or "healthy" amount is needed because heavy dependence on one's ethnic enclave could make immigrants feel disconnected and lacking the power to survive in mainstream society (Y. Kim, 2005). To be a resilient community member, a person needs to have perceived sufficiency in social capital, sense of community, collective efficacy, and community capacity/empowerment (Oetzel, 2009).

To strengthen young immigrants' resilience as community members and help them accumulate social capital, it is necessary to start with identity establishment. Newer immigrants often encounter an *identity dilemma*, or the questions of "who am I" and "where do I belong" in terms of the relationship between self and ingroups. As young immigrants in a new culture, they choose what cultural elements to keep or discard in terms of forming their identities. When they learn new cultural elements, they *acculturate*; when they unlearn their original ethnic cultural elements, they *deculturate* (Schwartz et al., 2010). Eventually a *cultural identity* becomes stable through the acculturation and deculturation processes.

Immigrant youth who lack a stable self-identity are susceptible to negative mental health outcomes, including stress, anxiety, and depression. These can develop from the youth's inability to integrate into the host society, especially if their ethnic backgrounds, cultural and/or religious values, and social relationships conflict with those of the host society (Paniagua & Yamada, 2013). Identity stability is desirable for immigrants because negative mental health outcomes are associated with the inability to adjust to cultural values, worldviews, religions, ethnic and racial identifications, social classes, gender roles, and social relationships (Paniagua & Yamada, 2013). The lack of a strong and clear identity can cause cognitive dissonance and negative emotions, which often lead to stress, anxiety, and depression (Berry, 2001; Mahmoud, Staten, Hall, & Lennie, 2012).

When experiencing high stress and perceived rejection from others, negative thoughts and expressions, including hatred and violence can become channels to connect with (or strike back at) the world. These negative associations can propel people to approach or form groups devoted to anti-social violence.

As such, effective and pro-social interventions during the acculturation and deculturation processes are key to the development of young immigrants' positive identities. Through these interventions, youth can develop resistance to the propaganda of violent extremism, participate in building positive narratives for themselves, and bring awareness and positive influences to those in their close social networks. Community engagement programs through strategic communication and relationship management can empower marginalized community members to establish or strengthen their sense of community belonging, and thereby build resistance against recruitment narratives from extremist groups, thus countering violent extremism.

Competency Building and Training

Having discussed the importance, dimensions, and processes of building intercultural communication competency for both public relations practitioners and members of the public, this section provides an overview of literature on training for such competency and intercultural adjustment. We note that some portion of intercultural communication competency is closely related to personality (i.e., trait-level competency), which is arguably difficult to change in the short term, or at all. However, with mindfulness and motivation to learn, it is highly possible that competency overall can be improved, as documented by literature in international business (e.g., Prestwich & Ho-Kim, 2009). In fact, as Sha and Ford (2007) argued, multicultural competencies as identified by Sheng (1995) are all "learned and learnable" (p. 394). In particular, they pointed out that anyone, regardless of whether they are a member of a particular cultural group, can become successful at managing multicultural public relations. This indicates that competence, especially culture-general competence, can be acquired through training.

This section starts by reviewing the current status of competency development and training for public relations practitioners, followed by various approaches to and strategies for competency training, and evaluation of competency building and training. It ends with a recommended framework for competency training.

Current Status of Competence Training for Practitioners

Sha and Ford (2007) highlighted the importance of multicultural competence that included the following factors identified by Sheng (1995): self-awareness, multicultural relational skills, multicultural sensitivity, and managerial skills.

Given the critical importance of competent practitioners in intercultural settings, it is surprising that not sufficient attention has been paid to this aspect in public relations education and training to help practitioners gain and enhance such competence. An empirical study by Freitag (2009) of members of the Public Relations Society of America (PRSA) indicated that only 16% of respondents had completed a course in cross-cultural or intercultural communication. In addition, although 90% of practitioners reported traveling outside of the United States, the level of preparedness for this travel was rather low, scoring the lowest among four related categories: preparation, success, satisfaction, and seeking attitude (desire for international assignments).

Freitag's (2009) model of ascending cultural competence potential predicts that success and satisfaction perceptions for international assignments are positively correlated with the desire for such assignments. Respondents felt that cross-cultural communication courses together with foreign language courses were the most important preparation for international assignments.

According to the *Public Relations Professional in 2015*, the PRSA Leadership Assembly completed a survey for what is needed for public relations professionals. PRSA defined ten areas of knowledge, skills, and abilities (KSAs): business literacy; communication models and theories; researching, planning, implementing and evaluating programs; media relations; ethics and law; management skills and issues; crisis communication management; using information technology efficiently; history of and current issues in public relations; and advanced communication skills (*Public Relations Professional in 2015*, 2011, p. 9). In response to the increasing trend toward globalization, the survey results also indicated the new requirement for "an ability to segment target publics, understand culture and belief systems and communicate in other languages" (p. 12).

Another major player in the professional field, the Commission on Public Relations Education, produced a summary report for the Industry-Educator Summit on Public Relations Education in 2015. The report identified some desirable characteristics of an entry-level public relations practitioner. The characteristics related to intercultural settings include personal traits (intellectual curiosity) and interpersonal skills or soft-skill competencies such as self-awareness, adaptability, assertiveness, collaboration, listening skills, and cultural sensitivity (Commission on Public Relations Education, 2015).

In terms of global knowledge, skills, and abilities (KSAs), global knowledge includes awareness of local sensitivities and cultural issues, and an understanding of ethical and legal issues across cultures. Global skills and abilities include speaking more than one language, having a global antenna, and embracing complexity and diversity. In another study on global standards for the public relations profession, the Global Body of Knowledge (GBOK) project (Valin, 2016, para. 10) identified a series of key knowledge, skills, and abilities, as well as behaviors needed for public relations professionals:

- *Knowledge*: The theoretical or practical understanding a practitioner requires in order to practice competently.
- *Foundational skills and abilities*: Universal and essential to practice anywhere in the world.
  - *Skills*: What practitioners need to learn and practice in order to act competently.
  - *Abilities*: The innate qualities of being able to act competently.
- *Behaviors*: How knowledge and skills are put into practice.

However, in this and most of the other projects, no systematic structure was provided for intercultural communication competency, nor was an integrated framework for training suggested. Only a few items were sporadically listed. These included "multi-cultural and global issues," "various world, social, political, economic and historical frameworks," "inclusiveness and accommodation: shows respect for and accommodation for diverse points of view, ethnicity and cultural differences," and "adaptability: is able to change course quickly due to events and scale activities in response to changing circumstances" (Valin, 2016).

To enhance competency in an intercultural setting, people should have self-awareness as well as the multidimensional nature of diversity. Tsetsura (2011) argued that, by looking at diversity as a multidimensional concept, public relations students could enrich their understanding and appreciation of one another. This realization would also help students examine and understand the complexities of their own identities, which may not have been evident and articulated in the past.

Approaches to Intercultural Communication Competency Training

Intercultural communication literature identified different perspectives and best practices for training in intercultural communication competency. Following the general theoretical approaches to intercultural communication competency discussed earlier in this chapter, training on such competency is classified into culture-general and culture-specific. Culture-general competency refers to areas of knowledge, skills, and enactment that are universal and go across different cultures. Culture-specific competency refers to knowledge and skills that are specific to one culture.

In addition to the different domains of competency, two routes to learning are proposed: didactic training (informative training based on the presentation of information) and experiential training (interaction-oriented). These two routes correspond to the two levels of competency, knowledge based and skill-enactment based (Rost-Roth, 2007).

Integrating these two dimensions of training, the following four types of training strategies emerged: culture-general informative training, culture-general interaction-oriented training, culture-specific informative training, and culture-specific interaction-oriented training. Typical activities in these four types of training are as follows (Rost-Roth, 2007).

Culture-General Informative Training

Activities include general cultural assimilator, seminars, training videos, case study analysis, and discourse analysis. This training emphasizes and is effective with cognitive learning, but the downside is that it may be too abstract.

Culture-General Interaction-Oriented Training

Activities include intercultural workshops, simulations, role-playing activities, and questionnaires. These mixed groups can experience cultural communication first hand, but the flaw is that tasks may not be taken seriously.

Culture-Specific Informative Training

Activities include culture-specific assimilator, language classes, specific seminars based on cultural areas, and case studies. This type of training can provide a thorough understanding of a specific culture, but it can also potentially increase and intensify stereotypes.

Culture-Specific Interaction Oriented Training

Activities include bicultural communication workshops, culture-specific seminars, negotiation role-plays, and sensitivity training. These training activities can provide an authentic experience created with a mixed group of individuals, but not all culture-specific knowledge can be included.

In addition to these training approaches with two main domains of competence, Prechtl and Lund (2007) identified six components of intercultural communication competency from the INCA project (2001–2004). Funded by the Commission of European Communities, the the INCA project aimed to develop a framework of intercultural competence and methods of assessing that competence. It was based primarily on three previous studies. Byram, Nichols, and Stevens (2001) included five components in their model: intercultural attitudes, knowledge, skills of interpreting and relations, skills of discovery and interaction, and critical cultural awareness. Kealey (1996) identified three key skill sets from studies of technical and managerial employees: adaptation, cross-cultural, and partnership skills. Kuhlmann and Stahl (1998) identified seven factors critical to success in an international working environment: tolerance for ambiguity, behavioral flexibility, goal orientation, sociability, as well as interest in other people, empathy, non-judgmentalness, and meta-communication skills.

The final six components of competence in INCA are: tolerance for ambiguity, behavioral flexibility, communicative awareness, knowledge discovery, respect for others, and empathy. The project also identified three elements in intercultural competency: motivation, skill/knowledge, and behavior, which roughly relate to the affective, behavioral, and cognitive (ABC) model of intercultural competency (see Ward, 2001). These domains and elements were summarized in a table (Prechtl & Lund, 2007, p. 476).

Very few studies in public relations have examined how exactly to train public relations practitioners. One such study (Benecke & Bezuidenhout, 2011) identified the view of educators regarding experiential learning and the different experiential learning methods used in the education and training of public relations learners in South Africa. The following section reviews some commonly used training strategies and methods.

Overview of Training Strategies and Methods

Some techniques of training typically used in international business contexts include the following (cf. Rost-Roth, 2007) and can be modified and adapted for use with both public relations practitioners and publics. After the review of these training methods, we summarize and integrate them under the different types of competencies in Table 5.2.

Simulations and role-plays are used frequently with the following three most common methods. Video conferences and experimental games are also used, and similar simulation games are to be expected with continuing technological advancements.

1. *Bafa-Bafa* is an experience-oriented method. Participants are divided into two groups, each representing a different culture (Alfa and Beta). Each group needs to first learn rules that are critical for their own culture and then engage in brief interactions with each other. The trainees then need to describe and explain what they experienced. Debriefing then follows, where issues like anxiety, culture shock, and attribution formation are discussed.
2. *Albatros* brings participants to a situation where they are confronted with new behaviors and experiences. They are asked to watch a role-play scenario and then describe what they see. Many will interpret and judge the characters based on their own experiences.
3. *Piglish* is a language-learning simulation. People are asked to learn a new language (Piglish) by following the specified rules of grammar, pronunciation, gestures, and vocabulary to repeat a familiar story in English (e.g., Three Little Pigs). Through this exercise, people experience some of the feelings associated with learning a new language.

Critical incidents and culture assimilators (also called intercultural sensitizers) are the types of training developed in the 1960s to prepare participants for encountering their own and other cultural orientation systems through cognitive insights. Critical incidents are conflict-relevant situations. They are used as case studies to disclose perspectives from both parties and understand how sometimes false interpretations occur (Rost-Roth, 2007).

The training concept of Linguistic Awareness of Cultures (LAC) places emphasis on differences in communication behaviors and aims to teach strategies for deriving cultural differences. It emphasizes psychological insights. Factors that are used include lexical items and social meanings, speech acts, conversational organization and convention of discourse, taboo subjects, levels of directness, register differences, paraverbal communication, nonverbal communication, value orientations and attitudes, and rituals. Each of these factors is to be analyzed to gain a deeper understanding of the culture.

Discourse analysis-based training aims to promote behavioral changes after participants reflect on their own work. It aims to reveal important communicative problems and to create behavioral changes by analyzing sound transcripts or video recordings and presenting these in role-play.

Coaching, consulting, and training on the job are recent tendencies in intercultural communication competency training. This on-the-job coaching and mediating is preferred over off-the-job training because it can offer more immediate reactions to "dysfunctional" situations.

Video and audio materials and websites containing training and assessment materials are also widely used and becoming more popular.

In addition to these individual techniques, Gudykunst (1998) provided a systematic training schedule based on the anxiety and uncertainty management theory applied to adjustment. This framework is focused on the perspective of the stranger, someone who just enters a new cultural environment, and the stranger's adjustment to the culture. It is noted that such adjustment is not a one-way process; hosts are included in the training as well.

The newcomer has two types of uncertainty about hosts. One is about hosts' attitudes, beliefs, values, and behaviors. The other is about why hosts behave the way they do. The newcomer's anxiety involves the heightened tense feeling of uneasiness when anticipating or engaging in communication with hosts. When anxiety and uncertainty are managed, strangers are more mindful, or more open to new information and aware of alternative perspectives, so that they can make more accurate predictions.

Overall, this theory-based adjustment training program helps trainees manage their uncertainty and anxiety and thus better adjust to new cultures. Here is a brief overview of the training program:

Session 1: Introductory session. The session focuses on trainees' long-term adjustment and immediate survival needs upon integrating into a new culture; cultural-general simulation (Bafa-Bafa) to help trainees understand how uncertainty and anxiety influence assimilating into the new culture.

Session 2: This session focuses on being more mindful. The training focuses on the three factors that lead to mindfulness, according to Langer (1989):

(1) creating new categories, (2) being open to new information, and (3) awareness of more than multiple perspectives.

Session 3: This session focuses on managing physical and mental effects of anxiety. Gudykunst (1998) states that techniques that work in the trainees' home culture will work in the new environment as well. These can be identified through role-playing.

Session 4: This session emphasizes managing uncertainty. To reduce uncertainty, trainees need to feel that they can "trust" host behaviors as "reliable" and responses as "predictable" according to Turner (1988). Trainees are taught the cultural variability framework to interpret host behavior. Within this framework, trainees are taught to reduce uncertainty in individualistic cultures (person-based information is emphasized) and collectivist cultures (group-based information is emphasized).

Session 5: Trainees interact with hosts using role-play to apply what has been learned, providing an opportunity to manage anxiety and uncertainty before joining the host culture in reality. This provides trainees with a context for behavior and cultural identity security.

Session 6: This session focuses on survival skills previously evaluated in a needs assessment, such as transportation, using telephones, ordering food, and finding a place to live in the host culture.

Session 7: Trainees summarize and evaluate what they have learned. Evaluation includes how useful simulations, role-plays, and other exercises have been in managing their anxiety and uncertainty.

Evaluation and Assessment of Intercultural Communication Competency Training

Assessment of training can be done through different methods, as summarized in Prechtl and Lund (2007): self-reports, judgments of significant others, archival and objective measures, evaluator observations, and measures of one's overt behavior; reactions, learning, transfer (use of the newly acquired knowledge, skills, and attitude), and results (improved quality); and changes in thinking, changes in feelings, and changes in behavior.

In the INCA project, after the team identified the components of intercultural communication competence, they sought to determine the various levels of competence by specifying the "basic," "intermediate," and "full" levels of competence. INCA developed a competence grid of descriptive "can-do" statements (Prechtl & Lund, 2007, p. 475) based loosely on the National Language Standards of the Languages National Training Organization.

Then, to assess such competence, INCA developed a procedure to map and record people's levels of competencies against the INCA grid. They determined that the assessment tools should be used for initial diagnosis and also for recognizing a candidate's potential for development. Borrowing from the European Language Portfolio used by the Council of Europe, they used three components to document a person's intercultural communication competence: *biography*, which was used to record an individual's intercultural events and situations; *passport*, which was used to provide the results of self-assessments or external assessments; and *dossier of evidence*, which contained certificates of completion, letters from peers, certificates of achievement, and so on.

Similar to the two types of training, information and experiential, INCA developed two types of tests for assessment: (a) cognitive and affective-oriented written exercises, which contained open-ended questions about intercultural situations, and (b) behavior-oriented exercises, which were conducted with participants from different cultural backgrounds.

Integrated Framework for Competency Training

Integrating the different dimensions and domains with the framework identified earlier in this chapter, we propose this revised model of intercultural communication competency training. This model provides nuanced levels of competency and suggests more targeted training and assessment methods.

In particular, as discussed earlier, one important perspective of ICC is that it is not just a self-reported concept, but a perceived concept. In other words, one can consider him- or herself competent, yet the other interactant or an observer may not feel so. In this case, the other's view is counted more heavily. Spitzberg's (2000) definition reflects this point. Thus, competency has both objective and subjective components. Biases are also often pointed out by others. For this reason, implicit bias needs to be acknowledged and assessed through objective reporting. In fact, the recent PWC Manifesto on diversity (CEO Action for Diversity and Inclusion, 2017) explicitly considers implicit bias as a problem and calls for the implementation and expansion of education regarding unconscious biases.

Below are the different dimensions of competency integrated into this new framework.

1. Culture-general: Personality traits
   a. Flexibility (van der Zee & van Oudenhoven, 2000).
   b. Empathy (Prechtl & Lund, 2007; van der Zee & van Oudenhoven, 2000).
   c. Emotional stability (van der Zee & van Oudenhoven, 2000).
   d. Tolerance for ambiguity; behavioral flexibility (Prechtl & Lund, 2007).
   e. Respect for others (Prechtl & Lund, 2007).
   f. Mindfulness (Ting-Toomey, 2005).
   g. Emotional regulation (van der Zee & van Oudenhoven, 2000).

TABLE 5.2 Integrated Framework for Intercultural Communication Competency Training

	Culture-general: Personality traits	Culture-general: Motivation	Culture-general: Knowledge	Culture-specific: Skill and knowledge	Enactment: Behavior
Informative training	Self-assessment to increase awareness of traits Exposure to alternative ways of thinking and behaviors	Self-assessment to increase awareness of motivation	Education programs in intercultural communication theory, anthropology, cultural psychology Culture-general assimilator Training videos Case study analysis Discourse analysis-based training	Self-assessment of implicitly held biases, via Implicit Association Test (IAT) Culture-specific assimilator Training videos Culture-specific seminars or education programs in history and cultural values, economic system, political system, and media system Language classes Linguistic awareness of cultures Case study analysis	n/a
Experiential training	Perspective-taking exercises	Intercultural identity awareness Stimulation of altruistic viewpoints and values	Intercultural communication workshops Simulations and role-plays for intercultural sensitization	Bicultural communication workshops Sensitivity training	Culture-specific simulations and role-plays Negotiation role-plays
Evaluation	Self-reports Judgments of significant others	Self-reports Judgments of significant others	Learning assessment	Learning assessment	Evaluator observation of overt behaviors

Note: For the Implicit Association Test (IAT) see https://implicit.harvard.edu/implicit/takeatest.html.

2. Culture-general: Motivation (refers to one's general eagerness to learn new things and adapt to new environments and people)

   a. Openness (Y. Kim, 2005; van der Zee & van Oudenhoven, 2000).
   b. Proactivity (motivation and willingness in Y. Kim, 2005).
   c. Communicative awareness (Prechtl & Lund, 2007).
   d. Knowledge discovery (Prechtl & Lund, 2007).
   e. Self-awareness (Sha & Ford, 2007; Tsetsura, 2011).

3. Culture-specific: Skill and knowledge

   a. Language.
   b. Cultural expectations and norms.
   c. Cultural contexts (including history, politics, economy, cultural values and practices, etc.).
   d. Implicit bias.
   e. Multicultural relational skills (Sha & Ford, 2007).
   f. Cultural values.

4. Enactment: Behavioral (refers to the capacity of encoding a message and performing an act through appropriate verbal and nonverbal communication). It is consistent with:

   a. Y. Kim's (2005) expression and enactment.
   b. Lustig and Koester's (2009) behavioral competence.
   c. Gudykunst's (2005) effective communication.
   d. van der Zee and van Oudenhoven's (2000) social initiative.

Both public relations practitioners and publics can use this model to enhance their intercultural communication competency to adapt and grow. To apply this to one particular case, for minority publics in different kinds of intercultural contexts, training can be done at individual, organizational, and societal levels. In particular, training on *culture-specific competence* should be focused on both linguistic and cultural competence. It is essential that minority publics such as immigrants recognize the importance of and actively participate in self-study at the individual level and that employing organizations or community organizations provide various training programs. Self-study and training could include language classes as well as seminars and workshops on cultural understanding about areas such as U.S. history, politics, economy, media, sports, literature, and entertainment or popular culture.

To enhance *enactment competence*, more work needs to be done at multiple levels because the frustration in communication and the perception of invisible lines cannot be overcome through individual efforts of immigrants only.

At the organizational level, immigrants' workplaces and community organizations could develop targeted training programs and social activities to help immigrants' integrative experience. Employing organizations can use more individual- or small-group centered social events rather than task-oriented interactions. Within community organizations serving immigrants, practitioners should conduct more training and intervention programs that involve immigrants and host culture members to establish goodness of fit between the two parties. The practitioners who work in organizations that facilitate immigration issues should focus on producing better cooperation between host culture and immigrant groups by establishing some basic ground rules for interaction, for example: (a) both groups should avoid using blame language toward either side, (b) the majority/host group members should refrain from accusing immigrants of "whining" and "over-sensitivity," and (c) immigrants should refrain from accusing members of the host culture of discrimination without substantive evidence. Community organizations should further provide services to facilitate mingling immigrants' children with those of host culture members. Introducing immigrants to various institutions in the host culture will be beneficial too, such as touring media, legal, and government facilities.

The overall host environment needs to be improved in terms of receptiveness to and an open and welcoming atmosphere for immigrants. At the societal level, policy changes need to take place that incorporate better integration efforts among various levels including governments, nonprofits, and corporations. As suggested by researchers from the Migration Policy Institute (2004), in order to address the integration needs of employment-based immigrants and their families effectively, governments at the national, regional, and local levels should work closely to assess how national migration policies affect state and local systems, such as education, health care, and social services. These societal institutions need to make efforts in the most cost-effective and fair way possible (see Papademetriou & Sumption, 2011). For example, the Building the New American Community Initiative (Migration Policy Institute, 2004) has done a fair job of emphasizing two-way interaction between immigrants and the receiving community, but it has not recognized explicitly the value of specific and communication-focused strategies such as social interaction training or awareness-building efforts. More such initiatives should be made.

Conclusion

In summary, intercultural communication competency at the interpersonal level is important for both public relations practitioners and members of publics themselves. This chapter advances the theoretical development in this area in two ways. First, by integrating various theoretical frameworks and identifying the common themes in these frameworks, this chapter proposes a new theoretical framework in ICC. This new framework includes three domains of competency (culture-general, culture-specific, and enactment competency), as well as three levels of competency: cognitive (knowledge), affective (emotive and motivational), and behavioral.

This chapter has discussed some initial research that examined the relationship between the intercultural communication competency of public relations practitioners and various practices and concepts in intercultural public relations. These include how different levels of public relations practitioner competency are related to relationship management (Wang et al., 2014), as well as how the different culture-general, trait-level competency of future public relations practitioners is related to their preferred public relations practices (Ni et al., 2015).

Future research should continue to examine and expand this framework to test the relationships between the intercultural communication competency of practitioners and public relations practices, as well as important outcome variables.

Further, following this new ICC framework and synthesizing the various approaches to and strategies for competency building and training, we have identified an integrated structure of competency training, with the corresponding approaches, strategies, and evaluation methods in this chapter. Little is known in public relations research on how to link the competency components needed with training or how to evaluate the effectiveness of different training strategies. Future research can employ the structure proposed in this chapter to fill this gap.

Taken together, this new model of intercultural communication competency adds value to public relations theory. In addition, it guides public relations practice in that it better informs both public relations practitioners and members of publics when they enter a new cultural environment. The perspective is that both practitioners and publics need to incorporate the different domains and dimensions of competency, initiate or participate in different training programs that aim for these domains and dimensions, and learn to adapt better to fulfill their personal goals and organizational goals.

References

Abe, H., & Wiseman, R. L. (1983). A cross-cultural confirmation of the dimensions of intercultural effectiveness. *International Journal of Intercultural Relations, 11*, 65–88.

Benecke, D. R., & Bezuidenhout, R.-M. (2011). Experiential learning in public relations education in South Africa. *Journal of Communication Management, 15*, 55–69.

Bernstein, A. G., & Norwood, R. S. (2008). Ethnic differences in public participation: The role of conflict communication styles and sense of community. *Journal of Intercultural Communication Research, 37*(2), 119–138. doi: 10.1080/17475750802533679

Berry, J. W. (1997). Immigration, acculturation, and adaptation. *Applied Psychology: An International Review, 46*(1), 5–34.

Berry, J. W. (2001). A psychology of immigration. *Journal of Social Issues, 57*(3), 615–631.

Bowen, S. (2008). A state of neglect: Public relations as "corporate conscience" or ethics counsel. *Journal of Public Relations Research, 20*, 271–296.

Byram, M., Nichols, A., & Stevens, D. (2001). *Developing intercultural competence in practice*. Clevedon, UK: Multilingual Matters.

CEO Action for Diversity and Inclusion (2017). *More than 150 CEOS make unprecedented commitment to advance diversity and inclusion in the workplace*. Retrieved from www.pwc.com/us/en/press-releases/2017/ceo-action-for-diversity-inclusion.html

Commission on Public Relations Education Industry-Educator Summit on Public Relations Education (2015). Retrieved from www.commpred.org/_uploads/industry-educator-summit-summary-report.pdf

Dozier, D. (1988). Breaking public relations' glass ceiling. *Public Relations Review, 14*(3), 6–14. doi: 10.1016/S0363-8111(88)80041-9

Freitag, A. (2009). Ascending cultural competence potential: An assessment and profile of U.S. public relations practitioners' preparation for international assignments. *Journal of Public Relations Research, 14*, 207–277. doi: 10.1207/S1532754XJPRR1403_3

Gordon, M. (1964). *Assimilation in American life*. New York, NY: Oxford University Press.

Gudykunst, W. B. (1998). Applying anxiety/uncertainty management (AUM) theory to intercultural adjustment training. *International Journal of Intercultural Relations, 22*, 227–250.

Gudykunst, W. B. (2005). An anxiety/uncertainty management (AUM) theory of strangers' intercultural adjustment. In W. B. Gudykunst (Ed.), *Theorizing about intercultural communication* (pp. 419–457). Thousand Oaks, CA: Sage.

Gudykunst, W. B., & Hammer, M. R. (1988). Strangers and hosts: An extension of uncertainty reduction theory to intercultural adjustment. In Y. Y. Kim & W. B. Gudykunst (Eds.), *Cross-cultural adaptation* (pp. 106–139). Newbury Park, CA: Sage.

Hon, L. C. (1995). Toward a feminist theory of public relations. *Journal of Public Relations Research, 7*, 27–88.

Hofstede, G. (2001). *Culture's consequences: Comparing values, behaviors, institutions, and organizations across nations* (2nd ed.). Thousand Oaks, CA: Sage.

Imahori, T. T., & Cupach, W. R. (2005). Identity management theory: Facework in intercultural relationships. In W. B. Gudykunst (Ed.), *Theorizing about intercultural communication* (pp. 195–210). Thousand Oaks, CA: Sage.

Jang, A., & Kim, H. (2013). Cultural identity, social capital, and social control of young Korean Americans: Extending the theory of intercultural public relations. *Journal of Public Relations Research, 25*, 225–245. doi: 10.1080/1062726X.2013.788444

Jimenez, T. R. (2011). Immigrants in the United States: How well are they integrating into society? *Migration Policy Institute*. Retrieved from www.migrationpolicy.org/research/immigrants-united-states-how-well-are-they-integrating-society

Kanihan, S., Hansen, K., Blair, S., Shore, M., & Myers, J. (2011). Communication managers in the dominant coalition: Power attributes and communication practices. *Journal of Communication Management, 17*(2), 140–156.

Kealey, D. J. (1996). The challenge of international personnel selection. In D. Landis & R. S. Bhagat (Eds.), *Handbook of intercultural training* (2nd ed., pp. 81–105). Thousand Oaks: Sage.

Kim, Y. Y. (2005). Adapting to a new culture: An integrative communication theory. In W. B. Gudykunst (Ed.), *Theorizing about intercultural communication* (pp. 375–400). Thousand Oaks, CA: Sage.

Kornegay, J., & Grunig, L. (1998). Cyberbridging: How the communication manager role can link with the dominant coalition. *Journal of Communication Management, 3*(2), 140–156.

Kuhlmann, T., & Stahl, M. (1998). Diagnose interkultureller kompetenz: Entwicklung und evaluierung eines Assessment-centers [Diagnosing intercultural competence: Development and evaluation of an assessment centre]. In C. Barmeyer & J. Bolten (Eds.), *Interkulturelle Personalorganisation* [*Intercultural Personnel Management*] (pp. 213–224). Sternenfels: Verlag fur Wissenschaft und Praxis.

Langer, E. (1989). *Mindfulness*. Reading, MA: Addison-Wesley.

Lustig, M. W., & Koester, J. (2009). *Intercultural competence: Interpersonal communication across cultures*. Upper Saddle River, NJ: Pearson.

Mahmoud, J. S. R., Staten, R. T., Hall, L. A., & Lennie, T. A. (2012). The relationship among young adult college students' depression, anxiety, stress, demographics, life satisfaction, and coping styles. *Issues in Mental Health Nursing, 33*(3), 149–156.

Martin, J. A., & Hammer, M. R. (1989). Behavioral categories of intercultural communication competence: Everyday communicators' perceptions. *International Journal of Intercultural Relations, 13*, 302–332.

Migration Policy Institute (2004). *Building the new American community initiative*. Retrieved from www.ncsl.org/Portals/1/documents/immig/BNAC_Report 1204.pdf

Neill, M. (2014). Building buy-in: The need for internal relationships and informal coalitions. *Public Relations Review, 40*(3), 598–605.

Ni, L., Wang, Q., & De la Flor, M. (2015). Intercultural communication competence and preferred public relations practices. *Journal of Communication Management, 19*, 167–183. doi: http://dx.doi.org/10.1108/JCOM-07-2012-0061

Ni, L., Wang, Q., & Gogate, A. (under review).

O'Neil, J. (2003). An investigation of the sources of influence of corporate public relations practitioners. *Public Relations Review, 29*(2), 159–169.

Oberg, K. (1960). Culture shock: Adjustment to new cultural environments. *Practical Anthropology, 7*(4), 177–182.

Oetzel, J. G. (2009). *Intercultural communication: A layered approach*. New York, NY: Vango Books.

Orbe, M. P., & Spellers, R. E. (2005). From the margins to the center: Utilizing co-cultural theory in diverse contexts. In W. B. Gudykunst (Ed.), *Theorizing about intercultural communication* (pp. 173–191). Thousand Oaks, CA: Sage.

Paniagua, F., & Yamada, A.-M. (2013). *Handbook of multicultural mental health: Assessment and treatment of diverse populations* (2nd ed.). New York, NY: Academic Press.

Papademetriou, D. G., & Sumption, M. (2011). *Eight policies to boost the economic contribution of employment-based immigration*. Migration Policy Institute. Retrieved from www.migrationpolicy.org/research/boosting-economic-contribution-employment-based-immigration

Plowman, K. (1998). Power in conflict for public relations. *Journal of Public Relations Research, 10*(4), 237–261.

Parker, P. S. (2002). Negotiating identity in raced and gendered workplace interactions: The use of strategic communication by African American women senior executives within dominant culture organizations. *Communication Quarterly, 50*(3/4), 251–268

Pompper, D. (2005). "Difference" in public relations research: A case for introducing Critical Race Theory. *Journal of Public Relations Research, 17*, 139–169. doi: 10.1207/s1532754xjprr1702_5

Prechtl, E., & Lund, A. D. (2007). Intercultural competence and assessment: Perspectives from the INCA project. In H. Kotthoff & H. Spencer-Oatey (Eds.), *Handbook of intercultural communication* (pp. 467–490). Berlin: Mouton de Gruyter.

Prestwich, R., & Ho-Kim, T.-M. (2009). Practical skills in international business: Training needs for workforce competence by Minnesota companies. *Journal of Teaching in International Business, 20*(2), 149–173. http://dx.doi.org/10.1080/0897 5930902827874

Public Relations Professional in 2015 (2011). Retrieved from http://apps.prsa.org/AboutPRSA/Documents/PRProfessionalIn2015.pdf

Rost-Roth, M. (2007). Intercultural training. In H. Kotthoff, and H. Spencer-Oatey (Eds.), *Handbook of intercultural communication* (pp. 491–517). Berlin: Mouton de Gruyter.

Rudmin, F. (2009). Constructs, measurements and models of acculturation and acculturative stress. *International Journal of Intercultural Relations, 33*, 106–123.

Salant, T., & Lauderdale, D. S. (2003). Measuring culture: A critical review of acculturation and health in Asian Immigrant populations. *Social Science & Medicine, 57*, 71–90.

Schwartz, S. J., Unger, J. B., Zamboanga, B.L., & Szapocznik, J. (2010). Rethinking the concept of acculturation: Implications for theory and research. *American Psychologist, 65*, 237–251. doi: 10.1037/a0019330

Sha, B.-L., & Ford, R. L. (2007). Redefining "requisite variety": The challenge of multiple diversities for the future of public relations excellence. In E. L. Toth (Ed.), *The future of excellence in public relations and communication management: Challenges for the next generation* (pp. 381–398). Mahwah, NJ: Lawrence Erlbaum Associates.

Sheng, V. W. (1995). *Multicultural public relations: A normative approach.* Unpublished master's thesis, University of Maryland, College Park.

Smith, R. A., & Khawaja, N. G. (2011). A review of the acculturation experiences of international students. *International Journal of Intercultural Relations, 35*, 699–713.

Spitzberg, B. H. (2000). A model of intercultural communication competence. In L. Samovar & R. Porter (Eds.), *Intercultural communication: A reader* (9th ed., pp. 375–387). Belmont, CA: Wadsworth.

Sriramesh, K. (2004). *Public relations in Asia.* Singapore: Thomson Asia Pte.

Sriramesh, K., & Vercic, D. (2009). *The global public relations handbook, revised and expanded edition: Theory, research, and practice* (2nd ed.). New York, NY: Routledge.

Srirmesh, K., & Vercic, D. (2012). *Culture and public relations: Links and implications.* New York, NY: Routledge.

Tindall, N. T. J., & Waters, R. D. (2012). Coming out to tell our stories: Using queer theory to understand the career experiences of gay men in public relations. *Journal of Public Relations Research, 24*, 451–475. doi: 10.1080/1062726X.2012.723279

Ting-Toomey, S. (2005). Identity negotiation theory: Crossing cultural boundaries. In W. B. Gudykunst (Ed.), *Theorizing about intercultural communication* (pp. 211–233). Thousand Oaks, CA: Sage.

Tsetsura, K. (2011). How understanding multidimensional diversity can benefit global public relations education. *Public Relations Review, 37*(5), 530–535. doi: 10.1016/j. pubrev.2011.09.020

Turner, J. H. (1988). *A theory of social interactions.* Stanford, CA: Stanford University Press.

Valin, J. (2016). *Pursuing global standards for the public relations profession/The GBOK project.* Retrieved from www.instituteforpr.org/pursuing-global-standards-public-relations-profession-gbok-project/

Van der Zee, K. I., & Van Oudenhoven, J. P. (2000). The multicultural personality questionnaire: A multidimensional instrument of multicultural effectiveness. *European Journal of Personality, 14*, 291–309.

Van der Zee, K. I., & Van Oudenhoven, J. P. (2001). The multicultural personality questionnaire: Reliability and validity of self- and other ratings of multicultural effectiveness. *Journal of Research in Personality, 35*, 278–288.

Wang, Q., Ni, L., & De la Flor, M. (2014). An intercultural competence model of strategic public relations management in the Peru mining industry context. *Journal of Public Relations Research, 26*, 1–22. doi: 10.1080/1062726X.2013.795864

Ward, C. (2001). The A, B, Cs of acculturation. In D. Matsumoto (Ed.), *The handbook of culture and psychology* (pp. 411–445). Oxford: Oxford University Press.

Wiseman, R. L. (2002). Intercultural communication competence. In W. B. Gudykunst & B. Mody (Eds.), *Handbook of international and intercultural communication* (pp. 207–224). Thousand Oaks, CA: Sage.

6

INTRA-ORGANIZATIONAL LEVEL

Identifying and Communicating with Publics

This chapter starts by explicating the relevance of identifying publics in different stages of the strategic management process of public relations programs, and by reviewing different approaches to identifying publics, ranging from the cross-situational to situational approaches, with different typologies of publics presented. The chapter then integrates previous chapters on the strategic management of public relations and discusses guidelines for identifying publics in different stages. The next sections examine identifying publics in intercultural settings, in particular, the challenges in the digital age, the various consequences of public formation, as well as the antecedents of public perceptions and formation. In the antecedents of public formation, we integrate the current literature by following a multilevel approach: micro-level influence, meso-level influence, and macro-level influence.

The chapter then reviews literature on how cultural influences play a role in communicating with diverse publics. Finally, the chapter touches on the challenges of pigeonholing, whereby practitioners of specific cultural backgrounds are restricted to working with those perceived as being culturally similar to themselves.

Approaches to Identifying Publics

The four-step strategic management process of public relations programs detailed in Chapter 2 includes research, planning, implementation, and evaluation. Within this framework, the identification of organizational publics has traditionally been taking place in both the research and planning stages. For example, research efforts should investigate the myriad cultural identities of organizational stakeholders, determining which identities are most salient in the intercultural communication situation at hand. Then, the planning effort requires the incorporation of appropriate cultural elements in the development of messages and messengers/channels.

However, in recent research (J.-N. Kim & Ni, 2013), the identification of publics is expanded to be relevant also in the evaluation stage of the strategic management of public relations programming. In particular, the different types of publics can be measured before and after a program to assess whether the program has effectively "activated" (in the case of organization-initiated public relations problems) or "de-activated" (in the case of public-initiated public relations problems) the publics based on the overall goals of the program.

In general, much current research in public relations identifies and segments publics based on the situational theory of publics, or its more-recent development, the situational theory of problem solving. However, as J.-N. Kim and Ni (2013) suggested, relationship management theory can also be used as a segmentation method. Within this broad context, J.-N. Kim, Ni, and Sha (2008) provided an overview of the multiple perspectives on identifying and segmenting organizational publics within the stakeholder environment. Following the strategic management stages of public relations (reviewed in Chapter 2), they discussed different approaches to identifying publics. The two main approaches are the *cross-situational approach* and the *situational approach*.

Cross-Situational Approaches to Identifying Publics

The uses and choices of the cross-situational and situational approaches to understanding and segmenting publics have been dynamically developed and preferred over the last few decades. The cross-situational approach focuses on the more static and enduring characteristics of individuals. These characteristics are usually easy to identify and share some similarities to marketing segmentation. This approach has been traditionally used in public relations planning and programming.

The importance of cross-situational approaches was challenged after J. Grunig (1966) developed the situational theory of publics in the 1960s, but recently, that approach has been readdressed. J. Grunig proposed and highlighted the importance of situational perceptions in shaping people's communication behaviors. Many early studies consistently found that situational perceptions predicted communication behaviors much more effectively than enduring, cross-situational perceptions such as attitudes (for a review, see J. Grunig, 1997). However, in recent years, the importance of cross-situational approaches to identifying publics has been re-examined and ideas of integrating both approaches have been proposed (e.g., Broom & Sha, 2013; J.-N. Kim & Ni, 2013).

Drawing from research in marketing and sociology, the cross-situational approach focuses on two kinds of organizational environments. The economic or task environment emphasized in marketing literature indicates the importance of resources needed by an organization. On the other hand, the social or institutional environment emphasized by public relations indicates the importance of consequences from organizational behaviors on the public, or vice versa. The consequences are important to consider for problem solving and relationship building. Specific methods of segmentation in this approach include geographics, demographics, psychographics, and membership (Broom & Sha, 2013).

Drawing from literature in business management and two important theories, stakeholder theory and resource dependency theory, the following segmentation methods are provided. The classic three-dimensional model in the stakeholder theory developed by Mitchell, Agle, and Wood (1997) focused on three key concepts: *power* (the influence on others to make decisions), *legitimacy* (the extent of having a legal, moral or presumed claim), and *urgency* (the extent to which the relationship or the claim is time sensitive or is critical to the stakeholder). Based on the different combinations of the three attributes, different stakeholder groups emerge. *Latent* stakeholders (with only one attribute and of low priority) include *dormant* (power only), *discretionary* (legitimacy only), and demanding (urgency only). *Expectant* stakeholders (with two attributes and of medium priority) include *dominant* (power and legitimacy), *dependent* (urgency and legitimacy), and *dangerous* (urgency and power) stakeholders. And the *definitive* stakeholders are those with all three attributes and of high priority.

Resource-dependency theory focuses on understanding who among the constituencies controls resources to minimize the organization's dependence on others and who controls resources to maximize the dependence of others on the organization.

In the public relations literature, the concept of linkages belongs to the cross-situational approach. Linkages are interpenetrating systems that are connected to an organization through consequences, whether these refer to the consequences of the organization on another system or vice versa. J. Grunig and Hunt (1984) proposed four major types of linkages. Enabling linkages are organizations or groups that provide authority and control resources that enable the existence of the focal organization. Functional linkages provide inputs (e.g., employees or unions and suppliers of raw material) and take outputs (e.g., other organizations who use the focal organization's products). Normative linkages are connections with organizations that face similar problems or share similar values. Finally, *diffused* linkages are with those groups that cannot easily be identified by formal membership but can mobilize and take action when needed.

Situational Approaches to Identifying Publics

The situational theory of publics (J. Grunig, 1997) and the recently developed situational theory of problem solving (J.-N. Kim & J. Grunig, 2011) have been used extensively in public relations to identify and segment publics. These theories fall under the situational approach because they focus on publics' non-enduring and dynamic characteristics. This approach has greater utility than cross-situational approaches because it can provide a more nuanced profile of publics. However it takes more time and resources in researching the publics.

The situational theory of publics has been used to explain when and how people communicate and when communication aimed at people is most likely to be effective. It contains three independent variables (problem recognition, constraint recognition, and level of involvement) and two independent variables (information seeking and information processing). Please refer to Chapter 2 for details. As discussed in an earlier section, this situational theory, typically used in the identification of publics, assumes members of a community communicate and act differentially in regard to the same problem. It defines what publics there are, how they behave, and how publics arise situationally.

One of the criticisms of the situational theory of publics and research as a result of that theory has been about the publics' role (i.e., publics seem to revolve around organizations' behaviors and react to problems that they consider to be a result of organizational actions). Attempting to examine the public's role as an active participant in the rhetorical process, Edwards (2006) applied a rhetorical approach to understanding publics in the case of the Avon Breast Cancer 3-Day Walk. Recognizing that although organizations may initiate a program that helps define issues and shape a community, the publics take an active part in sharing values, understanding, and experiences, Avon's discourse actually empowered participants and helped create a community (Edwards, 2006). This approach put emphasis on the public as partners in the dialogue, who help shape discourse at the forefront of a rhetorical situation. In other words, this was a public "defined by their beliefs and attitudes, not by their relationships with the organization" per se, because they were a public "seeking and finding meaning and . . . constructing identities, strategies, and goals of their own" (p. 856).

To address this and other criticisms of the original situational theory, a more recent development in this line of research has generated the situational theory of problem solving (J.-N. Kim & J. Grunig, 2011). In particular, the scope of communication has been expanded to include how publics themselves are communicating among themselves to build and empower their own communities. J.-N. Kim, J. Grunig and Ni (2010) proposed communicative action in problem solving, which encompasses broader aspects of communication behaviors related to a problematic life situation. Variables that explain information behaviors in this theory include three domains and two types: information acquisition, information selection, and information transmission. In these three domains, there are both proactive or active and reactive or passive variables. In information acquisition, the active one is *information seeking*, or "planned scanning of the environment for messages about a specific topic," and the passive one is *information attending*: "unplanned discovery of a message followed by continued processing of it" (J. Grunig, 1997, p. 9).

In terms of information transmission, the active variable is *information forwarding*, "a planned, self-propelled giving of information to others" about the problem, and the passive act is *information sharing*, or the "sharing of information reactively only when someone else requests one's opinion, idea, or expertise about the problem" (J.-N. Kim & J. Grunig, 2011, p. 127).

Finally in information selection, the active act is *information forefending*, or "the extent to which a problem solver fends off certain information in advance by judging its value and relevance for a given problem-solving task," and the passive one is *information permitting*, or "the extent to which a problem solver accepts any information related to a given problem-solving task" (J.-N. Kim & J. Grunig, 2011, p. 126).

Many factors or independent variables influence what kinds of information behaviors the different publics will have. These variables include three perceptual variables, one cognitive variable, and one situational motivation variable. The three perceptual variables are problem recognition, constraint recognition, and involvement recognition. Problem recognition refers to "one's perception that something is missing and that there is no immediately applicable solution" (J.-Kim & J. Grunig, 2011, p. 128). Constraint recognition is the "perceived obstacles in a situation that limit one's ability to do anything about the problem" (p. 130). Involvement recognition refers to "a perceived connection between the self and the problem situation" (p. 130). The cognitive variable is referent criterion, defined as "any knowledge or subjective judgmental system that influences the way in which one approaches problem solving." (p. 131). Finally, the motivational variable is situational motivation in problem solving, defined as "the extent to which a person stops to think about, is curious about, or wants more understanding of a problem" (p. 132).

Depending on the different types of problems (i.e., organization-initiated public relations problems or public-initiated public relations problems) and the corresponding goals of public relations programs (i.e., to activate publics or to "de-activate" publics), communicators need to influence public communication behaviors through influencing the different perceptual variables. These perceptions would then significantly influence motivational variables, which in turn influence the ultimate communication behaviors.

More recently, Moon, Rhee, and Yang (2016) developed a multidimensional model of publics' information transmitting behavior based on three criteria: activeness, valence, and expressivity. The resulting model has six dimensions: positive-proactive megaphoning, positive-reactive megaphoning, negative-proactive megaphoning, negative-reactive megaphoning, avoiding, and no-commenting. These different communication behaviors have led to different ways of identifying and segmenting the different types of publics, as reviewed below.

Types of Publics

The different combinations of the variables in the original situational theory of publics (see J. Grunig, 1997) helped identify eight types of publics. The four main ones are problem facing (those who recognize a problem and face no constraints), constrained behavior (those who recognize a problem but feel constrained), routine behavior (those who do not recognize a problem and feel free from constraints), and fatalistic behavior (those who have low problem recognition and high constraint recognition). These four types can have either high involvement or low involvement, generating eight kinds of publics altogether.

Some emerging and consistent patterns of publics can be identified across most major programs of public relations: typologies that are within issue (within the same issue) and cross issue (across different issues, J.-N. Kim et al., 2008). The within-issue typology includes the most commonly used types from J. Grunig (1997): nonpublic, latent public, aware public, and active public.

In addition, using the notions of knowledge and involvement, Hallahan (2000) identified four types of publics: active (high involvement and high knowledge), aroused (high involvement and low knowledge), aware (low involvement and high knowledge), and inactive (low involvement and low knowledge).

Other types for the within-issue typology are identified based on their role in the diffusion of innovation process or their connection with an organization. For example, Rogers (1995) included innovators, early adopters, early majority, late majority, and laggards in the diffusion of innovation. Center and Jackson (2002) identified primary public (who can or cannot do what the organization needs or wants to do), intervening public (a "gatekeeper" who delivers messages to the primary publics and typically includes news media, politicians, activists, and opinion leaders), and special publics (an organized group with formal rules and regular meetings,). Chay-Nemeth (2001)'s typology included circumscribed, co-opted, critical, and circumventing publics based on three historical conditions, resource dependency, discursive connectivity, and legitimacy.

Based on the three major characteristics in the problem-solving process of publics (openness to approaches in problem solving, extent of activeness in problem solving, and time or history of the problem solving), Ni and J.-N. Kim (2009) categorized eight types of publics: open dormant passive public, closed-dormant passive public, open-situational active public, closed-situational active public, open-situational activist public, closed situational activist public, open-chronic activist public, and closed-chronic activist public (also see J.-N. Kim & Ni, 2013). The specific procedure for getting such segmentations was discussed in J.-N. Kim (2011).

The cross-issue typology includes the all-issue public (active on all issues in a situation set), apathetic public (not involved or nonpublics on all issues), hot-issue public (active on issues that involve nearly everyone in the population), and single-issue public (focused on one issue and persistent in getting that issue resolved). These different typologies of publics have been used in public relations programs to better identify the different ways of communicating with different publics. This process appears to be critical in the strategic management of public relations.

Identifying Publics in Different Stages of Strategic Management of Public Relations

As clarified in Chapter 2, stakeholders and publics are not the same concepts, although sometimes the two terms are used interchangeably by scholars and practitioners. To see the differences between *stakeholders* and *publics*, please refer to "The Role of Public Relations in Strategic Management" section in Chapter 2.

In the stakeholder stage of the strategic management of public relations, which is the earliest stage, organizations are advised to use environmental scanning. In particular, practitioners are to find out what kinds of behaviors (and from whom) will influence the organization as well as who the organization's behaviors will influence. In this stage, the key concepts to note are consequences (whether negative or positive) and resources. The existence of consequences indicates a need to manage relationships, whereas the existence of resources indicates the availability of necessary assets to achieve desired goals. Therefore, particular attention needs to be paid to minimize strategic threats and maximize strategic opportunities.

In the publics stage, various publics will form on their own to exercise their influence with a targeted organization. When these publics perceive a problem from the consequences of a certain organizational behavior, feel highly involved in the problem, and consider themselves capable of doing something about this problem, they arise and approach the organization for acknowledging and correcting the problem.

It is particularly worth noting that segmentation can be done at different levels, based on different kinds of variables. J. Grunig and Repper (1992) identified a nested model of segmentation with multiple layers, where communication behaviors may be predicted by either inferred variables or objective variables. Whereas the inferred variables refer to variables that are not directly observable, such as individuals' perceptions, cognitions, or attitudes, the objective variables refer to those more-easily observable and identifiable, such as demographics, geographic location, or use of media.

The nested model of segmentation consists of seven layers: individual behaviors and effects of communication (including attitudes, cognitions, and situational perceptions); publics (active or passive); communities (which may sometimes overlap with the public nest); psychographics and lifestyles (e.g., activities, interests, and opinions), subcultures (with similar values, norms, customs, beliefs, and behaviors), and societal relationships (social classes, families, and reference groups); geodemographics (e.g., zip code clustering used for marketing products and services, identifying political parties, and understanding people's positions on issues); demographics and social categories; and mass audiences (see Figure 6.1). It is noted that the microsegments (or the inner nests) are segmented with inferred variables, whereas macrosegments (or the outer nests) are segmented with objective variables. The microsegments are usually time consuming and require high research costs, but once identified, they are useful for tailoring communication efforts. The macrosegments require fewer research costs but are not as useful because they include both passive and active publics.

In the issue (or crisis) stage, publics arise and make an issue out of a problem because the problem that needs to be resolved is becoming serious. The strategic threats outweigh strategic opportunities. In this stage, segmenting or identifying publics is usually easier than in other stages because these publics are more vocal and communicatively active. However, interacting with these publics becomes more difficult because they have already formed opinions and taken actions. By the time this stage is reached, organizational actions are becoming reactive.

Therefore, moving among the three stages, a tradeoff appears between the ease in segmentation of and the difficulty in interaction with these publics. Overall, the recommendations are that, in the first stage of strategic management (stakeholder stage), the publics should be segmented using cross-situational approaches grounded in the notions of "consequences" and "resources." In later stages (public and issue), the publics should be segmented using situational approaches, derived from notions of "problem" and "issue."

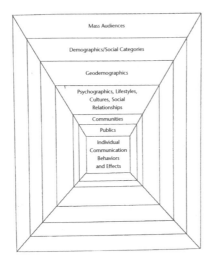

FIGURE 6.1 Nested Segmentation Concepts

Source: J. Grunig and Repper (1992, p. 133). Reprinted with permission of Lawrence Erlbaum Associates, Hillsdale, NJ.

In addition, it is recommended that segmentation be done by either a build-on combination or combine-with approach. The *build-on* combination approach means that, as the organization shifts between different stages (e.g., entering the public stage from the stakeholder stage), it should combine cross-situational methods with situational methods (e.g., demographics combined with the situational theory of publics). In other words, a segment starts with a cross-situational method, and then is sub-segmented using the situational theory to generate a more pinpointed segment. To our knowledge, little research has used this synthetic approach.

The *combine-with* method means that both situational and cross-situational methods are used simultaneously to better target a segment. For example, an active public segment based on the situational theory is identified and is asked questions about demographics and media-use habits so that this segment can be better reached and communicated with. Lee and Rodriguez's (2008) study on the publics in an anti-bioterrorism situation serves as an example for the *combine-with* method. Lee and Rodriguez examined how problem recognition, level of involvement, and constraint recognition affected publics' communication and protective behaviors. To segment the publics, they used cross-situational factors including media consumption habits and trust in information sources (i.e., news media, interpersonal communication sources, government agencies and institutions, and universities and advocacy groups). The four public types did turn out to have different kinds of media consumption habits, source trust evaluations, and behavioral intentions. In particular, the aware and active publics tended to be heavy consumers of newspapers compared to other types. The aroused and active publics showed more trust in interpersonal and mass media sources of bioterrorism-related information and demonstrated greater intentions to prepare against bioterrorist attacks than the other types. More research along this line is needed to better integrate the two approaches to identifying publics.

Identifying Publics in Intercultural Settings: Influence of the Digital Age

In the digital age of prevalent social media, it is increasingly a challenge for practitioners to identify and pinpoint various publics. Kruckeberg and Vujnovic (2010) questioned whether segmenting publics was still relevant and suggested the death of the concept of publics in its plural form because of the complexity and unexpected nature of how publics arise in today's world. They argued that, due to the vast amount of user-generated content on different platforms and the speed with which information travels on the Internet, "infinite numbers of volatile publics worldwide can form immediately and unpredictably and can act seemingly chaotically and with unforeseen power" (p. 124). This statement is supported in the cases with online public relations when a local event or campaign can all of a sudden turn into something that has gained international attention. One example is when a local, online public participation project focused on architectural design and transit planning that targeted everyday bus riders in Salt Lake City, Utah, suddenly attracted the attention of design professionals internationally (Brabham, 2012). These designers became "unexpected publics" and caused global–local and amateur–professional tensions.

Brabham (2012) examined managing such unexpected publics online and how to target specific groups within the context of the Internet age. He suggested a few guidelines, starting with not assuming that an online message targeted at a set of specific demographics will only reach the intended audience. The use of offline tools for online projects was also recommended because offline tactics such as word of mouth, community relations, and local media efforts may be better able to target a narrower, more specific public than online tactics that typically disseminate messages more widely than perhaps intended. Strategic management of these publics also includes, among other things, requiring user registration that provides demographic information and offering different filters to give different privileges and weights for different groups of publics. This way, public relations practitioners can still have maximum control over user behavior and data to best accomplish program goals.

In sum, despite the increasing difficulty to pinpoint publics in the digital age, basic guidelines can still be developed and applied. Differentiating publics based on their issue involvement is still needed.

Consequences of Public Formation: Effects of Public Types on Outcome Variables

It is important to understand the consequences of public formation because the purpose of understanding and segmenting publics is to design different, tailored messages for the different types of publics so the communication can be effective. Research in this area enhances the understanding of the behaviors of different publics and effective public relations approaches.

However, a clear correspondence between the strategic importance allocated to key publics and the level of research implemented has not been established (Oliveira & Capriotti, 2015). Oliveira and Capriotti (2015) examined the research of strategic publics in companies in the energy industry in Spain and noted that, although the companies conducted routine research on their key publics, no consistency was found between how important a group of publics was to the company and how much research was done on them.

The situational theory of problem solving (STOPS; J.-N. Kim & Grunig, 2011; J.-N. Kim & Krishna, 2014) has been recently applied and expanded in different contexts: hot-issue publics (J.-N. Kim, Ni, S.-H. Kim, & J.-R. Kim, 2012); employee relations (J.-N. Kim & Rhee, 2011), and problem chain recognition in organ donation issues (J.-N. Kim, Shen, & Morgan, 2011).

Different research has examined the effects of different segmented public types on outcome variables such as use and effectiveness of public relations strategy, trust, reputation, and behavior intentions. Werder (2005) examined how perceived attributes of publics, such as problem recognition, constraint recognition, involvement, and goal compatibility, influenced the use of different messaging strategies such as informative, facilitative, persuasive, and cooperative problem-solving strategies. Findings suggested significant influence of the perceived attributes of publics on not only the use of public relations strategy, but also the effectiveness of such strategy.

Hong, H. Park, Lee, and J. Park (2012) examined public segmentation in government public relations. They used cross-situational factors including cognitive perceptions of government, participation in social organizations, media use, and demographic characteristics to form public segments and then examined each segment's level of trust in government. This segmentation method was built upon the relationship-building perspective, rather than a problem-solving perspective. In a sense, this fits the scope of work identified by J.-N. Kim and Ni (2013) in using relationship management theory as a segmentation method. Y. Kim (2015) went a step further and adopted the synthetic approach to public segmentation as was identified in J.-N. Kim and Ni (2013) in the context of the government–public relationship. Synthesizing both situational and cross-situational variables, the study examined the different levels of trust that different types of publics have in federal, state, and local government.

Y. Kim (2016) explored different publics and their communicative behaviors in crisis situations. Specifically, Y. Kim studied the effects of crisis news framing and publics' communicative behaviors (information acquisition, selection, and transmission) in crisis situations on key outcome variables in crisis, such as reputation and behavioral intentions. Among other things, findings suggested that information attending, forwarding, and seeking were positively associated with reputation and behavioral intentions.

Identifying Publics in Intercultural Settings: (Cross-Situational) Antecedents to Public Perceptions and Public Formation

It is important to understand the antecedents of public formation because this can help inform how public relations practitioners can manage perceptual variables such as problem recognition, constraint recognition, and involvement recognition, so eventually they can help "activate" or "de-activate" publics depending on the different types of public relations problems. For example, for a public-initiated problem, the goal is to de-activate the publics and make them less active and angry. To do this, practitioners need to look into the real source of the problem and conduct some internal adaptation and adjustment to remove the problem in the first place, so that the publics' problem recognition would slowly decrease, until eventually they leave this situation mentally. In the process, doing cosmetic changes and using communication to divert people's attention are not effective. These and other manipulative behaviors will not appease the originally active publics in any substantial way. Rather, the public's anger would be further stoked, and their problem recognition and involvement increased. In any public relations program planning, both action strategy and communication strategy must be included.

For another example, if an organization initiates a problem that aims to improve public health, the organization should understand the antecedents to any constraints, both real and perceived, in the public's life. Only by removing the actual barriers to following a healthier lifestyle can the publics be truly "activated" to become active ones that engage in various information behaviors related to the health issue.

In intercultural settings, it is important to consider both cross-situational and situational factors in the formation of publics, as well as understanding and identifying these publics. The cross-situational factors include the traditionally used geographics, demographics, psychographics, and membership (Broom & Sha, 2013). In addition, some layers in the nested model of J. Grunig and Repper (1992) are also highly relevant. These include communities; psychographics and lifestyles, subcultures, and societal relationships; geodemographics; demographics; and social categories.

Drawing on these previously identified factors and integrating current literature on publics, we now continue to discuss three major, multiple-level cross-situational factors that are particularly relevant to intercultural settings. These factors can influence the formation of publics, and thereby influence public identification and tailored communication. These factors are classified under micro-level factors (cultural identity and life experiences), meso-level factors (organizational factors such as organization–public relationships), and macro-level factors (societal culture). The next section integrates current literature on publics using this classification and then proposes a synthesized framework.

Micro Level: Cultural Factors and Life Experiences

Cross-situational factors often play a substantial role in publics formation. At the micro, or personal level, these factors include demographics (e.g., Dozier, Shen, Sweetser, & Barker, 2016), life experiences, perceptions about focal issues, perceptions about media and messages (Aldoory, 2001), and acculturation and interest in politics (Len-Ríos, 2017).

Demographics and Life Experiences

Dozier et al. (2016) examined online political activism using a national probability sample of adult U.S. American Internet users. They found that certain demographics such as age, socioeconomic status, and political affiliation were correlated with the activeness of publics. Lifestyles such as Internet self-efficacy and search-engine usage also played a role in the formation of active publics.

Aldoory (2001) tested the situational theory of publics among women in terms of health issues. She explored the antecedents to perceived level of involvement and found four categories of antecedents: overall life experiences, perceptions about the issue at hand (health), information factors, and self-identity. The overall life experiences included the consciousness of everyday life, such as life situations, current environments, and everyday practices. Some examples included motherhood and pregnancy, employment, housing, and neighborhood. Consciousness of personal health and personal sensitivity to the body and to the importance of wellness, perceptions of healthiness, and invulnerability to health problems all formed some kind of cross-situational factors affecting women's level of involvement. Information factors included both the sources of information (source preference as reflected in source credibility and trustworthiness of media sources) and the cognitive analyses of message content (dissecting visuals and text of individual messages to decide how to make meaning of them, analyzing conflicting information, complexity of the message, and type of language used). In particular, self-identity, or a strong sense of self or strong identity to one's ethnicity, culture, sex, sexual identity, sexual orientation, or socioeconomic status, played a major role in how involved the women felt about health issues.

Len-Ríos (2017) examined how different factors influenced political participation and intention to vote among Latino publics. Cross-situational factors including demographic variables, acculturation, political ideology, and media use were examined to see how they were connected with the perceptions of the importance of immigration reform, political participation, and the likelihood to vote in the 2016 U.S. presidential election. Findings indicated that acculturation only predicted perceptions of the importance of immigration reform, but not other dependent variables, whereas interest in politics was the most important factor, predicting all of the dependent variables.

Perceived Shared Risk

Aldoory, J.-N. Kim, and Tindall (2010) examined the influence of perceived shared risk in crisis communication as antecedents to situational perceptions such as involvement as well as concern and desire to learn more about the issue. Findings supported the hypothesis that shared risk experience with media portrayals did influence various situational perceptions such as problem recognition, involvement recognition, and outcome variables such as information gaining.

Ethnocentrism

Illia, Lurati, and Casalaz (2013) explored a cultural ethnocentric bias in the perceptions and formations of publics. Using journalists as participants, the study found that this public's situational behavior was influenced by a referent criterion, in this case, a biased mindset toward the topic. An ethnocentric bias had a moderating effect only when journalists actively investigated an issue with no local connotations and did not feel personally involved in the issue. Journalists' communication behavior was influenced only by situational perceptions when they identified strongly with a topic. However, when they did not identify with a topic, their communication behavior was influenced by their ethnocentric view of the reality. These findings suggested that situational perceptions, in particular, involvement, seemed to outweigh cross-situational factors such as enduring ethnocentric bias in influencing these publics' behaviors.

Cultural Identity

Among all these factors, cultural identity is the most prevalent and most relevant to intercultural settings. Sha's (1995, 2006, 2008) work was the first that examined the influence of cultural identity on the public relations behaviors of organizations and their publics. Sha argued that self-identity affects how one reacts or does not react to certain situations. She examined two types of cultural identities: *avowed* identity, which occurs when one identifies with a cultural group and asserts that membership, and *ascribed* identity, which is assigned to a person based on some external features and which may not be the same as the person's avowed cultural identity. Her study (1995, 2006) found that non–White racioethnic groups were most likely to recognize racioethnic problems, to feel personally involved with those problems, and to engage in communication behaviors about those problems. The same effect was not found for constraint recognition. Linking cultural identity to the identification of publics makes intercultural public relations more effective by helping organizations to communicate in a culturally sensitive manner.

Other studies have since examined cultural identity. Focusing on the cultural identity of Korean Americans, Jang and H. Kim (2013) explored the connections among cultural identity, social capital, and social control of young Korean Americans and found that young Korean Americans have multifaceted, situational identities, which went beyond existing cultural stereotypes. Jang and H. Kim thus proposed situational cultural identity as a new category of understanding publics in intercultural public relations.

Ortiz Juarez-Paz (2017) examined undocumented identity storytelling in the Undocumented Student Movement (USM). These undocumented students were from historically misrepresented and excluded populations who used their identities to gain a voice in mainstream media and society. By documenting the communicative acts of the USM, she argued for a culture-centered approach to communication.

More recently, another expansion on this line of research is Ni, Wang, and Gogate (under review) where they examined not just cultural identity, but intercultural identity in understanding immigrant professionals in the United States. They examined the process of immigrants' intercultural identity development through their stress–adaptation–growth process and intercultural communication competence. They found that, in the context of intercultural identity development, the concepts of avowed and ascribed identities became even more nuanced.

It is also worth noting that, increasingly, multiracial individuals are becoming important due to their growing social visibility and recognized buying power. Most current research on multiracial individuals has been done among marketers, but not in public relations (except Sha, 2008). Harrison, Thomas, and Cross (2015) examined how multiracial individuals used consumption practices to develop and express their racial identities. They found that multiracial consumers tended to engage with the marketplace to relieve racial discordance and legitimize the liminal space they occupied. Future public relations research should be conducted to more fully capture the lived experiences in such acculturation and socialization processes for these individuals with two or more distinctly constructed racial backgrounds. The next section moves beyond the micro-level to the meso-level antecedents as to how different publics form.

Meso Level: Organization–Public Relationships

Not much research has been done to explore how organizational factors influence the formation of publics. Some earlier research has focused on messaging effects on the formation of publics. Werder (2006) examined the influence of public relations strategies on such attributes of publics as problem recognition, involvement, and constraint recognition. Results showed that problem recognition and involvement were influenced by public relations strategies. Ni (2012) examined the strategic importance of relationship management in the understanding of publics. Aiming to understand how organization–public relationships may serve as a meso-level cross-situational factor in the formation of publics, Ni explored how relationships can be managed strategically to influence the perceptual variables in the situational theory of problem solving. Based on this conceptual piece on the necessity of studying the formation of and potential change in publics using a quasi-cross-situational approach, some follow-up studies have been conducted in the context of community engagement. For example, Ni and colleagues have studied how community empowerment can be reflected in enhancing the publics' communication behaviors in public health issues (see Ni et al., 2016; Ni, de la Flor, Romero, & Wang, 2017; Ni, Xiao, Lu, & Gor, 2015). In doing so, these studies examined how relationship management at the organizational level had influences on the situational perceptions of publics and, consequently, the formation of publics and their communication behaviors.

Ni et al. (2015) studied how community empowerment was linked to its members' engagement and health in the Asian American community. Empowerment through quality organization–community relationships was reflected in, among other things, heightened communication activeness about health issues. In terms of the effect of situational perceptions on community members' *communication behaviors*, involvement recognition was the most prominent factor, affecting all four of the major communication behaviors: information seeking, attending, forwarding, and sharing. Problem recognition and constraint recognition had limited effects, affecting information attending and information forwarding, respectively. Members' sense of community and belonging contributed to their perceptual change, which in turn led to increased communication behaviors about health. These findings supported Ni's (2012) argument that relationship building plays a key role in public formation; in particular, when publics recognize the positive relationships organizations attempt to build with them, they change their perceptions and therefore communication behaviors.

In Ni et al.'s (2015) study, trust appeared to be the fundamental reason for this change mechanism. When community members acknowledged higher levels of trust, they perceived higher problem recognition and involvement recognition, and, to a lesser degree, lower constraint recognition. The less visible change in constraint recognition might be closely related to the particular health issue at hand, i.e., cancer status among Asian Americans. Because much of the outcome was beyond human control, constraint recognition was less likely to be removed, regardless of the organizations' engagement efforts. Control mutuality, on the other hand, only affected constraint recognition. This was consistent with Ni's (2012) argument: The more people feel empowered in an organizational setting, the fewer constraints they perceive in doing something about the issue.

Ni et al. (2017) continued to assess this theoretical framework in a Hispanic community empowerment and health study. Similar findings were obtained through qualitative interviews. Community members reported feeling empowered and started to actively communicate and help spread messages about health issues when they perceived high-quality relationships with community organizations.

In addition, internal publics have also been examined in terms of their relationships with organizations. Similar results have been found: Satisfying organization–public relationships encourage internal publics' communicative behavior as well. For example, J.-N. Kim and Rhee (2011) found that symmetrical internal communication and employee–organization relationships were significant antecedent variables to employee communication behaviors.

In conclusion, this series of research has found that a positive organization–public relationship empowers publics and makes them more communicatively active, thereby contributing to more activeness of the publics. Future research may continue to test the theory in different contexts.

Macro Level: Societal Culture and Others

Many studies have been conducted to test and apply the public segmentation theory in other countries or cultural contexts, although not all of them explicitly examined the influence of culture on the formation of publics. For example, Tkalac (2006) applied the situational theory of publics in Croatia but focused more on the role of cognitive schemata. Park and Jeong (2011) examined the application of the situational theory in Korea but focused on the formation of publics among Korean bloggers, with additional variables such as issue involvement and self-efficacy. Findings supported a typology of bloggers as active, constrained, latent, and routine publics. Neither of these studies incorporated different cultural aspects.

Sriramesh, Moghan, and Lim (2007) applied the situational theory to the examination of consumer publics in Singapore and their perceptions about customer service in the retail sector. Results indicated that the majority of the respondents perceived high problem recognition but also displayed constrained behavior in responding to the problem. Only a few respondents exhibited activist behavior. Sriramesh et al. argued that culture was not a constraint, but could be considered as one manifestation of referent criterion to play a role in the formation of publics. At the macro level, cultural factors such as deference to authority, benevolence, and collectivism played a significant role in the constrained behaviors of the respondents in their study.

Multiple and Intersected Identity

It is worth noting that the micro, meso, and macro levels of antecedents are interrelated and can affect each other. To complicate the situation even more, an individual's multiple layers of identity are intersected with each other, thus adding more depth to how publics are formed. For instance, Vardeman–Winter (2010) studied teen girls making health-related decisions. She found that multiple identities including race, gender, class, and parenthood status intersected in the process. Tindall and Vardeman–Winter (2011) studied the communication of women of color in the context of heart disease. Different cultural meaning-making factors such as perceptions of empowerment of knowledge, imagined sense of the heart-diseased body, and their understandings of heart disease through loss were all important factors.

Vardeman–Winter, Jiang, and Tindall (2013) examined antecedents to the constraints that prevent some publics from becoming active about their health concerns. They explored different levels of issues that could play a role simultaneously in the formation of publics, including cultural, social, and economic levels. They examined three levels of intersectionality of identity: *structural intersectionality* (the physical and legal systems that suppress the actual and perceived power of some groups because of the relationship that group has with dominant groups); *political intersectionality* (how organizational and legal policies and procedures are made, implemented, and maintained that subdue the rights of some groups according to their mix of identities); and *representational intersectionality* (how mediated texts represent some groups as disempowered because of their multiple identities, and how these texts, over time, contribute to stereotypes of marginalized groups).

Vardeman et al. (2013) found that, among other things, the levels of inter-sectionality interacted with one another in shaping and reinforcing disparate health public relations, making active health information seeking difficult or impossible for some women. Structural intersectionality was reflected in social structures that constituted "gendered socioeconomic disparities and restricted gendered physicality" (p. 398). Political intersectionality was reflected in poli-cies that ignored socioeconomic differences. Representational intersectionality was reflected in the lack of consciousness to race, class, gendered, and com-munity roles in media portrayals. Thus, this line of research has demonstrated that publics experience constraints on their information behaviors because of their multi-layered identities, as well as the intersectionality of societal structure, political environment, and media portrayals.

Incorporation of Culture in Implementation (Messaging, Messengers, and Channels)

Understanding publics in intercultural settings has important implications for the implementation of public relations programs. Knowing the cultural nuances of different audiences is critical in designing messaging strategies, selecting messengers, and utilizing channels. In the crisis and emergency management process, for example, planning should be done carefully so that the messages are culturally sensitive and messengers are culturally similar to the cultural groups targeted (Heath, Lee, & Ni, 2009).

In Ni et al.'s (2016) study on Asian American community health issues, at the message level, community members' input was sought in the design and implementation of various health events ranging from simple, one-time health seminars or workshops, comprehensive community fairs or resource days, to more sophisticated health campaigns. Community input was a key factor in the design of culturally sensitivity messages. In addition, community organizations emphasized the importance of cultural sensitivity in message design because of the diverse populations, cultures, and languages in the Asian American com-munity. For example, given the cultural stigma about mental health in this community, organizations chose to offer in-home services as an alternative so community members would not feel pressure. These organizations also decided to change their names to be less indicative of a mental health service provider and more of a community resource center. In addition, providing group coun-seling helped certain clients feel less isolated and realize that they were not alone.

Other examples include communicating about obesity and healthy diet (Ni et al., 2016). Because many immigrants in the Asian American community came as refugees, they had a cultural norm of not wasting any food and not being too skinny. When they came to the United States, they did not pay much attention to the content of their food. As a result, community organizations began to educate them about the nutrition facts of different types of food in the lunch program. One participant gave an example of educating about calories, taking into account Indian culture.

> [B]ecause if you're talking to people that first don't have a clear understanding of what calorie counts are and they don't have a high level of education and critical thinking, then you're going to have to break it down in a way that they do understand. They understand what is a chapati and what is a paratha. They know that when you hear a paratha, it's more filling. When you hear a chapati it's not. So you have to build off of that. From a nutrition health standpoint, if you can't do that and you're just going to do a lesson on you only have to eat 2000 calories a day and that's not going to be effective.
>
> (p. 18)

The gender of health providers also appeared to be an issue with certain cultural groups in the Asian American community, especially for women when they chose their ob/gyn (Ni et al., 2016). Then these members were also educated about the fact that they did not have to accept whoever was assigned as their primary-care physician, and they could choose the gender of their health providers.

Cultural considerations and sensitivity also emerged as key themes in a study on Hispanic community engagement and health (Ni et al., 2017). Such cultural considerations included linguistic appropriateness, choice of messengers, and tailoring of programs to community needs. First, many community organizations ensured that messages and messengers were bilingual so as to reach the community with limited English proficiency. Participants also acknowledged that translating materials should go beyond just translating from English to Spanish, but into terms and concepts that Hispanic community members could truly understand. In particular, the concept of *promotora* was repeatedly mentioned. This term referred to a layperson in the Hispanic community who acted as a community health worker. Having such liaisons with language and cultural fluency in the community was tremendously helpful to engage community members.

Practitioners' Challenges in Working with Specific Cultural Groups: Pigeonholing

Pigeonholing is a phenomenon in intercultural settings where a minority public relations practitioner is assigned work or clients with the cultural group that he or she identifies with and is therefore confined to these assignments and roles. Minority practitioners may not be expected to or have the opportunity to serve in additional organizational capacities and public relations roles. Through pioneering work by Kern-Foxworth (1989a, 1989b), Tillery-Larkin (1999), and Len-Ríos (1998), the problem of pigeonholing facing minority public relations practitioners was identified. Historically, pigeonholing in print journalism means that news reporters of color are relegated to covering stories that primarily deal with minority issues and, in the case of some Hispanic reporters, play the role of a translator. These practitioners were expected to be the designated ones to interact primarily with minority community members.

Brown, White, and Waymer (2011) found that prejudice in the public relations field often leads to pigeonholing. These pigeonholed positions offer limited opportunities for advancement and promotion (Kern-Foxworth, 1989a; Toth, 2009). Kern-Foxworth (1989b) found that pigeonholing and filling minority quotas were usually the only reasons firms hired minority practitioners at that time.

According to Len-Ríos (1998), rather than viewing pigeonholing as a form of subtle discrimination and an impediment to job advancement, some minority public relations professionals viewed it as a typical part of their job and good business practice to build and sustain relationships between their organizations and their publics. The practitioners felt that if they were the most qualified to identify with a minority public, then they considered it natural to take on that responsibility. However, in some situations, this practice was not considered appropriate, because sometimes assumptions about one's ethnic or racial cultural ties were made according to one's physical appearance and not one's real definition of him- or herself. Len-Ríos suggested that although practitioners of color may be able to identify with publics of their same race, other important factors such as education level, cultural background, and socioeconomic status could affect their ability to identify with a particular audience or cultural group. Through thorough research, audiences can be effectively reached.

This example can be taken to reflect the distinction between the avowed and ascribed cultural identities of public relations practitioners. As suggested by Len-Ríos (1998) and emphasized in this book, it is important to conduct genuine, two-way communication to understand a cultural group comprehensively, rather than just relying on one practitioner's assumed ties to that group.

A current research has been conducted with Hispanic practitioners (e.g., Radanovich, 2014) and African American practitioners (e.g., Tindall, 2009). Radanovich (2014) found that, consistent with the findings of Len-Ríos (1998), Hispanic public relations practitioners who were interviewed did not view being assigned to work on Hispanic outreach as pigeonholing. They perceived it to be a positive experience, because it gave them an opportunity to stay connected with and give back to the Latino community of which they were a part. Similarly, among African American public relations practitioners, pigeonholing did not seem to be a major barrier to career satisfaction.

Tindall (2009) found that few practitioners were hired to communicate solely with African American publics or minority audiences. Tillery-Larkin's (1999) and Ford and Applebaum's (2005) studies also indicated that the majority of African American public relations practitioners studied did not feel pigeonholed. An emphasis was placed on their career not being based on being a Black public relations professional, but being a public relations professional. Future research may assess pigeonholing among practitioners of other cultural groups to see whether culture-specific values might affect the practitioners' perceptions.

Despite the lack of explicit pigeonholing by organizations or departments, organizations should be aware of negative outcomes of pigeonholing. Although some practitioners may appreciate the chance to reach out to a group that shares their identities, the underlying factor is that they avowed that identity. In other cases, people may not avow an identity that is ascribed by others based on stereotypical external characteristics. In latter situations, perceived discrimination and conflicts may arise. Organizational leaders should first learn about their internal publics' avowed identities and help their career growth from there.

Figure 6.2 summarizes the theories and research discussed and synthesized in this chapter, following the different approaches to identifying publics and detailing both the (multilevel) antecedents to and consequences of public formation.

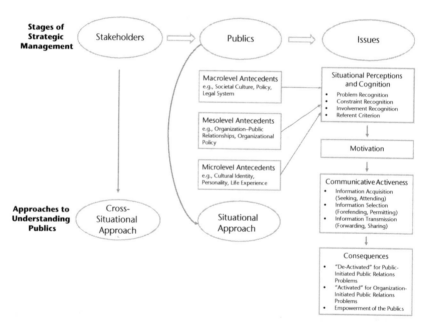

FIGURE 6.2 Theoretical Framework for Understanding Publics in Intercultural Settings

References

Aldoory, L. (2001). Making health communications meaningful for women: Factors that influence involvement. *Journal of Public Relations Research*, *13*, 163–185.

Aldoory, L., Kim, J., & Tindall, N. (2010). The influence of perceived shared risk in crisis communication: Elaborating the situational theory of publics. *Public Relations Review*, *36*(2), 134–140. doi: 10.1016/j.pubrev.2009.12.002

Brabham, D. C. (2012). Managing unexpected publics online: The challenge of targeting specific groups with the wide-reaching tool of the internet. *International Journal of Communication*, *6*, 1139–1158.

Broom, G., & Sha, B-L. (2013). *Cutlip and Center's effective public relations* (11th ed.). Upper Saddle River, NJ: Pearson.

Brown, K., White, C., & Waymer, D. (2011). African-American students' perceptions of public relations education and practice: Implications for minority recruitment. *Public Relations Review*, *37*, 522–529.

Center, A. C., & Jackson, P. (2002). *Public relations practices: Managerial case studies and problems*. Englewood Cliffs, NJ: Prentice Hall.

Chay-Nemeth, C. (2001). Revisiting publics: A critical archaeology of publics in the Thai HIV/AIDS issue. *Journal of Public Relations Research*, *13*(2), 127–161.

Dozier, D. M., Shen, H., Sweetser, K. D., & Barker, V. (2016). Demographics and Internet behaviors as predictors of active publics. *Public Relations Review*, *42*(1), 82–90. doi: 10.1016/j.pubrev.2015.11.006

Edwards, H. H. (2006). A rhetorical typology for studying the audience role in public relations communication: The Avon 3-day disruption as exemplar. *Journal of Communication*, *56*(4), 836–860. doi: 10.1111/j.1460-2466.2006.00322.x

Ford, R. L., & Applebaum, L. (2005). Top-line executive summary multicultural public relations practitioner study. Retrieved from www.ccny.uny.edu/prsurvey/recommendations.html

Grunig, J. E. (1966). The role of information in economic decision-making. *Journalism Monographs*, *3*, 1–51.

Grunig, J. E. (1997). A situational theory of publics: Conceptual history, recent challenges and new research. In D. Moss, T. MacManus, & D. Vercic (Ed.), *Public relations research: An international perspective* (pp. 3–48). London: International Thomson Business Press.

Grunig, J. E., & Hunt, T. (1984). *Managing public relations*. New York: Holt, Rinehart & Winston.

Grunig, J. E., & Repper, F. C. (1992). Strategic management, publics, and issues. In J. E. Grunig (Ed.), *Excellence in public relations and communications management* (pp. 117–157). Hillsdale, NJ: Lawrence Erlbaum.

Hallahan, K. (2000). Inactive publics: The forgotten publics in public relations. *Public Relations Review*, *26*(4), 499.

Harrison, R. L., Thomas, K. D., & Cross, S. N. (2015). Negotiating cultural ambiguity: The role of markets and consumption in multiracial identity development. *Consumption, Markets & Culture*, *18*(4), 301–332. doi: 10.1080/10253866.2015.1019483

Heath, R. L., Lee, J., & Ni, L. (2009). Crisis and risk approaches to emergency management planning and communication: The role of similarity and sensitivity. *Journal of Public Relations Research*, *21*, 123–141.

Hong, H., Park, H., Lee, Y., & Park, J. (2012). Public segmentation and government–public relationship building: A cluster analysis of publics in the United States and 19 European countries. *Journal of Public Relations Research, 24*(1), 37–68. doi: 10.1080/1062726X.2012.626135

Illia, L., Lurati, F., & Casalaz, R. (2013). Situational theory of publics: Exploring a cultural ethnocentric bias. *Journal of Public Relations Research, 25*(2), 93–122. doi: 10.1080/1062726X.2013.758581

Jang, A., & Kim, H. (2013). Cultural identity, social capital, and social control of young Korean Americans: Extending the theory of intercultural public relations. *Journal of Public Relations Research, 25,* 225–245. doi: 10.1080/1062726X.2013.788444

Kern-Foxworth, M. (1989a). Minorities 2000: The shape of things to come. *Public Relations Journal, 45,* 14–18, 21–22.

Kern-Foxworth, M. (1989b). Status and roles of minority PR practitioners. *Public Relations Review, 15*(3), 39–47. https://doi.org/10.1016/S0363-8111(89)80003-7

Kim, J.-N. (2011). Public segmentation using situational theory of problem solving: Illustrating summation method and testing segmented public profiles. *PRism, 8*(2), 1–12.

Kim, J.-N., & Grunig, J. E. (2011). Problem solving and communicative action: A situational theory of problem solving. *Journal of Communication, 61,* 120–149. doi: 10.1111/j.1460-2466.2010.01529.x

Kim, J.-N., & Krishna, A. (2014). Publics and lay informatics. *Communication Yearbook, 38,* 71–105.

Kim, J.-N., & Ni, L. (2013). Two types of public relations problems and integrating formative and evaluative research: A review of research programs within the behavioral, strategic management paradigm. *Journal of Public Relations Research, 25,* 1–29. doi: 10.1080/1062726X.2012.723276

Kim, J.-N., & Rhee, Y. (2011). Strategic thinking about employee communication behavior (ECB) in public relations: Testing the models of megaphoning and scouting effects in Korea. *Journal of Public Relations Research, 23,* 243–268.

Kim, J.-N, Grunig, J. E., & Ni, L. (2010). Reconceptualizing the communicative action of publics: Acquisition, selection, and transmission of information in problematic situations. *International Journal of Strategic Communication, 4*(2), 126–154. doi: 10.1080/15531181003701913

Kim, J.-N., Ni, L., & Sha, B.-L (2008). Breaking down the stakeholder environment: Explicating approaches to the segmentation of publics for public relations research. *Journalism and Mass Communication Quarterly, 85,* 751–768.

Kim, J.-N., Shen, H., & Morgan, S. (2011). Information behaviors and problem chain recognition effect: Applying situational theory of problem solving in organ donation issues. *Health Communication, 26,* 171–184. doi: 10.1080/10410236.2010.544282

Kim, J.-N., Ni, L., Kim, S.-H., & Kim, J. R. (2012). What makes people hot? Applying the situational theory of problem solving to hot-issue publics. *Journal of Public Relations Research, 24,* 144–164. doi:10.1080/1062726X.2012.626133

Kim, Y. (2015). Toward an effective government–public relationship: Organization–public relationship based on a synthetic approach to public segmentation. *Public Relations Review, 41*(4), 456–460. doi: 10.1016/j.pubrev.2015.06.020

Kim, Y. (2016). Understanding publics' perception and behaviors in crisis communication: Effects of crisis news framing and publics' acquisition, selection, and transmission of information in crisis situations. *Journal of Public Relations Research, 28*(1), 35–50. doi: 10.1080/1062726X.2015.1131697

Kruckeberg, D., & Vujnovic, M. (2010). The death of the concept of publics (plural) in 21st-century public relations. *International Journal of Strategic Communication, 4*(2), 117–125. doi: 10.1080/15531181003701921

Lee, S., & Rodriguez, L. (2008). Four publics of anti-bioterrorism information campaigns: A test of the situational theory. *Public Relations Review, 34*(1), 60–62. doi: 10.1016/j.pubrev.2007.11.007

Len-Ríos, M. E. (1998). Minority public relations practitioner perceptions. *Public Relations Review, 24*, 535–555.

Len-Ríos, M. E. (2017). The politics of Latino publics: Immigration reform, political participation and intention to vote. *Public Relations Review, 43*(1), 249–257. doi: 10.1016/j.pubrev.2016.11.003

Mitchell, R. K., Agle, B. R., & Wood, D. J. (1997). Toward a theory of stakeholder identification and salience: Defining the principle of who or what really counts. *Academy of Management Review, 22*, 853–886.

Moon, B. B., Rhee, Y., & Yang, S. (2016). Developing public's information transmitting behavior (ITB) model in public relations: A cross-national study. *Journal of Public Relations Research, 28*(1), 4–18. doi: 10.1080/1062726X.2015.1107482

Ni, L. (2012). Exploring the role of strategic relationship management in the formation of publics. *International Journal of Strategic Communication, 6*, 7–16. doi:10.1080/1553 118X.2011.634867

Ni, L., & Kim, J. (2009). Classifying publics: Communication behaviors and problem-solving characteristics in controversial issues. *International Journal of Strategic Communication, 3*(4), 217–241. doi: 10.1080/15531180903221261

Ni, L., Wang, Q., & Gogate, A. (under review).

Ni, L., De la Flor, M., Romero, B, & Wang, Q. (2017, March). *Community engagement and public health: A qualitative study of strategic communication of Hispanic community organizations.* Paper accepted at International Public Relations Research Conference, Orlando, FL.

Ni, L., Xiao, Z., Lu, Q., & Gor, B. (2015). *Effective communication and engagement to enhance Asian American health.* White Paper Submitted to Urban Communication Foundation. This white paper includes research funded by the Urban Communication Foundation White Paper Grant, 2014–2015.

Ni, L., Cui, Y., Xiao, Z., Lu, Q., Gor, B., & Ji, B. (2016). *The role of stakeholder engagement in the context of community health: A qualitative study on strategic communication and community empowerment.* Paper presented at the 2016 International Communication Association Conference in Fukuoka, Japan, June 13, 2016.

Oliveira, A., & Capriotti, P. (2015). The research of strategic publics in companies in the energy industry in Spain. *Public Relations Review, 41*(4), 541–543. doi: 10.1016/j.pubrev.2015.05.009

Ortiz Juarez-Paz, A. V. (2017). Undocumented identity storytelling: (Re)framing public relations. *International Journal of Media & Cultural Politics, 13*(1/2), 165–178. doi: 10.1386/macp.13.1-2.165_1

Park, N., & Jeong, J. (2011). Finding publics within the blogosphere: The blogger public segmentation model. *Asian Journal of Communication, 21*(4), 389–408. doi: 10.1080/01292986.2011.581299

Radanovich, D. (2014). A pilot qualitative study of the under-representation of Hispanics in public relations, *Public Relations Review, 40*, 835–837. doi.org/10.1016/j.pubrev.2014.10.003.

Rogers, E. M. (1995). *Diffusion of innovations* (4th ed.). New York, NY: The Free Press.

Sha, B.-L. (1995). *Intercultural public relations: Exploring cultural identity as a means of segmenting publics*. Unpublished master's thesis, University of Maryland, College Park.

Sha, B.-L. (2006). Cultural identity in the segmentation of publics: An emerging theory of intercultural public relations. *Journal of Public Relations Research, 18*, 45–65. doi: 10.1207/ s1532754xjprr1801_3

Sha, B.-L. (2008). Baseline study on diversity segments: Multirace Americans. *Institute for Public Relations*. Retrieved from www.instituteforpr.org/topics/diversity-multirace-americans/

Sriramesh, K., Moghan, S., & Lim, K.-W. (2007). The situational theory of publics in a different cultural setting: Consumer publics in Singapore. *Journal of Public Relations Research, 19*, 307–332.

Tillery-Larkin, R. (1999). Surveying perceived pigeonholing among African American public relations professionals. Unpublished doctoral dissertation, Southern Illinois University, Carbondale.

Tindall, N. J. (2009). In search of career satisfaction: African-American public relations practitioners, pigeonholing, and the workplace. *Public Relations Review, 35*, 443–445.

Tindall, N. J., & Vardeman-Winter, J. (2011). Complications in segmenting campaign publics: Women of color explain their problems, involvement, and constraints in reading heart disease communication. *Howard Journal of Communications, 22*(3), 280–301. doi: 10.1080/10646175.2011.590407

Tkalac, A. (2006). The application of situational theory in Croatia. In E. L. Toth (Ed.), *The future of excellence in public relations and communication management: Challenges for the next generation* (pp. 527–543). Mahwah, NJ: Lawrence Erlbaum.

Toth, E. (2009). Diversity and public relations practice. Retrieved from www.institute forpr.org/topics/diversity-and-pr-practice/

Vardeman-Winter, J. (2010). Using the cultural studies approach to understand health decision-making among a teen public. *Public Relations Review, 36*(4), 383–385. doi: 10.1016/j.pubrev.2010.06.004

Vardeman-Winter, J., Jiang, H., & Tindall, N. T. (2013). Information-seeking outcomes of representational, structural, and political intersectionality among health media consumers. *Journal of Applied Communication Research, 41*(4), 389–411. doi: 10.1080/00909882.2013.828360

Werder, K. P. (2005). An empirical analysis of the influence of perceived attributes of publics on public relations strategy use and effectiveness. *Journal of Public Relations Research, 17*(3), 217–266. doi: 10.1207/s1532754xjprr1703_2

Werder, K. P. (2006). Responding to activism: An experimental analysis of public relations strategy influence on attributes of publics. *Journal of Public Relations Research, 18*(4), 335–356. doi: 10.1207/s1532754xjprr1804_3

7

INTRA-ORGANIZATIONAL LEVEL

Relationship Management

This chapter first reviews recent developments on relationship management research and then focuses more specifically on relationship management in intercultural settings. As discussed in the overview in Chapter 2, relationship management research has been developed as a three-staged model (J. Grunig & Huang, 2000): antecedents, maintenance strategies (later called cultivation strategies), and outcomes. After reviewing recent developments in this literature in general and some specific work in intercultural settings, we revise and reformulate the model as a multilevel, multistage model.

Relationship management can be a challenge for both practitioners and publics because both parties face considerable anxiety and uncertainty in intercultural settings. Connecting intercultural competencies of public relations practitioners at different levels and their public relations practices, this chapter illustrates how practitioners manage their own anxiety and uncertainty in order to engage in strategic relationship management in intercultural settings. The chapter also examines the receivers' side, that is, how intercultural publics perceive the effectiveness of relationship management.

Based on a series of studies on relationship management in intercultural settings, involving international students in the United States (Ni & Wang, 2011), minority community members in the United States (Ni et al., 2016; Ni, De la Flor, Romero, & Wang, 2017; Ni, Xiao, Lu, & Gor, 2015), community members in Peru (Ni, Wang, De la Flor, & Penaflor, 2015), and public relations practitioners in Peru (Wang, Ni, & De la Flor, 2014), we propose a new theoretical framework that helps public relations scholars and practitioners better conceptualize and conduct effective relationship management with intercultural publics.

The new model consists of antecedents of relationships that are derived from the organizational side and the public side, the process of relationship management that describes overall approaches and specific strategies, measurements of relationships, and outcomes of relationships that are both organization-centered and public-centered. We briefly review these components below, followed by more detail for each stage. In this new framework, it is to be noted that each of these components involves factors unique to interactions with publics in intercultural settings.

Antecedents of relationship management used to focus on the situations through which organizations and their publics may interact with each other. Recently, more studies have revealed a clear pattern on when and why organizations and publics will enter a relationship, from either the organizational side (e.g., internal relationship dynamics; Cardwell, Williams, & Pyle, 2017) or the public side (e.g., motivations of publics in volunteer relationships as antecedents to relationship management; Bortree, 2015). In intercultural settings, intercultural communication competencies of both the practitioners and the publics also play a key role (Wang et al., 2014).

In the *process* of managing relationships, different overall approaches of communication exist (e.g., cultural, symmetrical, and interactive/two-way), as well as different strategies for the messengers, messaging, and channels. Some recent research has studied the influence of national cultures and cultural factors in relationship management. For example, Hung-Baesecke and Chen (2015) examined how traditional Chinese value orientations were incorporated in relationship cultivation strategies; and Y. Kim and J. Yang (2015) studied how the concept of *Chemyon*, a Confucian concept of social face, played a role in relationship management and conflicts. A new framework of engaging with intercultural publics or stakeholders has also been proposed and tested in several recent studies (Ni et al., 2016; Ni et al., 2017).

The third stage in the original model contained relational outcomes, and we argue that this stage should be examined through two related but separate categories: measurements of the relationship itself and the outcomes brought out by the relationship. For *measurements*, current research has identified multiple types and quality of organization–public relationships or OPRs (e.g., Hung, 2005; Waters & Bortree, 2012; personal network added by Jo, 2006; and emotions added by Muskat, 2014). Other recent studies have started to examine alternative dimensions of OPR measurements such as distrust in particular (Kang & Park, 2017) and negative dimensions of OPR as a whole (Moon & Rhee, 2013).

In this book, the *consequences* or outcomes of relationship management are divided into organization-centered and public-centered outcomes so that both parties' perspectives can be incorporated. The organization-centered outcomes have focused on either reducing negative impacts (e.g., conflict management and crisis management) or increasing positive impacts through a wide range of perceptual, attitudinal, communicative, and behavioral outcomes desired by organizations in different sectors such as business, non-profits, and political organizations. These outcomes include reputation (J. Grunig & Hung-Baesecke, 2015; S. Yang & Cha, 2015) and favorable behaviors from different publics such as employees' voluntary information behaviors (e.g., J.-N. Kim, Park, Krishna, & Martino, 2015). However, in studies on intercultural public relations, the focus has been increasingly placed on public-centered outcomes, or outcomes that matter to the publics or stakeholders themselves. These public-centered outcomes include community empowerment, either health empowerment or identity development (e.g., Ni et al., 2016). The rest of this chapter discusses these four components of relationship management (i.e., antecedents, process, measurements, and consequences) in more detail.

Antecedents to Intercultural Relationship Management

Coombs and Holladay (2015) expressed four concerns about the application of organization–public relationship (OPR) research in public relations practice: the problems associated with applying a concept from interpersonal communication to public relations, the role of identities in forming close relationships, the value of close relationships for publics, and the parasocial nature of organization–public relationships. They advised against over-concentrating on close relationships between organizations and publics and in favor of seeking appropriate re-formulations and alternatives that more accurately depict such connections.

Therefore, it is important and useful to differentiate between various antecedents to and outcomes of organization–public relationships. The new model we propose below focuses on this differentiation by incorporating both organizational and public perspectives in the conceptualization of antecedents and outcomes of OPR. Below, we discuss the antecedents to the formation and development of relationships from both the organizational side and publics side.

Organizational Factors

From the *organizational* side, internal relationship dynamics have been found to influence how public relations practitioners build relationships with external publics, including their orientation to dialogue and perceived challenges to external relationship building (Cardwell et al., 2017). Other organizational factors such as corporate-identity management (i.e., employee perceptions of how effectively their organization upholds its values; Holtzhausen & Fourie, 2013) have also been found to influence the strength of organization–employee relationships.

Public Factors

From the publics side, examined antecedents to relationship management have included the motivations of publics in the context of volunteer relationships

(Bortree, 2015), perceptions of young females in the United Arab Emirates in the context of digital engagement with foreign governments (Khakimova, 2015), and customer awareness of corporate philanthropy and community relations programs, which has been found to influence the strength of organization–customer relationships (Hall, 2006).

Particularly worthy of note, studies have examined the alternative views on the need for relationships and the role of identity in relationship management, both reflecting the cautions of Coombs and Holladay (2015). First, relationship-specific attachment styles help explain customers' preferences for relationship closeness, purchase intentions, and changes in relationship breadth (Mende, Bolton, & Bitner, 2013). This echoes the warning from Coombs and Holladay (2015) and illustrates that, despite the firms' attempts to create relationships with customers, not all customers are motivated to build close commercial relationships. This finding has implications for better public segmentation and tailored relationship building.

Second, a personal factor that relates to relationship building involves identity synergy as a driver of organizational identification. Fombelle, Jarvis, Ward, and Ostrom (2012) found that customers' multiple societal roles (e.g., parent, environmentalist, and professor) can be used to build and reinforce their relationships with the firm. Identity synergy, which is achieved when individuals' involvement with an organization (i.e., the identity of being a customer) facilitates their pursuit of other important social identities (e.g., the identity of being an environmentalist), is positively related to identification with an organization, which positively affects customer–firm relationships.

Factors Central to Both Parties: Intercultural Communication Competencies

In the special case of intercultural public relations, relationship building and interactions involve two parties with differing cultural backgrounds: the stakeholders living in a particular cultural environment and the public relations practitioners working with them to achieve particular organizational goals. In this process, both parties bring to the interaction multiple and diverse perspectives, personalities, assumptions, and perhaps suspicions. A satisfactory relationship requires both parties to have certain qualities.

Initially, the assumption was that the publics that are entering a new cultural environment needed to exhibit a certain level of competency when interacting with others (e.g., Ni & Wang, 2011). However, a study on practitioners working for multinational companies in local communities in Peru (Wang et al., 2014) has shown that these practitioners themselves needed to develop some critical competencies. Otherwise, they were not able to fully conduct public relations practices in an effective way, such as using symmetrical and two-way communication.

Wang et al.'s (2014) model proposed that public relations practitioners' trait-level intercultural competence (empathy, open-mindedness, and flexibility) would affect their perceptual-level competence (anxiety and uncertainty management), which in turn would affect their behavioral-level competence (public relations practices) and the consequent relational quality with the publics. Results indicated that trait competence components worked differently in reducing practitioners' uncertainty and anxiety. Such distress reduction enhanced the use of symmetrical and two-way public relations. Finally, use of symmetrical public relations and lowered anxiety increased practitioners' perceptions of trust and control mutuality in the relationships their organizations had with the publics (see detailed discussion in Chapter 5 on intercultural competencies).

Process of Intercultural Relationship Management

In managing relationships, different modes and approaches of communication exist, as well as different messengers, messaging, channels, and relationship cultivation strategies.

General Relationship Approaches

Current research in relationship management has focused in particular on interactivity and a need for attention to cultural differences. Interactivity of both messages and channels has been emphasized and argued to benefit relationship building. In particular, organizations' timely responses to publics' comments have been found to enhance relationship perceptions (Lee & Park, 2013), and interactivity on social media channels such as Twitter also contributes to organization-public relationships (Saffer, Sommerfeldt, & Taylor, 2013). However, lack of interactivity was still documented for different types of organizations (Waters, Friedman, Mills, & Zeng, 2011).

In addition, Valentini (2007) advocated for a cultural, instead of global, approach to relationship management, because different cultural contexts in different nations exert great effects. Sigala (2006) investigated the effects of cultural dimensions from the customers' side on the implementation of electronic customer relationship management. Findings provided empirical evidence on the impact of each cultural dimension on the implementation of certain practices and functionalities in electronic customer relationship management.

Relationship Management Strategies

It is noted that, although in the theoretical framework presented at the end of Chapter 4, messaging and relationship management are presented to be separate components, these two are also interrelated in that messaging helps with relationship building. Thus, messaging strategies are briefly described below, and more focus is placed on the synthesized framework of strategies in relationship cultivation.

Messengers

In addition to direct interaction between organizations and publics, the effective use of intermediaries (i.e., a mediator, or someone that acts as a link between people) helps relationship building as well (Frandsen & Johansen, 2015). These intermediaries can represent either the organization or its stakeholders, intervening in their relationships by furthering or impeding their interests and activities. This study identified a definition of intermediaries and a set of taxonomic criteria for the classification of intermediaries.

Messaging

Relationship management requires clear messages. Such messaging strategies that have been proven useful in relationship management include narrative (i.e., using transportation, or the engrossing effect of narrative, empathy, and personal response so that the recipients of stories get swept away and transported into the narrative world; Van Laer & de Ruyter, 2010), personification (Men & Tsai, 2015), and corporate social responsibility narratives as an organization–employee relationship management strategy (Dhanesh, 2014).

Channels

A big trend in both theory and practice in relationship management is the use of digital and social media platforms (e.g., tourism websites, Lei & Gang, 2014; blogs, Sweetser & Metzgar, 2007). Men and Muralidharan (2017) developed a social media peer communication model that links tie strength, social media dependency, and public-organization social media engagement to the peer communication process as well as to organization–public relationship (OPR) outcomes. Results showed that tie strength and public-organization social engagement were positive predictors of peer communication about companies on social media, which further led to quality OPRs.

Through analyzing social media usage patterns of organizations, Go and You (2016) found primary use of either a single social media application or multiple social media applications, emphasizing visualization, virtualization, and interactive collaboration. Levenshus (2010) examined the Obama presidential campaign's use of the participatory Internet to manage its grassroots campaign. This study identified the integration of online and grassroots strategy.

New Framework of Relationship Management Strategies

Past and current research has followed two main lines of literature in relationship management strategies: prominent public relations practices (i.e., symmetrical, ethical, two-way, interpersonal, and mediated communication, e.g., L. Grunig,

J. Grunig, & Dozier, 2002) and relationship cultivation strategies (i.e., access, openness, sharing of tasks, shared networks, assurance of legitimacy, and positivity, see Hon & J. Grunig, 1999).

In the first line of research, public relations practices include *symmetrical/ethical* (*symmetrical* henceforth) communication, which refers to balancing the interests of both an organization and its publics (L. Grunig et al., 2002; Huang, 2001). Two-way communication involves doing research on the publics and seeking their feedback in addition to disseminating information to them. Public relations can be conducted via *mediated communication* (using various media channels) and *interpersonal communication* (using face-to-face interactions).

This framework has been used in some intercultural contexts. Given the importance of and challenges in stakeholder engagement in the global context, Ni, Wang, de la Flor, and Penaflor (2015) examined the perceptions of local community members on the stakeholder engagement strategies of multinational corporations (MNCs) operating in Peru, as well as the relationship outcomes of such engagement. A survey with 300 local community members in Cajamarca, Peru, indicated that among the different engagement strategies, symmetrical/ethical communication was the most effective, whereas mediated communication was the least effective in increasing the effectiveness of stakeholder engagement for both stakeholders and organizations. In the process of stakeholder engagement, uncertainty reduction played a more important role than anxiety reduction in increasing perceived control mutuality and trust. Appropriate stakeholder engagement strategies and stakeholders' anxiety and uncertainty management significantly predicted organization–stakeholder relational outcomes.

In intercultural settings, Pratt and Omeunugha (2014) also applied the general theory of relationship management based on a two-way symmetrical model of public relations to two countries in sub-Saharan Africa. They developed theory-informed guidelines in managing conflicts and in engaging with stakeholders of disparate theological leanings. Their results showed that these communication strategies could be used to manage mutually respectful Muslim–Christian dialogue on intractable, sensitive issues.

The second line of research has examined the influence of six main cultivation strategies on OPR outcomes. Most studies use Hon and J. Grunig's (1999) conceptualizations. *Access* refers to an organization's making available to publics their organizational decision-making processes. *Positivity* is "anything the organization or public does to make the relationship more pleasant for the parties involved" (p. 14). *Openness* is the disclosure of "thoughts and feelings among parties involved" (p. 14). *Assurance of legitimacy* is the acknowledgment that publics' concerns are legitimate and that they are considered in the organization's decision-making processes. *Networking* is the organization's building of relationships or coalitions with the same groups that their publics do. Finally, *sharing of tasks* is mutual involvement of problem-solving processes in the areas of interest to the organization, the public, or both. Ki and Hon (2007) provided a detailed review of research that had used the six strategies, and the framework has continually received attention in the study of relationship cultivation (e.g., Men, Ji, & Chen, 2017; Ni & Wang, 2011).

Synthesized Framework

A close examination reveals that both conceptual and measurement overlaps exist between the public relations strategies in the Excellence theory and cultivation strategies. For example, assurance of legitimacy seems to be very similar to symmetrical communication, conceptually. The overlaps have led to much confusion. J. Grunig (2006) proposed some potential links between relationship cultivation strategies and public relations practices, but little research has been done to integrate these two lines of thoughts. In addition, criticisms about the nature of symmetrical communication argued that this strategy was merely used to give a false impression of organizations engaging with stakeholders without true actions to benefit these stakeholders

Recent studies have been conducted to sort through the similarities and differences as well as to examine how to achieve true symmetry. Synthesizing literature in both public relations and strategic management, Ni, Wang, et al. (2015) developed a typology based on a detailed discussion of the Excellent public relations practice strategies and cultivation strategies, both in concept and measurement. Conceptually, the study identified two dimensions: ends and means of engaging with stakeholders. Integrating organization-centered ends (achieving strategic goals of an organization) and public-centered ends (treating publics in an ethical and moral manner), the current typology adapts the "ethical strategists" approach in strategic management literature and identifies a relationship-centered typology of engaging with stakeholders.

Methodologically, Ni, Wang et al. (2015) used factor analysis to identify the underlying dimensions that would explain excellence in both public relations strategies and cultivation strategies. The results led to a typology of integrated stakeholder engagement strategies. Taking place in Peru, this study generated four distinctive types of stakeholder engagement strategies: substantive collaboration (capturing measurement items for assurance of legitimacy); relational collaboration (capturing items for two-way communication, interpersonal communication, and symmetrical communication); involvement through accessibility (capturing items for access); and involvement through sharing (capturing items for openness, task sharing, and network sharing).

Some follow-up studies were then done based on the typology. In the first study, Ni, Xiao, et al. (2015) interviewed both Asian American community organizations and community members and issued a survey with these community members. Results revealed best practices of community engagement and empowerment as reflected in communication and relationship management.

First, the qualitative interviews showed that stakeholder engagement in the community health context was most fruitful when such engagement took into consideration both organizational and community needs. The relationship-focused engagement was reflected at three levels: information, which mainly took the form of health education; consultation with community at the message, program, and community levels; collaboration with community through including them in decision-making; and facilitating joint resource attainment.

In addition, community organizations developed relationships with members ranging from more intimate and personal ones such as those between family and friends, to more functional and pragmatic ones such as serving as a bridge, platform, or window. Regardless, trust appeared to be the most important factor, and trust building needed to be culturally appropriate: Making community members feel warm and welcomed as well as helping them solve real-life problems were essential before they willingly engaged in active communication with the organizations.

The survey in this first project tested the relationship between strategic communication practices and outcomes of health concerns and perceived organization–public relationships. Results indicated that two-way communication and symmetrical communication were the most influential strategies in community engagement. The use of both strategies predicted enhanced control mutuality and trust. The use of interpersonal communication enhanced trust, whereas mediated communication had no effect.

In the second follow-up study on the Hispanic community, Ni et al. (2017) used interviews to examine the framework of engaging with community members. Results indicated four types of engagement strategies based on the modes (channels and direction), purpose, and nature of engagement: messaging/informational engagement, involvement or interactive engagement, collaborative engagement, and empowering engagement.

Mediators in Relationship Management Process

A series of studies (Ni & Wang, 2011; Wang et al., 2014) have demonstrated that, in intercultural settings, managing relationships can be more challenging than when the relationship involves parties coming from the same culture and sharing similar cultural beliefs and values. In this process, managing both parties' levels of anxiety and uncertainty has been found to be particularly critical.

Incorporating the Anxiety and Uncertainty Management (AUM) theory, these studies examined how positive communication outcomes, as demonstrated by relationship management, may result from successful management of two factors: the reduction of uncertainty and the reduction of anxiety. In other words, uncertainty and anxiety are mediators between causal variables and communication outcomes (Gudykunst, 2005; see a detailed review of this theory in Chapter 2). Briefly, uncertainty refers to the perception of lacking confidence in making attributions or predictions about others or the environment. Uncertainty reduction thus refers to an individual's capacity to effectively explain and predict the interactants' behaviors (Gudykunst & Hammer, 1988). Positive communication outcomes result from a successful management of uncertainty and anxiety (Gudykunst, 2005).

The general findings from those studies indicated that, in intercultural settings, both the publics and practitioners experience anxiety and uncertainty when interacting with each other, and effective anxiety and uncertainty management (AUM) leads to effective communication and satisfying relationship building. For example, in studying the multinational companies' (MNCs') operation in the mining industry in Peru, Wang et al. (2014) confirmed the importance of AUM from the practitioners' side. Later, Ni, Wang et al. (2015) collected data from local community members in Peru and confirmed that, equally important, this public's effective AUM positively predicted their trust and control mutuality toward the MNCs.

Interestingly, studies along this line have consistently found that uncertainty played a bigger role than did anxiety in relationship management (Ni & Wang, 2011; Wang et al., 2014). In the Asian American community health study (e.g., Ni, Xiao et al., 2015), anxiety did not contribute to any of the communication behaviors as a reflection of health empowerment, but uncertainty led to information sharing. This seemed to indicate that cognitive empowerment (uncertainty) played a bigger role than affective empowerment (anxiety) in certain information behaviors. Therefore, designing effective messages with right wording and channels that can help the publics understand the organization's intentions (as compared against mere social events) may be the most important way to build long-term satisfying relationships.

Outcomes of Strategic Relational Management

Measurements of OPR

Public relations researchers have identified several attributes of communication and relational outcomes between organizations and publics (see a summary in L. Grunig et al., 2002). Four outcomes—trust, control mutuality, relational satisfaction, and relational commitment—are the most widely accepted criteria to evaluate an organization's relationship with its publics (e.g., Huang, 2001; Jo, 2006; Ki & Hon, 2007; H.-S. Kim, 2007; Yang, 2007). Briefly, *trust* is the confidence in and willingness to be open to the other party (Hon & J. Grunig, 1999). *Control mutuality* refers to the "degree to which partners agree about which of them should decide relationships goals and behavioral routines" (Stafford & Canary, 1991, p. 224). *Relational satisfaction* refers to the degree to which both organization and publics are mutually satisfied with their relationship. *Relational commitment* refers to a lasting compliance to maintain a valued relationship, which includes two aspects: continuance commitment (endurance of a certain line of action) and affective commitment (endurance of a certain emotional attribute toward an object) (J. Grunig & Huang, 2000).

Current research has expanded this line of scholarship and identified additional types and qualities of organization–public relationships (e.g., Hung, 2005; Waters & Bortree, 2012). Jo (2006) added personal network and Muskat (2014) added emotions to the framework.

Organization–public relationships (OPRs) have also been examined in different contexts, i.e., political organization–public relationships (POPRs, Seltzer & Zhang, 2011a), internal OPRs (Seltzer, Gardner, Bichard, & Callison, 2012), organization–donor relationships (symmetry through coorientation, Waters, 2009; critical importance of trust, Wiggill, 2014), and marketing relationships (commitment both enables and undermines marketing relationships, Fullerton, 2005).

More recently, alternative dimensions of OPR measurements have emerged, including trust and distrust as well as negative dimensions of OPR as a whole. Kang and Park (2017) expanded the scope of the functions of trust and distrust in organization–public relationships. They found that trust and distrust might simultaneously exist during relational interactions and might play uniquely positive and negative functions in certain social contexts. Negative dimensions of OPR—dissatisfaction, distrust, control dominance, and dissolution—have also been identified, which were shown to influence publics' communication behaviors (Moon & Rhee, 2013). These studies helped understand how to restore damaged relationships between organizations and publics and how negative OPRs (NOPRs) can hamper public relations efforts. A related study on relationship dissolution was also conducted in the cultural context of South Korea (Moon & Yang, 2015).

Effects of Intercultural Relationship Management

OPRs matter to organizations as much as they do to publics. Organization-centered relationship management outcomes can help the organization achieve goals and implement effective conflict management (for more information on conflict management, please refer to Chapter 8). Meanwhile, organizational acts influence the publics' daily life. Research has examined public-centered outcomes such as health empowerment (e.g., Ni et al., 2016).

To resolve the two major types of public relations problems: public-initiated and organization-initiated (see more in Chapter 2), different kinds of relationship management outcomes are needed. In the public-initiated public relations problems where publics sense a problem in organizational decisions or actions, the relationship management outcomes would be reflected primarily in organization-centered outcomes, or benefits to the organization (i.e., reducing conflicts with angry publics). On the other hand, in organization-initiated public relations problems that arise because an organization has sensed potential problems affecting publics' or the organization's own interests, relationship management outcomes would be primarily reflected in public-centered outcomes, or benefits to the publics (i.e., what the publics gain from the relationship).

Organization-Centered Outcomes of Relationship Management

Given that most organizations build relationships for strategic purposes, it is worth exploring the specific outcomes that these relationships can help the organizations achieve. Whereas most early research on relationship management focused on the relationship cultivation strategies and the quality of these relationships (e.g., Ferguson, 1984; Ki & Hon, 2007), more recent studies have focused on the impact that relationship management can create. Overall, two major categories have been identified: reducing negative impact and increasing positive impact, reflecting the two approaches to demonstrating public relations value (cf. Huang, 2012).

Outcomes that *reduce negative impact* include conflict management and crisis management outcomes. Huang (2001) examined whether organization–public relationship quality would mediate the public relations effects on conflict management. Findings supported her proposition. A recent study on community (Ni, Wang et al., 2015) demonstrated the effect of relationship management on conflict management in Peru. Results indicated that effective relationship management with the local community helped smooth the conflict management process, leading to the publics' use of mostly positive conflict management strategies (see more in Chapter 8).

In crisis situations, the quality of OPRs has been found to influence attitudes of organizations in crisis (Park & Reber, 2011), as well as attributions of crisis responsibility (Brown & White, 2011). For example, Brown and White (2011) found that people with a positive relationship with the organization were less likely to place blame for the crisis on the organization regardless of its crisis response strategy. Although Park and Reber (2011) did not find the same effect of relationship on the judgment of crisis responsibility, they did find that relationships directly affected the attitude toward the organization in crisis. Those with a favorable relationship were more likely than were those with unfavorable relationships to have positive perceptions of the trustworthiness of the organization's internal sources and tended to support the organization's recovery from a critical situation. Therefore, effective cultivation of relationships with publics can work well with other crisis response strategies to contribute to effective crisis management.

In addition, quality of OPR moderates the negative spillover in the context of a corporate–nonprofit partnership when a crisis strikes a partner organization (Lee & Rim, 2016). Using an online experiment, this study showed that a crisis in an organization negatively affected participants' attitude and their word-of-mouth intention toward its partner organization. However, over time, the perceived congruence between a company and the cause of the nonprofit organization buffered the negative spillover effects. Thus, the publics seemed to positively interpret an organization's behavior when they had a high-quality relationship, showing the moderating effect of organization–public relationships.

The outcomes on *increasing positive impact* are reflected in multiple dimensions: attitude and behaviors toward the organization and its products, communication behaviors, and contribution to organizational strategies. For example, quality organization–public relationships are likely to bring favorable attitudes and behaviors, such as brand attitude formation (J. Kim & Chan-Olmsted, 2005), supportive behavioral intentions (e.g., Ki & Hon, 2007), favorable attitudes and support for political parties (Seltzer & Zhang, 2011b), and loyalty and behavioral intentions for nonprofits (e.g., volunteering and fundraising; Pressgrove & McKeever, 2016). In terms of communicative behaviors, relationships bring about positive word-of-mouth through the mediation of customer–company identification (Hong & Yang, 2009), public advocacy (Men & Tsai, 2014), and positive employee communication behaviors (J.-N. Kim & Rhee, 2011). Relationships also contribute to achieving organizational goals, such as employee–organization relationships in helping achieve different globalization strategies (Ni, 2006, 2009), as well as electoral support (Seltzer & Zhang, 2011b)

Public-Centered Outcomes of Relationship Management

Relationship management has implications for the publics, in particular, the formation of public types and the development of public empowerment. Ni (2012) examined the strategic importance of relationship management in the understanding of publics. The study explored how relationships can be managed strategically to influence the formation of important publics through influencing the perceptual variables in the situational theory of problem solving (STOPS, J.-N. Kim & Grunig, 2011). Although public formation brings value to an organization through potentially fostering or cultivating different types of publics that are critical to organizations, such formation can help the publics empower themselves in becoming more communicatively active about issues that matter to them (i.e., health issues).

Based on this conceptual piece on the necessity of studying the formation of and potential changes in publics through relationship management and incorporating public relations practices with stakeholder engagement, we propose that public-centered outcomes of intercultural relationship management can be reflected in public empowerment in the form of the publics' communication behaviors as well as their substantive behaviors regarding issues that they are concerned about. For example, a good relationship community members have with their community organizations can potentially encourage positive communication behavior and engagement in public health issues, political engagement, and developed efficacy in emergency situations.

For public health issues, relationship outcomes that are public-centered were reflected in community empowerment in the Asian American community (see Ni, Xiao et al., 2015). Empowerment was illustrated through (a) basic, personal empowerment; (b) health empowerment at the individual level as reflected in health awareness, health system navigation, and more communication activeness about health issues; (c) political/civic empowerment; and (d) community empowerment.

In that study, trust turned out to be the most impactful factor in the model. Trust significantly reduced uncertainty and anxiety (with a larger effect on uncertainty than on anxiety), increased community members' problem recognition and involvement recognition, reduced constraint recognition, and ultimately increased the likelihoods of all four communication behavior outcomes examined: information seeking, attending, forwarding, and sharing. In terms of the effects of situational perceptions on community members' communication behaviors, involvement recognition was the most prominent factor, positively affecting the likelihoods of all four communication behaviors. Problem recognition and constraint recognition had limited effects, only enhancing the likelihoods of information attending and forwarding.

The findings in the study indicated that a sense of belonging to a community greatly improved a person's perceptions of the community and willingness to adopt positive communication behaviors about health. It is important to continue this line of research and identify additional effects of relationship management on the well-being of the publics themselves.

Another potential line of research that integrates relationship management, community engagement, and the development of identities can be in the context of countering violent extremism (CVE). Community engagement can empower marginalized community members in establishing a sense of community and building resistance against recruitment narratives from terrorist groups, thereby countering violent extremism. This requires identity building of young immigrants. We here propose an initial model that has four distinct but integrated components: (a) community engagement strategies (i.e., informational, involvement, and collaborative); (b) empowerment through managing anxiety and uncertainty and through developing narratives for self-empowerment; (c) engagement outcomes at the community level as reflected in community trust and relationship building; and (d) engagement outcomes for individuals as reflected in positive identity development (e.g., Y. Kim, 2005) and heightened communication behaviors (e.g., J.-N. Kim & Grunig, 2011; Ni, 2012) about CVE.

As part of an effort to build and sustain local prevention efforts, building relationships based on trust with communities is key. Drawing on literature from strategic communication, intercultural communication, and community engagement, we refine a model that has been developed on community engagement and empowerment (e.g., Ni & Wang, 2011; Ni, Xiao et al., 2015; Wang et al., 2014) and apply it in the context of CVE.

Sense of Community and Intercultural Identity: A Special Case

Community and Bonding

Community refers to a group of people who have shared values, activities, social interactions, identity-hood, and sense of bonding. Community resembles an extended family that shares a common past and feels that they are building a common future. Feelings of strong bonds with a community are usually associated with psychological health and motivation to participate in vocational and social activities (Oetzel, 2009). For newer immigrants (i.e., first- and second-generation), having a sense of belonging to a specific community can be challenging because they have two different, and oftentimes conflicting, larger supra-communities. One consists of mainstream institutions that are represented by host-country members, mass media, and social media. The other is ethnic group community, composed of ethnic group members and ethnic media. As discussed in Chapter 5, immigrants need to keep a balanced way to associate with their ethnic group. Insufficient association leads to the lack of a comforting bond with their ethnic group, but excessive association leads to an isolation from other cultural groups (Y. Kim, 2005).

To be a resilient community member, a person needs to have perceived sufficiency in social capital, sense of community, collective efficacy, and community capacity/empowerment (Oetzel, 2009):

1. *Social capital*: The sum of economic and social resources related to social networks that enable a person to receive reciprocity, trust, and empowerment in social environments.
2. *Sense of community*: Feeling of caring and sharing that is shared (belonging).
3. *Collective efficacy*: Belief you can collectively achieve a goal as a community.
4. *Community capacity/empowerment*: Ability to address social problems and take social action.

To strengthen young immigrants' resilience as community members and make them feel like accumulating social capital, it is necessary to start with identity establishment.

Acculturation and Deculturation in Immigrant Identity Formation

Identity dilemma (see Chapter 5) can pose a big challenge for new immigrants. In the process of becoming permanent residents in a new culture, they have to decide, day to day, what to do when their "cultural practices, values, and identifications" are in conflict with those of the new culture (Schwartz, Unger, Zamboanga, & Szapocznik, 2010, p. 12). As they both acculturate (learn new cultural elements) and deculturate (unlearn their own ethnic cultural elements), they form their new identities, aptly labeled as a new cultural identity (Schwartz et al., 2010).

However, whether such new cultural identity is stable varies across individuals. A stable identity helps reduce the likelihood of mental health problems. When an immigrant fails to adjust to the new cultural environment, especially to new values, worldviews, or ways of positioning themselves in relation to others (e.g., identifications based on ethnicity, race, and social classes), negative emotions arise and lead to mental health problems such as depression (Berry, 2001; Mahmoud, Staten, Hall, & Lennie, 2012; Paniagua & Yamada, 2013). When overcome with such negative emotions and high stress, some immigrants perceive consistent rejections from others and resort to hatred as a way to cope with the world. They are thus more susceptible to narratives of violent extremism and may eventually turn to groups of violence. Relationship management in the form of pro-social interventions during the identity development process of young immigrants can be powerful in building a resilient community. The youth can be more resilient to narratives of violent extremism by actively building and sharing positive narratives for themselves and those around them.

People choose to acculturate and deculturate differently based on their backgrounds, goals, and experiences. Berry (1997) used acculturation (unsubscribing original ethnic culture) and deculturation (adoption of the new host culture) to predict four outcomes: integration (bicultural identity), assimilation (adoption of host culture mainly), separation (keeping ethnic culture mainly), and marginalization (not adopting either culture).

Marginalized Identity vs. Integrated Identity in Violent Extremism

Radicalization or extreme violence may be found mainly in individuals with a marginalized identity. The reason lies in the lack of strong attachments to a community, an ingroup, or any group, for that matter. Marginalized individuals do not have trusted others to feel mutual connection and care. They may have an unsatisfied need of self-esteem because of the lack of social capital (Berry, 1997). Instead, the perceived loneliness and subjectively interpreted hostility from others and the environment foster a strong sense of insecurity. Studies have shown that a strong ethnic identity brings positive health outcomes both physically and psychologically (Schwartz et al., 2010). The lack of bonding at the group or community level can leave individuals vulnerable to extremist groups' propaganda.

Therefore, it is essential to help immigrants, especially the youth, formulate healthy relationships with both ethnic and host-related cultural ingroups. Berry's (1997) term, *integration*, describes a "blended" identity that embraces both host and ethnic cultural elements. It allows the immigrant to appreciate both cultures and select cultural elements autonomously to form their identities. The integration process enables an immigrant to activate appropriate cultural schemata in any given situation and thus leads to high self-esteem and low psychological stress (Berry, 2001). A stable and resilient identity through integration also brings in ingroups and communities that the immigrants feel close to. This sense of bonding with communities may promote psychological health and build a stronghold against the propaganda of violence and anti-humanism.

Outcomes of Identity Transformation

The ultimate goal of integration is to build a transformed identity that helps immigrants to reach *functional fitness* (behavioral efficacy in social and vocational settings), *psychological health* ("life satisfaction, positive feelings, sense of belonging, and greater congruence in subjective meaning systems," Y. Kim, 2005, p. 391), and *global identity* (a stable self-image that loses its original cultural distinctiveness and rigidity while adopting an expanded and more flexible definition of self that benefits all human species; Y. Kim, 2005). In short, a healthy global self-identity is a healthy view of "who I am," stable and unique from any special groups but connected with many groups in a caring and altruistic manner.

A Model of Stakeholder Engagement and Relationship Management

Integrating what has been discussed in previous sections, we propose a new model of stakeholder engagement and relationship management that can be applied and adapted in various contexts. The new model consists of antecedents of relationships that are derived from the organizational side and the public side, processes of relationship management that describe overall approaches and specific strategies, measurements of relationships, and outcomes of relationships that are both organization-centered and public-centered (see Figure 7.1).

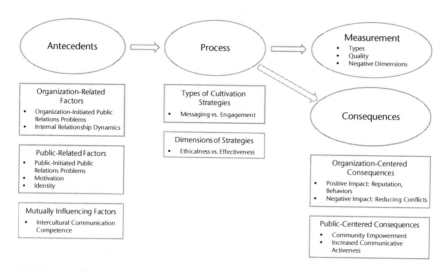

FIGURE 7.1 Theoretical Framework of Intercultural Relationship Management

References

Berry, J. W. (1997). Immigration, acculturation, and adaptation. *Applied Psychology: An International Review*, *46*(1), 5–34.

Berry, J. W. (2001). A psychology of immigration. *Journal of Social Issues*, *57*(3), 615–631.

Bortree, D. S. (2015). Motivations of publics: The power of antecedents in the volunteer–nonprofit organization relationship. In E.-J. Ki, J.-N. Kim, & J. A. Ledingham (Eds.), *Public relations as relationship management: A relational approach to the study and practice of public relations* (2nd ed., pp. 144–158). New York, NY: Routledge.

Brown, K. A., & White, C. L. (2011). Organization–public relationships and crisis response strategies: Impact on attribution of responsibility. *Journal of Public Relations Research*, *23*(1), 75–92. doi: 10.1080/1062726X.2010.504792

Cardwell, L. A., Williams, S., & Pyle, A. (2017). Corporate public relations dynamics: Internal vs. external stakeholders and the role of the practitioner. *Public Relations Review*, *43*(1), 152–162. doi: 10.1016/j.pubrev.2016.11.004

Coombs, W. T., & Holladay, S. J. (2015). Public relations' "relationship identity" in research: Enlightenment or illusion. *Public Relations Review*, *41*(5), 689–695. doi: 10.1016/j.pubrev.2013.12.008

Dhanesh, G. S. (2014). CSR as organization–employee relationship management strategy: A case study of socially responsible information technology companies in India. *Management Communication Quarterly*, *28*(1), 130–149. doi: 10.1177/0893318913517238

Ferguson, M. A. (1984, August). *Building theory in public relations: Interorganizational relationships.* Paper presented at the annual convention of the Association for Education in Journalism and Mass Communication, Gainesville, FL.

Fombelle, P., Jarvis, C., Ward, J., & Ostrom, L. (2012). Leveraging customers' multiple identities: Identity synergy as a driver of organizational identification. *Journal of the Academy of Marketing Science*, *40*(4), 587–604. doi: 10.1007/s11747-011-0254-5

Frandsen, F., & Johansen, W. (2015). Organizations, stakeholders, and intermediaries: Towards a general theory. *International Journal of Strategic Communication*, *9*(4), 253–271. doi: 10.1080/1553118X.2015.1064125

Fullerton, G. (2005). How commitment both enables and undermines marketing relationships. *European Journal of Marketing*, *39*(11/12), 1372–1388. doi: 10.1108/03090560510623307

Go, E., & You, K. H. (2016). But not all social media are the same: Analyzing organizations' social media usage patterns. *Telematics & Informatics*, *33*(1), 176–186. doi: 10.1016/j.tele.2015.06.016

Grunig, J. E. (2006). Furnishing the edifice: Ongoing research on public relations as a strategic management function. *Journal of Public relations Research*, *18*, 151–176.

Grunig, J. E., & Huang, Y. H. (2000). From organizational effectiveness to relationship indicators: Antecedents of relationships, public relations strategies, and relationship outcomes. In J. A. Ledingham & S. D. Bruning (Eds.), *Public relations as relationship management: A relational approach to the study and practice of public relations* (pp. 23–53). Mahwah, NJ: Lawrence Erlbaum Associates.

Grunig, J. E., & Hung-Baesecke, C.-J. F. (2015). The effect of relationships on reputation and reputation on relationships: A cognitive, behavioral study. In E.-J. Ki, J.-N. Kim, & J. A. Ledingham (Eds.), *Public relations as relationship management: A relational approach to the study and practice of public relations* (2nd ed., pp. 63–113). New York, NY: Routledge.

Grunig, L. A., Grunig, J. E., & Dozier, D. M. (2002). *Excellent public relations and effective organizations: A study of communication management in three countries*. Mahwah, NJ: Lawrence Erlbaum Associates.

Gudykunst, W. B. (2005). *Theorizing about intercultural communication*. Thousand Oaks, CA: Sage.

Gudykunst, W. B., & Hammer, M. R. (1988). Strangers and hosts: An extension of uncertainty reduction theory to intercultural adjustment. In Y. Y. Kim & W. B. Gudykunst (Eds.), *Cross-cultural adaptation* (pp. 106–139). Newbury Park, CA: Sage.

Hall, M. R. (2006). Corporate philanthropy and corporate community relations: Measuring relationship-building results. *Journal of Public Relations Research*, *18*, 1–21. https://doi.org/10.1207/s1532754xjprr1801_1

Holzthausen, L., & Fourie, L. (2013). The relationship between corporate identity-management constructs and relationship-management constructs: A case study of the North-West University. *Communicare*, *32*(1), 58–83.

Hon, L. C., & Grunig, J. E. (1999). *Guidelines for measuring relationships in public relations*. Gainesville, FL: The Institute for Public Relations. Commission on PR Measurement and Evaluation.

Hong, S. Y., & Yang, S. (2009). Effects of reputation, relational satisfaction, and customer-company identification on positive word-of-mouth intentions. *Journal of Public Relations Research*, *21*(4), 381–403. doi: 10.1080/10627260902966433

Huang, Y.-H. (2001). Values of public relations: Effects on organization–public relationships mediating conflict resolution. *Journal of Public Relations Research*, *13*(4), 265–301.

Huang, Y.-H. (2012). Gauging an integrated model of public relations value assessment (PRVA): Scale development and cross-cultural studies. *Journal of Public Relations Research*, *24*, 243–265. https://doi.org/10.1080/1062726X.2012.671987

Hung, C.-J. F. (2005). Exploring types of organization–public relationships and their implications for relationship management in public relations. *Journal of Public Relations Research*, *17*, 393–426. doi: 10.1207/s1532754xjprr1704_4

Hung-Baesecke, C.-J. F., & Chen, Y.-R R. (2015). Factoring culture into relationship management theory: Cultivation strategies and traditional Chinese value orientations. In E.-J. Ki, J.-N. Kim, & J. A. Ledingham (Eds.), *Public relations as relationship management: A relational approach to the study and practice of public relations* (2nd ed., pp. 217–239). New York, NY: Routledge.

Jo, S. (2006). Measurement of organization–public relationships: Validation of measurement using a manufacturer–retailer relationship. *Journal of Public Relations Research*, *18*(3), 225–248. doi: 10.1207/s1532754xjprr1803_2

Kang, M., & Park, Y. E. (2017). Exploring trust and distrust as conceptually and empirically distinct constructs: Association with symmetrical communication and public engagement across four pairings of trust and distrust. *Journal of Public Relations Research*, *29*(2/3), 114–135. doi: 10.1080/1062726X.2017.1337579

Khakimova Storie, L. (2015). Lost publics in public diplomacy: Antecedents for online relationship management. *Public Relations Review*, *41*(2), 315–317. doi: 10.1016/j.pubrev.2015.02.008

Ki, E., & Hon, L. C. (2007). Testing the linkages among the organization–public relationship and attitude and behavioral intentions. *Journal of Public Relations Research*, *19*(1), 1–23. doi: 10.1207/s1532754xjprr1901_1

Kim, H. (2007). A multilevel study of antecedents and a mediator of employee—organization relationships. *Journal of Public Relations Research*, *19*(2), 167–197. doi: 10.1080/10627260701290695

Kim, J., & Chan-Olmsted, S. M. (2005). Comparative effects of organization–public relationships and product-related attributes on brand attitude. *Journal of Marketing Communications*, *11*(3), 145–170. doi: 10.1080/1352726042000317214

Kim, J.-N., & Grunig, J. E. (2011). Problem solving and communicative action: A situational theory of problem solving. *Journal of Communication*, *61*, 120–149. doi: 10.1111/j.1460-2466.2010.01529.x

Kim, J.-N., & Rhee, Y. (2011). Strategic thinking about employee communication behavior (ECB) in public relations: Testing the models of megaphoning and scouting effects in Korea. *Journal of Public Relations Research*, *23*, 243–268.

Kim, J.-N., Park, S., Krishna A., & Martino, V. (2015). Risk management through employees: Testing employees' voluntary scouting and corporate readiness for cyber risks. In E.-J. Ki, J.-N. Kim, & J. A. Ledingham (Eds.), *Public relations as relationship management: A relational approach to the study and practice of public relations* (2nd ed., pp. 199–214). New York: Routledge.

Kim, Y. Y. (2005). Adapting to a new culture: An integrative communication theory. In W. B. Gudykunst (Ed.), *Theorizing about intercultural communication* (pp. 375–400). Thousand Oaks, CA: Sage.

Kim, Y., & Yang, J. (2015). Chemyon, relationship building, and conflicts. In E.-J. Ki, J.-N. Kim, & J. A. Ledingham (Eds.), *Public relations as relationship management: A relational approach to the study and practice of public relations* (2nd ed., pp. 240–257). New York: Routledge.

Lee, H., & Park, H. (2013). Testing the impact of message interactivity on relationship management and organizational reputation. *Journal of Public Relations Research*, *25*(2), 188–206. doi: 10.1080/1062726X.2013.739103

Lee, S. Y., & Rim, H. (2016). Negative spillover in corporate–nonprofit partnerships: Exploring the effects of company–cause congruence and organization–public relationships. *Public Relations Review*, *42*(4), 710–712. doi: 10.1016/j.pubrev.2016.06.003

Lei, Z., & Gang, K. H. (2014). Maintaining organization–public relationships on tourism Websites through relationship management strategies. *Public Relations Review*, *40*(5), 847–849. doi: 10.1016/j.pubrev.2014.06.006

Levenshus, A. (2010). Online relationship management in a presidential campaign: A case study of the Obama campaign's management of its internet-integrated grassroots effort. *Journal of Public Relations Research*, *22*(3), 313–335. doi: 10.1080/10627261003614419

Mahmoud, J. S. R., Staten, R. T., Hall, L. A., & Lennie, T. A. (2012). The relationship among young adult college students' depression, anxiety, stress, demographics, life satisfaction, and coping styles. *Issues in Mental Health Nursing*, *33*(3), 149–156.

Men, L. R., & Muralidharan, S. (2017). Understanding social media peer communication and organization–public relationships. *Journalism & Mass Communication Quarterly*, *94*(1), 81–101. doi: 10.1177/1077699016674187

Men, L. R., & Tsai, W. S. (2014). Perceptual, attitudinal, and behavioral outcomes of organization–public engagement on corporate social networking sites. *Journal of Public Relations Research*, *26*(5), 417–435. doi: 10.1080/1062726X.2014.951047

Men, L. R., & Tsai, W. S. (2015). Infusing social media with humanity: Corporate character, public engagement, and relational outcomes. *Public Relations Review*, *41*(3), 395–403. doi: 10.1016/j.pubrev.2015.02.005

Men, L. R., Ji, Y. G., & Chen, Z. F. (2017). Dialogues with entrepreneurs in China: How start-up companies cultivate relationships with strategic publics. *Journal of Public Relations Research*, *29*, 90–113. https://doi.org/10.1080/1062726X.2017.1329736

Mende, M., Bolton, R. N., & Bitner, M. J. (2013). Decoding customer–firm relationships: How attachment styles help explain customers' preferences for closeness, repurchase intentions, and changes in relationship breadth. *Journal of Marketing Research (JMR)*, *50*(1), 125–142

Moon, B. B., & Rhee, Y. (2013). Exploring negative dimensions of organization–public relationships (NOPR) in public relations. *Journalism & Mass Communication Quarterly*, *90*(4), 691–714. doi: 10.1177/1077699013503161

Moon, B. B., & Yang, S. (2015). Why publics terminate their relationship with organizations: exploring antecedents of relationship dissolution in South Korea. *Asian Journal of Communication*, *25*(3), 288–306. doi: 10.1080/01292986.2014.960876

Muskat, B. (2014). Emotions in organization–public relationships: Proposing a new determinant. *Public Relations Review*, *40*(5), 832–834. doi: 10.1016/j.pubrev.2014.06.004

Ni, L. (2006). Relationships as organizational resources: Examining public relations impact through its connection with organizational strategies. *Public Relations Review*, *32*, 276–281.

Ni, L. (2009). Strategic role of relationship building: Perceived links between employee–organization relationships and globalization strategies. *Journal of Public Relations Research*, *21*, 100–120.

Ni, L. (2012). Exploring the role of strategic relationship management in the formation of publics. *International Journal of Strategic Communication*, *6*(1), 7–16. doi: 10.1080/1553118X.2011.634867

Ni, L. & Wang, Q. (2011). Anxiety and uncertainty management in an intercultural Setting: The impact on organization–public relationships. *Journal of Public Relations Research*, *23*, 269–301. doi: 10.1080/1062726X.2011.582205

Ni, L., De la Flor, M., Romero, B., & Wang, Q. (2017, March). *Community engagement and public health: A qualitative study of strategic communication of Hispanic community organizations.* Paper accepted at the International Public Relations Research Conference, Orlando, FL.

Ni, L., Wang, Q., De la Flor, M., & Penaflor, R. (2015, May). *Stakeholder engagement and conflict resolution in the global environment: Strategies and outcomes.* Paper presented at the International Communication Association Annual Convention, San Juan, Puerto Rico.

Ni, L., Xiao, Z., Lu, Q., & Gor, B. (2015). *Effective communication and engagement to enhance Asian American health.* White Paper Submitted to the Urban Communication Foundation. This White Paper includes research funded by the Urban Communication Foundation White Paper Grant, 2014–2015.

Ni, L., Cui, Y., Xiao, Z., Lu, Q., Gor, B., & Ji, B. (2016). *The role of stakeholder engagement in the context of community health: A qualitative study on strategic communication and community empowerment.* Paper presented at the 2016 International Communication Association Conference in Fukuoka, Japan, June 13, 2016.

Oetzel, J. G. (2009). *Intercultural communication: A layered approach.* New York, NY: Vango Books.

Paniagua, F., & Yamada, A.-M. (2013). *Handbook of multicultural mental health: Assessment and treatment of diverse populations* (2nd ed.). New York, NY: Academic Press.

Park, H., & Reber, B. H. (2011). The organization–public relationship and crisis communication: The effect of the organization–public relationship on publics' perceptions of crisis and attitudes toward the organization. *International Journal of Strategic Communication, 5*(4), 240–260. doi: 10.1080/1553118X.2011.596870

Pratt, C. B., & Omenugha, K. A. (2014). "My God is not your God": Applying relationship management theory to managing ethnoreligious crises in sub-Saharan Africa. *International Journal of Strategic Communication, 8*(2), 100–125. doi: 10.1080/1553118X.2014.882338

Pressgrove, G. N., & McKeever, B. W. (2016). Nonprofit relationship management: Extending the organization–public relationship to loyalty and behaviors. *Journal of Public Relations Research, 28*(3/4), 193–211. doi: 10.1080/1062726X.2016.1233106

Saffer, A. J., Sommerfeldt, E. J., & Taylor, M. (2013). The effects of organizational Twitter interactivity on organization–public relationships. *Public Relations Review, 39*(3), 213–215. doi: 10.1016/j.pubrev.2013.02.005

Schwartz, S. J., Unger, J. B., Zamboanga, B. L., & Szapocznik, J. (2010). Rethinking the concept of acculturation: Implications for theory and research. *American Psychologist, 65*, 237–251. doi: 10.1037/a0019330

Seltzer, T., & Zhang, W. (2011a). Toward a model of political organization–public relationships: Antecedent and cultivation strategy influence on citizens' relationships with political parties. *Journal of Public Relations Research, 23*(1), 24–45. doi: 10.1080/1062726X.2010.504791

Seltzer, T., & Zhang, W. (2011b). Debating healthcare reform: How political parties' issue-specific communication influences citizens' perceptions of organization–public relationships. *Journalism & Mass Communication Quarterly, 88*(4), 753–770

Seltzer, T., Gardner, E., Bichard, S., & Callison, C. (2012). PR in the ER: Managing internal organization–public relationships in a hospital emergency department. *Public Relations Review, 38*(1), 128–136. doi: 10.1016/j.pubrev.2011.12.002

Sigala, M. (2006). Culture: The software of e-customer relationship management. *Journal of Marketing Communications, 12*(3), 203–223. doi: 10.1080/13527260600811787

Stafford, L., & Canary, D. J. (1991). Maintenance strategies and romantic relation-ship type, gender, and relational 725 characteristics. *Journal of Social and Personal Relationships, 8,* 217–242.

Sweetser, K. D., & Metzgar, E. (2007). Communicating during crisis: Use of blogs as a relationship management tool. *Public Relations Review, 33*(3), 340–342. doi: 10.1016/j.pubrev.2007.05.016

Valentini, C. (2007). Global versus cultural approaches in public relationship manage-ment. *Journal of Communication Management, 11*(2), 117–133

van Laer, T., & de Ruyter, K. (2010). In stories we trust: How narrative apologies provide cover for competitive vulnerability after integrity-violating blog posts. *International Journal of Research In Marketing, 27*(2), 164–174. doi: 10.1016/j.ijresmar.2009.12.010

Wang, Q., Ni, L., & De la Flor, M. (2014). An intercultural competence model of strategic public relations management in the Peru mining industry context. *Journal of Public Relations Research, 26,* 1–22. doi: 10.1080/1062726X.2013.795864

Waters, R. D. (2009). Comparing the two sides of the nonprofit organization–donor relationship: Applying coorientation methodology to relationship management. *Public Relations Review, 35*(2), 144–146. doi: 10.1016/j.pubrev.2009.01.011

Waters, R. D., & Bortree, D. S. (2012). Advancing relationship management theory: Mapping the continuum of relationship types. *Public Relations Review, 38*(1), 123–127. doi: 10.1016/j.pubrev.2011.08.018

Waters, R. D., Friedman, C. S., Mills, B., & Zeng, L. (2011). Applying relationship management theory to religious organizations: An assessment of relationship cultiva-tion online. *Journal of Communication & Religion, 34*(1), 88–104.

Wiggill, M. (2014). Donor relationship management practices in the South African non-profit sector. *Public Relations Review, 40*(2), 278–285. doi: 10.1016/j.pub rev.2013.10.005

Yang, S.-U. (2007). An integrated model for organization–public relational outcomes, organizational reputation, and their antecedents. *Journal of Public Relations Research, 19*(2), 91–121. doi: 10.1080/10627260701290612

Yang, S.-U., & Cha, H. (2015). A framework linking organization–public relation-ships and organizational reputations in public relations management. In E.-J. Ki, J.-N. Kim, & J. A. Ledingham (Eds.), *Public relations as relationship management: A relational approach to the study and practice of public relations* (2nd ed., pp. 114–129). New York: Routledge.

8

INTRA-ORGANIZATIONAL LEVEL
Conflict Management and Negotiation

Importance of Negotiation and Conflict Management in the Strategic Management of Public Relations

As discussed in Chapter 2, public relations should be a strategic management process. Public relations emphasizes interdependence and relationships among different entities, so it is critical for its practitioners to know the best practices in negotiation. Even with disagreements and conflicts, practitioners need to strive for a shared mission through openness, understanding, and trust building. The shared mission can only be achieved through negotiation and collaboration.

Negotiation in the process of conflict management is critical to the strategic management of public relations. In the stages of strategic management (see Chapter 2), the issues stage is where publics arise and pursue an issue with an organization. At this point, negotiation with these publics equals managing public relations strategically and requires the use of two-way and symmetrical communication.

Two-way and symmetrical public relations practice suggests that organizations and their publics need to simultaneously attempt to persuade each other, especially in times of conflict (J. Grunig & L. Grunig, 1992). Symmetry can also include the central route to persuasion when needed. For example, practitioners need to persuade both sides of a conflict: organizational management and the public. They need to persuade management that engaging with the public is not only moral (doing the right thing), but also strategic (contributing to organizational goals). On the other hand, they also need to persuade the public, when conserving certain organizational missions is needed (see Sha's work on organizational identity, 2004, 2009). However, when facing a conflict, both sides should typically switch to negotiation (J. Grunig & L. Grunig, 1992).

The use of two-way and symmetrical communication as public relations strategies essentially requires public relations practitioners to negotiate with stakeholders constantly, both externally and internally. Externally, issues of conflict can arise from activist groups (e.g., Target with its transgender bathroom policy) and community members (e.g., police–community relations). Internally, organizations may face dissatisfied employees with minority identities. Negotiating power within an organization can be a challenge to both organizations and their members (see Plowman et al., 1995).

In terms of channel choice for two-way and symmetrical communication, negotiation can occur through both mediated and interpersonal channels. Although negotiation traditionally relies more on interpersonal communication, mediated channels can today provide an important platform because the widespread use of social media has increasingly blurred the line between mediated and interpersonal communication.

Granted, two-way and symmetrical communication has its limitations. It may not work in certain situations, such as when the involved parties have sharp differences in ideologies and power differentials; when the conflict concerns multiple parties and historical antagonism; or when interventions in the past have failed (L. Grunig, J. Grunig, & Dozier, 2002). In such situations, mediation and other public relations strategies may be needed.

Given the importance of engaging with publics or stakeholders in a symmetrical and effective way, the role of conflict management is critical. In fact, conflict management is perhaps the most appropriate manifestation of two-way and symmetrical communication when different parties in a relationship disagree with each other. With the growing diversity and emerging influence of multiple cultural groups, whether grounded in race and ethnicity, countries of origin, or sexual orientation, conflicts between organizations and publics have become more frequent.

Today, social conflicts seem to occur more frequently in society, and many of them arise across cultures. Around the 2016 U.S. election, conflicts arose out of almost all manifestations of cultural differences: race (e.g., community–police tensions in the African American community; affirmative action in college admissions among Asian Americans); sexual orientation (e.g., transgender community and the use of bathrooms according to self-identified gender); ideological beliefs (e.g., gun control); religion (e.g., an anti-Muslim mentality in the wake of ISIS); countries of origin (e.g., resentment against refugees from Syria or undocumented immigrants from Mexico and South American countries); and Confederate statues and related issues (e.g., Charlottesville, 2017). Not surprisingly, all these issues have been heavily debated and taken a central stage during the 2016 U.S. presidential election period and long after that.

We cannot help but ask: Why are all these issues becoming more prominent now? And what can we do to address these conflicts? Granted, all these issues have highly complicated social, economic, and political roots and implications.

It is unrealistic to expect that these conflicts can be resolved using public relations only. However, when organizations engage with stakeholders or publics that are closely involved, it is likely that the conflicts might be managed better at least, if not completely resolved. We argue that such management of conflicts should include pre-conflict engagement, during-conflict interaction, and post-conflict engagement.

Current Theoretical Framework for Intercultural Public Relations Conflict Management

The current theoretical framework and relevant research on conflict management in the public relations context is primarily built upon the two-way and symmetrical practices of public relations and conflict resolution theory.

Symmetrical Communication

First of all, in defending the value of symmetry in the midst of criticism that symmetry potentially means giving up on the organization's underlying mission or manipulating the publics, L. Grunig et al. (2002) argued that symmetry implies a balance of the organization's and public's interest and does not equal accommodation at either party's expense. Symmetry is harder to achieve than any one-sided public relations, and that is why skill in negotiation and conflict management that requires the consideration of both parties' outcomes must become essential for public relations practitioners.

At the same time, symmetry is possible only with corresponding conservation (Sha, 2004). Applying Noether's Theorem, Sha (2004) argued and her findings supported that symmetry, or change on the part of the organization for the interest of the public, can only exist simultaneously with conservation or invariance. The implication for public relations is that, for organizations to change and adapt in response to public need, or for organizations to behave symmetrically, something else about the organization must remain constant in the organization–public relationship. For example, the organization should maintain certain beliefs, principles, or purposes that may never be relinquished (see more in Chapter 9 on organizational identity).

Symmetrical public relations does not equate to acquiescence in conflict management with publics. Symmetry emphasizes the principle of mutual communicating and listening, which does not imply agreeing. L. Grunig et al. (2002) argued that it would still be ethical to talk with representatives of a repugnant public, and such talking does not entail yielding to their perhaps unreasonable demands.

One incorrect judgment organizations lean toward is that, far too often, they consider their publics to be morally repugnant and the organization to be morally superior (i.e., paternalism on the part of organizations when they think and argue that they know what is best for the public) (L. Grunig et al., 2002).

In some situations, an organization or a public does have a more reasonable or more moral position than the other, but the point of symmetrical communication is that neither party would know the morality or reasonableness of the other side's interests without talking. Although it may be unethical to acquiesce to repugnant publics, it is ethical to talk to them. After having the dialogue, it is then possible to decide whether to engage in advocacy or to withdraw from further dialogue.

Multi-party conflict situations present a new layer of complication. In these situations, only symmetrical communication and sophisticated conflict management skills can potentially resolve the conflict, if at all, because asymmetrical communication or manipulative behaviors cannot be concealed to multiple publics at the same time.

Conflict Management Strategies

As discussed extensively in Chapter 4, conflict management theories have identified five major strategies as contending (contention), collaboration (cooperation), avoiding, compromise, and accommodation. Many classic books and articles from business negotiation and conflict management have also provided theoretical structure and practical applications to conflict management. The following section reviews some of the classic ones.

Principled Negotiation and Unconditional Constructiveness

Many researchers have examined models for maintaining good relations with an opponent without necessarily yielding on the issues at stake (Fisher & Brown, 1988; Fisher & Ury, 1983). They suggested a fourfold approach:

1. Separate the people from the problem (i.e., be tough or hard on the issues but soft or cooperative on the people).
2. Focus on interests, not positions.
3. Invent options for mutual gains.
4. Insist on using objective criteria to judge solutions.

One negotiation strategy called "best alternative to a negotiated agreement (BATNA)" was proposed. BATNA is adopted when parties fail to reach agreement and is usually identical with the status quo; that is, the situation that would have been obtained if negotiation had never taken place. This approach is based on the following:

1. *Rationality*: Balancing emotions with reason.
2. *Understanding*: Learning how the other party sees things.
3. *Good communication*: Consulting and listening before deciding.
4. *Reliability*: Being wholly trustworthy, but not wholly trusting.

5. *Persuasion instead of coercion*: Negotiating side by side.
6. *Mutual acceptance*: Dealing seriously with those with whom we differ, accepting them as worthy of our consideration, caring about them, and being open to learning from them.

The general guidelines are (a) to disentangle relationship issues from substantive goals so as to pursue each independently and vigorously, and (b) to think separately about the relationship as a process, otherwise we subordinate it to short-term substantive concerns. The strategy is to be unconditionally constructive.

Mutual-Gains Approach

As briefly reviewed in the conflict management section in Chapter 2, a mutual-gains approach to conflict management was proposed by Susskind and Field (1996). These authors started by defining anger as primarily defense, as response to either real or perceived pain, or the threat of such pain. Based on that, they considered it unfruitful to divide anger into rational or irrational. Labeling one's opponents as irrational leads to multiple practices not conducive to effective conflict management, such as limited ability to both absorb new information and consider information that counter one's initial belief.

Susskind and Field (1996) identified six sources of anger in conflicts: *hurt* where people are angry because they sensed that they have been hurt; *risk* where people are afraid of being hurt in the future; *belief* where people perceive that their identities and beliefs have been threatened; *weakness* where people feel angry because they have less power than the other party in the conflict; *lie* where people sense that they have been lied to; and *show* where people just want to strengthen their bargaining position or intimidate others.

Conflict management strategies in these situations may vary, but the underlying principles follow the mutual-gains approach outlined in Susskind and Field (1996):

1. Acknowledge the concerns of the other side (i.e., try to look at the issue from the standpoint of others).
2. Encourage joint fact-finding.
3. Offer contingent commitments to minimize impacts if they do occur; and promise to compensate knowable but unintended impacts.
4. Accept responsibility, admit mistakes, and share power.
5. Act in a trustworthy fashion at all times.
6. Focus on building long-term relationships.

In particular, for an angry public who has been *hurt* by accidents caused by corporations or public agencies, suggested guidelines include:

1. Share information to build trust and credibility.
2. Say what you mean and mean what you say.
3. Acknowledge the concerns of others.
4. Select an informed, experienced, capable, and eloquent spokesperson who is not condescending to the public.
5. Find an advocate who can defend and promote the company's or the agency's credibility from inside.
6. For government: seek voluntary rather than enforced compliance.

In cases of *risky* decisions, corporations and agencies should engage all relevant stakeholders in making decisions that pose risks to the public through the creation of consensus-building forums. Guidelines for dealing with angry publics over risks involve setting clear and believable performance standards.

1. Minimize the risks, not the concerns of others. (Corporations and agencies are better off communicating concrete and purposeful actions rather than merely attempting to educate the public about the risks.)
2. Make commitments you intend to keep, and then keep them.
3. Seek to know, not to hide information about your product or policy.
4. Engage stakeholders in making risky decisions through consensus-building forums.
5. Offer contingent commitment to alleviate worry and reduce uncertainty. Be certain that the basis for these offers is credible.

Determination of risk (which is the probability of a hazard occurring combined with impacts of the hazard) can generate enormous public controversy. Assessing risks by professionals involves differing assumption, errors of omission, unknown latent effects, animal studies versus human effects, and subjective bias. On the other hand, perceiving risks by a public involves factors such as research versus real life, weighing consequences differently, exposure versus harm (number of people versus the scope of the injuries), allocation of benefits and costs, and lack of trust. Therefore, having a consensus-building forum is essential. Such forums can take three forms:

1. A conference at which a neutral and respected body in the debate would organize a non-decision-making gathering. Its purpose is to highlight the extent of the scientific consensus already existing, as well as the reasons why technical experts might disagree. This conference attempts to give all credible scientific viewpoints a chance to debate the question.
2. Policy dialogues to help generate one or two specific policy options. Such dialogues could produce a small set of policy options and move the contending interests into a collaborative problem-solving mode.

3. Negotiated rule-making, through which people can come up with full-fledged regulations (not just recommendations) that become the subject of formal agency rule-making.

Anger related to *beliefs and values* is more challenging. Values involve strongly held personal beliefs, moral and ethical principles, basic legal rights, and, more generally, idealized views of the world. While interests are about what we want, values are about what we care about and what we stand for. Compromise on values-related conflicts means abandoning deeply held beliefs, values, or ideals. To negotiate away beliefs and values is to risk giving up one's identity. Thus, such conflicts are intense.

Three stages of de-escalating intractable value conflicts are proposed:

1. The disputants may agree on *peripheral* changes that do not eliminate the ongoing hostilities but do alleviate specific problems.
2. The disputants alter *some aspects* of the ongoing relationship, but fundamental values are not challenged or transformed, at least in the short-run. Find the common problems and work on them. Do not touch the core colliding values.
3. The disputants make a change in the *identity* they hold dear. This is most difficult.

The following guidelines are suggested for de-escalating value conflicts:

1. Search for shared or overarching principles on which to base a continuing dialogue.
2. Keep an open mind, be open to reason, and consider carefully that you might be wrong.
3. Seek to achieve real gains and substantial improvements, as seen through critics' eyes, rather than offering "appropriate" compensation to offset significant losses.
4. Stonewalling, belittling, and ignoring critics, especially when cultural differences are involved, create misunderstanding, polarize opinion, and increase criticism.
5. Look to history to better understand the critics' arguments and beliefs.
6. Acknowledge strong emotions but appeal to reasoned arguments.
7. Allow for and seek out diverse and complex views on all "sides."
8. Beware the pitfalls of "rights talk."
9. Seek forums for discussion to facilitate dialogue rather than adversarial debate, an airing of differences rather than attacks, and joint problem solving rather than unilateral, dominating decision-making.

Plowman and colleagues have applied and adapted these theories to the organizational level in the public relations context. The use of a continuum of conflict management strategies ranging from asymmetrical to symmetrical was suggested (Plowman, 2005; Plowman et al., 1995): contention, avoidance, compromise, accommodation, and cooperation, plus being unconditionally constructive and win–win or no deal.

It is also worth pointing out an important theory in public relations on conflict management, even though it was not proposed under the strategic management approach. The contingency theory developed by Cameron and colleagues specified many contextual factors facing any organization as it deals with conflicts. The contingency theory (see Cancel, Cameron, Sallot, & Mitrook, 1997) argued that two-way communication be considered as a continuum between pure advocacy and pure accommodation. In this view, multiple internal and external factors influence the ways that organizations communicate with their publics. The goal is to capture dynamics in organizational stances and decisions on public relations strategies along the advocacy-accommodation continuum.

On one end of the continuum, advocacy refers to public relations practitioners serving a similar role as that of when they advocate for the organizations' positions on an issue. And on the other end, accommodation refers to the organization giving in to the demands of the public. Both extreme ends may bring negative consequences. Pure advocacy of organizational interests may put too much emphasis on persuading the publics, which may bring about perceptions of manipulation, leading to a lack of trust from the public. Pure accommodation on the other hand completely disregards the organization's interest and position, which may lead to doubt about organizational mission.

Therefore, pure advocacy and pure accommodation are similar to the two sides in the reconceptualized symmetrical/asymmetrical communication in public relations (L. Grunig et al., 2002). Engaging in asymmetrical communication means ignoring completely either the organizational or the public's interest. Therefore, both theories of contingency and public relations strategies suggest the need to focus on some kind of middle, win–win zone along the continuum (organization-asymmetric vs. public-asymmetric and advocacy-accommodation).

In understanding the contextual factors of conflict management, the contingency theory identified an extensive list of 87 variables that affect the different organizational stances between pure advocacy and accommodation (see Cancel, Cameron, Sallot, & Mitrook, 1997). To summarize, these variables consist of external and internal categories. The variables in the external category are divided into five sets: (i) threats; (ii) industry environment; (iii) general political, social environment, and external culture; (iv) characteristics of the external public; and (v) the issue under question. The internal variables are divided into six sets: (i) characteristics of the organization; (ii) characteristics of the public relations department; (iii) characteristics of top management (i.e., dominant coalition); (iv) internal threats; (v) the individual characteristics of the public relations practitioner and managers; and (vi) characteristics of organization–public relationships.

Although the variables are detailed and comprehensive, they can be overwhelming to analyze and incorporate, which is a typical criticism of the contingency theory. In addition, no distinction about the different stages of public relations management is made in how these variables may play a role. Drawing from the strategic management approach of public relations reviewed in this book and the literature on conflict management and negotiation, we thus generate the following model of intercultural conflict management with multiple stages, each with its own influencing factors.

Model of Intercultural Conflict Management

We propose a model for intercultural conflict management that includes three stages: pre-conflict, during-conflict, and post-conflict. This model integrates theories reviewed in previous chapters that come from strategic management of public relations, including (a) environmental scanning, (b) identifying publics, (c) relationship management, (d) conflict resolution; as well as those from intercultural communication, including (e) identity and identification and (f) conflict management.

To resolve as efficiently as possible conflicts that may bring negative consequences, organizations need to be proactive about potential conflicts and take precautionary actions. They can do so via engaging in strategic management of public relations, i.e., by engaging in environmental scanning and identifying potential issues or signals that certain publics are about to arise regarding some problems. Organizations should then identify their strategic publics and engage with them by building relationships and gaining mutual understanding. With those conflicts involving fundamental value differences or identity clashes, organizations need especially to first engage with publics to gain some level of trust before a particular conflict occurs. Trust and relationship building help prevent conflicts from escalating to varying degrees and create a basic platform of dialogue and negotiation for if and when a conflict does occur. In the meantime, an organization needs to engage in training for its practitioners or other personnel that may engage in a conflict with organizational publics.

During a conflict situation, an organization needs to engage in conflict assessment by looking into the types and nature of conflict, goals assessment that includes both observable positions and fundamental values and interests, situational assessment that includes the different options and power issues, relational history between the two parties, and various characteristics of both parties in the conflict, such as cognitive, motivational, and behavioral. Based on these assessments, the organization can use appropriate conflict management strategies as well as negotiation strategies, if applicable.

For illustration purposes, we can analyze a recent controversial issue, the NFL "take a knee" movement, also termed the U.S. national anthem protests. The protests began when San Francisco NFL player Colin Kaepernick, instead of standing, sat and later kneeled during the national anthem before his team's preseason games in 2016. Later, various NFL and other sports team members engaged in similar protests. President Donald Trump called for NFL team owners to fire the protesting players, after which the NFL protests became more widespread when over 200 players sat or kneeled.

In this case, the type of conflict can be identified as relating to *values*. The overt positions are for or against NFL players taking a knee during the national anthem. The underlying interests in this case were not as relevant because the focus was on beliefs and values, which can be multiple. On the "for" side, the values included protesting social injustice, in particular race-based police brutality, and protesting the lyrics of the national anthem that used to be linked to slavery. On the "against" side, the values included patriotism, respect for the military, and the choice regarding the form of protest.

As we can see, the positions were observable through statements and behaviors of each party. They were rigid and hard to break down. If we stick to the examined positions only, there would be no way that any conflict could be resolved. However, multiple values were behind the two positions. It would be inappropriate to assume that any person taking a certain position necessarily believes in a certain value. For example, while the value held by many NFL players who take a knee is to fight against social injustice, in particular race-based police brutality, this does not mean that anyone opposed to taking a knee is actually in favor of such brutality or is OK with social injustice. Rather, opponents may be holding other values in mind, such as respecting the military and being patriotic.

It is exactly in these multiple values that some, if not all, potential solutions for resolving the conflict might be identified because these multiple values leave some room for discussion and for finding some potential common ground between the two parties. For example, in addition to the simple "for" or "against" position, some people have adopted the position that "while I behave in the way I deem appropriate (either taking the knee or not), I understand where the other side is coming from, and I can accept the behavior that is different from my own."

After a conflict is resolved or fails to be resolved, an organization needs to assess why certain strategies have worked or failed to work, identify any changes in the identity and positions of both parties, and determine if and how to repair or reestablish relationships. The following is the model in more detail.

1. Pre-conflict: Conflict management approach and preparation.

   a. Stakeholder engagement.

      i. Stakeholder engagement strategies.
      ii. Relationship building.

   b. Practitioner preparation and training.

      i. Cultural identity and values.
      ii. Intercultural communication competence and training.
      iii. Motivation/worldview: dual-concerns, two-way and symmetrical worldview.
      iv. Cognitive perspective training.
      v. Information behaviors.

2. During-conflict: Process of conflict management.

   a. Conflict assessment.

      i. *Types of conflict*: Is it about an accident (where publics are hurt), risk (where publics are concerned about potential risks), or values (where publics have fundamentally different values and beliefs, cf. Susskind & Field, 1996)?
      ii. *Goals assessment*: What are the positions as opposed to the fundamental interests and values (depending on the types of conflict) for the two parties involved in the conflict?
      iii. *Situational assessment*: What are the options, limits, power differences, and desired outcomes acceptable for the two parties involved in the conflict?
      iv. *Relational assessment*: What is the relationship history between the two parties involved in the conflict?
      v. *Negotiator assessment* (assessment of both parties in the conflict):

         1. *Cultural identity and values:* What is/are the most salient cultural identities for both parties involved in the conflict? What is/are the values they hold dear to heart? Are there any completing values at play?
         2. *Motivation/worldview:* Are the parties individualistic, altruistic, cooperative, or competitive? Where are the two parties in terms of their self-concern, other-concern, or both?
         3. *Cognition assessment*: What are the general perceptions of the two parties about the conflict (including certain heuristics and biases such as anchoring and adjustment, as well as conflict-related schemata such as fixed-pie perception and illusory conflict)? What are the situational perceptions of both parties

(including problem recognition, involvement recognition, constraint recognition, cf. Kim & Grunig, 2011, STOPS).

4. *Information behaviors*: How do those perceptions influence both parties' information behaviors (information acquisition, selection, and transmission, cf. Kim & Grunig, 2011, STOPS)

5. *Intercultural communication competence* (cf. Chapter 6).

b. Conflict management strategies: Integrative, distributive, and non-confrontational.

   i. Dual concerns.
   ii. Mutual-gains approach.

c. Negotiation stages: What strategies should be used at the global, regional, and local stages? (Refer to Chapter 4 for these stages.)

d. Negotiation tactics: What verbal and nonverbal acts should be adopted in each encounter? What personnel should be most appropriate in each encounter?

3. Post-conflict: Outcomes of conflict management.

a. Assessing strategies and outcomes: What are the outcomes (no agreement, victory for one party, simple compromise, or win–win)? What is the effectiveness of conflict strategies?

b. Assessing changes in identity and in positions of both parties as well as their relationships.

c. Developing goals for next stage: Do parties aim to re-establish and repair relationships or do they decide to withdraw? If the goals are to repair relationships, what needs to be done?

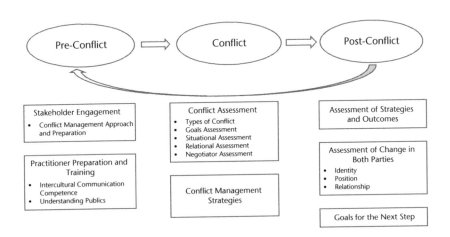

FIGURE 8.1 Theoretical Framework of Intercultural Conflict Management

Integration of Conflict Management in Public Relations

A review of current public relations research on negotiation and conflict management indicates that most research is aimed at external stakeholders, especially external activist groups. This research is reviewed and integrated in the sections below. For example, Murphy and Dee (1996) studied activism and Plowman et al. (1995) studied conflict management by retailer Walgreens. This section uses the revised theoretical framework and model to integrate current research on conflict management based on the three broad stages.

Pre-Conflict: Conflict Management Approach and Preparation

Importance of Stakeholder Engagement and Relationship Management

As recognized in the model of conflict management illustrated earlier, conflict management involves multiple stages, and the factors playing a role in each stage may overlap with and influence each other. Even during the active stage of dealing with conflicts when they occur, the specific strategies used are not just limited to the typical conflict strategies in the literature. Rather, the dimensions of public relations and relationship management strategies worked in conjunction with and served as pre-conflict preparation for different conflict management strategies.

In fact, Plowman (2007) argued for a long-term perspective for managing public relations. He suggested that a win–win solution is more likely to occur if the parties involved in a conflict have a long-term relationship. He also argued for the importance of environmental scanning ahead of any potential conflicts so the organization may be able to preempt or predict such conflicts.

As an overall testament to this model, when measuring public relations effects in the form of organization–public relationships and conflict resolution, Huang (2001) examined how both measures were related to public relations strategies. Specifically, she tested and supported the idea that public relations has value to an organization via reducing potential conflicts, among other things, and such an effect was mediated through relationship management. Therefore, her study demonstrated the value of public relations in terms of relationship management and conflict resolution.

Another example of the importance of pre-conflict relationship building and engagement in the conflict management process is the examination of the growing ethnopolitical and ethnoreligious conflicts and violence in sub-Saharan Africa. Pratt and Omenugha (2014) applied relationship management theory, with a special focus on the two-way symmetrical model of public relations. Their theory-informed guidelines in conflict management helped these African states of Sudan and Nigeria develop communication strategies to engage stakeholders with different theological leanings at the individual level. Essentially the study focused on communication strategies that facilitated mutually respectful dialogue between Muslim and Christian communities on some intractable and sensitive issues.

In addition, Hung's (2003) study integrated the then-models of public relations, relationship building, activism, and conflict resolution when examining how an organization manages conflicts with activist groups. Using a case study related to the termination of public prostitution in Taipei, Taiwan, Hung (2003) highlighted the importance of not only relationship management strategies in particular, but also the strategic management of public relations in general. Specifically, strategic management of public relations in the form of effective identification of issues and publics could help prevent existing conflicts from escalating. In adopting the then-models of public relations, the study showed the influencing role of power imbalance. In particular, the party with more power was argued to have the obligation to maintain symmetrical communication with the other party and reach a mutually agreeable solution. With regard to the role of relationship management, two particular strategies, assurance of legitimacy and sharing of tasks, were found to be useful in managing a conflict and building trust among the various parties involved.

Practitioner Preparation and Training

Not much research has been conducted on how public relations practitioners need to be trained to prepare for conflicts. Plowman (2005) argued that the value and contributions of public relations to strategic management lie partly in its functions and its practitioners' knowledge and experience in the mixed-motive model of public relations, which closely relates to conflict management. He noted in particular practitioner knowledge and experiences in using conflict strategies such as contention, avoidance, compromise, accommodation, cooperation, being unconditionally constructive, win–win or no deal, principled, preservation, and mediated strategy. To further incorporate culture into conflict resolution, Plowman (2007) also argued that the ability to negotiate cross-culturally is critical to global public relations practice. He suggested that, although cross-cultural communication can be difficult, creating mutually beneficial options would be easier in an intercultural setting where differences abound. It is differences, as opposed to similarities, that typically form the basis of such mutually agreeable solutions in conflicts. This is because differences in what each party demands can create the room for negotiation. We hope that the theoretical framework formed in this book on conflict resolution and practitioner competency and training can serve as a starting point for this line of research.

A good example to illustrate the pre-conflict stage preparation based on the theoretical framework laid out is using the case of police–community relations. In recent years, trust from both the African American community and the police toward each other has been sharply declining. Overall, the duty of police to protect our community is under serious scrutiny at the moment. Some suggestions for pre-conflict preparation can be made as follows.

The first suggestion is the need for more *competence training* in law enforcement personnel. Competence can be multi-level and multi-domain. Intercultural communication competence is critical because it directly affects how one social actor perceives and behaves in an encounter with another social actor from a dissimilar identity group. News stories about police training report that the police force actually lacks training on social intelligence and emotional intelligence. Police officers sometimes only have high school degrees and may have committed misdemeanors (Montagne & Haberfield, 2015).

The second suggestion is that the need for *more diversity* in law enforcement personnel may be imperative. Given the principle of "requisite variety," or the idea that there should be as much diversity inside an organization as there is outside (see Sha & Ford, 2007) in such a highly face-to-face interaction kind of setting, it is critical that we have more police officers who share some common characteristics with the community members they are trying to protect.

Related, the third suggestion is that despite the setback, frustration, and sometimes growing anti-police violence, it is perhaps more crucial than ever, for this exact reason, to launch, continue, or strengthen *community engagement* initiatives.

These steps fit with the theoretical framework of conflict management and the principles of the mutual gains approach we reviewed earlier in this chapter: to not dismiss the other party as irrational and to acknowledge others' concerns, frustrations, fears, even if you do not agree with them (Susskind & Field, 1996).

Specific strategies of community engagement have been implemented following the death of an unarmed black teenager shot by police in Ferguson, Missouri. The U.S. Justice Department launched a $5 million initiative to foster better relationships between communities and their police departments (Justice Department, 2014). This kind of community policing is used to better engage with communities. According to experts in this field, community policing is a community-based strategy to get community and residents involved in developing strategies for public safety. Further, it is collaborative in that these residents are acting as partners who work with law enforcement on strategies around public safety. It has the potential to change the police department both in its daily operations and in facilitating these operations. Instead of "us versus them," the community and the police force form an "us-together" identity.

The key here is building and rebuilding community trust and having the citizens and community members rate their satisfaction about law enforcement. The challenging part is the sustainability or resilience of that trust. When things happen, questions should be asked around how quickly the trust "erupts and breaks again," whether trust has been completely broken, or whether it can be healed. Finding answers to these questions requires time and research, but doing so brings effective conflict resolution over the long term.

Constance Rice once said that the primary goal of community engagement projects is building trust (National Public Radio Staff, 2014). She talked about how White police officers had a fear of Black men, even though these officers themselves may not be racists in any way. Engaging with the community makes the officers fear less and be embraced more by the community. One statement summarizes it all: "You are not in the arrest business; you are in the trust business" (National Public Radio Staff, 2014). One example would be the police officers playing basketball with kids in the neighborhood. In 2015, Los Angeles Police Department started implementing the program where some police officers moved in to the neighborhood they patrolled to embed themselves, engage with the community, and learn about the residents there. It was hard at first; the police faced resistance. The police said: "We know you hate us, but we're here to serve. We're going to win your trust." Over time, the murder rate in the community went down (National Public Radio Staff, 2014).

The African American community is not the only community in need of such engagement. Law enforcement needs to engage in community outreach with various communities to make them more secure. The International Association of Chiefs of Police formed a Committee on Terrorism Countering Violent Extremism (CVE) Working Group, which proposed the following national security community outreach and engagement goals and principles:

- Build and maintain relationships and partnerships with diverse communities.
- Establish transparency, mutual understanding, and trust between the diverse communities and law enforcement.
- Ensure public safety and address threats by building law enforcement's knowledge and awareness of diverse communities.
- Ensure equal and respectful treatment of communities and partners (IACP-COT, 2012).

According to that report, the types of engagement ranged from tailored engagement to broad-based engagement; the levels of engagement ranged from virtually no contact to the existence of an extensive network (IACP-COT, 2012). Several similar recommendations have been proposed by the Major Cities Chiefs Association, the Major County Sheriffs Association, and the Federal Bureau of Investigation National Executive Institute (Engagement-based policing, 2015).

The first challenge is changing police culture from a mentality of warriors to one of guardians (21st century policing). The second is a perceived reluctance in giving officers more discretion in implementing community-oriented policing, problem-solving policing, and intelligence-led policing into a policy, practice, and culture of engagement-based policing with our communities.

Process of Conflict Management: During Conflict

We integrated the literature on negotiation processes (e.g., Murphy & Dee, 1992, 1996; Plowman, 2007; Susskind & Field, 1996) that we reviewed and identified four common themes:

1. Separate positions from interests and people from problems.
2. Perspective taking and refraining from labeling the other party (avoid "rights" talk or stereotyping the "evil other").
3. Communication efforts (depending on situations).

   a. *Principles*: Open and transparent.
   b. *Strategies*: Shared platform, trusted mediators, and flexibility with options.
   c. *Goals*: Finding common ground and principles, no matter how small.

4. Consider situational factors and relationship factors (and ideally work on these prior to the conflict).

Conflict Assessment

Given the complexities of some issues of conflict, identifying the types of conflict is the first step in assessing conflicts. Susskind and Field (1996) identified six sources of anger in conflicts: *hurt, risk, beliefs and values, weakness, lie*, and *show*. Among the six, they acknowledged that conflicts arising from values clashes are the most difficult to resolve. Conflicts arise from diverse values, e.g., pro-choice vs. pro-life, death penalty, equality vs. equity, compassion for those hurt by economic times versus belief in self-reliance. Values tell us what is preferred and identity tells us who we are. Both values and identity are deep-rooted and fundamental to a person, which makes it extremely challenging and oftentimes impossible to resolve a conflict arising from differences in values and identity.

Values contain different components (Hofstede, 2001). The *direction* of value indicates whether something is good or bad (sign). The *intensity* of value indicates its relevance (size). Taking an example from Hofstede (2001): Having money is important (intensity), more is good/less is bad (direction), but not applicable in the Christian view (less is good). Values vary in kinds. Desired values are what people actually desire whereas desirable values are what people think they ought to desire. Classification of values includes terminal values (desired goals) and instrumental values (methods/ways to reach the goals)

As a major part of conflict assessment discussed earlier in the framework, the factor of conflict *goals* is also critical to understand. It is worth noting that it is not necessarily in the best interests of both parties to actually "resolve" the conflict. Assessment of conflict management also includes the existence of compatible ground rules. Murphy and Dee (1992) examined the "tit for tat" games between Du Pont and Greenpeace. Interestingly, both entities used incompatible approaches to dispute resolution, resulting in little hope for resolution. Specifically, Du Pont used tit for tat, and Greenpeace used a pure zero-sum model. However, both met their objectives by *not* resolving the conflict in the end, because their objectives lay more in satisfying the demands of their respective constituencies and getting the attention of important audiences. In essence, instead of aiming for resolving conflicts, prolonged conflict served as a central strategy.

Another key situational antecedent in understanding negotiation is the *cultural expectations* and *identities* of both parties. Murphy and Dee (1996) examined the positions of environmental activists and corporate policymakers and noted the difference between environmentalism and economic benefits. However, both parties' positions were rarely as radical as each might have assumed. Differences in positions existed but were exaggerated because of polarization of cultures (i.e., culture clashes exaggerated by research approaches looking for differences). So their research focused on finding commonalities and zones of agreement.

The relationship between extreme environmental activists and traditional corporate targets shows characteristics of "malignant social conflict" (Murphy & Dee, 1996). To analyze the cognitive nature of this conflict, they used multiple regression-based judgment analysis to generate decision profiles. Through a co-orientation approach, based on Hammond's (1973) approaches social judgment theory (SJT), they compared two sets of decision profiles: those specified by each group as an ideological statement and those derived from respondents' assessments of 30 hypothetical environmental policies.

Results showed that both groups' ideological statements differed substantially from their actual judgment behavior; and each group's estimate of its counterpart's decision structure was highly stereotyped. They found many commonalities. The ideological judgment profiles of activists were highly correlated with those of the corporate policymakers, as were their assessments of the hypothetical policies. However, the policy impasse would probably still continue as neither group accepted a compromise set of environmental values.

Murphy and Dee (1996) indicated that both parties showed solid consensus in the weight given to decision attributes and in the level of attributes they favored most. However, there was little correlation between judgment profiles derived from these attributes and decision values that each group self-reported. Such disparities are damaging for mediation because of "stereotyping of the evil other." The researchers suggested that participants in a conflict should partition the problem into separate components (decision cues) on which specific trade-offs can be considered.

That study has great implications for conflict resolution. Because of stereotyping and misperceptions, it is easier to categorize information and identify differences in opinions. However, highlighting differences also tunes out information and leads to the "freezing of beliefs," making these beliefs extreme and rigid. These rigid perceptions do not help in productive negotiations. When such inaccurate self-perceptions of both parties (i.e., exaggerated claims to maximize each party's gains) are prolonged, communication will not help any more. In other words, encouraging dialogue may actually entrench the cause and sharpen the sense of grievance. In particular, for some parties in a conflict, refusal to talk may actually be an effective strategy: Playing ignorant makes it easier to assert one's own position. This phenomenon relates to the challenges in negotiations with activists in some cases. They may actually require the prolonged conflict to conserve their own identity (cf. Sha, 2004).

Relational Assessment

Various factors influence and determine the kind of conflict strategies adopted by either the organization or the public. Christen (2004) examined the effects of perceived power and trustworthiness on the willingness of organizations and external interest groups to consider a negotiated solution to a conflict. Willingness to negotiate was measured by a seven-item index in a simulated conflict on recreation management. Results largely supported the prediction that perceived trustworthiness of an external group was positively related to an organization's willingness to negotiate with that group. Both a linear and a curvilinear relationship existed between perceived power and willingness to negotiate. Overall, the perceived trustworthiness of the external public strongly predicted the organization's willingness to negotiate when considering the influence of perceived power. It will be equally interesting to examine how the trustworthiness of the organization influences the publics' willingness to negotiate, which we recommend researching.

Conflict Strategies

Many studies have examined the use of specific strategies during conflicts. Plowman et al. (1995) examined conflicts surrounding the retailer Walgreens and its stakeholders and possible strategies. Combining conflict management theory with the situational theory of publics and public relations theories, these researchers provided the general conflict management process that included identifying overt positions, underlying interests, and best alternatives for management.

Most public relations literature on conflict management has suggested the use of a continuum of conflict management strategies ranging from asymmetrical to symmetrical (Plowman, 2005; Plowman et al., 1995): contention, avoidance, compromise, accommodation, and cooperation, with some new strategies added such as being unconditionally constructive and win–win or no deal, both used when it is not possible to reach any kind of agreement (Plowman, 2007).

Contention, avoidance, compromise, accommodation, and cooperation conflict management strategies were discussed in Chapter 4. *Being unconditionally constructive* (cf. Fisher & Brown, 1988) refers to following the guidelines that will benefit both the relationship and the party using the principles, regardless of whether the other party reciprocates or not. In other words, one party decides to take an altruistic, unilateral strategy after doing research to understand the interests of the other party and of the relationship. *Win–win or no deal* (cf. Covey, 1990) refers to another positive way to get past a negotiation stalemate. Both parties either collaborate to find a win–win solution or agree to disagree.

There are also two tactics that are one-way or two-way respectively: principled and perseverance. *Principled* means to hold to higher ethics that cannot be compromised (Plowman, 2007, p. 94). *Perseverance* refers to a combination of humility, will power, and persistent determination to endure to the end. Finally, *mediation* in conflict management is also a widely used conflict management strategy in public relations (Plowman, 2007). Three important trends and evolution in the use of mediation have been discussed: mediator being neutral or unbiased, mediator being independent, and mediator being knowledgeable and credible. All of these strategies are integrated in a model of conflict resolution in public relations (Plowman, 2007, p. 95). Later, using a qualitative role-playing design, Plowman (2009) examined the hot waste issue in Utah. After framing the issue and defining different parties' self-interests, the study employed all nine conflict management strategies that were paired against each other in different combinations. Contention was found to be the most-often used strategy, typically used in combination with principled strategy. Avoidance was then used if these strategies failed. Cooperation and compromise were used next, which made it less confrontational and easier to discuss alternatives. The most useful strategy overall was mediation.

Incorporating the cultural role of religion, Shin (2008) conducted a national survey among religious public relations practitioners working for mainstream Protestant Christian churches. With strategic communication strategies, religious public relations professionals were more likely to use collaborating, contending, or compromising in a conflict with a given public, but they were likely to use concession or corrective action in a crisis situation. The influencing factors for more accommodative strategies such as accommodating, avoiding, and concession were more likely to be used for internal conflicts whereas those for contending were used most often for external conflicts.

Jin, Park, and Len-Ríos (2010) examined the role of emotion in conflict management with multiple publics. Through examining newspaper stories about the 2006 Duke University lacrosse team crisis, they noted that the media coverage focused on the expressions of hope from the university and the expressions of anger from the public. The university's conflict stances were more accommodative toward internal publics than they were toward external publics. The conflict strategies of concession and adjustment were used for litigation and conflict management with multiple publics, respectively.

Cultural Influence on Conflict Management

Many cross-cultural tests of various theories in conflict management have been conducted, although not all such studies have actually identified or incorporated cultural factors unique to different countries (Shin, Cheng, Jin, & Cameron, 2005). A quantitative test of the contingency theory in China (Li, Cropp, & Jin, 2010) examined the influence of the 80 contingent variables as perceived by Chinese public relations practitioners. Among them, the most influential variables were individual characteristics as related to conflict management and political-social factors. The findings helped demonstrate how to strategically identify and combine the most influential factors in conflict management in China.

Choi and Cameron (2005) tested the contingency theory and psychocultural conflict theory in the context of multinational corporations (MNCs) practicing public relations in Korea. When identifying the contingency factors that impacted MNCs' stances in conflict situations, results found the critical role of "fear factor," a fear of Korean media and local culture to be specific, in why MNCs took more accommodative stances, regardless of whether two-way communication was used. Therefore, cultural factors seemed to play a role in the ambiguous role of one-way communication. In other words, one-way communication did not result in the use of advocacy, which is typical in Western cultures, but actually led to accommodation.

Taylor (2000) explored more directly the role and challenge of cultural differences in global public relations. This study provided some analysis of different national cultures and highlighted certain cultural characteristics (e.g., power distance and uncertainty avoidance) that led to different reactions to perceived threats. Using the Coca-Cola scare as a case, the study also examined the dynamics of organization–public relationships in an international context when a controversy occurred.

The role of culture on the preferred use of different conflict management strategies, including mediation, was examined in Huang (2008). She explored the use of third-party mediation, integration, distribution, and avoidance in general conflict resolution in the Taiwanese government's executive–legislative relations. Additionally, third-party mediation *mianzi* (face) and *renqing* (favor) in relation to Chinese culture were explored. Findings showed that third-party mediation, across two independent samples, had the strongest correlations with nonconfrontation/avoidance strategies, as opposed to integration and distribution. Face and favor, the two cultural factors, were first associated with distribution, then with third-party mediation, avoidance, and finally integration.

Use of Communication Channels and Messages

Conflicts are managed not only through negotiation, but also via different communication channels and messages, or symbols. Rasmussen (2015) examined the role of new media in strategic communication when dealing with conflicts. Results showed that public relations theories could be put into practice on new media as organizations aim to manage conflicts while considering new communication platforms. Using a case study on the conflict between the pro-life nonprofit Live Action and the pro-choice institute Planned Parenthood, the study looked at how an undercover video footage released by Live Action on multiple social media sites such as Blog and YouTube channels purportedly showed Planned Parenthood clinic staff disregarding the reporting laws and aiding sex traffickers. Facing the threat of funding cuts by the federal government as well as public attention on social media, Planned Parenthood began a campaign on new media to repair its image and maintain its funding, through shifting attention to the societal need for the organization. However, Live Action strived to keep the videos at the forefront of the issue.

The study exemplified the use of contention strategy between the two parties. However, the uses of strategies during this conflict were primarily framed in terms of crisis management, and through different channels, but not in terms of how the two parties directly interacted with each other in resolving this conflict.

Using the political debate over the Tasmanian wilderness, Lester (2006) examined the use and adoption by industry and government of powerful symbols that had been typically used by and connected to the environment movement. Using textual analysis and interviews with different parties in the conflict, including journalists, activists, government and industry, the researcher identified three key mechanisms for symbolizing the environment movement—words, images, and protest. The symbolic power was then taken over and used by the other side of the conflict, i.e., industry and government.

Another study on the use of words or symbols was conducted by García (2011), who examined the framing of U.S. newspapers in the "Go Green" conflict between BP and Greenpeace over a period of ten years. The study identified six dominant frames and attributes: credibility frame, power frame, hero frame, villain frame, causal attribution, and social responsibility attribution. These frames and attributes were used to portray the two parties.

Multiple Parties and Publics

Conflicts involving multiples publics are understandably more difficult to manage than those with only two parties. The situation becomes even more complicated when multiple parties from multiple cultures are involved. Springston, Keyton, Leichty, and Metzger (1992) did some early work on multi-public conflicts through the application of field dynamics. However, that line of research has not been extended in recent years.

Molleda (2004) expanded the dynamic of "cross-national conflict shifting" in the context of global public relations management. Using four cases involving issues affecting more than one country and several parties, this study highlighted the roles of different parties in such cross-national conflict shifting: host, home, and transnational publics, as well as how the interactions among the various players played out. Among the ten propositions, he identified the main source of cross-national conflict shifting, the magnitude of such conflict shifting, and the nature of shifting of conflicts to the international arena.

Outcomes of Conflict Management: Post-Conflict

Assessment of Outcomes

Linking relationship management with conflict management, a study on a Peru community (Ni, Wang, de la flor, & Penaflor, 2015) demonstrated the effect of relationship management on conflict management. This study's overall results indicated that effective management of relationships with the local community helped smooth the conflict management process, leading to publics adopting mostly positive conflict management strategies. The study used a new typology of relationship strategies and incorporated anxiety and uncertainty management as empowerment mediators.

This particular study supported the ethicalness–effectiveness framework, that is, beyond only being possible, collaborative and involvement stakeholder engagement strategies are crucial in building equal and trustworthy organization–public relationships, as well as encouraging integrative and dialogical conflict management strategies. Further, the study corroborated the findings in the business and communication literature that engagement strategies have both direct and indirect effects—via anxiety and uncertainty management (AUM)—on relational and conflict management outcomes (e.g., Huang, 2001; Ni & Wang, 2011; Wang, Ni, & De la Flor, 2014).

In responding to the debate about *effectiveness* versus *ethicalness* as the end of stakeholder engagement strategies in the literature on business and public relations (e.g., Cheney & Christensen, 2001; L. Grunig et al., 2002; Noland & Phillips, 2010), Ni et al.'s (2015) study revealed that, whereas collaborative and involvement engagement strategies (largely reflecting both ethicalness and effectiveness), were essential in anxiety and uncertainty management, relational building, and conflict management, informational engagement did not appear to be influential.

Limits and Challenges to Negotiation and Dialogue

Despite its usefulness, public relations does not work in all conflict situations. Negotiation or the practice of communication has its limits. Kelleher (2003), for example, examined the theoretical models of public relations in terms of conflict theory in the context the 2001 University of Hawaii faculty strike. The study found that, although public relations models were useful in discussing relationships, the use of public relations was limited by the circumstances of collective bargaining. Therefore, public relations was used as an alternative to negotiations between the different parties in the conflict, rather than as an actual mechanism to resolve the conflict.

In questioning two-way symmetrical communication as the most effective and ethical model for public relations, Stoker and Tusinski (2006) challenged the usefulness of dialogue, especially in terms of the potential of dialogue for selectivity and tyranny as well as its emphasis on reciprocal communication. They argued that one-way dissemination of information could be more just than dialogue because it demands more integrity of the source and recognizes the freedom and individuality of the source. As an alternative, they proposed reconciliation as a new model of public relations that recognizes and values individuality and differences, as well as putting integrity above agreement.

A similar discussion on the use of dialogue in conflict management was provided in Varma's (2011) case study that used relationship management and negotiation as the theoretical lens to examine how Louisiana State University managed relationships and restored its image after a crisis involving its women's head basketball coach and charges of inappropriate conduct with former basketball players.

Among others, one of the key findings pointed to the important role that negotiation could play when the different parties involved in the conflict were not willing to engage in dialogue. Specifically, dialogue promotes the "co-creation of joint outcomes and mutuality of interests" (Varma, 2011. p. 375). It may be more effective where relationships are important. However, dialogue may not result in a solution to the identified problem. Negotiations may prove to be more useful when resolution of problems is more important than maintaining relationships. Another finding was that, in aiming to find a win–win situation for this conflict, the university realized that the lack of transparency and openness in the initial stages brought negative effects. Varma (2011) argued that in conflict management, honesty, openness, and having a clear policy should be maintained throughout the process.

Assessment of Changes in Identity

Assessing changes in identity or in positions, and assessing re-established relationships, has not been extensively examined in public relations literature. These areas may thus be useful directions for future research.

References

Cancel, A. E., Cameron, G. T., Sallot, L. M., & Mitrook, M. A. (1997). It depends: A contingency theory of accommodation in public relations. *Journal of Public Relations Research, 9*, 31–63.

Cheney, G., & Christensen, L. T. (2001). Public relations as contested terrain: A critical response. In R. L. Heath (Ed.), *Handbook of public relations* (pp. 167–182). Thousand Oaks, CA: Sage.

Choi, Y., & Cameron, G. T. (2005). Overcoming ethnocentrism: The role of identity in contingent practice of international public relations. *Journal of Public Relations Research, 17*(2), 171–189. doi: 10.1207/s1532754xjprr1702_6

Christen, C. T. (2004). Predicting willingness to negotiate: The effects of perceived Power and trustworthiness in a model of strategic public relations. *Journal of Public Relations Research, 16*(3), 243–267.

Covey, S. R. (1990). *The seven habits of highly effective people: Restoring the character ethics.* New York, NY: Fireside.

Engagement-based policing: The what, how, and why of community engagement (June 2015). Retrieved from https://majorcitieschiefs.com/pdf/news/community_engagement_5_27_15.pdf

Fisher, R., & Brown, S. (1988). *Getting together: Building a relationship that gets to yes.* Boston, MA: Houghton Mifflin.

Fisher, R., & Ury, W., (1983). *Getting to yes: Negotiating agreement without giving in.* New York, NY: Penguin Books.

García, M. M. (2011). Perception is truth: How U.S. newspapers framed the "Go Green" conflict between BP and Greenpeace. *Public Relations Review, 37*(1), 57–59. doi: 10.1016/j.pubrev.2010.10.001

Grunig. J. E., & L. A. Grunig (1992). Models of public relations and communication. In J. E. Grunig (Ed.), *Excellence in public relations and communication management* (pp. 285–326). Hillsdale, NJ: Lawrence Erlbaum.

Grunig, L. A., Grunig, J. E., & Dozier, D. M. (2002). *Excellent public relations and effective organizations: A study of communication management in three countries.* Mahwah, NJ: Lawrence Erlbaum Associates.

Hammond. K. R. (1973). The cognitive conflict paradigm. In L. Rappoport & D. A. Summers (Eds.), *Human judgment and social interaction* (pp. 188–205). New York: Holt, Rinehan & Winston.

Hofstede, G. (2001). *Culture's consequences: Comparing values, behaviors, institutions, and organizations across nations* (2nd ed.). Thousand Oaks, CA: Sage.

Huang, Y. (2001). Values of public relations: Effects on organization–public relationships mediating conflict resolution. *Journal of Public Relations Research, 13*(4), 265–301

Huang, Y. (2008). The role of third-party mediation and face and favor in executive–legislative relations and conflict. *Asian Journal of Communication, 18*(3), 239–263. doi: 10.1080/01292980802207249

Hung, C.-J. F. (2003). Relationship building, activism, and conflict resolution. *Asian Journal of Communication, 13*(2), 21–49.

IACP Committee on Terrorism Countering Violent Extremism (CVE) (2012). Working Group Community Outreach and Engagement Principles. Retrieved on September, 26, 2017 from www.theiacp.org/portals/0/pdfs/IACP-COT_CommPolicingPrinciples__FINALAug12.pdf

Jin, Y., Park, S., & Len-Ríos, M. E. (2010). Strategic communication of hope and anger: A case of Duke University's conflict management with multiple publics. *Public Relations Review, 36*(1), 63–65. doi: 10.1016/j.pubrev.2009.08.015

Justice Department aims to rebuild trust in police with community engagement initiative (2014). Retrieved from www.pbs.org/newshour/bb/justice-department-aims-rebuild-trust-police-community-engagement-initiative/

Kelleher, T. (2003). PR and conflict: A theoretical review and case study of the 2001 university of Hawaii faculty strike. *Journal of Communication Management, 8*(2), 184–196.

Kim, J.-N., & Grunig, J. E. (2011). Problem solving and communicative action: A situational theory of problem solving. *Journal of Communication, 61*, 120–149. doi: 10.1111/j.1460-2466.2010.01529.x

Lester, L. (2006). We too are green: Public relations, symbolic power and the Tasmanian wilderness conflict. *Media International Australia Incorporating Culture & Policy, 121*, 52–64.

Li, C., Cropp, F., & Jin, Y. (2010). Identifying key influencers of Chinese PR practitioners' strategic conflict management practice: A survey on contingent variables in Chinese context. *Public Relations Review, 36*(3), 249–255. doi: 10.1016/j.pubrev.2010.05.006

Molleda, J. (2004). Cross-national conflict shifting: A global public relations dynamic. *Public Relations Review, 30*(1), 1–9. doi: 10.1016/j.pubrev.2003.11.001

Montagne, R. (Interviewer), & Haberfeld, M. (Interviewee). (2015). Effective hiring can help police departments build community trust [Interview transcript]. Retrieved from Houston Public Media News 88.7 website, www.npr.org/2015/04/28/402735968/the-right-hire-can-help-police-departments-build-community-trust

Murphy, P., & Dee, J. (1992). Du Pont and Greenpeace: The dynamics of conflict between corporations and activist groups. *Journal of Public Relations Research, 3*, 3–20. https://doi.org/10.1207/s1532754xjprr0401_02

Murphy, P., & Dee, J. (1996). Reconciling the preferences of environmental activist and corporate policymakers. *Journal of Public Relations Research, 8*, 1–33. https://doi.org/10.1207/s1532754xjprr0801_01

National Public Radio Staff. (2014). Civil rights attorney on how she built trust with police. KPBS. Retrieved from www.kpbs.org/news/2014/dec/05/civil-rights-attorney-on-how-she-built-trust-with/

Ni, L. & Wang, Q. (2011). Anxiety and uncertainty management in an intercultural Setting: The impact on organization–public relationships. *Journal of Public Relations Research, 23,* 269–301. doi: 10.1080/1062726X.2011.582205

Ni, L., Wang, Q., de la Flor, M., & Penaflor, R. (May, 2015). Stakeholder engagement and conflict resolution in the global environment: Strategies and outcomes. Paper presented at the International Communication Association Annual Convention, San Juan, Puerto Rico.

Noland, J., & Phillips, R. (2010). Stakeholder engagement, discourse ethics and strategic management. *International Journal of Management Reviews, 12,* 39–49.

Plowman, K. D. (2005). Conflict, strategic management, and public relations. *Public Relations Review, 31*(1), 131–138. doi: 10.10l6/j.pubrev.2004.10.003

Plowman, K. D. (2007). Public relations, conflict resolution, and mediation. In E. L. Toth (Ed.). *The future of excellence in public relations and communication management: Challenges for the next generation* (pp. 85–102). Mahwah, NJ: Lawrence Erlbaum Associates.

Plowman, K. D. (2009). Hot waste in Utah: Conflict in the public arena. *Journal of Public Relations Research, 20*(4), 403–420. doi: 10.1080/10627260802153371

Plowman, K. D., ReVelle, C., Meirovich, S., Pien, M., Stemple, R., Sheng, V., & Fay, K. (1995). Walgreens: A case study in health care issues and conflict resolution. *Journal of Public Relations Research, 7,* 231–258.

Pratt, C. B., & Omenugha, K. A. (2014). "My God is not your God": Applying relationship management theory to managing ethnoreligious crises in sub-Saharan Africa. *International Journal of Strategic Communication, 8*(2), 100–125. doi: 10.1080/1553118X.2014.882338

Rasmussen, L. (2015). Planned Parenthood takes on Live Action: An analysis of media interplay and image restoration strategies in strategic conflict management. *Public Relations Review, 41*(3), 354–356. doi: 10.1016/j.pubrev.2015.01.004

Sha, B.-L. (2004). Noether's theorem: The science of symmetry and the law of conservation. *Journal of Public Relations Research, 7,* 391–416.

Sha, B.-L. (2009). Exploring the connection between organizational identity and public relations behaviors: How symmetry trumps conservation in engendering organizational identification. *Journal of Public Relations Research, 21,* 295–317. doi: 10.1080/10627260802640765

Sha, B.-L., & Ford, R. L. (2007). Redefining "requisite variety": The challenge of multiple diversities for the future of public relations excellence. In E. L. Toth (Ed.), *The future of excellence in public relations and communication management: Challenges for the next generation* (pp. 381–398). Mahwah, NJ: Lawrence Erlbaum Associates.

Shin, J. (2008). Contingency, conflict, crisis: Strategy selection of religious public relations professionals. *Public Relations Review, 34*(4), 403–405. doi: 10.1016/j.pubrev.2008.06.007

Shin, J., Cheng, I., Jin, Y., & Cameron, G. T. (2005). Going head to head: Content analysis of high profile conflicts as played out in the press. *Public Relations Review, 31*(3), 399–406. doi: 10.1016/j.pubrev.2005.05.001

Springston, J. K., Keyton, J., Leichty, G. B., Metzger, J. (1992). Field dynamics and public relations theory: Toward the management of multiple publics. *Journal of Public Relations Research, 4,* 81–100. https://doi.org/10.1207/s1532754xjprr0402_02

Stoker, K. L., & Tusinski, K. A. (2006). Reconsidering public relations' infatuation with dialogue: Why engagement and reconciliation can be more ethical than symmetry and reciprocity. *Journal of Mass Media Ethics, 21*(2/3), 156–176. doi: 10.1207/s15327728jmme2102&3_5

Susskind, L., & Field, P. (1996). *Dealing with an angry public: The mutual gains approach to resolve disputes.* New York, NY: The Free Press.

Taylor, M. (2000). Cultural variance as a challenge to global public relations: A case study of the Coca-Cola scare. *Public Relations Review, 26*(3), 277.

Varma, T. M. (2011). Crisis communication in higher education: The use of "negotiation" as a strategy to manage crisis. *Public Relations Review, 37*(4), 373–375. doi: 10.1016/j.pubrev.2011.08.006

Wang, Q., Ni, L., & De la Flor, M. (2014). An intercultural competence model of strategic public relations management in the Peru mining industry context. *Journal of Public Relations Research, 26,* 1–22. doi: 10.1080/1062726X.2013.795864

9

ORGANIZATIONAL LEVEL

Organizational Identity and Identification

Defining Organizational Identity

The concept of organizational identity or corporate identity has received significant attention from both academics and practitioners in different fields in the last few decades. As noted succinctly by Sha (2009), "Fundamentally, organizational identity deals with the question of 'who are we?' The answer to that question is not simple" (p. 297).

Most commonly, scholars of organizational identity refer to work by Albert and Whetten (1985) connecting this concept to core organizational attributes that are distinctive and enduring. Sha (2009) connected this approach to the notion of "conservation" (not in terms of ideology on a political spectrum, but in terms of organizational efforts to maintain, retain, preserve or otherwise conserve).

Stuart, Ashforth, and Dutton (2000) published a special issue of the *Academy of Management Review* on organizational identity and identification, arguing that:

> Increasingly, an organization must reside in the heads and hearts of its members. Thus, in the absence of an externalized bureaucratic structure, it becomes more important to have an internalized cognitive structure of what the organization stands for and where it intends to go—in short, a clear sense of the organization's identity. A sense of identity serves as a rudder for navigating difficult waters.
>
> *(Stuart et al., 2000, p. 13)*

These authors likewise acknowledged the lack of clear definitions of organizational identity and identification, seeking perhaps to proactively reduce intellectual angst by noting:

> Although some may be dismayed at the lack of consensus regarding the
> meaning and definition of the terms *organization identity* and *identification*,
> we prefer to see this diversity as reflecting a creative process that will
> evolve through cycles of divergence and convergence.
>
> *(Stuart et al., 2000, p. 15)*

Organizational *identity* and organizational *identification* appear consistently in the literature as separate but related constructs (cf. He & Brown, 2013; Ravasi & van Rekom, 2003). Management scholars Stuart et al. (2000) note that "[a]s noun (identity) and verb (identify), they can be used as versatile concepts, frames, or tools that open up possibilities for theoretical development and revelation" (p. 13). In public relations scholarship, Sha, Tindall and Sha (2012) similarly noted that the term "organizational identity" can be "related both to the identification that employees have with their employing organization and to the identity of that organization itself" (p. 78). Likewise, He and Brown (2013) reviewed literature in both organizational identity (OI) and organizational identification (OID). Hodgkinson (2013) upheld the importance of distinguishing OI constructs from OID constructs (p. 146), while criticizing scholars for inhibiting the progress of research in both areas due to their own "identity barriers" (p. 147) within management and organization studies, whereby disciplinary silos prevent creative cross-fertilization of ideas.

This chapter on "organizational identity" will thus address both organizational identification (OID) and organizational identity (OI) itself. The OID perspective essentially examines how employees and other organizational stakeholders reach out to and seek connection with organizations, in an ongoing process of identification, i.e., creating and maintaining a sense of belonging. The OI perspective essentially considers the collective identity of "the organization" and includes not only how identity is articulated or presented by the organization (i.e., avowed identity), but also how it is received by organizational stakeholders (i.e., ascribed image), as well as how it is perceived by those stakeholders (i.e., ascribed reputation).

This dual-pronged approach is appropriate for this text on intercultural public relations, in that extant literature has already claimed employees as organizations' top-priority public or stakeholder group (e.g., Broom & Sha, 2013), while increasing numbers of studies have delved into the notions of corporate image and organizational reputation, which may be considered critical components of the identity of an organization.

Identification *with* the Organization

Organizational identification pertains to how employees and other stakeholders feel that they belong to an organization, i.e., their self-identity in relation to their organizational membership (see Ashforth & Mael, 1989). Research in

OID has largely been grounded in social identity theory (see Tajfel & Turner, 1979, 1986), which basically posits "the organization" as one social category that people might identity with (see Ashforth, Harrison, & Corley, 2008).

Management research in organizational identification has included the examination of both outcomes and antecedents of this construct (see He & Brown, 2013). Positive OID outcomes in terms of employee performance have included employee creativity (Hirst, van Dick, & van Knippenberg, 2009; Madjar, Greenberg, & Chen, 2011), financial performance (Homburg, Wieseke, & Hoyer, 2009; Weiseke, Ahearne, Lam, & Von Dick, 2008), and task and job performance (Walumbwa, Avolio, & Zhu, 2008; Weiseke et al., 2008).

Research on antecedents to organizational identification has examined the role of various factors, including perceived attributes of the organization (e.g., Dutton, Dukerich, & Harquail, 1994), organizational leadership (e.g., Walumbwa et al., 2011), and social exchange variables. See He and Brown (2013) for an overview of this scholarship in the management literature.

In public relations literature, when the term "organizational identity" is used in the sense of employee (or other stakeholders') identification with an organization, related concepts often come up, including organizational commitment, organizational engagement or involvement, and organizational well-being. Drawn from research in organizational psychology (e.g., *Resources for Employers*, 2017), these terms typically refer to employees' psychological, cognitive and affective states and how they impinge on the employee experience with an employing organization (e.g., Sha & Ahles, 2009; White, Vanc, & Stafford, 2010).

In other words, OID research in public relations has centered on social exchange factors, i.e., what employees are willing to offer (e.g., commitment, engagement) as these are related to what benefits they are deriving from their employing organizations (e.g., procedural justice, sense of belonging, job satisfaction). For example, Sha (2009) found that "identification with the organization" separated statistically into two dimensions: identification with the organization's mission (*mission identification*) and feeling of belonging to the organization (*organizational belonging*). In the context of internal communication and employee relations, Walden, Jung, and Westerman (2017) found that job engagement mediates the relationships between employee communication and organizational commitment; they concluded that, when employees are engaged in their work, their commitment to the organization is enhanced and the likelihood of them leaving the organization decreases.

Similarly, in organizational psychology, Loi, Chan, and Lam (2014) found that organizational identification mediates the positive relationship between leader-member exchange and job satisfaction. Furthermore, the relationship between leader-member exchange and organizational identification is moderated by job security (Loi et al., 2014). In consumer research, multiple studies have indicated that when consumers have strong identifications with companies and products (i.e., consumer–brand identification), there are consequences on their brand loyalty (Stokburger-Sauer, Ratneshwar, & Sen, 2012). Furthermore, consumer–brand identification is usually brought about by strong consumer–company relationships (Bhattacharya & Sen, 2003).

What all these studies have in common is a grounding of organizational identification in the concepts of social identity theory (see Tajfel & Turner, 1979, 1986), which in turn grew out of studies in intercultural communication and conflict reduction between cultural groups. Thus, this book on intercultural public relations appropriately includes this chapter on organizational identity and identification, as well as chapters on intercultural communication and conflict management.

Identity *of* the Organization

He and Brown (2013) reviewed literature on organizational identity and found four scholarly approaches to this concept: functionalist, social constructionist, psychodynamic, and postmodern. In the *functionalist* approach, organizational identity typically is studied as an objective and tangible aspect to an organization, such as company logos, brand elements, and executive speeches. Studies undertaking a *social constructionist* approach typically investigate how organizational identity is created collectively by organizational members through shared language and experience (e.g., Theunissen, 2014). Research in the *psychodynamic* perspective typically emphasizes unconscious processes at play in the shaping of organizational identity, such as self-esteem and emotions. *Postmodern* approaches to organizational identity typically problematize the very notion of "identity" itself and question the "authorship" of identity in collective enterprises. See He and Brown (2013) for detailed examples of studies undertaking each approach to organizational identity.

In their foundational work on organizational identity, Albert and Whetten (1985) argued that an organization's identity was composed of that which was central, enduring and distinctive about it. Subsequently, research across a variety of disciplines has investigated organizational identity, but often without actually defining the term (Stuart et al., 2000). Ultimately, however, scholarly consensus is that organizational identity involves, in one way or another, "an entity's attempts to define itself" (Corley et. al., 2006, p. 87).

Furthermore, this self-definition comes not only from within an organization itself, but also from others and what they know or believe about a focal organization. Indeed, Brown, Dacin, Pratt, and Whetten (2006) pointed out that four related but different concepts can be used to describe such knowledge and belief of individuals regarding organizations: identity, intended image, constructed image, and reputation. First, *identity* refers to "mental associations about the organization held by organizational members" and answers the essential question "Who are we as an organization?" Second, *intended image* refers to "mental associations about the organization that organization leaders want important audiences to hold," which addresses the question of "What does the organization want others to think about the organization?" Third, *construed image* refers to "mental associations that organizational members believe others outside the organization hold about the organization" and asks "What does the organization believe others think of the organization?" Last, *reputation* refers to "mental associations about the organization actually held by others outside the organization," which answers "What do stakeholders actually think of the organization?" (pp. 100–102).

The four concepts identified by Brown et al. (2006) in relation to organizational identity equate roughly to dimensions of organizational identity articulated by Sha et al. (2012): avowed organizational identity, ascribed image, and ascribed reputation, respectively, which is how the remainder of this chapter is organized.

Organizational Identity: Avowed Identities and Intended Images

Just as individuals claim or avow their identities, so do organizations of all kinds, in all sectors of activity. These include governmental organizations, nongovernmental nonprofits, corporations, educational institutions, etc. The avowed identity is both determined or shaped by internal or external organizational environments and proactively managed or negotiated within an organization. The notion of an organization's avowed identity as defined by Sha et al. (2012) relates to Brown et al.'s (2006) concepts of identity and intended image.

Environmental Factors Shaping Organizational Identity Avowals

The avowal of organizational identity may be shaped by organizational types, as well as by organizational culture.

Organizational Types

In the context of public relations, organizational types vary in the age of globalization. Vercic (2009) reviewed the literature on Stohl's typology of organizations, which described the transformation and convergence of domestic to global forms of organizing. These organizations are classified based on various important dimensions: predominance of a single national or cultural identity, perceived importance of an international orientation and perspective, legitimacy of multiple voices and authority, type of structure, and the interconnected nature of interactions across diverse cultural groups. As a result, five types of organization were labeled with the following names and dimensions: domestic, multicultural, multinational, international, and global. These dimensions would shape the kind of avowed identity of different organizations.

In particular, a *domestic* organization has a national orientation with the focus on one country and one dominant culture. It does not have an international orientation nor does it perceive such an orientation to be important. The organization is in general parochial, and it has hierarchical, traditional bureaucratic, and matrix structures. Its management model is monocultural and its international interaction is limited to some import and export goods with a few representatives abroad.

A *multicultural* organization also has one predominant national identity, but with the recognition by the management team of the diversity in its workforce. It accords very little importance to international orientation. It is typically ethnocentric but emphasizes teamwork and flattening hierarchy. It shows cultural dominance; and imports and exports goods with some representatives abroad, and has intercultural communication among the workforce. A *multinational* organization has one national identity while doing business in several countries. The international orientation is considered to be important. The organization is moved to polycentric, with a hierarchical structure managed from a central location with national subsidiaries. It shows cultural compromise and favors intercultural communication among workforce, management, clients, and customers.

An *international* organization identifies with two or more countries. It perceives extreme importance to its international orientation and is typically regiocentric. It has hierarchical and international divisions that integrate global activities with teamwork within subsidiaries but not across. It emphasizes cultural synergy and is internationally loosely coupled. Finally, a *global* organization identifies not with any particular country or culture, but with the global system. An international orientation is dominant in such an organization, which is geocentric. It is structured in a way with decentralized decision-making and sharing of responsibilities. It emphasizes global integration and exists in global networks that are integrative and tightly coupled.

Organizational Culture

Organizational culture is another environmental factor affecting (and affected by) the expression of organizational identity (see Downey, 1986; Hatch & Schultz, 1997; Melewar, 2003; Melewar & Jenkins, 2002). According to Sriramesh, Y. Kim, and Takasaki (1999), organizational culture may be thought of as the personality of an organization. Different definitions and descriptions of organizational culture exist, but Sriramesh, J. Grunig, and Buffington (1992) found some common patterns. These researchers defined organizational culture as "the sum total of shared values, symbols, meanings, beliefs, assumptions, and expectations that organize and integrate a group of people who work together" (p. 591).

In their Excellence study, L. Grunig, J. Grunig, and Dozier (2002) found two major types of organizational culture, authoritarian and participative. In *authoritarian* cultures, decision-making is centralized; departmental agendas conflict with each other; employees believe they are given little flexibility in innovation and that senior managers are interested in them only as workers not as whole people; employees may express fear of their supervisors; and such cultures are generally closed and resistant to external ideas. In organizations with *participative* cultures, the common value is teamwork; employees believe management values them as whole people; and the organizations are open to ideas from both external and internal environments.

Researchers have also used alternative frameworks to explore different types of organizational culture. Al-Khalifa and Aspinwall (2001), for example, used the competing values framework (CVF). Applied to issues such as leadership development and organizational change, CVF was extended to examine organizational culture by Quinn and Kimberly (1984). This framework contains two dimensions: the vertical dimension deals with the degree of control and the horizontal dimension focuses on internal versus external functioning.

Daft (2001) discussed other ways to look at organizational culture. His four categories of culture include: *adaptability/entrepreneurial* culture, which has a strategic focus on external environment through flexibility and change to meet customer needs; *mission* culture, which is more concerned with serving customers in the external environment without the need for rapid change and that has an emphasis on a clear vision of organization's purpose and on achievement of goals; *clan* culture, which is primarily focused on the involvement and participation of the organization's members and on rapidly changing expectations from the external environment; and *bureaucratic* culture, which has an internal focus and a consistency orientation for a stable environment. Robbins (1990) listed the following as key characteristics of organizational culture: individual initiative, risk tolerance, direction, integration, management support, control, identity, reward system, conflict tolerance, and communication patterns.

Avowing Organizational Identities and Conveying Intended Images

In addition to environmental factors, public relations practices play a role in the creation, management, and negotiation of organizational identity. In practice, the creation and management of organizational identity as a process of identity avowal often falls into the purview of public relations. In research, most scholarly work on organizational identity comes from management fields, rather than from public relations.

Avowing Organizational Identity

Organizations avow or assert their identities in numerous ways, including via their graphic representations (such as logos) (van Riel & Balmer, 1997), their mission statements (Sha, 2009), their mission slogans (Verboven, 2011), and their corporate narratives as controlled by organizational elites (Humphreys & Brown, 2002), etc. David, Kline, and Dai (2005) suggested as another component to corporate identity the dimension of "corporate expertise," which they define as "the ability of an organization to detect, assess, and satisfy consumers' needs, wants, and desires by being the leader in a product or service category" (p. 293). This allusion to corporate leadership and competitive advantage links the concept of corporate expertise to the avowal of corporate identity.

Perhaps most importantly, Whetten and Mackey (2002) argued that organizational identities are revealed through what organizations do, i.e., through their actions as collective entities. This argument was underscored by Melewar (2003), whose review of the literature on corporate identity yielded several determinants including both corporate communication and the behaviors of employees, managers, and the organization as an entity.

The idea that the expression of organizational identity is linked inextricably to organizational action places the study of organizational identity avowal squarely within the realm of public relations, which involves not only organizational communication, but also organizational action (cf. Broom & Sha, 2013; *The Page Principles*, 2017). Indeed, while studying how organizations use public relations behaviors to create, maintain, and strengthen their identities, Sha (2009) found that organizations were more able to generate stakeholder identification through the use of symmetrical communication than through the use of conserving communication. Because the definition of "symmetrical communication" involves organizational willingness to change (see Sha, 2004), the term implicitly connotes organizational actions.

Similarly, Holtzhausen and Fourie (2011) recognized the importance of internal stakeholders such as employees in forming part of an organization's external corporate identity and advocated for an inward shift of identity management. They suggested that employees were more concerned about the actual *behaviors* of an organization than about the visual representation of the organization. Ultimately, their findings supported the relationship between employees' perceptions of the effectiveness of an organization's upholding its values (as part of corporate identity) and the quality of its employee relationships.

Conveying Intended Image

Organizations seek to convey their identities in various ways, including through design elements (see He & Brown, 2013; Olins, 1989; van Riel & Balmer, 1997).

Melewar (2003) explained that the very emergence in the 1970s of the notion of corporate identity lay in its origins as a design concept, and then subsequently as a tool for building both support among stakeholders and strategic advantages against competitors. Citing Topalian (1984, p. 56), Melewar (2003) defined corporate identity as "the set of meanings by which a company allows itself to be known and through which it allows people to describe, remember and relate to it" (p. 195). Both Melewar (2003) and Melewar and Jenkins (2002) offer excellent overviews of elements of corporate identity investigated by scholars up to that time.

Sha et al. (2012) argued that "corporate identity" had great research potential in public relations, noting that, "in discussing 'corporate identity,' we do not mean the identity of organizations that are classified as for-profit 'corporations.' Rather, we mean the term 'corporate' in the sense of 'corporal' or pertaining to the whole" (p. 79). Areas identified by these scholars for research on corporate identity included reputation and coalition building, message development and branding, social responsibility and ethics, among others (see Sha et al., 2012).

Today, the conveying of corporate identity (i.e., the avowing of organizational identity to organizational stakeholders) continues to include such design elements as logos, brands, slogans, and even organization names. In this vein, scholars have investigated corporate visual identity (CVI) as a component of organizational identity research and practice. For example, Van den Bosch, de Jong, and Elving (2004) found that the consistent self-presentation of organizations in their corporate visual identity was affected by both structural and cultural elements. Structural elements included technical tools such as design templates and access for all employees to design guidelines. Cultural elements included managers setting an example of consistent CVI presentations.

In terms of corporate identity being that which sets organizations apart from each other, Schmeltz and Kjeldsen (2016) studied how an organizational name change could accomplish strategic goals, in terms of both operations and branding. Organizational name changes are not only about internal concerns, however, as environmental factors also shape the avowal of organizational identities. As one example, the use of Native American names for the organizational identities of sports teams has become increasingly controversial (e.g., Wahlberg, 2004). This example demonstrates the challenges of conveying an intended organizational identity while balancing an organization's responsibility to society.

Claiming Corporate Social Responsibility

Moving beyond the design-centric origins of corporate identity, organizations now also avow their identities or convey their intended images in increasingly sophisticated ways, including the articulation of corporate social values and the claiming of corporate social responsibility. While numerous definitions exist for this concept, we appreciate this one:

Corporate social responsibility, often abbreviated "CSR," is a corporation's initiatives to assess and take responsibility for the company's effects on environmental and social wellbeing. The term generally applies to efforts that go beyond what may be required by regulators or environmental protection groups.

(Investopedia, 2018, n.p.)

CSR initiatives offer many opportunities for organizations to convey their corporate identities, because the assertion of "who we are" is often implicit (intentional or not) in the demonstration of "what we value." Organizations' strategic engagement in specific CSR activities compels specific organizational behaviors that avow corporate identity, as noted above. Furthermore, CSR activities have been shown to affect the reputation of organizations, at least insofar as this is related to corporate image, to be discussed below.

For now, suffice to mention that organizational participation in CSR activities is one means by which an organization might avow its identity as a "good citizen" of society. As David et al. (2005) suggested, "Corporate social responsibility . . . is a citizenship function with moral, ethical, and social obligations that provide the scaffolding for mutually beneficial exchanges between an organization and its publics" (p. 293). Relatedly, Atakan–Duman and Ozdora–Aksak (2014) found that banks in Turkey constructed their online identities using CSR, again illustrating the connection between CSR and corporate identity avowal.

Corporate citizenship and corporate social responsibility are connected to the notion of social values (David, 2004), which—as generally accepted societal norms—must necessarily evolve with shifts in cultural and social norms. A similar-sounding concept, "social value," is about providing a benefit to society. For example, Atakan–Duman and Ozdora–Aksak (2014) found that banks in Turkey portrayed themselves online as providing social value through their CSR efforts, not through their core banking functions. Similarly, Ozdora–Aksak (2015) found that Turkish telecommunications companies constructed their corporate identities in part by focusing on the benefits they provided to the community, i.e., their social value. In other words, our present societal norms include the notion of "social value" to be provided by organizations as one of many social values held by society. See Ho Lee (2017) and Pompper (2015) for recent overviews of scholarship connecting CSR to the public relations function.

Managing Corporate Identity

The importance of corporate identity, both as avowed by the organization and as conveyed to organizational stakeholders, necessitates its careful and strategic management. David (2004) explicitly connected the advent of corporate citizenship with the increased professionalism of public relations practice, which he indicated would be enhanced by a focus on public relations as a managerial function as advocated in the Excellence study (cf. L. Grunig et al., 2002).

The management of organizational identity may extend beyond a specific organization to the broader industry or sector to which that organization belongs. For example, Lellis (2012) found evidence of a "cause identity," a strong collective identity shared among numerous disability organizations, which they expressed more strongly than they did their individual organizational identities. Similarly, Feldner and Fyke (2016) found that identity work among social entrepreneurship organizations happened at both the level of the organizations and the level of this emergent sector. The findings from these studies affirm the assertion by Sha et al. (2012) that coalition building would be another means by which organizations could avow their identities in relation to a larger collective.

Indeed, the management of corporate identity has generated its own subfield: corporate identity management (CIM). Simões, Dibb, and Fisk (2005) believed that CIM involves (1) the endorsement of consistent behavior through the diffusion of a company's mission, values, and goals; (2) the expression and pursuit of brand and image consistency in the organization's symbols and forms of communication; and (3) the implementation, support, and maintenance of visual systems. In many ways, these notions of CIM are consistent with the public relations ideal of organizational words matching organizational behavior (see Broom & Sha, 2013; *The Page Principles*, 2017).

The notion that public relations is not just about organizational communication, but also about organizational action (see above) leads directly to the aspect of organizational identity that is ascribed by stakeholders to organizations, insofar as those ascriptions are grounded not only in what the organization's promotional activities say about itself, but also in how the organization's leadership behaves. Thus, we turn now to consider the identities of organizations as they are ascribed by stakeholders in the forms of image and reputation.

Organizational Identity: Ascribed Images and Reputations

How an organization's identity is perceived by external stakeholders may not always be the same as that which the organization has worked so hard to construct. Sha et al. (2012) asserted that how an avowed organizational identity is *received* by organizational stakeholders constitutes its ascribed image, whereas how that avowed organizational identity is *perceived* by those stakeholders constitutes its ascribed reputation.

For Sha et al. (2012), the key point about *both* image and reputation was that each concept involves *ascriptions* of identity to an organization by others. Whereas the locus of definition for "identity" is the organization itself, the locus for definition of "image" and "reputation" is the organizational stakeholder. For example, Barnett, Jermier, and Lafferty (2006) defined image as "*observers' general impressions of a corporation's distinct collection of symbols, whether that observer is internal or external to the firm*" (p. 34, emphasis added).

Whereas they have in common being defined by others and not by the organization, "image" and "reputation" also are distinct from each other, although exactly how, no one seems certain. In fact, Whetten and Mackey (2002) noted that identity, image, and reputation—while all important elements in an organization's conception of itself—have each suffered from a lack of clear conceptualization and together have suffered from indistinct relationships to each other. For an excellent overview of the literature on these concepts up to its publication year, see Whetten and Mackey (2002).

Two examples will suffice in this chapter for making the point about conceptual confusion: First, Bromley (2000) described corporate image as "the way an organization presents itself to its publics, especially visually," although this definition is reflective of corporate visual identity (discussed earlier in this chapter as a dimension of corporate identity avowal), rather than ascription. Second, in describing the corporate citizenship dimension of corporate social values (discussed above as a form of corporate identity avowal), David et al. (2005) asserted them to be "perceptions or schemas that the consumer has about a corporation" (p. 297), thus alluding to corporate "image."

Along with "image," the concept of organizational reputation has received growing attention from scholars and practitioners in public relations, marketing, and management, among other fields. This focus on reputation has also been shared by lay audiences of non-experts, for whom various reputation rankings have been created to purportedly evaluate a wide range of collective entities, from corporations and nonprofits, to educational institutions and even countries.

Yet, conceptualizations of corporate reputation have varied in different disciplines of research (Helm, 2005; Mahon, 2002). Just as Hodgkinson (2013) criticized scholars for letting their own disciplinary identities impede progress on cross-disciplinary research in organizational identity and identification, Mahon (2002, p. 415) lamented that:

> Reputation is . . . (fill in the blanks please)? Reputation has been subjected to research for some time and has periodically been "rediscovered" by scholars in different disciplines, with different definitions and perspectives, so the answer to what is reputation is not as clear as it might initially seem to a casual observer. What makes it even more troubling is that the research in these different disciplines often makes little or no reference to the parallel research being conducted elsewhere. As a consequence, we do not seem to achieve the great breakthroughs that we would if we used the existent research across disciplines.

Bromley (2000) noted that corporate reputation refers to "the way key external stakeholder groups or other interested parties actually conceptualize that organization" (p. 240). This approach recalls Brown et al.'s (2006) definition of "reputation" as "mental associations about the organization actually held by others outside the organization" (p. 102).

Aside from the confusion about what reputation actually *is*, scholars in management have often conceptualized reputation in terms of *what is it good for?* Reputation has been considered as a resource for the company and, as such, something that can be managed and that can create a competitive advantage for the organization (Dowling, 2006; Fombrun, 1996; Rindova & Fombrun, 1999). In this resource-based view, scholars have examined reputation from the perspective of how it will bring value to an organization, typically as an intangible asset, more so than a tangible one (Fombrun, 1996; Mahon, 2002). As an intangible asset, reputation is very difficult to reproduce from one organization to the next, because of two factors that lead to the development of reputation: time (historical aspect) and connections among the organization and its stakeholders across contexts (relational aspect) (see Hall, 1992; Mahon, 2002).

The notion of corporate reputation as an intangible asset built up over time as a result of complex relationships points to the important role of public relations in managing, if not the ascribed reputations themselves, then at least the relational implications of those ascriptions of corporate identity. This is a key point that connects management research on reputation with public relations scholarship in the same area, and it's a point that is too infrequently articulated explicitly.

In public relations research, scholars have found organization–public relationships (OPRs) to exert important influence in the reputation management process (Sung & Yang, 2009; Yang, 2007; Yang & J. Grunig, 2005). Essentially, high quality OPRs predict positive organizational reputations (Sung & Yang, 2009).

Furthermore, Bromley (1993) differentiated between primary organizational reputation and secondary organizational reputation. *Primary reputations* are based on direct experience with an organization; *secondary reputations* result from the lack of such direct experience and hence are more superficial, stereotypical, and conforming to preexisting ideas. This differentiation implies that publics with and without direct experience will perceive an organization's reputation differently and suggests that the quality of organization–public relationships impacts reputation, as such relationships are based on certain levels of experience and involvement.

Influence of Organizational Identity and Identification on Public Relations Practices

The connections between organizational identity (OI) and organizational identification (OID) on the one hand and public relations on the other are obvious, and we summarize them in Table 9.1.

TABLE 9.1 Summary of the Influence of Organizational Identity and Organizational Identification on Public Relations

Organizational identity (OI)/organizational identification (OID)	Claim from the literature	Connection to public relations
Process of OID	How employees see their self-identity in relation to their organizational membership (see Ashforth & Mael, 1989)	Public relations as internal and employee communication, plus related social-exchange factors such as work-life fit, diversity, job engagement, organizational commitment, etc. (e.g., Sha & Ahles, 2009; Walden et al., 2017; White et al., 2010)
Avowing OI (defining self)	Affected by environmental factors (e.g., Hatch & Schultz, 1997; Melewar, 2003; Melewar & Jenkins, 2002)	Public relations as an environmental scanning function (Broom & Sha, 2013; L. Grunig et al., 2002)
Avowing OI (defining self)	Revealed in part through what organizations *do* (Whetten and Mackey, 2002)	Public relations is about organizational behaviors, not just organizational communications (Broom & Sha, 2013)
Avowing OI (conveying intended image)	Communicated through design elements (Hu & Brown, 2013; Melewar, 2003; Olins, 1989; van Riel & Balmer, 1997)	Public relations as creation and dissemination of organizational symbols via media and interpersonal channels (Broom & Sha, 2013)
Avowing OI (conveying intended image)	Communicated through social values and corporate social responsibility (David, 2004; David et al., 2005)	CSR as a public relations function (Ho Lee, 2017; Pompper, 2015)
Ascribed image and ascribed reputation as components of OI	OI as received and as perceived by stakeholders (see Brown et al., 2006; Sha et al., 2012)	High-quality organization–public relationships predict positive organizational reputations (e.g., Sung & Yang, 2009)

In closing, we believe that organizational identity and identification are, and will continue to be, important concepts in the practice of public relations, especially in the intercultural context. Increasingly, organizations are facing not only internal and external publics that have varying degrees of identification with the organization, but also publics whose own identities are not the same as, and sometimes clash with, those of the organization. These layers of complexity make it even more imperative for organizations to approach intercultural public relations in two ways:

First, organizations must continue to strengthen their environmental scanning efforts, as well as their identification of internal and external publics so as to better engage in strategic communication and relationship building. Second, organizations must engage in internal reflection to understand their own organizational identity, i.e., *who we are*. When their identity is inevitably challenged in interactions with various organizational publics, organizations will need to determine which aspects of their identities are to be kept and which are to be discarded, negotiated, and reshaped.

Thus, in the terminology propounded by Sha (2004), the question of organizational identity ultimately becomes a question of symmetry (i.e., which things will be adapted) and conservation (i.e., which things will be maintained). Much, much more research is needed—preferably across disciplinary identity barriers (cf. Hodgkinson, 2013)—to enhance our understanding and thinking along these lines.

References

Albert, S., & Whetten, D. A. (1985). Organizational identity. *Research in Organizational Behavior, 7*, 263–295.

Al-Khalifa, K. N., & Aspinwall, E. M. (2001). Using the competing values framework to investigate the culture of Qatar industries. *Total Quality Management, 12*, 417–428.

Ashforth, B. E., & Mael, F. A. (1989). Social identity theory and the organisation. *Academy of Management Review, 14*, 20–39.

Ashforth, B. E., Harrison, S. H., & Corley, K. G. (2008). Identification in organizations: An examination of four fundamental questions. *Journal of Management, 34*, 325–374.

Atakan-Duman, S., & Ozdora-Aksak, E. (2014). The role of corporate social responsibility in online identity construction: An analysis of Turkey's banking sector. *Public Relations Review, 40*, 862–864. doi:10.1016/j.pubrev.2014.07.004

Bardhan, N., & Weaver, C. K. (2010). *Public relations in global cultural contexts. Multiparadigmatic perspectives.* New York, NY: Routledge.

Barnett, M. L., Jermier, J. M., & Lafferty, B. A. (2006). Corporate reputation: The definitional landscape. *Corporate Reputation Review, 9*, 26–38. doi: 10.1057/palgrave.crr.1550012

Bhattacharya, C. B., & Sen, S. (2003). Consumer–company identification: A framework for understanding consumers' relationships with companies. *Journal of Marketing, 67*(2), 76–88. https://doi.org/10.1509/jmkg.67.2.76.18609

Bromley, D. B. (1993). *Reputation, image and impression management.* West Sussex, UK: Wiley.

Bromley, D. B. (2000). Psychological aspects of corporate identity, image and reputation. *Corporate Reputation Review, 3*, 240–252. doi.org/10.1057/palgrave.crr.1540117

Broom, G. M., & Sha, B.-L. (2013). *Cutlip and Center's effective public relations* (11th ed.). Upper Saddle River, NJ: Pearson.

Brown, T. J., Dacin, P. A., Pratt, M. G., & Whetten, D. A. (2006). Identity, intended image, construed image, and reputation: An interdisciplinary framework and suggested terminology. *Journal of the Academy of Marketing Science, 34*(2), 99–106.

Corley, K. G., Harquail, C. V., Pratt, M. G., Glynn, M. A., Fiol, M., & Hatch, M. J. (2006). Guiding organizational identity through aged adolescence. *Journal of Management Inquiry, 15*, 85–99.

Daft, R. L. (2001). *Essentials of organization theory & design.* Cincinnati, OH: South-Western College Publishing.

David, P. (2004). Extending symmetry: Toward a convergence of professionalism, practice, and pragmatics in public relations. *Journal of Public Relations Research, 16*, 185–211.

David, P., Kline, S., & Dai, Y. (2005). Corporate social responsibility practices, corporate identity, and purchase intention: A dual-process model. *Journal of Public Relations Research, 17*(3), 291–313. doi:10.1207/s1532754xjprr1703_4

Dowling, G. (2006). How good corporate reputations create corporate value. *Corporate Reputation Review, 9*, 134–143.

Downey, S. M. (1986). The relationship between corporate culture and corporate identity. *Public Relations Quarterly, 31*(4), 7–12.

Dutton, J. E., Dukerich, J. M., & Harquail, C. V. (1994). Organizational images and member identification. *Administrative Science Quarterly, 39*, 239–263.

Feldner, S. B., & Fyke, J. P. (2016). Rhetorically constructing an identity at multiple levels: A case study of social entrepreneurship umbrella organizations. *International Journal of Strategic Communication, 10*(2), 101–114. doi:10.1080/1553118X.2016.1144188

Fombrun, C. J. (1996) *Reputation: Realizing value from the corporate image.* Boston, MA: Harvard Business School Press.

Grunig, L. A., Grunig, J. E., & Dozier, D. M. (2002). *Excellent Public relations and effective organizations: A study of communication management in three countries.* Mahwah, NJ: Lawrence Erlbaum Associates.

Hall, R. (1992). The strategic analysis of intangible resources. *Strategic Management Journal, 13*, 135–144.

Hatch, M., & Schultz, M. (1997). Relations between organizational culture, identity, and image. *European Journal of Marketing, 31*(516), 356–365.

He, H., & Brown, A. D. (2013). Organizational identity and organizational identification: A review of the literature and suggestions for future research. *Group and Organization Management, 38*, 3–35.

Helm, S. (2005). Designing a formative measure for corporate reputation. *Corporate Reputation Review, 8*, 95–109.

Hirst, G., van Dick, R., & van Knippenberg, D. (2009). A social identity perspective on leadership and employee creativity. *Journal of Organizational Behavior, 30*, 963–982.

Ho Lee, T. (2017). The status of corporate social responsibility research in public relations: A content analysis of published articles in eleven scholarly journals from 1980 to 2015. *Public Relations Review, 43*(1), pp. 211–218.

Hodgkinson, G. P. (2013). Organizational identity and organizational identification: A critical realist design science perspective. *Group & Organization Management, 38*(1), 145–157.

Holtzhausen, L., & Fourie, L. (2011). Employees' perceptions of institutional values and employer–employee relationships at the North-West University. *Journal of Public Affairs, 11*(4), 243–255.

Homburg, C., Wieseke, J., & Hoyer, W. D. (2009). Social identity and the service-profit chain. *Journal of Marketing, 73,* 38–54.

Humphreys, M., & Brown, A. D. (2002). Narratives of organizational identity and identification: A case study of hegemony and resistance. *Organization Studies, 23,* 317–337.

Investopedia. (2018). Corporate social responsibility. Retrieved from www.investope dia.com/terms/c/corp-social-responsibility.asp#ixzz55c1Erm64.

Lellis, J. C. (2012). Cause identity: A measurement of disability organizations' communicated values. *Public Relations Review, 38*(3), 508–510. doi:10.1016/j.pubrev.2012.02.005

Loi, R., Chan, K. W., & Lam, L. W. (2014). Leader-member exchange, organizational identification, and job satisfaction: A social identity perspective. *Journal of Occupational and Organizational Psychology, 87,* 42–61. doi:10.1111/joop.12028.

Madjar, N., Greenberg, E., & Chen, Z. (2011). Factors for radical creativity, incremental creativity, and routine, noncreative performance. *Journal of Applied Psychology, 96,* 730–743.

Mahon, J. F. (2002). Corporate reputation: A research agenda using strategy and stake-holder literature. *Business and Society, 41,* 415–445.

Melewar, T. C. (2003). Determinants of the corporate identity construct: A review of the literature. *Journal of Marketing Communications, 9*(4), 195–220.

Melewar, T. C., & Jenkins, E. (2002). Defining the corporate identity construct. *Corporate Reputation Review, 5*(1), 76–90.

Olins W. (1989). *Corporate identity: Making business strategy visible through design.* Boston, MA: Harvard Business School Press.

Ozdora-Aksak, E. (2015). An analysis of Turkey's telecommunications sector's social responsibility practices online. *Public Relations Review, 41*(3), 365–369. doi:10.1016/j. pubrev.2015.01.001

The Page Principles. (2017). Arthur W. Page Society: Author. Retrieved from https:// awpagesociety.com/site/the-page-principles.

Pompper, D. (2015). *Corporate social responsibility, sustainability and public relations: Negotiating multiple complex challenges.* New York, NY: Routledge.

Quinn, R. E., & Kimberly, J. R. (1984). Paradox, planning, and perseverance: Guidelines for managerial practice. In J. R. Kimberly & R. E. Quinn (Eds.), *Managing organiza-tional translations* (pp. 295– 313). Homewood, IL: Dow Jones-Irwin.

Ravasi, D., & van Rekom, J. (2003). Key issues in organizational identity and identi-fication theory. *Corporate Reputation Review, 6,* 118–132. doi.org/10.1057/palgrave. crr.1540194

Resources for Employers. (2017). American Psychological Association: Author. Retrieved from www.apaexcellence.org/resources/creatingahealthyworkplace/

Rindova, V., & Fombrun, C. J. (1999). Constructing competitive advantage: The role of firm-constituent interactions. *Strategic Management Journal, 20,* 691–710.

Robbins, S. P. (1990). *Organizational theory: Structure, design, and applications* (3rd ed.). Englewood Cliffs, NJ: Prentice Hall.

Schmeltz, L., & Kjeldsen, A. K. (2016). Naming as strategic communication: Understanding corporate name change through an integrative framework encom-passing branding, identity and institutional theory. *International Journal of Strategic Communication, 10*(4), 309–331. doi:10.1080/1553118X.2016.1179194

Sha, B.-L. (2004). Noether's theorem: The science of symmetry and the law of conservation. *Journal of Public Relations Research, 16*(4), 391–416.

Sha, B.-L. (2009). Exploring the connection between organizational identity and public relations behaviors: How symmetry trumps conservation in engendering organizational identification. *Journal of Public Relations Research, 21*(3), 295–317. doi:10.1080/10627260802640765

Sha, B.-L., & Ahles, C. B. (2009, March). *Identity vs. survival: Communicating with employees while adjusting to the changing business environment.* Paper presented at the International Public Relations Research Conference, Miami, FL.

Sha, B.-L., Tindall, N. T. J., & Sha, T.-L. (2012). Identity & culture: Implications for public relations. In K. Sriramesh & D. Vercic (Eds.), *Culture and public relations: Links and implications* (pp. 67–90). New York: Taylor & Francis/Routledge.

Simões, C., Dibb, S., & Fisk, R. P. (2005). Managing corporate identity: An internal perspective. *Journal of the Academy of Marketing Science, 33*(2), 153–168.

Sriramesh, K., & Vercic, D. (2009). *The global public relations handbook, revised and expanded edition: Theory, research, and practice* (2nd ed.). New York, NY: Routledge.

Srirmesh, K., & Vercic, D. (2012). *Culture and public relations: Links and implications.* New York, NY: Routledge.

Sriramesh, K., Grunig, J. E., & Buffington, J. (1992). Corporate culture and public relations. In J. E. Grunig (Ed.), *Excellence in public relations and communication management* (pp. 577–595). Hillsdale, NJ: Lawrence Erlbaum.

Sriramesh, K., Kim, Y., & Takasaki, M. (1999). Public relations in three Asian cultures: An analysis. *Journal of Public Relations Research, 11*, 271–292. https://doi.org/10.1207/s1532754xjprr1104_01

Stokburger-Sauer, N., Ratneshwar, S., & Sen, S. (2012). Drivers of consumer-brand identification. *International Journal of Research in Marketing, 29*, 406–418. doi.org/10.1016/j.ijresmar.2012.06.001

Stuart, A., Ashforth, B., & Dutton, J. (2000). Organizational identity and identification: Charting new waters and building new bridges. *Academy of Management Review, 25*(1), 13–17.

Sung, M., & Yang, S.-U. (2009). Student–university relationships and reputation: A study of the links between key factors fostering students' supportive behavioral intentions towards their university. *Higher Education, 57*, 787–811.

Tajfel, H., & Turner, J. C. (1979). An integrative theory of intergroup conflict. In W. G. Austin & S. Worchel (Eds.), *The social psychology of intergroup relations* (pp. 33–47). Monterey, CA: Brooks-Cole.

Tajfel, H., & Turner, J. C. (1986). The social identity theory of intergroup behavior. In S. Worchel & W. G. Austin (Eds.), *Psychology of intergroup relations* (pp. 7–24). Chicago, IL: Nelson-Hall.

Theunissen, P. (2014). Co-creating corporate identity through dialogue: A pilot study. *Public Relations Review, 40*(3), 612–614. doi:10.1016/j.pubrev.2014.02.026

van den Bosch, A. L. M., de Jong, M. D. T., & Elving, W. J. L. (2004). Managing corporate visual identity: Use and effects of organizational measures to support a consistent self-presentation. *Public Relations Review, 30*(2), 225–234. doi:10.1016/j.pubrev.2003.12.002

van Riel C. B., & Balmer J. M. T. (1997). Corporate identity: The concept, its measurement, and management. *European Journal of Marketing, 31*, 341–355.

Verboven, H. (2011). Communicating CSR and business identity in the chemical industry through mission slogans. *Business Communication Quarterly, 74*(4), 415–431. doi:10.1177/1080569911424485

Vercic, D. (2009). Public relations of movers and shakers: Transnational corporations. In K. Sriramesh & Vercic (Eds.), *The global public relations handbook, revised and expanded editions: Theory, research, and practice* (2nd ed., pp. 795–806). New York: Routledge.

Vercic, D., Zerfass, A., & Wiesenberg, M. (2015). Global public relations and communication management: A European perspective. *Public Relations Review, 41*, 785–793.

Wahlberg, D. (2004). Ending the debate: Crisis communication analysis of one university's American Indian athletic identity. *Public Relations Review, 30*(2), 197–203. doi: 10.1016/j.pubrev.2004.02.002

Walden, J., Jung, E. H., & Westerman, C. Y. K. (2017). Employee communication, job engagement, and organizational commitment: A study of members of the Millennial Generation. *Journal of Public Relations Research, 29*(2–3), 73–89. http://tandfonline.com/doi/full/10.1080/1062726X.2017.1329737

Walumbwa, F. O., Avolio, B., & Zhu, W. (2008). How transformational leadership weaves its influence on individual job performance: The role of identification and efficacy beliefs. *Personnel Psychology, 61*(4), 793–825.

Walumbwa, F. O., Mayer, D. M., Wang, P., Wang, H., Workman, K., & Christensen, A. L. (2011). Linking ethical leadership to employee performance: The roles of leader-member exchange, self-efficacy, and organizational identification. *Organizational Behavior and Human Decision Process, 115*, 204–213. doi.org/10.1016/j.obhdp.2010.11.002

Weiseke, J., Ahearne, M., Lam, S. K., & Von Dick, R. (2008). The role of leaders in internal marketing: A multilevel examination through the lens of social identity theory. *Journal of Marketing, 73*(2), 123–146.

Whetten D. A., & Mackey A. (2002). A social actor conception of organizational identity and its implications for the study of organizational reputation. *Business & Society, 41*, 393–414.

White, C., Vanc, A., & Stafford, G. (2010). Internal communication, information satisfaction, and sense of community: The effect of personal influence. *Journal of Public Relations Research, 22*, 65–84.

Yang, S.-U. (2007). An integrated model for organization–public relational outcomes, organizational reputation, and their antecedents. *Journal of Public Relations Research, 19*, 91–121.

Yang, S.-U., & Grunig, J. E. (2005). Decomposing organizational reputation: The effects of organization-public relationship outcomes on cognitive representations of organizations and evaluations of organizational performance. *Journal of Communication Management, 9*, 305–325.

10

SOCIAL MEDIA

Overview of Social Media Use in Public Relations

Social media use has been adopted in public relations across different industry *sectors* and across *cultures*. However, different factors have played roles in the extent to which social media is used. Social media use and adoption have been examined in the contexts of government agencies at different levels (Avery et al., 2010; Graham, Avery, & Park, 2015; Lee & VanDyke, 2015); institutes of higher learning (among university communicators, Kelleher & Sweetser, 2012; Twitter use among colleges and universities, Linvill, McGee, & Hicks, 2012); multinational companies (Bingqi & Han, 2009); and non-profits (Curtis et al., 2010; Gao, 2016). Social media use also has been examined in different functions of public relations, such as donor engagement (Smitko, 2012) and investor communication (Koehler, 2014).

Among these studies, advantages and disadvantages of social media adoption were identified. Avery and Graham (2013) examined the role that various community features played on local governments' social media use in promoting participatory and transparent government. Among other things, citizen expectations and perceived social media effectiveness by government officials strongly predicted social media use. Graham et al. (2015) found that the extent of social media use in crises by local government was positively associated with local city officials' assessments of their ability to control a crisis situation and strength of crisis responses.

Challenges in social media adoption exist. Avery et al. (2010) examined the diffusion of social media use in health departments in different communities. The study identified reasons for slow social media adoption in some areas, which led to health information disparities. In addition, adoption of social media among government agencies communicating science is still found to be mostly one-way use (Lee & VanDyke, 2015).

Adoption of social media is also examined in different countries, such as the use of social media among public relations practitioners in Turkey (Alikilic & Atabek, 2012) and response to digital trends among public relations agencies in Greece (Triantafillidou & Yannas, 2014).

The Effects of Social Media Use on Public Relations Practitioners

The use of social media has professional and personal implications for public relations practitioners. Professionally, social media usage has become a part of the professional activities of practitioners and a part of the strategic planning process (Charest, Bouffard, & Zajmovic, 2016). In turn, such social media use is related to the perceptions of decision-making power and public relations roles (Diga & Kelleher, 2009).

Personally, practitioners use social media according to field-constrained norms, occupational publicness, and the need to be visible online outside of the workplace (Walden & Parcha, 2017). This personal use has cultural implications and influences the strategies to negotiate practitioners' personal identity and identity of their organization (Vardeman-Winter & Place, 2015). In addition, such use involves emotional labor and has implications for practitioners' personal brands. The pros and cons, including long working hours, are examined by Bridgen (2011).

Integrating both professional and personal implications, a series of studies has examined public relations leaders' as well as strategic communicators' perceptions of the impact of social media use on their work, leadership behaviors, and work–life conflict (Jiang, Luo, & Kulemeka, 2016; Luo, Jiang, & Kulemeka, 2015). Jiang et al. (2016) found that perceived importance of the role of social media positively predicted the use of "Facebook, RSS Feeds, Blogging, YouTube, [as well as] use of social media in media relations and environmental scanning" (p. 497). The use of these social media platforms was also positively related to their perceived leadership. Luo et al. (2015) interviewed 43 public relations leaders to explore leadership behavior and social media use. They discovered four reasons why these leaders used social media: demonstrating expertise, showing beneficial outcomes to gain decision-making power, demonstrating leadership vision, and maintaining leadership power within the peer group. These studies indicated that public relations leaders tended to used social media to establish their leadership roles, and that they used social media platforms selectively to realize this goal. Luo et al. (2015) called for future research to study how such leadership use might influence the organizational use of social media as a whole.

The Effects of Social Media Use on the Publics

Social media has shifted the power of communication from public relations practitioners to the publics, or to social media users who may not have a recognized role or defined interest in an organization (Smith, 2010). As a result, traditional public relations responsibilities are being distributed to social media users. These publics themselves have become increasingly able to better negotiate their own identities, feel empowered through social media use, and form their own communities to achieve their goals. These effects are reflected in advocacy and activism, awareness building, and community building.

Advocacy and Activism

Social media has been tremendously helpful in mobilizing otherwise disconnected publics and engaging them in advocacy efforts. Sometimes, social media has directly facilitated social movement and activism efforts.

For example, online advocacy campaigns have been conducted by nongovernmental organizations to promote active participation of supporters in the case of Greenpeace Mediterranean's anti-genetically engineered food campaign in Turkey (Pınar Özdemir, 2012). Digital activism has reached an all-time high because social media can be used effectively to express dissensus, as was examined in the case of Chick-fil-A's Facebook page (Ciszek, 2016). Kaur (2015) examined digital environmental publics where online advocacy efforts had created an anti-corporate public sentiment to slow down the operations of Lynas, an Australian rare earth mining company that wanted to set up a refinery in Malaysia. The environmental publics successfully achieved their goals through the strategic use of digital media that united activists with voters.

Paek, Hove, Jung, and Cole (2013) examined how promoting a cause-related public relations campaign on child welfare was conducted across three social media platforms (Blog, Facebook, and Twitter) and found that people's use of each platform was significantly related to these people's engagement as well as to all the campaign's intended behavior outcomes. Similarly, advocacy of interest organizations has been enhanced through social media. For example, Chalmers and Shotton (2016) examined the determinants of the use of social media tools by interested organizations as part of a larger set of news media lobbying strategies. They argued for and identified two factors that determined social media use: the importance an organization places on trying to shape lobbying debates through the new media and the importance placed on shaping public image through the new media.

Awareness Building

Social media is used to support or boost marketing public relations because it is relatively inexpensive, has instant wide reach, and allows real-time feedback (Papasolomou & Melanthiou, 2012). Other researchers have found that social media can quickly generate conversations, facilitate brand positioning, and maintain brand sustenance (Allagui & Breslow, 2016). These functions of social media help the one-way information dissemination purpose of public relations.

Community Building

In the context of health care, social media changes how people access health care information online. The power of consumer-driven critical mass helps organizations improve health care literacy and health outcomes through online engagement. Geoghegan and Monseau (2011) reviewed Johnson & Johnson's social media efforts that enabled the launch and initial growth of two Facebook communities for the attention-deficit hyperactivity disorder (ADHD) therapeutic community: ADHD Moms for caregivers of children with ADHD and ADHD Allies for adults with ADHD. Their study identified three priorities for a disease-awareness social media program: (a) to redefine the impact of social media dynamics and change from focusing on selling (i.e., "return on investment") to sharing, from being transactional to relational, from establishing authority to affinity; (b) to help organizations recognize that social media is different—it is a true consumer democracy; and (c) to reflect and reinforce the true value of generating disease awareness in social media by serving patient needs and creating the foundation for new relationships in their comfort zones.

Cultural Identity

In the context of intercultural public relations, interacting groups' cultural values, beliefs, traditions, and norms form the backdrop of social media use. The cultural groups are also embedded in their dominant political, economic, and historical backgrounds. The access to and impact of social media may differ across interacting groups. Therefore, environmental analysis and public identification in intercultural public relations become even more crucial than in the intracultural context.

For example, faced with Lowe's decision to pull advertising from TLC's *All-American Muslim* program and with Susan G. Komen (SGK) *for the Cure's* announcement of new granting criteria that impacted Planned Parenthood, many angry voices emerged on social media, followed by apologies from both organizations (Kinsky, Drumheller, Gerlich, Brock-Baskin, & Sollosy, 2015). People were angry in the former case because they considered the program to be an anti-Muslim move and in the latter case because they believed the policy change at SGK to be politically motivated, which was opposed to the stakeholders' expectations because in general SGK is supposed to be an apolitical organization with an apolitical cause. Kinsky et al.'s (2015) study found that, given the importance of the involved stakeholders' values in the above situations, their attitudes and social norms best predicted the publics' reported intentions to donate or buy. Kinsky et al. (2015) thus argued that social media has expanded the scope of strategic publics that influence how people listen and pay attention to issues.

Some cases of *hashtag hijacking*—when a hashtag on social media is used for a different purpose than the one originally intended—illustrate the increasingly prominent role of culture and the different cultural identities of publics in social media responses. In the case of #AskJameis, this public relations campaign was hijacked by audiences through an investigation of the #AskJameis campaign, essentially mocking and criticizing both the organization (Florida State University) and the individual involved in the lawsuit, Jameis Winston. Sanderson, Barnes, Williamson, and Kian (2016) noted the need to consider the potential "pulse" of the audience before launching social media campaigns. They also concluded that, at times, not using social media is a more effective public relations practice.

Another case, of #myNYPD, illustrated the power of social media dissent and networked counterpublics. These counterpublic narratives about racial profiling and police misconduct played a big role in hijacking a hashtag that was originally supposed to demonstrate the positive role of the New York Police Department (NYPD). In such cases, one needs to understand the evolving nature of counterpublics and how media shapes public debates around marginalization (Jackson & Welles, 2015). Because hashtag labels attract readers both for and against the issue, the high involvement level may mobilize both sides more quickly than ever, and thus produce viral effects that sharply differ from what was intended.

Finally, cultural influences may affect individual concerns about privacy in the use of social media. While the massive amount of data collected from users' social media usage behaviors is beneficial to strategic communication professionals and practices, the pervasive nature of social media use significantly impacts users' privacy concerns as a result of these big data applications. Yang and Kang (2015) incorporated a cultural dimension framework in examining cross-cultural data on how cultural context shapes what is considered to be private and how individuals should respond to any infringement upon their own privacy. The individualism and collectivism dimension was found to explain cross-cultural variations.

Effects of Social Media Use on Organizational Identity

In addition to exerting effects on individuals, social media also affects and potentially changes an organization's identity. The functions of social media for organizations can vary depending on the nature of the organization and the issues. Four major functions included maintaining organizational identity, building relationships, controlling issues management, and promoting corporate social responsibility (Reitz, 2012). To attract and retain publics in today's competitive world, any organization needs to build and maintain strong organizational identities (see more in Chapter 9). Reitz (2012) argued that social media could serve as the "feedback mechanism" through which organizational publics voice their opinions and impressions of the organization during the repeated interactions with the organization, which is crucial for the social construction of organizational identity (p. 48). In fact, publics could use social media to shape an organizations' identity, in the sense of its reputation. We believe that organizational identity is not only to be maintained but also challenged, and negotiated through social media in intercultural settings.

Social Media Use and Public Relations Practices

Social media use has significantly changed every aspect of public relations practice, ranging from environmental scanning, identifying and understanding publics, engaging with publics through messaging and relationship management, as well as resolving conflicts and crises. Current public relations research has addressed some, but not all, of these areas, with a heavy focus on identifying and understanding publics, engaging with publics through messaging, relationship management, and conflict management and crisis management. These four areas of research are synthesized in the following section.

Environmental Scanning

We believe that the use of social media has played a huge role in how organizations engage in environmental scanning to contribute to issues management. Reitz (2012) identified issues management as one function of social media use by organizations. There are both advantages and disadvantages. On one hand, the use of social media has made it much easier for organizations to proactively identify potential issues, concerns, and opinions of their publics. Doing research for a public relations program is faster and less costly because organizations can monitor and observe the interactions between the publics and the organizations online. They can even initiate dialogue by asking for publics' opinions on certain issues (Reitz, 2012).

On the other hand, social media has also made it harder for organizations to communicate with their publics because of instant changes in the social environment, the potential for "unexpected publics" online (e.g., Brabham, 2012) to arise, and the difficulty of appealing to different publics with diverse interests and values at the same time. Because more and more people have access to social media and many tend to be vocal about their opinions, organizations can no longer assume that their policies or positions can meet every public's need. Therefore, the illusory sense of "control" is lost. As of now, not much research has been done along this line. Future research should begin to address the effects and changes social media bring to environmental scanning.

Identifying and Understanding Publics

In the context of social media, we identify the following types of publics as essential because they have been the focus of study in the current literature: the users, the creators, and the influencers of social media content. These publics are often interconnected and overlap.

The most comprehensive model on different types of publics in social media has been developed in the context of crisis communication. In particular, the social-mediated crisis communication (SMCC) model (Jin & Liu, 2010; Liu, Jin, Briones, & Kuch, 2012) described the interaction between a focal organization with a crisis and three types of publics relating to crisis information via social media (SM), traditional media (TM), and offline word of mouth (WOM) communication:

> (a) influential SM creators, who create crisis information for others to consume; (b) SM followers who consume the influential SM creators' crisis information; and (c) SM inactives, who may consume influential SM creators' crisis information indirectly through offline WOM communication with SM followers and/or TM who follow influential SM creators and/or SM followers.
>
> *(Liu, Jin, & Austin, 2013, p. 54)*

Liu et al.'s (2013) study examined the reasons and means that the publics used to communicate about crisis. They identified that humor value and having/seeking insider information were the major motivations for participants to communicate online about crises. For one particular type of social media—blogs—they identified six primary motivators for communication: information seeking and media checking, convenience, personal fulfillment, political surveillance, social surveillance, and expression and affiliation. Liu et al. also found that traditional media still had heavier influence than did social media in crisis communication.

Outside of the crisis context, for the users of social media content, research has identified how personal profiles could be analyzed to gain an understanding of the users. For example, Len-Ríos, Hughes, McKee, and Young (2016) studied adolescents as publics and their media use preferences, parental mediation, and perceived Internet literacy. In particular, they found that early adolescents with social media accounts spent more time with television than they did with social media, indicating that traditional media outlets such as TV were still useful channels for the youth. Len-Ríos et al. (2016) also found that adolescents were more likely to observe the posts on social media than to post information themselves. Therefore, public relations practitioners should actively look for those adolescents who do spread messages online, or "opinion leaders."

Finally, Len-Ríos et al. (2016) found that adolescents tended to be multitaskers and all-around media consumers. The greater the number of social media accounts they had, the more time they spent with magazines, music, streaming video, email, and social media. Parental limits on social media were not significantly related to the participants' time spent with social media.

The creators of social media content for organizations are the public relations practitioners in most cases. These individuals are responsible for strategically planning for and implementing social media messages. Some people from outside an organization can also create social media content on organizations, for example, industry analysts or media representatives covering specific sectors. St. John III and Johnson (2016) studied a special case of public, citizen journalists. The participants reported that they were not sure of the value of public relations practitioners or the usefulness of their materials, but they voiced a positive regard for public relations practitioners who had more interactions with them.

Influencers on social media help spread the word quickly and therefore are of great value to organizations that aim to build relationships with their publics online. Studying the public perceptions of personality to identify influencer features has been considered important and useful (Freberg, Graham, McGaughey, & Freberg, 2011). Social media influencers (SMIs) are defined as "a new type of independent third party endorser who shape audience attitudes through blogs, tweets, and the use of other social media" (Freberg et al., 2011, p. 90). Freberg et al. used the Q-sort method to quantify and compare publics' subjective impressions of people or entities online. The method was found to be a more useful measure for assessing the SMI's influence than using the number of followers.

Related research has been conducted in the global context. Pang, Tan, Lim, Kwan, and Lakhanpal (2016) conducted interviews with ten Singapore SMIs to explore how organizations could build effective relations with them. They found that, whereas SMIs' media ideology was irrelevant, their judgments on content, routine usage, performed roles and goals in the society, and perceived extra-media forces were highly relevant. Pang et al. proposed a social media influencer engagement model to depict these key concepts and consequential strategies for the organizations to consider.

Himelboim, Golan, Moon, and Suto (2014) used a social network framework to examine how social mediators connected the U.S. State Department with its publics globally. They identified and characterized social mediators, both formal (i.e., through government agencies) and informal (i.e., through nongovernmental organizations, or NGOs, and individuals). Interestingly, whereas the informal social mediators exerted key influence on the relationships with people in the Middle East and North Africa, formal social mediators influenced the relationships with people in the rest of the world. They also found that the formal and informal social mediators had similar levels of influence in the bilateral relationships, but the traditional public relations mediators (i.e., news media) only functioned for unilateral relationships. This study illustrated the need to identify key publics and the consequentially effective social media channels to connect the U.S. Statement Department with its international public.

It is also worth noting that social media platforms can hinder some people from becoming SMIs, especially those who hold different positions than popular views. Although social media can be used to convey different ideas and engage in point-to-point debates, *argumentum ad hominem* is more likely to happen online than in face-to-face situations; and some may stoop to dig out their opponents' background information completely unrelated to the issue to attenuate their arguments. Trolling and insults from others inhibit many people's willingness to engage in any argument or debate online. These concerns may explain to a certain degree the silent majority phenomenon and serve as reasons for the publics as well as the organizations to not develop relationships via social media. However, this area of research on publics on social media has been lacking and should be a direction for future research.

Communication and Messaging

Having identified and understood publics, organizations and practitioners need to engage with publics via social media using different approaches, platforms, and messaging strategies, which may involve relationship management in new contexts.

Interestingly, the use of social media can also change the traditional elements in overall public relations programming and communication. Allagui and Breslow (2016) argued that the effective use of social media might disrupt the traditional public relations campaign cycle. In other words, while typically campaign events were used to generate publicity to help with a public relations campaign, in the future, the act of sharing social media content itself might be used to generate publicity, replacing a campaign event.

Different Platforms and Media

McLuhan's (1964) famous saying that "the medium is the message" still applies today. His analysis of different media platforms and effects on the general public were bounded by the media available in the 1960s, yet the method and meaning analysis can still help users understand the combined meanings of a message and its dissemination channel. Based on specific functions of a social media platform, the message creator can use it to serve as a communication strategy.

In the context of crisis communication, Liu et al. (2013) found that, although social media had been used more frequently than before, traditional media still played an integral role in predicting whether publics were likely to communicate positively about organizational crises via social media or offline word-of-mouth communication. They also found that study participants preferred to communicate about crises in person, followed by text messaging and Facebook. These findings indicated that interpersonal communication and traditional media cannot be replaced by social media communication in crisis situations.

With the emergence and prevalence of social media, a new media model for organizations has emerged. Macnamara, Lwin, Adi, and Zerfass (2016) examined whether the original PESO model would still be relevant in the current social media environment. Specifically, *paid media* refers to "traditional advertising and other forms of content commercially contracted between organizations and mass media" (p. 377). *Owned media* are "publications and digital sites established and controlled by organizations, such as corporate magazines, newsletters, reports and, more recently, organization Web sites, blogs, and official Facebook pages" (p. 377). *Earned media* refers to "editorial publicity that is generated by organizations through media releases, interviews, and other media relations activities" (p. 377). *Shared media* are "those that are open for followers, friends, and subscribers to contribute and comment" and include popular social media platforms such as Facebook, Twitter, YouTube, Tumblr, Instagram, and Pinterest, as well as blogs that allow comments to be posted (p. 378).

Macnamara et al. (2016) found that the PESO model no longer reflected the priorities in media strategies of organizations. Instead, because of growing technology and access to the Internet and social media, shared social media was more likely to move to the top of the priority list, followed by owned media, mostly digital and online. The move of shared and owned media to the top has radically changed content production and distribution strategies. Therefore the PESO model has been replaced by the SOEP model (shared, owned, earned, paid).

Waters, Tindall, and Morton (2010) examined the phenomenon of "media catching," or how the news media targeted public relations practitioners for content for story ideas. Specifically, instead of public relations practitioners pitching stories to journalists as traditionally had been done, journalists were asking for sources of information for their stories. In response to such needs, Peter Shankman created the Help-A-Reporter-Out (HARO) group on a social networking site and encouraged journalists to send out specific information requests to the group so people who had the sources could respond to these journalists.

These new models of media can be useful for marginalized groups when they need to get media attention via social media. Instead of waiting passively for the news media to pick up and spread their stories, they can use social media to respond to journalists' needs and target their stories better.

Another major theme in the study of social media channels is on the use of platforms. The general consensus for social media use is that more platforms are to be used to appeal to different audiences (Shin, Pang, & H. Kim, 2015). In particular, Shin et al.'s study took an integrated approach and found that top global organizations used brand Web sites, Facebook, and Twitter together to cultivate relationships with stakeholders. However, these online media were used more for information dissemination (one-way communication) than user engagement (two-way communication).

It is thus important to assess the effectiveness, believability, and credibility of motion media (Lee, Park, Lee, & Cameron, 2010) and other types of social media, such as Wikipedia (Thompson, 2016), and micro-blogs (Gao, 2016). Thompson (2016) aimed to understand the motivations of public relations practitioners who breached the norms on Wikipedia and engaged in illicit editing. Findings suggested that the open and transparent governance approach on Wikipedia and on other common-pool media works against any free-rider or polluting effects when public relations practitioners attempt illicit alterations. As a result, the economic value of information held by public relations professionals has been undermined by the collaborative nature of common-pool media.

Gao (2016) examined how social media, more specifically, Sina Weibo (a micro-blogging site in China), was used by the top 300 nonprofit public-fundraising foundations in China to advance their missions. Findings suggested that this micro-blogging site was mainly used to disseminate information, especially for promoting issues and activities as well as calling for help; only occasionally was the use of two-way communication found. Although micro-blog posts with certain multimedia and dialogic/interactive features were significantly more likely to be commented on, shared, and liked, such multimedia and dialogic features were not fully used.

Lee et al. (2010) examined motion media (e.g., video stories on TV, web, cell phones, handheld devices) by assessing two media features: media modality (text, text+picture, video) and source (public relations, news, user-generated content [UGC]) and their effects on source credibility, perceived veridicality (a perception of an object as being accurate and believable), and impact of messages. The findings revealed that motion media modality significantly enhanced believability judgments and perceived veridicality, regardless of source cue. Thus, the audio-visual functions of media platforms were also important sources to construct effective and believable messages.

Different Messaging Strategy

Messages can be conveyed through effective strategies. Some critical messaging strategies examined in the literature include digital storytelling (Allagui & Breslow, 2016), personification (Men & Tsai, 2015), and exemplification (Spence, Sellnow-Richmond, Sellnow, & Lachlan, 2016). Allagui and Breslow (2016) examined the best practices of and trends in the effective use of social media through four award-winning public relations campaigns. Findings suggest that *digital storytelling* techniques that were both immersive and emotive were critical to social media campaigns and could promote content sharing. In particular, these stories needed to involve members of the target audience in at least one form of open-ended offline engagement that involved sharing behaviors.

Other effective strategies included making sure the content was optimized for mobile displays and controls and was timely.

By linking the factors central to social media communications, including perceived corporate character, parasocial interaction, and community identification, to public engagement and organization–public relationships, Men and Tsai (2015) identified the effectiveness of a *personification* approach in social media communication to construct an agreeable corporate character to increase public engagement and to create intimate, interpersonal interactions and community identification. This in turn improved organization–public relationships.

Another messaging strategy, exemplification, was found to be effective (Spence et al., 2016). *Exemplification* is the use of highly emotional and arousing messages to elicit responses and to influence perceptions. Spence et al.'s (2016) study examined the use of social media (specifically video-sharing sites) to combat the negative effects of news coverage concerning lean finely textured beef (LFTB). Respondents reported stronger perceptions of threat severity, susceptibility, behavioral intentions to avoid LFTB, and lower levels of organizational trust and reputation when exposed to an exemplification-only condition than to conditions with countering video-sharing sites. The findings were consistent with exemplification theory and indicated that message ordering could influence exemplification effects.

Relationship Management

Social media has also been used as an online mechanism of relationship management. In fact, relationship management was one of the four major functions of social media use of an organization (Reitz, 2012). In particular, the inherent interactive nature of social media may have greatly facilitated the process of relationship management. Other features important in relationship management, such as establishing emotional bonds and authentic connections, are also enhanced through social media use.

As with relationship building offline, the concepts of being interactive and participatory have been critical to engaging with publics via social media. Avidar, Ariel, Malka, and Levy (2015) examined users' perceptions about social media use and found that participatory engagement was particularly needed. Unfortunately many uses of social media still remain one-way and information only, as Waters, Ghosh, Griggs, and Searson (2014) found with corporate blogs. They found that the lack of two-way interaction and conversation between the organizations and their publics was not just because the technology was new, but also because keeping the kind of transparency required by two-way communication could be risky and hard to incorporate into traditional business models.

Interestingly, while the concept of dialogue or interactivity is highly emphasized in managing relationships via social media, some have argued that it is not necessary to prefer dialogue over persuasion. Theunissen (2015), for example, suggested that in social media, dialogue and persuasion both have a role to play in relationship building and do not have to be mutually exclusive. These two elements can occur simultaneously and be effective in engagement. This view is consistent with the ideas regarding symmetrical communication in that, while engaging with publics and understanding their needs and expectations, public relations practitioners still need to engage in persuasion, either to persuade the organization to adjust its internal policies or behaviors, or to persuade the publics, depending on the situation (L. Grunig, J. Grunig, & Dozier, 2002).

In addition to the general principles of interactivity and dialogue, many specific concepts in relationship management research have been re-examined or modified using social media as a context. For example, Sisson (2017) examined the role of control mutuality in social media engagement and found it to be a useful social media strategy for nonprofit organizations.

In addition, some specific concepts in digital dialogic theory (Kent & Taylor, 1998) have been examined, such as *propinquity* (immediacy of presence, temporal flow and engagement; Sutherland, 2016) and *usefulness of information* (Watkins, 2017). Sutherland (2016) examined the social media phenomenon of the amyotrophic lateral sclerosis (ALS) Ice-Bucket Challenge by applying Kent and Taylor's dialogic theoretical component of propinquity. Sutherland found that the ALS Ice-Bucket Challenge leveraged a propinquital loop to enable participants to move between online (social media) and offline spaces, while creating relational elasticity between participants and the cause itself. Another key dialogic principle of usefulness of information was found to have significant influence on public engagement on social media and public attitudes (Watkins, 2017).

Researchers have also examined factors that influence the quality of relationships, such as public engagement with CEOs (Men & Tasi, 2016) and political digital interaction (Sweetser, English, & Fernandes, 2015). Men and Tsai (2016) found a positive relationship between CEO–public engagement on social media and the interpersonal communication variables of perceived authenticity and approachability. Such engagement also directly affected organization–public relational outcomes. They further found that publics were primarily motivated by reasons of thought leadership and task attraction when they engaged with CEOs on social media. In the political context, using Twitter to examine the cultivation of political organization–public relationships, Sweetser et al. (2015) found that active engagement with an organization on Twitter on the part of the public increased the perception of conversational exchange, enhancing the organization–public relationship. Some individual political dispositions, such as political cynicism, political information efficacy, or strength of ideology, could also help predict organization–public relationships.

One area of special note for social media is relationship management with bloggers. Public relations practitioners have been actively building relationships with bloggers to obtain brand mentions and reviews that have high credibility (Hayes & Carr, 2015). In the process of managing relationships with bloggers, public relations practitioners must balance between maintaining control over (negative) messages by limiting blogger comments and maintaining social features of blogs. Socialness has been found to increase perceptions of blogger expertise, brand attitudes, and purchase intention, but not credibility (Hayes & Carr, 2015).

Conflict Management and Crisis Communication

A heavy focus has been placed on the role of social media in managing conflicts and crises. Studies have typically examined the creation of crises or paracrises (cf. Coombs & Holladay, 2012) through social media, organizational crisis responses via social media, and public reaction to crises via social media.

First, social media can be the creator of crises and can be used by public relations practitioners to scan for crises. The Red Cross scandal (Long, 2016) involved a legitimacy crisis when the lack of attention to actional legitimacy escalated on social media. Social media can also serve as an element of scanning for crisis risks, or paracrisis. Coombs and Holladay (2012) further examined how to identify, assess/appraise, respond, and evaluate paracrisis responses. In particular, they defined a paracrisis as "a publicly visible crisis threat that charges an organization with irresponsible or unethical behavior" (p. 409). A paracrisis should be assessed based on the reputational threat to the organization through analyzing both the stakeholders and their power, legitimacy, and urgency, as well as organizational constraints (Mitchell, Agle, & Wood, 1997).

When responding to such paracrises, both strategic and tactical (what specific communication resources to employ) concerns should be addressed. Strategic levels mainly concern what outcome is desired and what communication strategy is needed. There are three primary communicative response strategies for a paracrisis involving a challenge: refute (fight back against the challenge), reform (change organizational practices to reflect the demands of the stakeholders), and refuse (do not acknowledge or respond to the challenge publicly in the hope that the paracrisis will disappear due to lack of attention).

At the tactical level, Coombs and Holladay (2012, p. 413) suggested that one major rule still applies to social media despite the rapid change in technology and communication platforms, that is, there should be a fit between the channels selected and the stakeholders targeted. Other important social media tactical rules are:

1. Be where the action is.
2. Be there before the paracrisis appears.
3. Be redundant and sprawl.

Among the various components identified in Coombs and Holladay (2012), the response to crises on social media is more heavily researched, from the perspective of public reactions. For example, Twitter was used as a means of coping with emotions and uncontrollable crises (Brummette & Sisco, 2015). Publics can react, respond, and communicate about crises through social media (Liu et al., 2013). Publics may also display different levels of intention to comply with crisis messages via social media (Freberg, 2012).

Specifically, Brummette and Sisco (2015) analyzed stakeholder tweets to help organizations gauge the public's collective sentiment and construct coping messages during a crisis. They analyzed stakeholders' tweets after a crisis, based on perceived controllability and predictability, the emotions, and coping strategies. They argued that such an online dialogue between an organization's external stakeholders would make these people become social media creators of crisis communication content and directly influence followers. These creators could sometimes respond on behalf of organizational communities when little information comes from the organization itself. In the process, these creators might influence the emotions of their followers and, in turn, influence the public perception of the organization and its crisis response. Organizations thus need to be aware of the inherent uncertainty and inaccuracy in this process and manage it on top of managing the initial crisis.

Freberg (2012) examined consumer responses to food recall messages that varied in source (generated by the organization or by users) and reliability (confirmed versus unconfirmed). She found that the consumer intent to comply with such messages was stronger in response to organizational messages than to user-generated messages, but did not vary according to message reliability. These studies have indicated that social media works as a double-edged sword. It can help manage and control crises and conflicts, but it can also escalate crises and conflicts to a direction hardly predictable or controllable from the organization's perspective. Future research should continue searching for key players, characteristics of social media platforms, and types of issues involved, so that effective models can be built.

Effectiveness of Social Media Use

Evaluation of social media use can be conducted at multiple levels: platform, messaging, engagement, and outcome variables. Research has also documented concerns about the moral values of social media use.

Message and Platform Evaluation

Saxton and Waters (2014) examined public reactions to different kinds of messages from nonprofit organizations: informational, promotional, and community building. Results indicated that the publics preferred reading and commenting on dialogic and some mobilizational messages, but preferred sharing one-way informational messages only. The publics also showed more liking of Facebook than other social media platforms.

Expanding on the research of how companies use individual social media channels, DiStaso, McCorkindale, and Agugliaro (2015) explored an organization's social media presence across several channels and identified differences among industries. Results indicated differences across industries regarding their adoption and integration of best practices into their social media accounts. For example, in terms of adoption of social media channels, Twitter was the most commonly adopted platform across all the industries. YouTube was the second-most commonly adopted platform for all the industries except the entertainment/leisure industry. The retail/wholesale industry had the highest rate of adopting Facebook and Twitter among all industries, while the technology industry, had the highest adoption of YouTube.

Engagement and Outcome Evaluation

Different strategies of engagement have been evaluated in social media practices. For example, transparency was found to be of great value when organizations provided information on social media to help publics make informed decisions (DiStaso & Bortree, 2012). Ott and Theunissen (2015) found that, during social media crises, authenticity of voice and transparency were crucial factors for success, whereas engaging indiscriminately with emotional individuals could potentially escalate an issue. Evaluation of social media messages has also been conducted using value modeling, and a number of top-ranked attributes included links to further information, use of strong voice, and multimedia (Freberg, Saling, Vidologff, & Eosco, 2013).

In terms of outcomes, Sweetser (2010) examined the strategy of nondisclosure in social media and how that had an impact on organization–public relationships. The study found that unethical behaviors, such as lack of disclosure, damaged organization–public relationships, especially communicated relational commitment. Maiorescu (2015) assessed the use of social media by the Stillbirth and Neonatal Death Society (SANDS) in the United Kingdom. Results indicated that this organization only engaged in one-way communication even on social media and therefore failed to take full advantage of the potential of the Web 2.0 to increase awareness, raise funds, and break the taboo around stillbirth and neonatal death.

Potential Ethics Consequences of Social Media Use

The postmodern approach views the current use of social media as perpetuating the privileged, rational models of social engagement (Kennedy & Sommerfeldt, 2015). In this view, the challenge of the "digital divide" should be acknowledged and researched. The digital divide refers to the gap between those who have access to media technologies and those who do not. As social media use increases, the gap between the two groups become larger, and so does their access to social and economic resources. Valentini (2015) examined whether using social media is actually "good" for the public relations profession. Valentini argued that although social media is popularly considered "good" because of its role in helping organizations engage and build relationships with publics, this assumption should be questioned because social media was created to enhance social capital, and to enable more human connectedness, rather than to promote organizational business interests (van Dijck, 2013, as cited in Valentini, 2015). Valentini (2015) criticized the "using social media is good" discourse in public relations, by showing that the use of social media is not necessarily as beneficial to either organizations or publics as has been depicted. Risks exist that can undermine relations, both among publics and between publics and organizations. Valentini further indicated that social media measurements may lack reliability and validity. Thus, social media use is not necessarily "good," due to conceptual, methodological, and functional issues.

Research has also explored the role of ethics as it relates to social media and crisis communication. In particular, Tusinski (2017) argued for the need to be aware of ethical concerns in the context of crisis communication across different organizations and industry areas. Practitioners' attitudes toward ethics challenges in their use of social media have been studied in different countries, such as New Zealand and Israel (Toledano & Avidar, 2016). The study found that Israeli practitioners consistently scored below New Zealander practitioners in responses to ethics statements such as publishing a disclaimer about sponsored messages, negative campaigns on social media, payments to bloggers, and the use of social media for the creation of front groups. Toledano and Avidar (2016) identified major challenges as clustering around transparency in the use of social media: fake identities in comments, payments to bloggers in general, and payments to social media experts for conducting smear campaigns.

Similar issues with transparency have been identified, such as blogger engagement ethics (Langett, 2013), where the research argued for promoting a dialogic approach to blogger outreach ethics. In addition to bloggers, other new influencers such as Instagrammers bring about ethics challenges to public relations because these influencers wish to be compensated for the activities. Archer and Harrigan (2016) argued that such payments should be disclosed to the public and acknowledged as not pure relationship building. Future research should acknowledge and examine these and other ethics concerns in the use of social media, such as "fake news" on social media, digging up personal information, and violations of privacy because of data mining.

Directions for Future Research

Social media is a hot topic in public relations research, teaching, and practice. As can be observed from our discussion earlier in this chapter, social media has affected the identities of individuals, including both publics and public relations practitioners themselves, as well as those of organizations. The prevalence of social media has significantly changed many critical areas in public relations practice, including environmental scanning, identifying publics, messaging strategies, relationship management, and conflict management.

At the moment, research has been heavily focused on some areas and has ignored others. In particular, research has relied primarily on replication or application of theories in offline communication, such as relationship management theory, to the new context of social media. However, more research is needed in the following areas.

First, social media forms a public image that may or may not be the same with the creator. Because of multiple identities of culturally diverse publics, it is important to understand how these publics use social media to express their multifaceted identities and associate with others to form publics. These publics also need to constantly negotiate their identities to adjust and adapt to different groups (e.g., ethnic group at home and mainstream cultural group at work). Their social media use may reflect their stable and flexible identities. Researchers and practitioners can study what types of publics they assume; what online communication behaviors they adopt regarding particular issues; how these behaviors and others' responses influence their senses of identification with either an organization or a community (physical or virtual); and how they are empowered in pursuing their goals through such social media interaction. In this process, it is important to acknowledge the reality of the "digital divide" and the challenge it brings to marginalized publics.

Second, organizations' social media use needs to be examined systematically in terms of how their identities are constructed, challenged, negotiated, and redefined; how different platforms and messaging interact; and how such use and interactions affect their branding, reputation, and relationship with internal and external stakeholders. While the essence of symmetrical communication is to take into consideration both organizational and public interests, how organizations achieve such symmetry while maintaining or conserving (cf. Sha, 2004) certain key aspects of their own identity can be a challenge.

Finally, in public relations practice, although social media has been used more extensively and is critical in environmental scanning, not much research has been conducted systematically to understand the mechanisms and effectiveness of such use. In addition, in this book, the practices of engagement and conflict management with culturally diverse publics are examined through the theoretical framework. How social media affects these practices should be further explored.

References

Alikilic, O., & Atabek, U. (2012). Social media adoption among Turkish public relations professionals: A survey of practitioners. *Public Relations Review, 38*(1), 56–63. doi: 10.1016/j.pubrev.2011.11.002

Allagui, I., & Breslow, H. (2016). Social media for public relations: Lessons from four effective cases. *Public Relations Review, 42*(1), 20–30. doi: 10.1016/j.pubrev. 2015.12.001

Archer, C., & Harrigan, P. (2016). Show me the money: How bloggers as stakeholders are challenging theories of relationship building in public relations. *Media International Australia (8/1/07–Current), 160*(1), 67–77. doi: 10.1177/1329878X16651139

Avery, E. J., & Graham, M. W. (2013). Political public relations and the promotion of participatory, transparent government through social media. *International Journal of Strategic Communication, 7*(4), 274–291. doi: 10.1080/1553118X.2013.824885

Avery, E. J., Lariscy, R., Amador, E., Ickowitz, T., Primm, C., & Taylor, A. (2010). Diffusion of social media among public relations practitioners in health departments across various community population sizes. *Journal of Public Relations Research, 22*(3), 336–358. doi: 10.1080/10627261003614427

Avidar, R., Ariel, Y., Malka, V., & Levy, E. C. (2015). Smartphones, publics, and OPR: Do publics want to engage? *Public Relations Review, 41*(2), 214–221. doi: 10.1016/j. pubrev.2014.11.019

Bingqi, F., & Han, L. (2009). An analysis of consumer-generated media's application in multicultural public relations practice. *China Media Research, 5*(4), 20–30.

Brabham, D. C. (2012). Managing unexpected publics online: The challenge of targeting specific groups with the wide-reaching tool of the internet. *International Journal of Communication, 6*, 1139–1158.

Bridgen, L. (2011). Emotional labour and the pursuit of the personal brand: Public relations practitioners' use of social media. *Journal of Media Practice, 12*(1), 61–76. doi: 10.1386/jmpr.12.1.61_1

Brummette, J., & Sisco, F. H. (2015). Using Twitter as a means of coping with emotions and uncontrollable crises. *Public Relations Review, 41*(1), 89–96. doi: 10.1016/j. pubrev.2014.10.009

Chalmers, A. W., & Shotton, P. A. (2016). Changing the face of advocacy? Explaining interest organizations' use of social media strategies. *Political Communication, 33*(3), 374–391. doi: 10.1080/10584609.2015.1043477

Charest, F., Bouffard, J., & Zajmovic, E. (2016). Public relations and social media: Deliberate or creative strategic planning. *Public Relations Review, 42*, 530–538.

Ciszek, E. L. (2016). Digital activism: How social media and dissensus inform theory and practice. *Public Relations Review, 42*(2), 314–321. doi: 10.1016/j.pubrev.2016.02.002

Coombs, W. T., & Holladay, S. J. (2012). The paracrisis: The challenges created by publicly managing crisis prevention. *Public Relations Review, 38*(3), 408–415. doi: 10.1016/j.pubrev.2012.04.004

Curtis, L., Edwards, C., Fraser, K. L., Gudelsky, S., Holmquist, J., Thornton, K., & Sweetser, K. D. (2010). Adoption of social media for public relations by non-profit organizations. *Public Relations Review, 36*(1), 90–92. doi: 10.1016/j.pub rev.2009.10.003

Diga, M., & Kelleher, T. (2009). Social media use, perceptions of decision-making power, and public relations roles. *Public Relations Review, 35*(4), 440–442. doi: 10.1016/j.pubrev.2009.07.003

DiStaso, M. W., & Bortree, D. S. (2012). Multi-method analysis of transparency in social media practices: Survey, interviews and content analysis. *Public Relations Review, 38*(3), 511–514. doi: 10.1016/j.pubrev.2012.01.003

DiStaso, M. W., McCorkindale, T., & Agugliaro, A. (2015). America's most admired companies social media industry divide. *Journal of Promotion Management, 21*(2), 163–189. doi: 10.1080/10496491.2014.996799

Freberg, K. (2012). Intention to comply with crisis messages communicated via social media. *Public Relations Review, 38*(3), 416–421. doi: 10.1016/j.pubrev.2012.01.008

Freberg, K., Graham, K., McGaughey, K., & Freberg, L. A. (2011). Who are the social media influencers? A study of public perceptions of personality. *Public Relations Review, 37*(1), 90–92. doi: 10.1016/j.pubrev.2010.11.001

Freberg, K., Saling, K., Vidoloff, K. G., & Eosco, G. (2013). Using value modeling to evaluate social media messages: The case of Hurricane Irene. *Public Relations Review, 39*(3), 185–192. doi: 10.1016/j.pubrev.2013.02.010

Gao, F. (2016). Social media as a communication strategy: Content analysis of top nonprofit foundations' micro-blogs in China. *International Journal of Strategic Communication, 10*(4), 255–271. doi: 10.1080/1553118X.2016.1196693

Geoghegan, T., & Monseau, M. (2011). Moving from 2.No: Building strategic consensus to create communities for attention-deficit hyperactivity disorder awareness on Facebook®. *Journal of Communication in Healthcare, 4*(1), 4–12. doi: 10.1179/175380 611X12950033990052

Graham, M. W., Avery, E. J., & Park, S. (2015). The role of social media in local government crisis communications. *Public Relations Review, 41*(3), 386–394. doi: 10.1016/j.pubrev.2015.02.001

Grunig, L. A., Grunig, J. E., & Dozier, D. M. (2002). *Excellent public relations and effective organizations: A study of communication management in three countries.* Mahwah, NJ: Lawrence Erlbaum Associates.

Hayes, R. A., & Carr, C. T. (2015). Does being social matter? Effects of enabled commenting on credibility and brand attitude in social media. *Journal of Promotion Management, 21*(3), 371–390. doi: 10.1080/10496491.2015.1039178

Himelboim, I., Golan, G. J., Moon, B. B., & Suto, R. J. (2014). A social networks approach to public relations on Twitter: Social mediators and mediated public relations. *Journal of Public Relations Research, 26*(4), 359–379. doi: 10.1080/1062726X.2014.908724

Jackson, S. J., & Welles, B. F. (2015). Hijacking #MYNYPD: Social media dissent and networked counterpublics. *Journal of Communication, 65*, 932–952. https://doi.org/10.1111/jcom.12185

Jiang, H., Luo, Y., & Kulemeka, O. (2016). Leading in the digital age: A study of how social media are transforming the work of communication professionals. *Telematics & Informatics, 33*(2), 493–499. doi: 10.1016/j.tele.2015.10.006

Jin, Y., & Liu, B. F. (2010). The blog-mediated crisis communication model: Recommendations for responding to influential external blogs. *Journal of Public Relations Research, 22*, 429–455.

Kaur, K. (2015). Social media creating digital environmental publics: Case of Lynas Malaysia. *Public Relations Review, 41*(2), 311–314. doi: 10.1016/j.pubrev.2014.12.005

Kelleher, T., & Sweetser, K. (2012). Social media adoption among university communicators. *Journal of Public Relations Research, 24*(2), 105–122. doi: 10.1080/1062726X.2012.626130

Kennedy, A. K., & Sommerfeldt, E. J. (2015). A postmodern turn for social media research: Theory and research directions for public relations scholarship. *Atlantic Journal of Communication, 23*(1), 31–45. doi: 10.1080/15456870.2015.972406

Kent, M. L., & Taylor, M. (1998). Building dialogic relationships through the World Wide Web. *Public Relations Review, 24*(3), 321–334.

Kinsky, E. S., Drumheller, K., Gerlich, R. N., Brock-Baskin, M. E., & Sollosy, M. (2015). The effect of socially mediated public relations crises on planned behavior: How TPB can help both corporations and nonprofits. *Journal of Public Relations Research, 27*(2), 136–157. doi: 10.1080/1062726X.2014.976826

Koehler, K. (2014). Dialogue and relationship building in online financial communications. *International Journal of Strategic Communication, 8*(3), 177–195. doi: 10.1080/1553118X.2014.905477

Langett, J. (2013). Blogger engagement ethics: Dialogic civility in a digital era. *Journal of Mass Media Ethics, 28*(2), 79–90. doi: 10.1080/08900523.2013.751817

Lee, H., Park, S., Lee, Y., & Cameron, G. T. (2010). Assessment of motion media on believability and credibility: An exploratory study. *Public Relations Review, 36*(3), 310–312. doi: 10.1016/j.pubrev.2010.04.003

Lee, N. M., & VanDyke, M. S. (2015). Set it and forget it: The one-way use of social media by government agencies communicating science. *Science Communication, 37*(4), 533–541. doi: 10.1177/1075547015588600

Len-Ríos, M. E., Hughes, H. E., McKee, L. G., & Young, H. N. (2016). Early adolescents as publics: A national survey of teens with social media accounts, their media use preferences, parental mediation, and perceived internet literacy. *Public Relations Review, 42*(1), 101–108. doi: 10.1016/j.pubrev.2015.10.003

Linvill, D. L., McGee, S. E., & Hicks, L. K. (2012). Colleges' and universities' use of Twitter: A content analysis. *Public Relations Review, 38*(4), 636–638. doi: 10.1016/j.pubrev.2012.05.010

Liu, B. F., Jin, Y., & Austin, L. L. (2013). The tendency to tell: Understanding publics' communicative responses to crisis information form and source. *Journal of Public Relations Research, 25*, 51–67. doi: 10.1080/1062726X.2013.739101

Liu, B. F., Jin, Y., Briones, R., & Kuch, B. (2012). Managing turbulence in the blogosphere: Evaluating the blog-mediated crisis communication model with the American Red Cross. *Journal of Public Relations Research, 24*, 353–370.

Long, Z. (2016). Managing legitimacy crisis for state-owned non-profit organization: A case study of the Red Cross Society of China. *Public Relations Review, 42*(2), 372–374. doi: 10.1016/j.pubrev.2015.09.011

Luo, Y., Jiang, H., & Kulemeka, O. (2015). Strategic social media management and public relations leadership: Insights from industry leaders. *International Journal of Strategic Communication, 9*(3), 167–196. doi: 10.1080/1553118X.2014.960083

McLuhan, M. (1964). *Understanding media: The extensions of man.* New York, NY: McGraw-Hill.

Macnamara, J., Lwin, M., Adi, A., & Zerfass, A. (2016). "PESO" media strategy shifts to "SOEP": Opportunities and ethical dilemmas. *Public Relations Review, 42*(3), 377–385. doi: 10.1016/j.pubrev.2016.03.001

Maiorescu, R. (2015). Public relations for the bereaved: Online interactions in a community for stillbirth and neonatal death charity. *Public Relations Review, 41*(2), 293–295. doi: 10.1016/j.pubrev.2014.11.015

Men, L. R., & Tsai, W. S. (2015). Infusing social media with humanity: Corporate character, public engagement, and relational outcomes. *Public Relations Review, 41*(3), 395–403. doi: 10.1016/j.pubrev.2015.02.005

Men, L. R., & Tsai, W. S. (2016). Public engagement with CEOs on social media: Motivations and relational outcomes. *Public Relations Review, 42*(5), 932–942. doi: 10.1016/j.pubrev.2016.08.001

Mitchell, R. K., Agle, R. A., & Wood, S. J. (1997). Toward a theory of stakeholder identification and salience: Defining the principle of who and what really counts. *Academy of Management Review, 22*(4), 853–886.

Ott, L., & Theunissen, P. (2015). Reputations at risk: Engagement during social media crises. *Public Relations Review, 41*(1), 97–102. doi: 10.1016/j.pubrev.2014.10.015

Paek, H., Hove, T., Jung, Y., & Cole, R. T. (2013). Engagement across three social media platforms: An exploratory study of a cause-related PR campaign. *Public Relations Review, 39*(5), 526–533. doi: 10.1016/j.pubrev.2013.09.013

Pang, A., Tan, E. Y., Lim, R. S.-Q., Kwan, T. Y.-M., & Lakhanpal, P. B. (2016). Building effective relations with social media influencers in Singapore. *Media Asia, 43*(1), 56–68. doi: 10.1080/01296612.2016.1177962

Papasolomou, I., & Melanthiou, Y. (2012). Social media: Marketing public relations' new best friend. *Journal of Promotion Management, 18*(3), 319–328. doi: 10.1080/10496491.2012.696458

Pınar Özdemir, B. (2012). Social media as a tool for online advocacy campaigns: Greenpeace Mediterranean's anti genetically engineered food campaign in Turkey. *Global Media Journal: Canadian Edition, 5*(2), 23–39.

Reitz, A. (2012). Social media's function in organizations: A functional analysis approach. *Global Media Journal: Canadian Edition, 5*(2), 41–56.

St. John III, B., & Johnson, K. (2016). Perspectives of an underconsidered stakeholder group: Citizen journalists' views of public relations practitioners and their materials. *Public Relations Review, 42*(1), 184–191. doi: 10.1016/j.pubrev.2015.09.010

Sanderson, J.; Barnes, K., Williamson, C., & Kian, E. T. (2016). "How could anyone have predicted that #AskJameis would go horribly wrong?" Public relations, social media, and hashtag hijacking. *Public Relations Review, 42*(1), 31–37. doi: 10.1016/j.pubrev.2015.11.005

Saxton, G. D., & Waters, R. D. (2014). What do stakeholders like on Facebook? Examining public reactions to nonprofit organizations' informational, promotional, and community-building messages. *Journal of Public Relations Research, 26*(3), 280–299. doi: 10.1080/1062726X.2014.908721

Sha, B.-L. (2004). Noether's theorem: The science of symmetry and the law of conservation. *Journal of Public Relations Research, 7*, 391–416.

Shin, W., Pang, A., & Kim, H. J. (2015). Building relationships through integrated online media: Global organizations' use of brand web sites, Facebook, and Twitter. *Journal of Business & Technical Communication, 29*(2), 184–220. doi: 10.1177/1050651914560569

Sisson, D. C. (2017). Control mutuality, social media, and organization–public relationships: A study of local animal welfare organizations' donors. *Public Relations Review, 43*(1), 179–189. doi: 10.1016/j.pubrev.2016.10.007

Smith, B. G. (2010). Socially distributing public relations: Twitter, Haiti, and interactivity in social media. *Public Relations Review, 36*(4), 329–335. doi: 10.1016/j.pubrev.2010.08.005

Smitko, K. (2012). Donor engagement through Twitter. *Public Relations Review, 38*(4), 633–635. doi: 10.1016/j.pubrev.2012.05.012

Spence, P. R., Sellnow-Richmond, D. D., Sellnow, T. L., & Lachlan, K. A. (2016). Social media and corporate reputation during crises: The viability of video-sharing websites for providing counter-messages to traditional broadcast news. *Journal of Applied Communication Research, 44*(3), 199–215. doi: 10.1080/00909882.2016.1192289

Sutherland, K. E. (2016). Using propinquital loops to blend social media and offline spaces: A case study of the ALS Ice-Bucket Challenge. *Media International Australia (8/1/07–Current), 160*(1), 78–88. doi: 10.1177/1329878X16651138

Sweetser, K. D. (2010). A losing strategy: The impact of nondisclosure in social media on relationships. *Journal of Public Relations Research, 22*(3), 288–312. doi: 10.1080/10627261003614401

Sweetser, K. D., English, K., & Fernandes, J. (2015). Super PACs and strong relationships: The impact of digital interaction on the political organization–public relationship. *Journal of Public Relations Research, 27*(2), 101–117. doi: 10.1080/1062726X.2014.976824

Theunissen, P. (2015). The quantum entanglement of dialogue and persuasion in social media: Introducing the Per–Di Principle. *Atlantic Journal of Communication, 23*(1), 5–18. doi: 10.1080/15456870.2015.972405

Thompson, G. (2016). Public relations interactions with Wikipedia. *Journal of Communication Management, 20*(1), 4–20. doi: 10.1108/JCOM-12-2014-0083

Toledano, M., & Avidar, R. (2016). Public relations, ethics, and social media: A cross-national study of PR practitioners. *Public Relations Review, 42*(1), 161–169. doi: 10.1016/j.pubrev.2015.11.012

Triantafillidou, A., & Yannas, P. (2014). How public relations agencies in Greece respond to digital trends. *Public Relations Review, 40*, 815–817. doi: 10.1016/j.pubrev.2014.09.004

Tusinski Berg, K. (2017). Trends in public relations: Exploring the role of ethics as it relates to social media and crisis communication. *Journal of Media Ethics, 32*(1), 61–66. doi: 10.1080/23736992.2016.1260992

Valentini, C. (2015). Is using social media "good" for the public relations profession? A critical reflection. *Public Relations Review, 41*(2), 170–177. doi: 10.1016/j.pubrev.2014.11.009

van Dijck, J. (2013). *The culture of connectivity: A critical history of social media.* Oxford, UK: Oxford University Press.

Vardeman-Winter, J., & Place, K. (2015). Public relations culture, social media, and regulation. *Journal of Communication Management, 19*(4), 335–353. doi: 10.1108/JCOM-11-2013-0079

Walden, J. A., & Parcha, J. M. (2017). "This is a stage": A study of public relations practitioners' imagined online audiences. *Public Relations Review, 43*(1), 145–151. doi: 10.1016/j.pubrev.2016.11.002

Waters, R. D., Tindall, N. J., & Morton, T. S. (2010). Media catching and the journalist–public relations practitioner relationship: How social media are changing the practice of media relations. *Journal of Public Relations Research, 22*(3), 241–264. doi: 10.1080/10627261003799202

Waters, R. D., Ghosh, P., Griggs, T. D., & Searson, E. M. (2014). The corporate side of the blogosphere: Examining the variations of design and engagement among Fortune 500 blogs. *Journal of Promotion Management, 20*(5), 537–552. doi: 10.1080/10496491.2014.946207

Watkins, B. A. (2017). Experimenting with dialogue on Twitter: An examination of the influence of the dialogic principles on engagement, interaction, and attitude. *Public Relations Review, 43*(1), 163–171. doi: 10.1016/j.pubrev.2016.07.002

Yang, K. C., & Kang, Y. (2015). Exploring big data and privacy in strategic communication campaigns: A cross-cultural study of mobile social media users' daily experiences. *International Journal of Strategic Communication, 9*(2), 87–101. doi: 10.1080/1553118X.2015.1008635

11

CONCLUSIONS

The world in which you were born is just one model of reality. Other cultures are not failed attempts at being you; they are unique manifestations of the human spirit.

(Wade Davis)

We may have all come on different ships, but we're in the same boat now.
(Martin Luther King, Jr.)

Intercultural encounters tend to pose challenges, and intercultural public relations does more so because the communication is not between only two culturally dissimilar individuals, but between an organization with its complicated identity and culturally varied groups of people with labyrinthine connections both with the organization and with each other. We hope that this book can serve as a useful guide for researchers, teachers, practitioners, and students who are interested in a comprehensive examination of theoretical foundations in intercultural public relations. This book systematically examines and integrates theories in public relations and intercultural communication, among other disciplines. The end product is the proposal of various general and specific theoretical frameworks for understanding, explaining, or predicting the various stages, levels, and—most importantly—players in intercultural public relations.

Following the behavioral, strategic management approach of public relations (L. Grunig, J. Grunig, & Dozier, 2002; Kim & Ni, 2013), this book illustrates the stages in the strategic management of public relations: stakeholder, public, and issues. Multiple levels of public relations practice are discussed, ranging from the interpersonal level of competencies and training; to the intraorganizational level of identifying and understanding publics, relationship management, and conflict management and negotiation; to the organizational level of culture and identity.

More importantly, the book focuses on both organizations and publics. Synthesizing literature and theories from different fields, we propose an overall theoretical structure of public relations practice in intercultural settings, which contains elements that are both public- and organization-centered. Although the behavioral, strategic management approach to public relations has often been criticized for being organization-centric, this approach actually does acknowledge and highlight the active role of publics. This is seen from the way that the public is conceptualized in the situational theory of publics, i.e., publics arise on their own and are not created or controlled by any particular organization.

Nevertheless, we do recognize that the behavioral, strategic management approach to public relations tends to place an emphasis on the role of an organization. For example, when conceptualizing most public relations programs through this approach, an organization is typically either an initiator of an issue (i.e., because an organization needs to bring awareness to something) or a responder to an issue (i.e., when activist publics demand something from the organization).

Therefore, the structure in our book further expands this approach by highlighting both public-centric and organization-centric perspectives. To achieve this goal, we have conceptualized and analyzed the publics by acknowledging and highlighting their proactive nature, especially in the cases when they arise and form collectives on their own when they are highly concerned about certain issues. In this process, micro-level factors (such as the publics' identity) and macro-level factors (such as societal culture and structure) will play major roles, none of which is directly related to or under the control of any particular organization.

Meanwhile, it is equally important to conceptualize the publics and their behaviors as independent of any relationship with any particular organization in generic contexts. In other words, a public may arise and form regarding a particular issue or issues without actually being connected with a particular organization in any way. Their issue may be purely based on values and beliefs, and not on relationships. They may not be interested in forming or maintaining any kind of relationship with a particular organization or organizations at all. Keeping both approaches in mind helps public relations researchers and practitioners stay flexible and equipped to respond effectively to various situations, case by case.

These dual perspectives will be discussed in more detail as we illustrate our models in the next section.

Overarching Intercultural Public Relations Management Model

After reviewing and integrating foundational theories in public relations (Chapter 2), we propose the strategic management model of public relations that synthesizes the goals of different public relations programs with the classic public relations management process of research, planning, implementation, and evaluation (see Figure 2.2). To give a brief overview of this model, research is first conducted to identify the type of public relations problem, that is, organization-initiated public relations problems (OPRP) or public-initiated public relations problems (PPRP), as well as research on the organization and the publics. In the planning stage, the goal for the public relations program is determined, that is, to "activate" publics and make them more communicatively active for OPRPs or to "de-activate" the publics by removing the root cause of the problem for PPRPs. The objectives for different publics are then determined based on these goals. The objectives now go beyond the traditional knowledge, attitude, and behavioral objectives to include also situational perceptions, communicative activeness, and organization–public relationships. In the implementation stage, again different types of strategies are used, motivating publics to enhance their awareness, attitude, and behavior, through messaging or communication strategies in the case of OPRPs, and relationship management and conflict management through face-to-face interaction and perspective-taking in the case of PPRPs. Finally, the evaluation stage needs to take into consideration both outputs and outcomes as specified in the planning stage.

We then provide an overarching theoretical model for intercultural public relations management at the end of Chapter 4 based on both Kim and Ni's (2013) taxonomy of public relations problems and the strategic management model of public relations proposed in this book. Different theories in public relations are usually examined separately without integration. The model in this book provides a comprehensive view by proposing relationships among the major components in the strategic management of public relations that includes environmental scanning, identification of publics, relationship management, and conflict management.

This expanded model of intercultural public relations management (Figure 4.3.) not only puts these theoretical development areas into context, but also identifies the crucial roles of culture and identity in managing public relations in intercultural settings. It provides a platform for examining such intercultural interactions from multiple levels and multiple players. The next section summarizes the model based on these players and levels.

Multiple Players: Both Public- and Organization-Centered Perspectives

Public-Centered Perspective

We highlight the critical and sometimes independent role of the public by placing it at the center of our model. In particular, we recognize and examine the importance and strategies of identifying publics by looking into the antecedents to the formation and/or change of publics (Chapter 6). We also acknowledge that these antecedents include multiple levels of factors and that only the meso level is related to organizational behaviors. At the micro level, publics' perceptions and communication behaviors are influenced by their individual cultural identities (Chapter 3) and personal life experiences (Chapters 4 and 5), among other things. At the meso level, public perceptions and communication behaviors may be influenced by organizational factors, such as how organizations manage the relationships with these publics (organization–public relationships, Chapter 7), as well as how they manage conflicts with them (conflict management, Chapter 8). At the macro level, societal cultures, including supra-organizational level factors such as cultural dimensions (Chapter 3 and Chapter 9), may play a role in the formation of publics.

Also highlighted in this book is the proactive nature of publics who do not necessarily exist in relation to a particular organization. They are organically formed when the publics themselves need to adjust to a new cultural environment and build their own competencies (Chapter 5); when they can be empowered to communicate about issues that are important to themselves (Chapter 6); as well as when they perceive and manage a conflict not because they have a particular relationship with an organization, but because of their own values and identities (Chapter 8).

We note that public relations practitioners, serving as the boundary spanners between an organization and its public, need to develop intercultural competencies themselves in adjusting to both internal and external organizational environments.

Organization-Centered Perspective

Because this book adopts the strategic, managerial approach to public relations, we examine how different kinds of organizations can practice intercultural public relations in the most effective and ethical way. Kim and Ni (2013) distinguished between the public relations problems that are initiated by an organization and those initiated by publics. We extend their model by sketching and emphasizing different strategies to achieve different goals facing these two different types of problems.

In particular, the top of the model follows the stages of strategic management: stakeholder, public, and issues. To cope with these stages, the organization can approach with environmental scanning and the identification of publics (Chapter 6), as well as relationship management (Chapter 7) and conflict management (Chapter 8), correspondingly.

The bottom of the model incorporates the taxonomy of public relations problems (PPRPs vs. OPRPs) as well as the corresponding goals and objectives of these two types of problems. At the same time, these objectives can be the outcomes of relationship management (i.e., organization–public relationships can bring about different outcomes).

The goal of organization-initiated public relations problems is to "activate" the publics, from latent to aware or even to active publics. This is accomplished primarily through public relations in the more traditional sense, such as messaging and persuasion (Chapter 2). On the other hand, the goal of public-initiated public relations problems is to "de-activate" the publics, from active (and usually angry) to aware or latent publics. This is accomplished primarily through relationship management and conflict management (Chapters 7 and 8), because messaging alone will not be sufficient or ethical. The publics cannot simply be persuaded if the organization does not engage in substantial, internal adjustment and change in terms of policies, procedures, and behaviors. However at the same time, organizations have their own organizational identities (Chapter 9) that are constantly negotiated and that play a role in symmetrical communication.

Multiple Levels

At the interpersonal level, our model connects the intercultural communication competencies of both public relations practitioners and members of diverse publics (Chapter 5). At the intra-organizational level, the model proposes subsequent links between theoretically interrelated components of public relations management: public identification (Chapter 6), relationship management (Chapter 7), and conflict management (Chapter 8). At the organizational or supra-organization level, the model incorporates the influence of organizational identity (Chapter 9) and societal cultures (Chapter 3) on the practice of public relations and the roles of publics.

The following sections summarize each of the individual models or frameworks about the different components.

Model of Intercultural Competencies and Training

The literature integrated in Chapter 5 and the proposed framework of competency training (Table 5.2) provide more nuanced levels of competency and suggest more targeted training and assessment methods. In doing so, theoretical development in the area of intercultural communication competency (ICC) is advanced in two ways. First, by integrating various theoretical frameworks and identifying the common themes, we propose in Chapter 5 a new theoretical framework in intercultural communication competency. This new framework includes three domains of competency (culture-general, culture-specific, and enactment competency), as well as three levels of competency: knowledge (cognitive), affective (motivational), and behavioral.

This chapter has discussed some initial research that examined the relationship between the intercultural communication competency of public relations practitioners and the various practices and concepts in intercultural public relations. Future research can continue to examine and expand this framework to further test the relationship between the intercultural communication competency of practitioners and public relations practices, as well as important outcome variables.

Second, following this new ICC framework and synthesizing the various approaches to and strategies of competency building and training, the chapter identifies an integrated structure of competency training (Table 5.2.), with corresponding approaches, strategies, and evaluation methods. Very little is known in public relations research on how to link the competency components needed with training or how to evaluate the effectiveness of different training strategies. Future research can use our structure to fill this gap.

The integrated framework for competency training (Table 5.2) provides a useful structure for both public relations practitioners and culturally diverse publics in developing their multi-level, multi-domain competencies. Public relations practitioners are interacting with increasingly diverse publics, either at home or abroad. The practitioners who bear culturally diverse or various minority identities face two separate levels of challenges.

Within the organization, at the personal level, they need to adapt to a new environment with their unique identity development. At the professional level, some may be considered as outsiders by other practitioners, even within the same organization. Thus, these practitioners need to manage their own intercultural identities at both the personal and the professional levels.

Externally, public relations practitioners need to interact with culturally diverse publics and to develop an in-depth understanding of the challenges, dynamics, and outcomes of these publics' identity development. This process is essential in helping practitioners better engage and build relationships with these publics.

At the same time, diverse groups may encounter multiple challenges in learning how to identify their own competence to handle stressors from various sources and how they achieve optimum adaptation and identity building, if at all. For culturally diverse publics, the outcomes of their adaptation can be reflected in similar aspects, including health, career advancement, identity development, and political engagement.

Taken together, this new model of intercultural communication competency adds value to public relations theory. In addition, it guides public relations practice in that it better informs both public relations practitioners and publics when they enter a new cultural environment. Specifically, both practitioners and publics need to incorporate the different domains and dimensions of competency, initiate or participate in different training programs that aim for these domains and dimensions, and learn to adapt better to fulfill their personal goals and organizational goals.

Model of Identifying Intercultural Publics

In intercultural settings, it is important to consider cross-situational and situational factors in the formation of publics, as well as the understanding and identification of these publics. Cross-situational factors include the traditionally used geographics, demographics, psychographics, and memberships (Broom & Sha, 2013). In addition, some layers in the nested model of J. Grunig and Repper (1992) are also highly relevant. These are communities; psychographics and lifestyles, subcultures, and societal relationships; geodemographics; and demographics and social categories.

Drawing on these factors and integrating current literature on publics, Chapter 6 proposes a theoretical framework of understanding publics in intercultural settings (Figure 6.2) that discusses three multilevel, cross-situational factors that are particularly relevant to intercultural settings. These are classified under micro-level factors (cultural identity and life experiences), meso-level factors (organizational, or organization–public relationships), and macro-level factors (societal culture). These factors can influence the formation of publics and hence help both researchers and practitioners understand how these publics should be identified and communicated with.

Model of Intercultural Relationship Management

The theoretical framework of intercultural relationship management (Figure 7.1) in Chapter 7 consists of antecedents of relationships (organizational level and public level), processes of relationship building (approaches and strategies), measurements of relationships, and outcomes of relationships (organization-centered and public-centered).

Antecedents of relationship management used to focus on the situations through which organizations and their publics may interact with each other. Recently, some studies have revealed a clear pattern on when and why organizations and publics will enter a relationship, from either the organizational side or the publics side. Unique to intercultural settings, both parties' (publics or stakeholders and public relations practitioners) intercultural communication competencies (discussed in Chapter 5) also play a key role.

In the *processes* of managing relationships, different overall approaches of communication exist (e.g., cultural, symmetrical, and interactive/two-way), as well as different strategies regarding messengers, messaging, and channels. In particular, the incorporation of culture and cultural factors in relationship management has been reflected in recent research, especially in the process of relationship management via anxiety and uncertainty management.

The third stage is now split into two categories: *measurements* of the relationship itself and the *outcomes* brought about by the relationship. Our model divides the outcomes of relationships into organization-centered (reducing negative impact and increasing positive impact) and publics-centered (community empowerment).

Model of Conflict Management and Negotiation

The model of conflict management and negotiation illustrates the importance of following a strategic managerial approach to public relations before a conflict arises. Specifically, an organization needs to be proactive about potential conflicts and take precautionary actions. It needs to do so via engaging in the strategic management of public relations by conducting environmental scanning and identifying potential issues or signals that certain publics are about to arise about some problems. The organization should then identify its strategic publics and engage with them by building relationships and gaining mutual understanding. Especially with those conflicts involving fundamental values differences or identity clashes, an organization needs to first engage with its publics to gain some level of trust before a particular conflict occurs. This helps prevent a conflict from escalating to varying degrees and creates a basic platform of dialogue and negotiation if and when a conflict does occur. In the meantime, an organization needs to engage in training for its practitioners or other personnel that might engage in a conflict with its publics.

During a conflict situation, an organization needs to assess the conflict by looking into the types and natures of conflict; conduct a goals assessment that includes both the observable positions and fundamental values and interests; and engage in situational assessments that include the different options and power issues, relational history between the two parties, and various characteristics of both parties in the conflict such as cognitive, motivational, and behavioral. Based on these assessments, the organization can use appropriate conflict management strategies, as well as negotiation strategies, if applicable.

After a conflict deescalates or fails to reach any kind of resolution, an organization needs to assess why certain strategies have worked or failed to work, identify any changes in the identities and positions of both parties, and determine if and how to repair or reestablish relationships.

Practical Contributions

We hope this book can shed light for current and future public relations practitioners on how to best practice public relations in intercultural settings. At the same time, the theoretical structure we offer can be used by organizational publics themselves, whether they are individuals entering new a cultural environment who need to adapt or groups of activists aiming to push forward their agendas. We hope that the theoretical frameworks presented here can be used, either in their entirety, or as individual components, to address real-life cases of intercultural public relations, i.e., "public relations in which the salient cultural identity avowed by the organization differs from the salient cultural identity avowed by the public" (Sha, 2006, p. 54).

References

Broom, G., & Sha, B.-L. (2013). *Cutlip and Center's effective public relations* (11th ed.). Upper Saddle River, NJ: Pearson.

Grunig, J. E., & Repper, F. C. (1992). Strategic management, publics, and issues. In J. E. Grunig (Ed.), *Excellence in public relations and communication management* (pp. 31–64). Hillsdale, NJ: Erlbaum.

Grunig, L. A., Grunig, J. E., & Dozier, D. M. (2002). *Excellent public relations and effective organizations: A study of communication management in three countries.* Mahwah, NJ: Erlbaum.

Kim, J.-N., & Ni, L. (2013). Two types of public relations problems and integrating formative and evaluative research: A review of research programs within the behavioral, strategic management paradigm. *Journal of Public Relations Research, 25,* 1–29. http://dx.doi.org/10.1080/1062726X.2012.723276

Sha, B.-L. (2006). Cultural identity in the segmentation of publics: An emerging theory of intercultural public relations. *Journal of Public Relations Research, 18,* 45–65. doi: 10.1207/ s1532754xjprr1801_3

INDEX

access 215, 216
accommodation 125, 128–129, 235, 245, 251; co-cultural theory 158–159; contingency theory 42, 239; MNCs in Korea 252
acculturation 97, 100, 224; intercultural communication competency 9, 152, 163, 164–165, 167–168; multiracial individuals 198; public formation 195, 196
action strategy 26, 27, 31, 195
activism 23, 157; conflict management 244, 245, 249; environmental 253–254; Excellence theory 5; political 196; social media 281
adaptability 169, 170
adaptation 9; cross-cultural adaptation theory 73, 96–98; minority public relations practitioners 162; outcomes of 163, 164–168
Adi, A. 287–288
adjustment 142, 144, 153, 154
adolescents 285
advocacy 239, 252, 281
affect 34; positive 138; see also emotions
affective autonomy 83
Africa 215, 244–245
African Americans: conflict management 233; police-community relations 245–247; public relations practitioners 160, 162, 203–204; professional women 158–159; public participation 166

aggression 128, 129, 158–159
Agle, B. R. 186
Agugliaro, A. 294
Al-Khalifa, K. N. 266
Albatros 172
Albert, S. 260, 263
Aldoory, L. 196
Allagui, I. 287, 289
altruism 36, 137
Amason, A. C. 119
ambiguity 92, 171, 175
analytic remarks 132
anchoring and adjustment 138
Anderson, R. B. 35
anger 119, 121, 236, 238, 248
anthropology 8, 60, 61, 62–64, 134
anticipation 161–162
anxiety 68, 69, 92–95, 109, 154; conflict 121–122; expectancy violation theory 92; immigrants 167, 224; intercultural communication competency 155, 156–157; relationship management 39, 209, 213, 215, 217, 222, 254, 309
anxiety and uncertainty management theory (AUM) 92–95, 154, 156–157; conflict management 254–255; relationship management 217–218, 309; training 173–174
Applebaum, L. 204
appraisal 91
arbitration 135
Archer, C. 295

argument strategies 36
Ariel, Y. 290
ascribed image 264, 270–272, 273
ascription versus achievement 82, 92
Ashforth, B. 260–261
Asian Americans: community
  empowerment 199, 216, 222; conflict
  management 233; cultural sensitivity in
  message design 201–202; relationship
  management 218; *see also* Korean
  Americans
Aspinwall, E. M. 266
assertiveness 158–159, 161, 169
assimilation 98, 100, 158–159, 162,
  164, 224
Atakan-Duman, S. 269
attitudes 3, 187; change in 27; conflict
  124; Countering Violent Extremism
  campaign 48; motivations behind 34;
  prior 34; relationship management 221
audiences 33–35; capability of 32;
  Countering Violent Extremism
  campaign 48, 51; evaluation stage 27
AUM *see* anxiety and uncertainty
  management theory
Austin, L. L. 37, 285
Australia 88
authoritarian cultures 23, 266
autonomy 83, 99
Avery, E. J. 37, 279
Avidar, R. 290, 295
avoidance 42, 125, 128–129, 235, 239,
  245, 251, 252–253
Avon Breast Cancer 3-Day Walk 187
avowed identities 264–270, 273

back-translation 107
Bafa-Bafa 172, 173
Banks, S. 1, 4
Bardhan, N. 6, 11
Barki, H. 118, 119
Barnes, K. 283
Barnett, M. L. 271
BATNA *see* "best alternative to a
  negotiated agreement"
Baxter, L. A. 99, 119
Becker, E. 68–69, 72, 109
behavior: behavioral acculturation 164–165;
  change in 27; communication
  accommodation theory 95; Countering
  Violent Extremism campaign
  48; intercultural communication
  competency 170, 172

behavioral analysis 134
behavioral intentions 192, 194, 221
beliefs 3, 71, 187, 303; conflict
  management 233, 238, 250;
  organizational culture 265–266; social
  media 282
Bendersky, C. 118
Benedict, Ruth 63
Benoit, P. J. 135–136
Bernstein, A. G. 166
Berry, J. W. 100, 108, 224, 225
"best alternative to a negotiated
  agreement" (BATNA) 41, 135, 136,
  235–236
biases 138, 139, 175, 177, 197
bicultural identity 99, 224
biculturalism 165
Birdwhistell, Ray 64, 65
Blair, S. 161
Blake, R. R. 8–9, 125–126, 127, 136
blogs/bloggers 200, 280, 285, 288, 290,
  291–292, 295
Boas, Franz 61, 62–63
Bond, Michael 81
bonding 223, 225
Bortree, D. S. 39
BP 253–254
Brabham, D. C. 193
brand attitudes 221
brand awareness 281
brand loyalty 262–263
Breslow, H. 287, 289
Bridgen, L. 280
Brislin, R. W. 107
Bromley, D. B. 271, 272
Broom, G. M. 31, 32
Brown, A. D. 261, 262, 263
Brown, K. A. 203, 220
Brown, P. 88, 89, 90, 105
Brown, T. J. 263–264, 272
Brown, W. J. 86, 87–88
Brummette, J. 293
Buffington, J. 265–266
Building a New American Community
  Initiative 178
Bullis, C. 119
Burgoon, J. K. 91–92
Byram, M. 171

Cai, D. A. 120, 127
Cameron, G. T. 42, 239, 252
Canary, D. J. 39
capability of audience 32

Capriotti, P. 193
CAPS *see* communicative action in problem solving
Cardwell, L. A. 39
Carnevale, P. J. 127, 135, 136–138, 139–140
Casalaz, R. 197
Casmir, Fredrick 67
CAT *see* communication accommodation theory
Center, A. C. 189
CEOs *see* chief executive officers
Chalmers, A. W. 281
Chan, K. W. 262
change 27, 34
channels 27, 32, 36–38; conflict management 253–254; Countering Violent Extremism campaign 49, 50; cross-cultural adaptation theory 97; negotiation 233; relationship management 214; social media 294
Chay-Nemeth, C. 189
Chen, N. 1, 4, 5
Chen, Y.-R. R. 40, 210
Chick-fil-A 281
chief executive officers (CEOs) 291
China: conflict management 252, 253; face-negotiation theory 109; relationship management 40, 210; social media 289
Choi, Y. 252
Christen, C. T. 250
CIM *see* corporate identity management
circumvention 36
clarity 32, 90
class 200, 201; *see also* socioeconomic status
co-cultural theory 157–159, 161, 162
coalitions 161
Coca-Cola 252
code switching 95
cognition: conflict management 242–243; information processing 138; self-construal theory 87
Cole, R. T. 281
collaboration 216, 235, 255
collaborative research 107
collective efficacy 223
collectivism 67, 79–81, 84, 85; expectancy violation theory 92; face-negotiation theory 88–89; identity negotiation competence 154; interactive constraints theory 90;

privacy concerns 283; self-construal theory 86, 87, 88; uncertainty reduction 174
Collier, M. J. 102–104, 105
colonialism 60, 61, 63
Commission on Public Relations Education 169
communication 10, 187; anxiety and uncertainty management theory 92–94, 95; co-cultural theory 158–159; conflict management 42, 130, 131–132, 233, 234–235, 244–245, 248, 252; Countering Violent Extremism campaign 46, 48, 49, 50, 51; culture 71; definition of 61; as dialogue 51; direction of 22; Excellence theory 23; expectancy violation theory 90–91; high-context and low-context cultures 84, 92; interactive constraints theory 90; issues stage 25; negotiation as 133–134, 141; relationship management 40, 210, 214–215, 216, 217, 309; self-construal theory 85–86, 87–88; seven Cs of 32; social media 287–290; strategy 26, 27, 31, 195, 304; worldview of organization 45–46; *see also* intercultural communication competency; messaging; symmetrical communication; two-way symmetrical communication
communication accommodation theory (CAT) 95–96
communicative action in problem solving (CAPS) 30
communicative activeness 48, 52, 53, 187–188, 204, 221, 226, 304
communicative awareness 171, 177
communicator valence 91, 92
communitarianism 82
community empowerment 40, 167–168, 187, 198–199, 211, 216–217, 222–223, 226
community engagement 168, 216–217, 222, 223, 246–247, 248
community segmentation 190–191, 195
community, sense of 166, 223
compensating variation 19
competencies *see* intercultural communication competency
competing values framework (CVF) 18, 266
competition 116–117, 137
compromise 42, 125, 128–129, 141, 235, 239, 245, 251

Comte, Auguste 62, 63
concession-making 139
conciliatory remarks 132
conflict 8–9, 116; antecedents,
consequences and constants 124;
defining 117–125; newsworthiness 36;
schematic information processing 138;
social identity theory 100, 101, 102;
strategies 130; task-oriented 133
conflict management 8–9, 10–11,
12, 40–42, 52, 116–132, 232–256;
assessment 240–241, 242–243,
248–250, 309; "de-activation" of
publics 13; defining conflict 117–125;
ethnic differences 166; expanded
model of intercultural public relations
management 141, 142, 143, 304, 305,
306; face-negotiation theory 88, 89;
identity goals 129–130; integration
in public relations 244–256; issues
stage 25; model of 240–243, 309–310;
negotiation distinction 133; outcomes
254–256; relationship management
220, 226; social media 292–293;
strategies 126–127, 128–129, 130,
235–240, 241, 243, 248, 250–252,
309; symmetrical communication
234–235; tactics 130–132; two-
dimensional models 125–129, 136,
139; see also negotiation
conformity pressure 98
confrontational remarks 132
Confucianism 108, 210
consensus-building forums 237–238
conservatism 83
consistency 32
constraint recognition 30, 187, 188,
200, 204; antecedents of public
formation 194; communication
behaviors 199; Countering Violent
Extremism campaign 48, 49–50; public
relations strategies 198; relationship
management 222; segmentation of
publics 192; types of publics 194
content 32
contention 42, 139, 235, 239, 245,
251, 253
context 32; conflict management
239–240; intercultural communication
competency 177; self-construal theory
87; socio-historical 95
contingency theory 42, 239–240, 252
continuity 32

control mutuality 37, 39, 157; constraint
recognition 199; relationship
management 213, 217, 218; social
media 291; stakeholder engagement 215
controlled media 36–37, 38
convergence 74, 95–96
Coombs, W. T. 211, 212, 292
Coon, H. M. 79
cooperation 42, 116–117, 137, 138, 235,
239, 245, 251
Corley, K. G. 263
corporate citizenship 269–270, 271
corporate identity management
(CIM) 270
corporate social responsibility (CSR)
268–269, 273
corporate visual identity (CVI) 268, 271
countering violent extremism (CVE)
46–51, 167–168, 222–225, 247
credibility 32, 196; bloggers 291–292;
conflict management 237; Countering
Violent Extremism campaign 51;
motion media 289
crisis communication 34, 201; channel
and media choices 37; perceived
shared risk 196; relationship
management 220–221; situational
crisis communication theory 35;
social media 287, 292–293, 294;
social-mediated 37, 285; types of
publics 194
critical approach 4, 6, 63–64, 66, 104
critical incidents 172–173
Croatia 200
cross-cultural adaptation theory 73,
96–98
cross-cultural approach 4–6, 7, 73, 245
cross-national conflict shifting 254
Cross, S. E. 76
Cross, S. N. 198
cross-situational approaches 185–186,
192, 194, 195–196, 204, 308
CSR see corporate social responsibility
Culbertson, H. M. 1, 4, 5
cultivation strategies 215–216, 220, 226
cultural convergence 74
cultural dimensions theory 79–85; Hall
84; Hofstede 79–82; Schwartz 83–84;
Trompenaars and Hampden-Turner
82–83
cultural empathy 154, 156–157
cultural evolutionary theories 62
cultural identification 104

cultural identity 2, 12, 76, 77–78, 98–99, 100; conflict management 242; cultural identity theory 102–104, 105; identification of publics 184–185, 195, 197–198, 305, 308; identity management theory 105, 106; immigrants 167; Korean Americans 166; publics 143; social media 282–283; *see also* identity
cultural relativism 62–63, 67, 75
culture 7, 60, 109, 157, 201–202; anxiety and uncertainty management theory 94; concept of 5, 8, 67–73; conflict management 245, 252–253; cross-cultural adaptation theory 73, 96–98; cultural dimensions theories 79–85; cultural identity theory 104; definitions of 3, 67, 68, 69, 70–73, 102; Excellence theory 5; expanded model of intercultural public relations management 142; expectancy violation theory 91–92; face-negotiation theory 89; Hall on 64–65; intercultural communication competency 104–105, 153, 155; levels of 3; methodological issues 107, 108–109; pigeonholing 202–204; privacy concerns 283; public formation 195, 200, 303, 305, 308; relationship management 40, 210, 212, 213, 217, 309; self-construal theory 86; social and cultural environment 38
Cupach, W. R. 104–106, 152, 153
Currall, S. C. 127–128
Curtin, P. A. 4–5, 6
customer relationship management 212, 213
CVE *see* countering violent extremism
CVF *see* competing values framework
CVI *see* corporate visual identity
cyber-bridging 161

Dacin, P. A. 263–264
Daft, R. L. 266
Dai, Y. 267
Darwin, Charles 61–62, 65, 116
data collection 29
David, P. 267, 269–270, 271
Davis, Wade 302
De Dreu, C. K. W. 118
de Jong, M. D. T. 268
De la Flor, M. 7, 156, 215
decentering 107
decoding 163

deculturation 97, 163, 164, 167–168, 224
deductive methods 130–131
Dee, J. 244, 249–250
demographics 37, 186, 190–192, 193, 194, 195–196, 308
denial 131
derived etic method 108
Deutsch, Morton 117
development communication 66
dialogue 51; conflict management 238, 240, 250, 255, 309; policy 237; social media 290–291
Dibb, S. 270
didactic (informative) training 170–171, 176
differentiation 134, 137
digital age 192–193
digital divide 294–295, 296
digital gap 74–75
digital storytelling 289
digitalization 52
Dillard, J. P. 120, 129
disability 158, 162
discrimination 67, 77, 94, 178, 204
DiStaso, M. W. 294
divergence 74, 95–96
diversity 20, 162, 307; Excellence theory 5; minority public relations practitioners 160; multiculturalism 6, 73; multidimensional nature of 170; police 246; PWC Manifesto on 175
Doerfel, M. L. 6
domestic organizations 265
domination 125, 128, 129
Donohue, W. A. 135–136
Dozier, D. M. 161, 196, 266
drunken driving 35
Du Pont 249
dual-concern model 125–126, 127, 129, 243
Duke University 252
Dutta-Bergman, M. J. 6
Dutta, M. J. 6
Dutton, J. 260–261

ecological fallacy 80, 84–85, 86, 107, 108
economic development 5, 157
eCRM *see* electronic customer relationship management
Edwards, H. H. 187
effectiveness 17–19, 254–255, 293–294
egalitarisnism 83
ego 68
Ekman, Paul 65

Elaboration Likelihood Model (ELM) 33, 36
electronic customer relationship management (eCRM) 213
Elving, W. J. L. 268
emic approach 79, 108
emotional regulation 175
emotional stability 154, 155, 175
emotions 34, 235; conflict management 118–119, 120, 121–122, 123, 125, 238, 252; cross-cultural adaptation theory 97; cultural dimensions theory 82; immigrants 224; intercultural communication competency 153; organizational identity 263; self-construal theory 87; social media 293
empathy 154, 155, 156–157, 171–172, 175, 213
employees: communication behaviors 199; conflict management 233; organizational culture 266; organizational identification 261–263, 273; organizational identity 267; relationship management 211, 214, 221
empowerment 142, 144, 204, 305; community 40, 167–168, 187, 198–199, 211, 216–217, 222–223, 226; countering violent extremism 222; public relations function 20; relationship management 211, 218, 221, 222, 226, 254
enactment competence 155, 159, 163–164, 176, 177
encoding 163
Engels, Friedrich 62
environmental activism 253–254
environmental scanning 28–29; conflict management 11, 240, 244, 309; cyber-bridging 161; definition of 28; expanded model of intercultural public relations management 142, 143, 306; organizational identity 273, 274; situational analysis 26; social media 284, 296; stakeholder stage 24, 190; strategic management model 53; value of public relations 18
equal opportunities 20, 23
equality 137
equivalence 107
ethics: anxiety and uncertainty management theory 94; conflict management 234–235, 254–255; Excellence project 22; Excellence

theory 5; intercultural communication 75; negotiation 136–137; organizational identity 268; social media 294–295
ethnic group strength 98
ethnic identity 98–99, 100, 103, 165, 225
ethnicity: co-cultural theory 158; conflict management 233; cultural identity 102–103; intercultural communication competency 152, 162, 170; sensitivity to ethnic differences 166–167; *see also* race
ethnocentrism 3, 67, 101, 108, 197
etic approach 79, 107, 108
evaluation 52–53; Countering Violent Extremism campaign 50–51; evaluation stage 27, 28, 304; identification of publics 185
events 37
evolutionary perspectives 62, 63, 64
EVT *see* expectancy violation theory
Excellence theory 5, 18, 19–23, 216
exclusion 75
exemplification 289, 290
expectancy violation theory (EVT) 90–92
expectations 18, 153, 177, 249
experiential (interaction-oriented) training 170–171, 176
"extension transference" 72
extremism 46–51, 167–168, 222–225, 247

face 76, 81, 88–89; Chinese culture 253; expectancy violation theory 92; facework 89, 105; identity management theory 105, 106; interactive constraints theory 90
face-negotiation theory (FNT) 85, 87, 88–89, 109, 127
Facebook 280, 282, 288, 293; activism 281; Countering Violent Extremism campaign 49, 50; crisis communication 287; retail/wholesale industry 294
fairness 136–137
fear 119, 121
Feldner, S. B. 270
femininity 80, 81, 92; *see also* gender; women
Ferguson, M. A. 38
Field, P. 41, 236, 246, 248
filial piety 108
Fine, M. G. 74
Fink, E. L. 120, 127
Fisher, R. 41

Fisk, R. P. 270
Fiske, A. P. 84
flexibility 154, 155, 156–157, 171,
    175, 213
FNT *see* face-negotiation theory
focus groups 24–25
Fombelle, P. 212
Ford, R. L. 154, 168, 204
Foreign Service Institute (FSI) 8, 60,
    64–66
Fourie, L. 267
framing 36
Freberg, K. 286, 293
Freitag, A. R. 5, 169
Freud, Sigmund 61, 63, 65, 116
Friedman, R. A. 127–128
functional fitness 225
functional theory of attitudes 34
functionalism 263
Fyke, J. P. 270

Gaither, T. K. 4–5, 6
Gallois, C. 95, 96
game theory 133, 134, 135
Gao, F. 289
García, M. M. 253–254
Gelfand, M. J. 84
gender 3; Asian Americans 202;
    co-cultural theory 158; cultural
    identity 102–103; equal opportunities
    20, 23; intercultural communication
    competency 152, 162; intersectionality
    200, 201; masculinity-femininity
    cultural dimension 80, 81; Mead's
    work 63; minority public relations
    practitioners 160; multicultural
    approach 6; social identity 98; *see also*
    femininity; masculinity; women
geodemographics 191, 195, 308
Geoghegan, T. 282
geographics 186, 195, 308
Germany 109
Ghosh, P. 290
Giles, Howard 95
Global Body of Knowledge (GBOK)
    project 169
global identity 225
global knowledge, skills and abilities
    169–170
global organizations 265
global public relations 3, 5, 6
global village 74
globalization 2, 3, 5, 74–75, 169, 221

Go, E. 214
goals 18, 52–53, 187, 308; conflict
    119–125, 128–131, 242, 243, 248,
    249; corporate identity management
    270; expanded model of intercultural
    public relations management 306;
    goal-attainment approach 18; goal
    compatibility 35; goal orientation 171;
    goal statements 26; identity 129–130,
    137; negotiation 135–136; public stage
    24; types of publics 194
goals-plans-action theory 129
Goffman, E. 88, 105
Gogate, A. 166, 198
Golan, G. J. 286
government public relations 194, 279
Graham, M. W. 279
Greece 280
Greenpeace 249, 253–254, 281
Griggs, T. D. 290
Grunig, James E.: communicative action
    187–188; Excellence theory 5; linkages
    186; organizational culture 265–266;
    relationship management 38–39, 215–216;
    relationships 31; segmentation 31, 189,
    190, 195, 308; situational theory of
    problem solving 30, 138; situational
    theory of publics 30, 185, 186; strategic
    management 17, 24
Grunig, L. A. 18, 21, 24, 234, 266
Gudykunst, W. B.: anxiety and
    uncertainty management theory 92–94,
    154; cross-cultural adaptation theory
    73; enactment competence 155, 177;
    individualism and collectivism 84, 88;
    methodological issues 107; training
    173, 174

Hall, Edward T. 64–65, 66, 70, 71–72,
    73, 84, 109
Hallahan, K. 31, 36, 189
Hammond, K. R. 249
Hampden-Turner, C. 72, 79, 82–83
Hansen, K. 161
Hardiman, R. 76, 77–78
Hargie, O. 6
Harinck, F. 118
harmony 83, 85
Harrigan, P. 295
Harrison, R. L. 198
Hart, W. B. 61, 66, 67
Hartwick, J. 118, 119
hashtag hijacking 282–283

Hawaii 90
He, H. 261, 262, 263
health issues 196, 198, 199, 200–201;
    community engagement 217; cultural
    sensitivity in message design 201–202;
    media channels 37; relationship
    management 218, 219, 222; social
    media 279, 282
Helms, J. 76, 77
Heuristic and Systematic Model (HSM)
    33, 36
heuristics 138
hierarchy 83, 85, 134
high-context cultures 84, 92
Himelboim, I. 286
Hispanics 202, 203, 217; see also Latinos
Hockett, Charles 64, 65
Hodgkinson, G. P. 261, 271
Hofstede, Geert 5, 69, 79–82, 83, 157;
    definition of culture 3, 70–71, 72–73;
    ecological fallacy 85; values 248
Hofstede, Gert Jan 3, 70–71, 80–81
Hogg, M. A. 75
Holahan, P. J. 119
Holladay, S. J. 211, 212, 292
Holtzhausen, L. 267
Hon, L. C. 38–39, 160, 215–216
honesty 256
Hong, H. 194
Hong Kong 81
host communication competence 153
Hove, T. 281
HSM see Heuristic and Systematic Model
Huang, Y.-H. 38, 220, 244, 252–253
Hubbard, A. S. E. 91–92
Hughes, H. E. 285
Humboldt, Wilhelm von 61
Hung-Baesecke, C.-J. F. 40, 210
Hung, C.-J. F. 38, 245
Hunt, T. 31, 186

IABC Excellence Study 17–18, 22–23
IBM 79, 80
identification: conflict management 240;
    cultural 104; organizational 11, 212,
    260, 261–263
identity 75–78; acculturation 164–165;
    African Americans 162; conflict
    management 11, 238, 240, 248,
    256, 309–310; countering violent
    extremism 222, 224–225; ethnic
    98–99, 100, 103, 165, 225; expanded
    model of intercultural public relations

management 142; global 225;
    identity goals 129–130, 137; identity
    negotiation theory 98–100; immigrants
    167–168, 223–225; intercultural 97,
    165–166, 198; Korean Americans 166;
    organizational 11, 142, 144, 260–274,
    283–284, 306; pigeonholing 204;
    public relations practitioners 155, 307;
    publics 187, 197, 200–201, 296, 303;
    relationship management 212, 226;
    social media 280, 296; women's health
    issues 196; see also cultural identity;
    social identity
identity management theory (IMT)
    104–106
identity negotiation theory 105,
    153–154, 164
identity politics 74
ideology 77
Illia, L. 197
image 263–264, 267–268, 270–272, 273
Imahori, T. T. 104–106, 152, 153
immigrant professionals (IPs) 166, 198
immigrants: anxiety and uncertainty
    management theory 92–93, 154;
    Asian Americans 202; conflict
    management 233; conformity pressure
    98; countering violent extremism
    47–48, 51, 222, 223–225; intercultural
    communication competency 9, 162,
    163–168; training 177–178
implementation 27, 28, 52–53, 304;
    Countering Violent Extremism
    campaign 49–50; minority public
    relations practitioners 161–162;
    understanding publics 201–202
imposed etic approach 108
IMT see identity management theory
INCA project 171, 174–175
inclusion 75, 161
independent self-construal 86–88, 89, 90
individualism 67, 79–81, 82, 84, 85;
    expectancy violation theory 92;
    face-negotiation theory 88–89;
    identity negotiation competence 154;
    interactive constraints theory 90;
    negotiators 137–138; privacy concerns
    283; self-construal theory 86, 88;
    uncertainty reduction 174
individualization 97, 165–166
inductive methods 130–131
information acquisition 187, 194,
    204, 243

information attending 30, 187, 194, 199, 204, 222
information processing 30, 33, 38, 138
information seeking 30, 35, 38, 187, 194, 199, 204, 222
information selection 187, 188, 194, 204, 243
information transmission 187, 188, 194, 204, 243
informative training 170–171, 176
infrastructure 5, 7, 157
innovation 32, 189
inoculation theory 34
Instagram 49, 50, 288, 295
integration: conflict management 125, 128–129, 252–253; immigrants 164, 165, 224, 225
integrative analysis 134
intellectual autonomy 83
interaction-oriented training 170–171, 176
interactive constraints theory 85, 87, 90
interactivity 36, 37, 38, 213, 290
intercultural adjustment 93, 94, 95
intercultural communication:
    conceptualization of culture 67–73; conflict management 11; definition of 61; history of 8, 60–67; identity management theory 105, 106; key concepts related to 73–78; key theories 78–106; methodological considerations 106–109; multinational organizations 265
intercultural communication competency 7, 9, 142, 306–308; conflict management 242, 243; cross-cultural adaptation theory 97; culture-general 155, 156–157, 163–164, 170–171, 175–177; culture-specific 155, 157–159, 163, 170–171, 176, 177; diverse publics 162–168; enactment 155, 159, 163–164, 176, 177; identity management theory 104; importance of 151–152; minority public relations practitioners 160–162; relationship management 39, 210, 212–213, 226; theoretical frameworks 152–155, 178–179; training 168–178, 179
intercultural communication competence 209, 246, 305
intercultural identity 97, 165–166, 198
intercultural public relations 4, 6–7, 302–310; concept of 2; expanded model 141–144, 304–306

interdependence 120–121, 122, 124
interdependent self-construal 86–88, 89, 90
intermediaries 214
International Association of Business Communicators (IABC) 17–18
international communication 66
international organizations 265
international public relations 2, 3, 4–5
Internet 161, 192–193; *see also* social media
interpersonal interaction 105, 106
interpretivist paradigm 63–64, 103, 104
intersectionality 200–201
intracultural communication 73, 105, 106
involvement 30, 187, 188, 204; antecedents of public formation 194; communication behaviors 199; Countering Violent Extremism campaign 48, 49, 51; media channels 37; messaging 33; perceived shared risk 196; public relations strategies 35, 198; relationship management 222; segmentation of publics 31, 192; stakeholder engagement 255; types of publics 189, 194
IPs *see* immigrant professionals
irrelevant remarks 132
Israel 295
issue groups 135
issues 135, 204, 303; expanded model of intercultural public relations management 142, 143; issues stage of strategic management 25, 40, 191; social media 284; types of publics 189–190

Jackson, P. 189
Jamarani, M. 61
Jandt, F. E. 74
Jang, A. 166, 197
Japan 84, 87, 88, 109
Jarvis, C. 212
Jehn, K. A. 118
Jenkins, E. 268
Jeong, J. 200
Jermier, J. M. 271
Jiang, H. 200–201, 280
Jin, Y. 37, 252, 285
Jo, S. 219
job engagement 262
job satisfaction 23
Johnson & Johnson 282
Johnson, K. 286

journalists 6, 197, 288
Jung, E. H. 262
Jung, Y. 281

KAB *see* knowledge, attitude and
  behavior
Kabanoff, B. 128
Kanagawa, C. 76
Kang, M. 219
Kang, Y. 283
Kanihan, S. 161
Kaepernick, Colin 122, 123, 241
Kealey, D. J. 171
Kelleher, T. 255
Kemmelmeier, M. 79
Kent, M. L. 291
Kern-Foxworth, M. 203
Keyton, J. 254
Ki, E. 216
Kian, E. T. 283
Kilmann, R. H. 125, 128, 136
Kim, H. 166, 197, 288
Kim, J.-N.: communicative action
  187–188; employee communication
  behaviors 199; expanded model
  of intercultural public relations
  management 51–52, 143; integrated
  model for public relations management
  42–45; perceived shared risk 196;
  public relations problems 304, 305;
  relationship management 185, 194;
  segmentation 31, 185, 189; situational
  theory of problem solving 30, 138;
  theoretical structure 12
Kim Jong Un 134
Kim, M.-S. 87, 90
Kim, S. 35, 37
Kim, S. H. 118
Kim, Y. 40, 210, 265
Kim, Y. Y.: adaptation 163; crisis
  communication 194; cross-cultural
  adaptation theory 73, 96–98;
  enactment competence 155, 177;
  intercultural communication
  competency 153; intercultural identity
  165–166; psychological health 225
Kimberly, J. R. 266
King, Martin Luther Jr. 302
Kinsky, E. S. 282
Kitayama, S. 75, 85–87
Kjeldsen, A. K. 268
Kline, S. 267
Kluckhohn, Clyde 60, 61, 70, 78–79

Kluckhohn, Florence 69, 78–79, 82, 83
knowledge: Countering Violent
  Extremism campaign 48, 51; cross-
  cultural approach 7; evaluation 27;
  expectancy violation theory 92;
  global 169–170; identity negotiation
  competence 153–154; intercultural
  communication competency 157,
  172; knowledge discovery 171, 177;
  segmentation of publics 31; types of
  publics 189
knowledge, attitude and behavior (KAB)
  45, 46, 48, 53, 142
Koester, J. 152, 153, 155, 177
Korea: bloggers 200; interactive
  constraints theory 90; multinational
  corporations 252; relationship
  management 40, 219; self-construal
  theory 88
Korean Americans 166, 197; *see also* Asian
  Americans
Kroeber, Alfred 70
Kruckeberg, D. 192
Kudoh, T. 87
Kuhlmann, T. 171
Kuhn, Thomas 63
Kurogi, A. 89, 127
Kwan, T. Y.-M. 286

LAC *see* Linguistic Awareness of Cultures
Lafferty, B. A. 271
Lakhanpal, P. B. 286
Lam, L. W. 262
Landis, Daniel 67
Langer, E. 93, 173–174
language 61, 63; cross-cultural adaptation
  theory 97; Hispanics 202; intercultural
  communication competency 177;
  linguistic equivalence problem 107;
  paralanguage 65; Piglish training
  simulation 172; *see also* linguistics
Latinos 196; *see also* Hispanics
leadership 280
Lee, H. 37, 289
Lee, S. 192
Lee, Y. 194
legal systems 5, 157
legitimacy 186, 215, 216, 245
Leichty, G. B. 254
Lellis, J. C. 270
Len-Ríos, M. E. 196, 203, 252, 285
Lester, L. 253
Leung, K. 107–108

Levenshus, A. 214
Levine, R. 63
Levine, T. R. 88
Levinger, G. 120
Levinson, S. 88, 89, 90, 105
Levitt, Theodore 2
Levy, E. C. 290
Lewicki, R. 118
Lewin, Kurt 117
life experiences 12, 143, 195, 196, 305
lifestyle 190–191, 195, 196, 308
Lim, K.-W. 200
Lim, R. S.-Q. 286
limits 135
Linguistic Awareness of Cultures (LAC) 173
linguistics 8, 60, 61, 64, 65; see also language
linkages 24, 186
Liu, B. F. 37, 285
Live Action 253
Loi, R. 262
long-term orientation 81
Louisiana State University 255
low-context cultures 84, 92
Lowe 282
loyalty 221
Lund, A. D. 171, 174
Luo, Y. 280
Lurati, F. 197
Lustig, M. W. 7, 152, 153, 155, 177
Lwin, M. 287–288
Lynas 281

McCorkindale, T. 294
McKee, L. G. 285
Mackey A. 267, 271
McLuhan, Marshall 72, 73, 74, 287
Macnamara, J. 287–288
Mahon, J. F. 271
Maiorescu, R. 294
majority groups 77–78
Malka, V. 290
managerial grid 8–9, 125–126, 136
managerial skills 155, 168–169
managers 20–21
maps 37
marginalization 164, 224–225
marketing 185–186, 219
Markus, H. R. 75, 76, 85–87
Marshall Program 64, 65–66
Martin, J. N. 61
Marx, Karl 61, 62, 116

Marxism 63, 64
masculinity 80, 81, 92; see also gender
mastery 83
Matsumoto, D. 87
Mead, Margaret 61, 63
meanings 68, 69, 71, 72, 102, 265–266
media 36–38, 74, 157; conflict management 253; Countering Violent Extremism campaign 50; cross-cultural adaptation theory 97; cross-cultural approach 7; Excellence theory 5; immigrants 223; international communication 66; newsworthiness 36; PESO media model 287–288; relationship management 214; segmentation of publics 192; see also channels; social media
media relations role 20
mediated communication 215, 233
mediation 135, 251, 252–253
medium theory 36
Melewar, T. C. 267, 268
Men, L. R. 214, 290, 291
messaging 31–38, 52, 306; Countering Violent Extremism campaign 49; cultural sensitivity in message design 201–202; identification of publics 185; public formation 198; relationship management 213, 214; social media 289–290, 293; strategies 27, 36, 304; types of publics 194
meta-communication 171
methodological issues 106–109
Metzger, J. 254
micro-blogging 289
Migration Policy Institute 178
mindfulness 93–95, 138, 154, 155, 168, 173–174, 175
minority groups 9, 77–78, 152, 162; see also immigrants
minority public relations practitioners 160–162, 202–204, 307
Minton, J. M. 118
mission 262, 266, 270
Mitchell, R. K. 186
mixed motives 21, 117, 160, 245
MODE 128
modeling 35
models of public relations 21–22
Mody, B. 73
Moghan, S. 200
Molleda, J. 254
monetary value 19

Monseau, M. 282
Moon, B. B. 188, 286
Mooney, A. C. 119
moral inclusion 75, 94
moral standards 130, 137
morality 234–235
Morgan, Lewis Henry 62
Morton, T. S. 288
motion media 289
motivation 34, 188, 204; conflict
   management 242; intercultural
   communication competency 172,
   177; negotiators 137; relationship
   management 226; self-construal theory
   87; situational theory of problem
   solving 30
Mouton, J. S. 8–9, 125–126, 127, 136
multicultural approach 4, 6
multicultural organizations 265
multicultural relational skills 154, 155,
   168, 177
multicultural sensitivity 154–155, 168
multiculturalism 73–74
multinational corporations (MNCs) 7,
   212, 215, 218, 252, 265, 279
multiracial individuals 198
Muralidharan, S. 214
Murphy, P. 244, 249–250
Muskat, B. 219
mutual-gains approach 41–42, 236–239,
   243, 246
Myers, J. 161

names, organizational 268
National Football League (NFL)
   122–123, 241
naturalism 8, 60
nature 83
negotiation 11, 41, 116, 133–141,
   232–233; activists 250; antecedents
   136–139; definition of 133; issues
   stage 25; key terms 135–136; limits
   to 255–256; minority public relations
   practitioners 160–161; model of
   conflict management 240, 243, 309;
   outcomes of 140–141; principled 141,
   235–236, 251; strategies 135–136,
   139–140, 141; willingness to negotiate
   250; see also conflict management
Neill, M. 161
networking 215, 216
New York Police Department (NYPD) 283
New Zealand 6, 295

newsworthiness 36
NFL see National Football League
Ni, L.: communicative action 187;
   community health issues 201;
   expanded model of intercultural public
   relations management 51–52, 143;
   immigrant professionals 166, 198;
   integrated model for public relations
   management 42–45; intercultural
   communication competency 156;
   public relations problems 304, 305;
   relationship management 6, 7, 39,
   185, 194, 198–199, 215, 216–218,
   221; segmentation 31, 185, 189;
   stakeholder engagement 255;
   theoretical structure 12
Nichols, A. 171
Nigeria 244–245
Noether's Theorem 234
noncommittal remarks 131–132
nonverbal communication 63,
   64, 67; Birdwhistell's work 65;
   communication accommodation
   theory 95; conflict management 130;
   expectancy violation theory 90–91
norms: acculturation 164–165;
   communication accommodation
   theory 95; culture 71, 72, 102,
   109; intercultural communication
   competency 177; open-mindedness
   154; social media 282
Norwood, R. S. 166
novelty 36, 99
nutrition 202
NYPD see New York Police Department

Oakes, P. J. 75
Obama, Barack 214
objectives 48, 52–53, 304, 306; see also
   goals
OCCI see Organizational
   Communication Conflict Instrument
Oetzel, J. G. 71, 72, 74–75, 76, 85,
   89, 109
Ogay, T. 95
OI see organizational identity
OID see organizational identification
Oliveira, A. 193
Omenugha, K. A. 215, 244–245
O'Neil, J. 161
open-mindedness 154, 156–157, 213
openness 155, 177, 215, 216, 232, 256
opinion change 27

OPRPs *see* organization-initiated public relations problems
options 135
Orbe, M. P. 158–159, 161, 162
organization-initiated public relations problems (OPRPs) 43–44, 45–46, 143; Countering Violent Extremism campaign 46; expanded model of intercultural public relations management 142, 304, 306; relationship management 219–220, 226; strategic management model 51–52, 53
Organizational Communication Conflict Instrument (OCCI) 126–127
organizational culture 11, 23, 265–266
organizational identification (OID) 212, 260, 261–263, 272–274
organizational identity (OI) 11, 142, 144, 260–274, 283–284, 306
organizational structure 264–265
organizational types 264–265
Ortiz Juarez-Paz, A. V. 197
Ostrom, L. 212
Ott, L. 294
outcomes 45–46, 53; of adaptation 163, 164–168; conflict management 124, 254–256; Countering Violent Extremism campaign 51; expanded model of intercultural public relations management 306; negotiation 135, 140–141; relationship management 40, 210–211, 218–226, 309; social media 294; types of publics 194
outputs 50, 53
Oyserman, D. 79, 84, 85
Ozdora-Aksak, E. 269

Paek, H. 281
Pal, M. 6
Pang, A. 286, 288
paracrises 292
paralanguage 65
Park, H. 37, 194, 220
Park, J. 194
Park, N. 200
Park, S. 252
Park, Y. E. 219
Parker, P. S. 162
participative cultures 23, 266
particularism 82, 92
paternalism 234–235
Penaflor, R. 215

perseverance 251
personal identity 98–99
personality 63, 65, 70; conflict management styles 127–128; cross-cultural adaptation theory 97; intercultural communication competency 153, 154, 155, 168, 175
personification 289, 290
persuasion 13, 35, 232, 306; negotiation 133–134, 236; social media 290–291; theory of 45
Peru 209, 212, 215, 216, 218, 220, 254
PESO media model 287–288
Phinney, J. S. 76, 77
pigeonholing 10, 202–204
Piglish 172
Pinterest 288
Planned Parenthood 253, 282
planning 26, 28, 52–53, 304; Countering Violent Extremism campaign 47–48; identification of publics 185; negotiation 135
platforms 288, 294
Plowman, K. D. 42, 239, 244, 245, 250, 251
police-community relations 245–248
policy dialogue 237
politeness theory 88, 90, 105
political system 5, 7, 157
Pondy, L. R. 123–124
Popper, Karl 63
Porter, R. E. 66
positivity 215
post-colonialism 66
post-positivism 63
postmodernism 6, 263, 294
power: conflict management 233, 245, 250; critical approach 4; cultural dimensions theory 83; hidden 72; minority public relations practitioners 160–161; multicultural approach 6; negotiation 134, 139; stakeholder theory 186
power distance 80, 81, 83, 88–89, 92
PPRPs *see* public-initiated public relations problems
Pratt, C. B. 215, 244–245
Pratt, M. G. 263–264
Prechtl, E. 171, 174
prejudice 67, 203
preparation 161–162
press agentry model 21
principled negotiation 141, 235–236, 251

prior attitudes 34
privacy 283, 295
proactivity 155, 177
problem recognition 29–30, 187, 188, 200, 204; antecedents of public formation 194; communication behaviors 199; Countering Violent Extremism campaign 48, 49, 51; "de-activation" of publics 43, 195; perceived shared risk 196; public relations strategies 35, 198; relationship management 222; segmentation of publics 192; types of publics 194
problem solving 45, 186; conflict management 238; negotiation 133–134, 139–140; sharing tasks 215–216; situational theory of 138, 186–187, 193, 198, 221; types of publics 189
problem statements 26
PRSA *see* Public Relations Society of America
Pruitt, D. G. 118, 125–126, 135, 136–138, 139–140
psychodynamic perspective 263
psychographics 186, 190–191, 195, 308
psychological health 225
psychology 60, 85, 116, 134
public-centered outcomes 40, 305
public information model 21
public-initiated public relations problems (PPRPs) 43–44, 45–46, 143; Countering Violent Extremism campaign 46–47; expanded model of intercultural public relations management 142, 304, 306; relationship management 219, 226; strategic management model 52, 53
public media 36, 38
public relations: buffering and bridging functions 51; empowerment of public relations function 20; expanded model of intercultural public relations management 141–144; integrated model 42–46; integration of conflict management 244–256; models and dimensions 21–22; organization of 22; organizational identity 266, 267, 270, 272–274; role in strategic management 23–25; roles 20–21; social media 280, 284–293, 296; strategic management model 8, 17–53; value of 18–19; *see also* intercultural public relations

Public Relations Society of America (PRSA) 169
publics 6, 7, 184–204, 303; "activation" of 12–13, 44, 46–47, 51–53, 142–143, 185, 194, 204, 304, 306; antecedents of public formation 194–201; conflict management 240, 243, 309; Countering Violent Extremism campaign 46–47, 48; cross-situational approaches 185–186, 192, 194, 195–196, 204, 308; "de-activation" of 13, 43, 46–47, 52–53, 142–143, 185, 194, 204, 304, 306; digital age 192–193; expanded model of intercultural public relations management 142, 143–144, 305; identification of 9–11, 12, 18, 25, 29–31, 142–143, 184–201, 240, 284–287, 306, 308; intercultural communication competency 9, 151, 152, 156, 159, 162–168, 179; media channels 38; messaging 33, 35; pigeonholing 202–204; public stage of strategic management 24–25, 43, 190, 191; relationship management 211–212, 221–223, 226; self-study and training 177; social media 280–283, 284–287, 296; stakeholder distinction 25; types of 31, 189–190, 193–194; value of public relations 19; *see also* segmentation; situational theory of publics; stakeholders
Putnam, L. L. 126–127, 129, 133, 134, 135–136, 137, 141
PWC Manifesto on diversity 175
Pyle, A. 39

Quinn, R. E. 266

race: conflict management 233; cultural identity 102–103; intercultural communication competency 152, 162; intersectionality 200, 201; multicultural approach 6; multiracial individuals 198; pigeonholing 203; publics 197; *see also* ethnicity
racism 78
Rahim, M. A. 126, 127, 128
Rasmussen, L. 253
Reber, B. H. 220
receptivity 98
Red Cross 292
referent criterion 188, 200, 204
Reicher, S. D. 75

Reitz, A. 283–284
relational commitment 39, 218–219
relational identity 105
relational satisfaction 39, 218–219
relationship management 6–7, 10, 38–40,
    52, 198–199, 209–226; antecedents
    of 210, 211–213, 225–226, 308–309;
    community engagement 168; conflict
    management 11, 240, 244–245,
    254; Countering Violent Extremism
    campaign 47; "de-activation" of publics
    13; expanded model of intercultural
    public relations management 142, 143,
    304, 306; intercultural communication
    competency 179; measurement of 40,
    210, 218–219, 225–226, 309; model
    of 225–226, 308–309; outcomes 40,
    210–211, 218–226, 309; process of 210,
    213–218, 225–226, 309; segmentation
    185, 194; social media 287, 290–292
relationships 6–7, 18, 307; conflict
    management 236; exchange and
    communal 39; monetary value
    19; mutual-gains approach 42;
    organization-public 12, 52–53, 142,
    195, 198–199, 210–221, 240, 272–273,
    291, 304, 305–306; segmentation of
    publics 44; symbolic and behavioral 31;
    types of 44–45
relativism 62–63, 67, 75
religion 3, 152, 233, 251
Repper, F. C. 24, 190, 195, 308
reputation: corporate social responsibility
    269; Countering Violent Extremism
    campaign 51; crisis communication 35,
    194; organizational identity 264, 268,
    270–272, 273; relationship management
    40, 211, 226; website interactivity 37
research 25, 26, 28; Countering Violent
    Extremism campaign 47; expanded
    model of intercultural public relations
    management 52–53; identification of
    publics 184–185; methodological issues
    106–108
resilience 155, 167, 223, 225
resource-dependency theory 186
respect 134, 135, 171–172, 175
Rhee, Y. 188, 199
Rhoades, J. A. 127
Rice, Constance 247
risk: channel and media choices 37;
    conflict management 236, 237, 242;
    perceived shared risk 196

Robbins, S. P. 266
Rodriguez, L. 192
Rogers, E. M. 32, 61, 66, 67, 189
Róheim, G. 67–68, 72
role-play 172, 174
Roloff, M. E. 133, 134
RPIE (Research, Planning,
    Implementation, and Evaluation)
    25–28, 31
Rubin, J. Z. 118, 120, 125–126
rule-making 238

Samovar, L. A. 66
Samp, J. A. 131
sampling 108–109
sanction strategies 36
Sanderson, J. 283
SANDS see Stillbirth and Neonatal Death
    Society
Sapir, Edward 61, 63, 65
Sapir-Whorf hypothesis 61, 63
Saunders, D. M. 118
Saxton, G. D. 293
SCA see Speech Communication
    Association
SCCT see situational crisis
    communication theory
scenario building 29
schematic information processing 138
Scherer, K. 87
Schmeltz, L. 268
Schrader, D. C. 129
Schwartz, S. H. 79, 83–84
Schwartz, S. J. 164, 165
Searson, E. M. 290
segmentation 24, 31, 43, 169, 186,
    190–192; government public relations
    194; issues stage 25; nested model
    of 190–191, 195, 308; planning 26;
    relationship management 185, 194,
    212; types of methods 44–45; types of
    publics 189
self-awareness 154, 155, 168, 169,
    170, 177
self-concept 75–76, 94, 98, 165–166
self-construal: face-negotiation
    theory 88, 89; interactive constraints
    theory 90; self-construal theory
    85–88
self-efficacy 35, 47
self-esteem 225, 263
sense of community 166, 223
separation 158–159, 164, 224

seven Cs 32
sexual orientation 3; co-cultural
theory 158; conflict management
233; intercultural communication
competency 152, 162; minority
public relations practitioners 160;
multicultural approach 6
Sha, B.-L.: communication and action
strategies 31; cultural identity 2, 197;
multicultural competence 154, 168;
organizational identification 262;
organizational identity 260, 261, 264,
267, 268, 270, 274; segmentation
185; seven Cs of communication 32;
symmetrical communication 234
Sha, T.-L. 261
Shankman, Peter 288
Sharifian, F. 61
sharing tasks 215–216, 245
Shell, G. R. 136
Sheng, V. W. 154, 168–169
Sherif, M. 100
Shin, J. 251
Shin, W. 288
Shore, M. 161
short-term orientation 81
Shotton, P. A. 281
Sigala, M. 213
Sillars, A. L. 121, 131
Simões, C. 270
Sina Weibo 289
Singapore 200, 286
Singelis, T. M. 86, 87–88
Singer, M. R. 3
Sisco, F. H. 293
Sisson, D. C. 291
situational analysis 26
situational crisis communication theory
(SCCT) 35
situational perceptions 52, 53, 196, 197,
198–199, 204, 304
situational theory of problem solving
(STOPS) 30, 138, 186–187, 193,
198, 221
situational theory of publics 25, 29–30,
33, 185, 186–190, 303; channels 37; life
experiences 196; messaging strategies
35; pigeonholing 204; public formation
195; segmentation 44, 45, 192
SMCC see social-mediated crisis
communication
SMIs see social media influencers
Smith, R. D. 35

Snapchat 50
SNSs see social networking sites
sociability 171
social capital 166, 167, 197, 223,
225, 295
social categories 191, 195, 308
social categorization 94, 102
social change 101
social comparison 101, 102
social competition 102
social constructionism 263
social constructivism 103
social creativity 102
social Darwinism 62
social environment 38
social evolution theory 62
social exchange 135, 262, 273
social identity 76, 212; communication
accommodation theory 96; identity
negotiation theory 98; social identity
theory 100–102, 261–262, 263
social initiative 154, 177
social interaction 95, 103, 105
social justice 75, 104
social media 11–12, 144, 279–296;
communication and messaging
287–290; conflict management
123, 253, 292–293; Countering
Violent Extremism campaign
49, 50; effectiveness 293–294;
effects on organizational identity
283–284; effects on public relations
practitioners 280; effects on publics
280–283; environmental scanning
284; ethics 294–295; expanded
model of intercultural public relations
management 142; future research
296; identification of publics 192,
284–287; immigrants 223; mediated
communication 233; relationship
management 213, 214, 290–292;
Trump/Kim conflict 134
social media influencers (SMIs) 286
social-mediated crisis communication
(SMCC) 37, 285
social mobility 101
social networking sites (SNSs) 37; see also
social media
social responsibility 5, 19, 268–269, 273
social value 269
social values 269, 273
socioeconomic status 3, 158, 162, 203;
see also class

sociology 8, 60, 134, 185
SOEP media model 288
Solomon, D. H. 131
Somerville, I. 6
Sorenson, R. L. 127
Speech Communication Association
  (SCA) 67
Spellers, R. E. 158–159, 161, 162
Spence, P. R. 290
Spencer, Herbert 62, 63
Spencer, M. E. 73–74
Spitzberg, B. H. 152, 153, 175
Springston, J. K. 254
Sriramesh, Krishnamurthy 1, 5–6, 11,
  157, 200, 265–266
St. John III, B. 286
Stafford, L. 39
Stahl, M. 171
stakeholders: conflict management 242,
  243, 244–245; engagement 11, 215,
  216–217, 225, 233, 242–243, 244–245;
  expanded model of intercultural
  public relations management 142, 143;
  identification of 26; organizational
  identification 261–263; organizational
  identity 267, 270–271, 273; publics
  distinction 25, 190; stakeholder stage
  of strategic management 24, 190, 191;
  stakeholder theory 186; *see also* publics
Starosta, William 66, 67
stereotypes 92, 101, 160, 249–250
Stevens, D. 171
Stillbirth and Neonatal Death Society
  (SANDS) 294
Stoffels, J. 28, 29
Stoker, K. L. 255
Stokes, A. Q. 5
STOPS *see* situational theory of problem
  solving
strategic constituencies 18
strategic management 8, 17–53, 144,
  152, 303; conflict management 40–42,
  232, 240, 245, 309; Countering
  Violent Extremism campaign 46–51;
  development of messages and media
  channels 31–38; effectiveness 18–19;
  environmental scanning 28–29;
  evaluation 27, 28; excellence 19–23;
  expanded model of intercultural public
  relations management 51–53, 142,
  143, 304, 306; identification of publics
  29–31, 184–185, 190–192, 193, 204;
  implementation 27, 28; integrated

model for public relations management
  42–46; planning 26, 28; relationship
  management 38–40; research 25, 26,
  28; role of public relations 23–25;
  value of public relations 18–19
strategies 26, 27, 35, 195, 304; conflict
  management 126–127, 128–129, 130,
  235–240, 241, 243, 248, 250–252,
  309; messaging 36, 194; negotiation
  135–136, 139–140, 141; publics 187;
  relationship management 213–217
stress 97, 128, 163–164, 166, 167–168, 224
Strodtbeck, Fred 69, 78–79, 82, 83
struggle 135
Stuart, A. 260–261
subcultures 191, 195, 308
Sudan 244–245
Sung, K.-H. 35, 37
Sung, M.-J. 29
Susan G. Komen (SGK) 282
Susskind, L. 41, 236, 246, 248
Sutherland, K. E. 291
Suto, R. J. 286
Sweetser, K. D. 291, 294
SWOT analysis 26
symbols: culture 71, 102; identity
  management theory 106; image 271;
  organizational culture 265–266;
  organizational identity 270, 273
symmetrical communication 13; conflict
  management 234–235; organizational
  identity 267; persuasion 291;
  relationship management 212–213;
  social media 296; *see also* two-way
  symmetrical communication
systems approach 18

tactics 26; conflict management 130–132;
  Countering Violent Extremism
  campaign 50; minority public relations
  practitioners 161; negotiation 135–136,
  139, 243
Taiwan 245, 252–253
Tajfel, H. 75, 100–102
Takai, J. 71, 73
Takasaki, M. 265
"taking the knee" 122–123, 130, 241
Tan, E. Y. 286
Tanno, D. V. 74
targeting 193
task sharing 215–216, 245
Taylor, M. 6, 252, 291
technicians 20–21

technology 52
television 36, 66
Theunissen, P. 290–291, 294
Thomas and Kilmann's Instrument
    (TKI) 136
Thomas, K. D. 198
Thomas, K. W. 125, 128, 136
Thomas, M. 102–103, 105
Thompson, G. 289
Tidd, S. T. 127
Tillery-Larkin, R. 203, 204
time orientation 81, 82, 92
Tindall, N. T. J. 160, 196, 200–201,
    204, 261, 288
Ting-Toomey, Stella: conflict 119;
    definition of culture 70, 71, 73; face-
    negotiation theory 87, 88–89, 127;
    identity 75; identity negotiation theory
    98–100, 105, 153–154, 164
Tjosvold, Dean 118, 119
Tkalac, A. 200
TKI see Thomas and Kilmann's
    Instrument
TLC 282
Toledano, M. 6, 295
Topalian, A. 268
topic management 131
traditions 71
Trager, George Leonard 64, 65
training: conflict management 240,
    242, 243, 245–248, 309; intercultural
    communication competency 9,
    151–152, 168–178, 179, 306–308
transparency 294, 295
Triandis, H. C. 84
Trompenaars, F. 72, 79, 82–83
Trump, Donald 122, 134, 241
trust 161, 199; conflict management
    232, 235–237, 240, 245, 250, 309;
    countering violent extremism
    222–223; government public relations
    194; intercultural communication
    competency 157; media trustworthiness
    196; negotiation strategies 140;
    police-community relations 246–247;
    relationship management 38, 213, 215,
    217, 218–219, 220, 222; segmentation
    of publics 192
Tsai, J. C. 127–128
Tsai, W. S. 290, 291
Tsetsura, K. 170
Tumblr 288
Turkey 269, 280, 281

Turner, J. C. 75, 100–102
Turner, J. H. 174
Tusinski Berg, K. 295
Tusinski, K. A. 255
Twitter 281, 288, 294; Countering
    Violent Extremism campaign 49,
    50; crisis communication 292–293;
    interactivity 213; relationship
    management 291
two-dimensional models 125–129,
    136, 139
two-way asymmetrical model 21
two-way symmetrical communication
    21, 22, 156–157, 160, 212–213;
    conflict management 41, 232–233,
    234–235, 255; contingency theory 42,
    239; Countering Violent Extremism
    campaign 49; Excellence theory 5;
    relationship management 214–215, 217
Tylor, Edward Burnett 62

uncertainty 67, 92–95, 154; conflict
    management 237; expectancy violation
    theory 92; intercultural communication
    competency 155, 156–157; relationship
    management 39, 209, 213, 215, 217,
    222, 254, 309; training 173–174
uncertainty avoidance 81, 92
unconditional constructiveness 42, 141,
    235–236, 239, 245, 251
Undocumented Student Movement
    (USM) 197
United States: face-negotiation theory
    109; Foreign Service Institute 8, 60,
    64–66; immigrant professionals 198;
    interactive constraints theory 90;
    political activism 196; relationship
    management studies 209; self-construal
    theory 87, 88; U.S. State Department
    286; see also African Americans; Asian
    Americans
universalism 75, 82, 92
universality 3, 69, 92
universalization 97, 165–166
University of Hawaii 255
urgency 186
Ury, W. 41
USM see Undocumented Student
    Movement

Valentini, C. 213, 295
validity 107
Valin, J. 170

value of public relations 18–19
values 34, 144, 303, 305; acculturation 100, 164–165; communication accommodation theory 95; competing values framework 18, 266; conflict management 238, 240, 241, 242, 248–249, 309; cultural dimensions theory 85; culture 3, 71, 72, 109; Excellence theory 5; expectancy violation theory 91–92; intercultural communication competency 177; open-mindedness 154; organizational culture 265–266; organizational identity 267, 270; social 269, 273; social media 282; value content 98; value orientation theory 69, 78–79
Van de Vijver, F. 107–108
Van de Vliert, E. 128
Van den Bosch, A. L. M. 268
Van der Zee, K. I. 74, 154, 155, 177
Van Oudenhoven, J. P. 74, 154, 155, 177
Van Vianen, A. E. M. 118
Vardeman-Winter, J. 200–201
Varma, T. M. 255–256
Vercic, Dejan 2, 5–6, 11, 264
Vilanilam, J. V. 5
violent extremism 46–51, 167–168, 222–225, 247
visuals 37
Vujnovic, M. 192

Walden, J. 262
Walgreens 244, 250
Wallbott, H. 87
Wang, Q.: conflict management 120, 126, 128–129, 131; immigrant professionals 166, 198; intercultural communication competency 156; relationship management 6, 7, 39, 213, 215, 216–218
Ward, J. 212

Waters, R. D. 160, 288, 290, 293
Watson, T. 5
Waymer, D. 203
Weaver, C. K. 6, 11
websites 37, 49, 50
Werder, K. P. 35, 194, 198
Westerman, C. Y. K. 262
Wetherell, M. S. 75
Whetten, D. A. 260, 263–264, 267, 271
White, C. L. 203, 220
Whorf, Benjamin 61, 63, 65
Wiesenberg, M. 2
Wikipedia 289
Williams, S. 39
Williamson, C. 283
Wilmot, W. W. 121, 131
Wilson, C. E. 126–127, 129, 135–136
win-win solutions 42, 139–140, 141, 239, 244, 245, 251, 256
Winston, Jameis 283
women: Asian Americans 202; health issues 196; minority public relations practitioners 160, 162; *see also* femininity; gender
Wood, D. J. 186
word-of-mouth communication 221, 285
worldviews 45–46, 79, 167, 242

Xiao, Z. 216

Yamada, A. M. 88
Yang, J. 40, 210
Yang, K. C. 283
Yang, S. 188
Yee-Jung, K. 89
Yep, G. A. 75, 104
You, K. H. 214
Young, H. N. 285
YouTube 253, 280, 288, 294

Zerfass, A. 2, 287–288

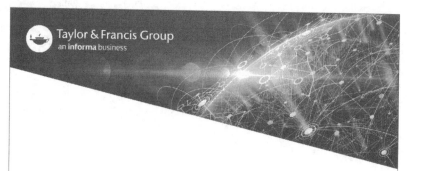